'In my opinion this book is unrivalled – it sets out to give detailed solutions to coaching problems. It asks for technical excellence, without letting small mistakes slip by – demanding thorough preparation and attention to detail.'
*Clive Woodward, England Head Coach*


'Jim Greenwood's books are my inspiration; they are my "bible".'
*Bill Freeman, former Director of Coaching, NZ Rugby Football Union*


'It took maybe 20 minutes to recognise that Jim's way of coaching was the most effective I'd come across. I was an All Black then, and when I became the All Blacks coach I was into his methods, helped by his books. I still turn to them and thoroughly recommend them.'
*Wayne Smith, Northampton Saints Coach and former All Blacks Coach*


'Jim Greenwood remains the most important influence in my career. He was ahead of his time in every respect … without him women's rugby in the UK would not have been the same.'
*Lisa Burgess, Captain of Wales*


'I didn't feel I'd started coaching properly until I'd read Jim Greenwood.'
*Ian McGeechan OBE, British Lions Coach*


'Jim Greenwood was fantastic. He taught us everything and encouraged us to learn and experiment.'
*Emma Mitchell, Captain of England*

# TOTAL RUGBY

# TOTAL RUGBY

**5th edition**

# Jim Greenwood

A&C Black • London

Fifth edition published 2003 by
A & C Black (Publishers) Ltd
37 Soho Square, London W1D 3QZ

First edition 1978
Second edition 1985
Third edition 1992
Fourth edition 1997

ISBN 0 7136 6672 2

A CIP catalogue record for this book is available from the British Library.

Printed and bound in Great Britain by Biddles Ltd, Guildford and King's Lynn.

## Acknowledgements
Cover photograph and all other photographs courtesy of Empics.

## Other Rugby Union titles available from A & C Black

**Think Rugby** by Jim Greenwood (ISBN 0 7136 5440 6)
This companion to Total Rugby explains how a well prepared team can initiate carefully planned moves and so win matches. The text is fully supported by illustrations, worked examples and suggestions for training activities.

**Know the Game Rugby Union** (ISBN 0 7136 5823 1)
Produced in collaboration with the Rugby Football Union
A helpful book for beginners, players and spectators, providing information on skills, laws, equipment, the field and officials' duties.

**Rugby Lesson Plans for Three-quarters with Jonathan Webb** by Peter Johnson(ISBN 0 7136 4041 3)
An invaluable aid to all coaches, in particular to those unsure of how to physically structure and operate practice sessions for three-quarters. Provides lesson plans and coaching guidance. Endorsed by Jonathan Webb.

**The R.F.U. Rugby Union Referee's Manual** (ISBN 0 7136 4614 4)
Produced in collaboration with the Rugby Football Union
The official R.F.U. manual for both qualified and aspiring referees, this comprehensive guide discusses the role of the referee in every major aspect of play – the scrummage, line-out, ruck and maul – as well as the philosophy and principles of the referee, and the mental and physical demands of the game.

**The R.F.U. Handbook of Safe Rugby** (ISBN 0 7136 4520 2)
Produced in collaboration with the Rugby Football Union
An official publication from the R.F.U. on the increasingly topical issue of safety within the game. Touching on a range of safety aspects including insurance, good and bad technique, women's rugby and the treatment of injuries on the field of play, the handbook is invaluable to every participant in this inherently physical game.

**The author in Argentina, starting a session at about 10 pm.**

My coaching books have done exceptionally well in the southern hemisphere, and have led to widespread coaching tours. I was shown a manuscript translation of *Total Rugby* in Spanish, completed by an enthusiast who didn't speak English but had puzzled out the meaning with the help of a dictionary. So don't complain about its length in English!

Jim Greenwood

for

# MARGOT

and in memory of

# LAURIE O'REILLY

# CONTENTS

## PART 5 BASIC PREPARATION - TECHNICAL

## PART 6 BASIC PREPARATION - PHYSICAL

# Foreword

I believe I was extremely fortunate as a player as I came under the influence of three great coaches – Earl Kirton, Chalky White but most importantly Jim Greenwood, who coached me for the four years I was at Loughborough University. He was well ahead of his time then and I was a student at Loughborough when I first read *Total Rugby*. Twenty five years later, its still the only rugby coaching book I regularly refer to and I am delighted that I am still in regular contact with Jim.

This book has been in continual publication during that twenty five year period and has been through five editions – considering how many changes the game of rugby has been through in that time, it illustrates how important the concept of *Total Rugby* is to the game.

In my opinion this book is unrivalled – it sets out to give detailed solutions to coaching problems. It asks for technical excellence, without letting small mistakes slip by – demanding thorough preparation and attention to detail.

During the last four years as England Head Coach, our game has become more expansive, more exciting and more successful. I agree totally with Jim's concept that continual improvement, continual learning and striving for excellence in everything that we do is vital to success and this is what England Rugby is all about today.

Enjoy the book, enjoy learning and enjoy the game.

Clive Woodward
*England Head Coach*

# Introduction

Play and games are socially and specially rooted in our culture. Our national philosophy has recognised, much more than most other nations, the contribution of play and games both to the balanced development of the young and the sensible integrated lifestyle of adults. Our educationists have consistently pointed to the cognitive, social and cultural values of play and games in child development, and our psychologists and philosophers seeking a formula for a satisfying and integrated adult lifestyle recommend a balance or harmony between aspects of our life which may be described as intellectual ('homo sapiens'), work ('homo laborans') and play ('homo ludeus'). The balance or harmony to be sought is not simply a matter of investing an equal amount of time in each of those aspects of life, but rather a problem of integrating the three appropriately in every human activity. This would mean, for example, that the play aspect of our lives must not only be an opportunity for spontaneous exuberant recreative activity but, if it is properly to serve its purpose, it must offer challenges to man the intellectual and man the worker.

In this book Jim Greenwood has set out, as one might expect of a man with his pedigree in rugby football, a thoroughly enlightened prospectus for the 'second generation' coaches. But for me he has also produced something of equal value – a sound and sensitive philosophy for the athletic sports which is firmly based on the total needs of the athlete towards becoming an integrated, capable, stable and fulfilled person. Playing rugby football is thus revealed as an ideal environment for those suitably endowed with ability to satisfy at the same time the integrating needs of man as a thinker, as a worker and as a player. In setting out his views the author uncovers his own attitudes and behaviour as an outstanding coach and as an experienced and perceptive educator. In his own words his purpose is 'to help the player to become a complete player in so far as his physical, mental and emotional limitations allow. My job is to encourage him to enjoy and extend his abilities . . . I specifically do not want him to feel that his chief cause for self esteem is his rugby or that a bad game diminishes him as a person'. He could have added in support of his philosophy something I've heard him repeat often to players . . . *'but you've got to work hard and intelligently if you want to be a good player'.*

On the technical side Total Rugby represents a synthesis of the effective arts and sciences of coaching rugby football which Jim Greenwood has carefully evolved over years of analysing, experimenting and developing. I have had the great pleasure of observing and admiring him teaching, advising and coaching at Loughborough which has been his 'laboratory' in recent years. In the process I have come to recognise and appreciate not only his impressive wisdom about the game, but his generous willingness to share with others his accumulated knowledge in order to advance the level of coaching for all. The publication of this book represents, in my opinion, a significant advance for rugby football coaching. The concepts, methods and materials that are included represent a resource that has so far not been available to coaches. In a sense rigorous coaching methods have come to be fully accepted only recently in rugby football compared with many of the other athletic sports, and as a result the application of sound principles and method may have lagged behind. The leeway would now seem to have been more than adequately made up, particularly in respect of Jim Greenwood's notions of 'total rugby' which may take the understanding and interpretations of the game onto a new and exciting level. It certainly deserves the most serious attention of coaches, players and administrators.

J. E. Kane
*Principal, West London Institute of Higher Education*

# TOTAL RUGBY AND ITS DEVELOPMENT

## Tim Stimpson kicks another penalty

Paulo di Canio is reported to have asked 'Why, in England, when people miss a target, is it always "Unlucky, unlucky!"?' Usually, he implies, it's not a matter of luck but lack of know-how. It's:

1. lack of an appropriate mechanical model of the technique

2. lack of intervention from the coach, to explain and educate

3. lack, as a result, of informed quality practice leading to confidence, composure, concentration and success.

Alan Hansen spent fourteen years at Liverpool and says he was *never* coached. And throughout UK sport this is the great technical weakness. Coaches rely on repetition practices when they should use these to spot weaknesses and intervene with technical advice to improve performance. I

remember demonstrating active coaching to an England women's hockey coach, who said she'd never seen anything like it. Active coaching is the central technical theme of this book: study it actively and you can learn to do it, and dramatically accelerate the improvement of your team. The great aim is to put each player in a position where he can coach himself — where he understands what he needs to do, and can practise until he does it, as it were, unconsciously.

Tim Stimpson has scored over 1500 points for Leicester. All players note — he has probably gone through this process for *himself*, and you can do the same. All coaches note — like Tim, you start off with a certain amount of talent, and this book will help you *maximise* it (see pp. 151–7).

# 1 THE MEANING OF TOTAL RUGBY

## TOTAL RUGBY AND PLAY-SAFE RUGBY

The rugby I'm concerned with as a coach is rugby at its most exciting – the fifteen-man handling game, in which every player is equipped to play an active role as attacker, defender, and supporting player, and in which the overall style of play gives him a chance to do so. This open, ebullient form of rugby is the most satisfying to players and potential players, spectators, officials, and coaches. It's where the game's most memorable expression has been found in the past, and where – because of its wide appeal – its future should lie.

We need a new name for it, for play-safe coaches have found it expedient to equate 'fifteen-man rugby' with reckless abandon, typified by a slavish commitment to spinning the ball wide. I believe in fifteen-man rugby, but the quality I prize most highly in a player is judgement, and one of the qualities I most deplore in a team is a strict adherence to any single aspect of play. Total rugby is a convenient title to describe rugby that subsumes all simpler forms of the game and uses them tactically as judgement dictates, but which seeks whenever possible to play the fifteen-man handling game.

What characterises this game is well-judged risk-taking. Much of the immediate pleasure in games, for player and spectator, comes from successful risk-taking, the spice of adventure, perhaps because it affords a more complete expression of the player, or because it offers a glimpse of values that go beyond the safe and conventional. Even in winning – that safest and most conventional measure of success – the best that the game can offer is the pleasure of winning with panache, of getting beyond the banal, the humdrum, the workaday.

To show it consistently you must be committed to winning. What clearly distinguishes total rugby is the variety and enterprise of its attacking methods, based on the all round competence of its players.

To help define this position it's useful to consider the polar alternative – play-safe rugby, which sets out to win by minimising the risk of defeat. This is based on two excellent tactical precepts – to restrict risk, and to play to your strength. Both of these figure in total rugby as elements in a mix; in play-safe they tend to define and limit the aspirations of the team. As part of the mix, they bring security and confidence; in isolation, lack of adventure and lack of variety.

The critical weakness of playing minimum-risk rugby is that it gives the players little chance to exercise the full range of their talents. The critical flaw in constantly playing to the team's strength, is that it tends to perpetuate the team's weaknesses. Concentration on these elements produces, at its best, a formidable but dull efficiency always based on the power of the pack. When the basic tactics

– typically, tactical kicking or taking the ball on the short side – are countered, there's often a lack of resource in alternative ways of playing the game. At its worst, possession becomes almost a liability, an embarrassment, so limited in variety is their attack. Yet paradoxically, the power of their pack creates the perfect base on which to build a really enterprising team performance. What stands in the way is a lack of vision and know-how.

The primary losers are the players. They become the victims of the play-safe syndrome: denied the preparation that would develop their talent, and the opportunity to use it, they gradually lose the techniques, the judgement, and the attitude of mind that makes enterprising rugby possible. They then become an excuse for the system – for of course you can't play enterprising rugby with players like that. This happens at all levels, but most blatantly at the top – some of the most prestigious teams throughout the world of rugby play this negative form of the game, teams with genuinely talented players whose talents are all too often allowed to atrophy. As a result everyone connected with the game suffers, and most of all the game itself.

This battle has now been won. By the '95 World Cup, total rugby was dominant – the style for the future. The book has always been concerned with the primary need to improve the individual player in the variety and quality of his skills. At first it concentrated on the lack of coaching for the back, later on freeing the forwards from outworn assumptions about their role in the game. And it's fair to say that both aims have been successfully attained.

# 2 IMPLICATIONS OF TOTAL RUGBY FOR THE COACH

## TOTAL RUGBY AND COACHING

There was a time when the restricted form of the game was, for most teams, inevitable as coaching expertise on how to improve performance was simply not available. Teams that played something like total rugby did so through a happy coincidence of players, whose abilities and temperaments made it possible. The great justification of coaching – to my mind its only justification – is to make total rugby possible for a far greater number of players. The technical knowledge now available makes it possible for any team with adequate commitment to play more enterprising, enjoyable and entertaining rugby.

The basic challenge facing the coach is obvious enough: the quality of the rugby his team can play is dictated by the thoroughness with which he has pre-pared individual players, and the attitudes he has encouraged in them to the playing of the game. He may not now have the players to play enterprising rugby; he could be on the way to producing them. He has to devote more time, thought, and energy to ensuring that individual players can function effectively in a greater variety of situations – the more successful he is in this, the more acceptable become the risks of employing them fully, extending the range and enterprise of team tactics.

For most established coaches this will represent a shift of emphasis. First gen-eration coaches have tended to see their job as organisational – assembling the players available into an effective team rather than improving the quality of the individual players. They have tended also to concentrate on the pack in first phase at the expense of the backs, and on the more mechanical aspects of play rather than those involving judgement. What is needed is a more systematic, more comprehensive approach to the needs of the game.

A shift of emphasis towards the individual and enterprising play would, of course, be timely. Team games are under increasing pressure from individual pursuits, and an approach that seeks to realise the individual's potential and evolve a style of play that gives him a maximum chance to show it is going much of the way to meet the challenge. Again, with educational change all around, the game will need to attract the younger player – as mini-rugby does – and keep him happy in a way that formerly was not felt to be necessary. Again, to solve the game's financial problems it's desirable that we attract not only more players but more spectators, and the slow handclap at Twickenham leaves no doubt what kind of rugby they want to see. At international level, it's becoming increasing-ly obvious that the team has to be firing on all cylinders to stand a chance of winning. From every point of view, an approach to coaching that emphasises the importance of the individual and the need for enterprising play must pay off.

Of course, the realisation of these objectives won't come overnight. Extending the reliable range of play of the individual and the team is a gradual process. Unless you set out to do it, however, it may not come at all. There is no need to sacrifice success on the way – even if you measure success only in the most conventional way, by winning without regard to how you won. You can prepare to play enterprising rugby, and rehearse it before you put it on the pitch; you can revert to play-safe when circumstances demand it. But how much sweeter to win with flair!

## COACHING AND ORGANISING

What's been said so far links coaching to the individual player, and focuses on that aspect of coaching that aims at producing fifteen players capable of playing effective, exciting, rugby. Another aspect of coaching deals with the organising of players into units and the team. The distinction between coaching and organising is real enough: I first used it when the West Midlands squad came together before we played (and beat) the All Blacks. The bulk of the players, from Coventry and Moseley, had no club coaches and I wasn't at all sure how they'd react to the idea of a coach. (In fact, they were all very keen to learn.) The first point I made was that I wasn't going to coach them, I was going to organise them. In the time we had, there was no way I could make a substantial improvement to their individual abilities. All we could do was organise so that we functioned effectively. This entailed sorting out: *common policies* in terms of e.g. mauling techniques or back row defence; *basic tactics*, when we had the ball e.g. our main striking points, or when they had the ball e.g. how we'd defend from mauls and rucks; *basic roles* for the players, e.g. that our inside-centre should be in charge of defence, or that our outside-centre should be our focal attacker. Once out on the field we were working to make these ideas effective, practising what we intended to do. This wasn't too difficult since the selections had been made with a basic game-plan in mind.

Out on the field, too, organising and coaching began to fade into each other. We had to get the ball to outside-centre with room to move and this meant working on *depth* at fly-half, *ball-speed* at inside-centre, and *width* across the front-three. But what we couldn't do – and certainly would have done had we been a club side meeting regularly – would have been to work on such aspects as improving the length of the scrum-half's pass, or the effectiveness of the winger's defence against an overlap. This distinction is important, because it helps define the role of the club coach: in the interests of the players, he cannot simply see himself as an organiser – if *he* doesn't improve the players' abilities, no-one will. He must see organising as simply one part of being the coach. It should also focus the club committee's attention on one aspect of their responsibilities to the player: to what extent does the club help the player maximise his potential, and to what extent does it simply offer him a game?

At levels above the club, with coaches under ever greater pressure to gain results, there's a danger of organisation completely replacing coaching. I've watched the preparation of representative sides in which individual weaknesses went unnoticed and, equally, in which individual strengths were ignored.

The great danger is the sterility of trying to create cohesion in a team by the simple expedient of forcing a pattern upon them. This is as bad as a club coach's failure to work towards a discernible strategy for his side. When we talk about a team's strategy – that staple pattern of play in which it finds its most effective expression – we're talking about something that has been fostered carefully. It has an organic quality: it has grown with the players. It can only thrive where there is real care for continuity of purpose. But simply to decide that, in this match, the stand-off, no matter what the qualities for which he was selected, should kick the ball high in the air, is an exercise in futility. Selection and method of play and preparation of the players, the units, and the team must be coherent and continuous.

## COACHING AND 'FLAIR'

The major charge laid against coaching is that it inhibits 'flair' – that it subordinates the individual to the team, and subordinates spontaneity and initiative to mechanical efficiency. This is, in fact, one result of confusing 'organising' with coaching. However, the case is usually overstated because of a limited understanding of the nature of the game, and of games in general. What distinguishes the good player is *judgement* – his risk-taking (i.e. decision-making) is justified by results: he rarely makes mistakes. This implies a limitation on simple spontaneity. The good player is constantly looking to maximise the team's advantage, and this requires forethought and a continuous summing up of the situation. Behind all his play lies a sense of *purpose*, and in the best rugby the whole team is working with purpose. The purpose is often to give a single player (and often a player with flair) the maximum chance to make a break. If players don't co-operate in this disciplined way then the chances of the individual are limited (see p. 268 ff).

The danger that faces the 'organiser' is that he fails to prepare the individuals adequately in terms of variety of possibilities, judgement, and freedom of action. These are exactly the qualities with which the coach is most concerned. Please look at p. 268 ff, where I've tried to suggest the coach's responsibility to the player with flair: coaching offers the chance to maximise his talent and to make the fullest use of it.

An extension of this is the relationship between the coach and the tactical decision-makers (TDMs) on the pitch. You must have such decision-makers: people whose flair in performance is that they can read the game accurately and determine the most effective way to attack or defend. It's simplistic to think of *either* the captain or the coach being in charge: the coach must be closer to the decision-makers than to anyone else, and an excellent measure of his coaching is the quality of their understanding. They must be free to make decisions on the pitch, and must accept that freedom responsibly. And it should never be forgotten that every player is in some degree constantly making decisions within the patterns created by the tactical decision-makers.

## TOTAL RUGBY AND PROFESSIONAL RUGBY

Two conditions are necessary to allow total rugby to flourish – the opportunity to develop coaching and playing talents fully, and the will to do it. In the past these conditions have led to the odd passionate visionary coach or player, in a favourable environment, with a driving ambition to maximise his talents, encouraging those around him. But substantial numbers, a critical mass, are needed if a total rugby culture is to develop. That's what happened in the southern hemisphere, with open rugby – full-time professionalism – providing the opportunity and the motivation. Given this opportunity, total rugby has become the selected dominant form of the game. It provides a high-scoring, lively, exciting spectacle – an eminently marketable consumer product – and has become the dominant form in international and global competition. If you want to compete, that's the form you aspire to.

The new professionalism has created a world pool of coaches and players. If you can afford it, you can recruit globally. There will soon be as many foreigners in English rugby – coaches and players – as in English soccer, and for the same reason: the UK has been left behind in the development of games we invented. But unless people of influence are converted to a total rugby culture, and create the conditions in which it becomes the dominant 'natural' vision of the game, it won't display the robust health here that characterises it in the south. A cautious, piece-meal, flavour-of-the-month approach is totally devoid of the creative vitality that's needed to develop and improve it. We don't need second-rate copy-cat coaches, we need original thinkers who will take the vision into new dimensions. And we need to make sure they are supported.

At international level, great strides have been made. There was a time when it was possible for an England coach to adopt a major strategy irrespective of the strengths and weaknesses of the players selected. He simply ignored them, and imposed a pattern – e.g. kick and rush – with dire results for all involved. Now, there is a vision that players and coaches share, and a development programme to ensure that the vision will grow as the abilities of the players expand – a genuinely organic process. Selection is based on clear priorities for all positions. A corps of coaches fosters the development of individual players, units and phases of the game. The squad has been enlarged, in part by giving talented youngsters a chance. This simultaneously creates greater competition within the squad, and safeguards the future. Technical structures have been created that promise to give enduring success. Such bold initiatives were all but unimaginable when the first edition of this book came out – in the year that Clive Woodward captained Loughborough – but in that year the notion of professionalism was also inherently unlikely. Commercial pressures, no doubt, have eased the way for these radical, visionary changes. You need a winning team to attract all the forms of support that are available, and that is a persuasive argument for even the most amateur-thinking of administrators in a professional era. Nevertheless, someone had to have the vision, courage and persuasiveness to put it forward and the energy to implement it. It's on a scale that should make every Union think, and with an attention to detail that will continue to develop.

And for every club throughout the world of rugby the basic message is clear: you need a coherent continuous development policy for your teams. You recruit with that in mind, you select with that in mind, you coach with that in mind. This book makes the basic assumption that you won't have access to star players – its aim is to help your coaches make the most of the players you've got. But if it works, it'll be down to their commitment, patience, enthusiasm, and capacity for dedication. If you do have star players, remember: there's never been a player who couldn't be improved. The talented, above all, merit the coach's attention.

# 3 IMPLICATIONS OF OPEN RUGBY FOR THE CLUB

## THE CLUB AND THE PLAYER

The critical technical question for the coach or committee man to ask is '*to what extent has being a member of our club accelerated that player's progress?*'. Every player likes to feel his ability is growing, and detailed, personal help towards that improvement is perhaps the most valuable thing the club has to offer – it's at once technical aid and a guarantee of the club's interest in him.

Beyond that, every player can be helped to feel that he has a contribution to make to the preparation and development of the team. There's little scope for discussion on the practice field – you need decisive leadership to get high work-rate – but time can be made for it off the field. The aim of team playing policy must be to offer every player the chance to use in the match the abilities he has developed. Everybody in rugby knows how many exciting and talented players are denied the chance, game after game, to show what they can do and to build confidence in their ability to do it.

Beyond the club team, the player has his sights legitimately set on some form of representative honours. The higher the level, the greater the part that sheer talent must play in success, but at every level solid preparation by the club should be evident. The player's talent is often specialised and takes the form of one commanding talent – his strength at prop, for example; the club's contribution should be the all-round competence of his other play, the range of skills he has acquired, the attitude of mind he has developed.

A club that is seriously ambitious should be offering challenges to its players, and especially its best players, for the good of the players, the coach, the club, and ultimately the national team. An ambitious club needs ambitious players, ambitious coaches – and the way to keep them is to offer them a demanding programme of development, and inspire them with a passion for excellence.

Most of the best players will become members of representative squads, and there they should meet the same challenges, intensified. As representative rugby grows in importance, and the squad meets more frequently, the representative coach has a real chance to command allegiance from the players by offering a seriously better programme of development for the individual player, the units, and the team. If the representative team is to flourish, its members must feel allegiance primarily to it; feel that there their talents are being maximised.

Competition of this kind should lift both club coach and representative coach, but it should be accompanied by an on-going dialogue on how best to develop the player. The club coach should attend representative sessions, and the representative coach club sessions.

The most important step the player himself can make is to accept responsibility for his development – and that means demanding far more of himself than any outsider would. He's got to:

- set his own fitness/strength standards – it's useless doing just enough to satisfy the coach: he must be intent on exacting increasing maxima from his body and his mind
- eliminate avoidable mistakes from his routine skills by prolonged concentration in practice
- extend the range of his skills to cope with all but the most specialised situations in the game
- feel that if he gives enough he can win the match by himself right up to the final whistle
- be more concerned with what he does badly than with what he does well
- reject completely any tinge of complacency about his abilities
- enlist whatever help's available, inside or outside his club/rugby
- underline his commitment to his team-mates in practice and in matches
- adopt an athletic lifestyle, staying focused throughout the year.

The message is clear: don't wait for other people to help you, don't accept their idea of working hard – get in there and help yourself.

## THE COMMITTEE AND TOTAL RUGBY

Committee men are, in most sports, chosen less for their consciousness of technical developments than for their administrative ability and willingness to serve. They are, however, inevitably those most protective of their club's reputation – they are the people who helped to create it. It's particularly important, therefore, that they should move beyond the 'all that counts is not losing' attitude. They might take pride in the fact that their club has very much more to offer than a desperate need to win; that they have a coherent preparation policy, so that the prospective player will have a real chance of maximising his potential; that they play enterprising rugby in which every player has a part; that their talented players are given all round competence; that they often win, and that they win by playing quality rugby. If they can add to that that they offer coaching at all levels, that every team is watched, that there is a coherent, fair, selection process and that, in fact, the individual player is seen as an important club member – they will have real grounds for pride in their club.

In one other respect the club, and especially the coach and committee, can enhance their reputation and make an important contribution to the health and attractiveness of the game. They are the people in the best position to establish and maintain high standards of conduct on the field. The referee, with the backing of Disciplinary Committees and the Union, can certainly curb the excesses of the few, but the club is in the best position to encourage a positive outlook in all its players. The reputation of the game itself has not been helped by the image of the rugger hearty, the bar-room hero from the undistinguished XV whose claim to fame is his capacity for beer and song. But the image of manliness that finds expression in deliberate intimidation and foul play is destructive of the game itself.

The stakes are higher in professional sport; the temptation to win at any cost is greater. It's reflected in technical offences – using a hand to play the ball back in the scrum, for example, and in crude brutality. Unhappily, there's little or no use in appealing to moral principle: the judgement by TV commentators was based on the same risk/reward materialism that prompted the offence. He was likely to get away with it; even if he didn't the consequences were acceptable; but he did get away with it, so his judgement was spot-on and his conduct was validated. It's even more disturbing to see violence on the increase. In what was to be my last match for Scotland, I was clumsy enough to dislocate my left shoulder, silly enough to have it put back in on the pitch, and stupid enough to carry on playing with it bound up. Late in the game, I managed to tackle Niall Brophy, the Irish left wing. I must have whined when we hit the ground. Niall bounced up, kicked the ball into touch, asked 'Are you alright, Jim?', and helped me to my feet. Rugby had more to offer then than the 'triumph' of winning, or the 'disaster' of losing, at least for some players, and it still could have if coaches and schoolmasters fostered it.

The committee concerned with the club's reputation can make it clear that there is no place in their team for the habitually dirty player. If we are to attract players to the game it's got to be on the basis of a robust, enjoyable, and positive activity. The atmosphere in the club itself is the best guarantee of this positive approach on the field.

It's difficult, too, to dissociate a negative approach to the style of play from a negative attitude to the game's ethics. Play-safe, nine-man rugby, by placing an emphasis on physical confrontation and often esteeming strength more highly than skill creates more situations where violence can erupt, and predisposes the team towards it. Those with a responsibility for the club's reputation might bear this in mind.

## THE SPECTATOR AND TOTAL RUGBY

When this book first appeared, spectators were not normally mentioned in books on rugby. 'The game is for the players' was a sentiment sure to win applause. It was unnecessarily exclusive even then; rugby is in part a display activity, and to be a focus of attention may well enhance a player's efforts and enjoyment.

Since then, the need for the game to attain a higher profile and earn more money has meant that the spectator on the line or in the armchair has assumed new importance. He has become the key that unlocks the door to financial security. I've no doubt that total rugby will prove more attractive to the spectator, and especially to the casual television watcher, than any other kind.

There always have been rugby grounds where the spectators took a simple partisan approach to the match. I remember in Paris a touch-judge being bombarded with oranges because he'd given a decision against France. In Madrid, there was some doubt at the end of the match whether we'd make it to the changing rooms. Indeed, at Langholm as a lad of tender years, I was amazed at the energy with which the crowd advised the referee 'Get yon fair-haired bugger off the pitch, Ref: he's aye off-side'. But I think there's little doubt that with league structures and cup competitions – both devised in 19th century soccer to maintain and boost spectator appeal by adding external importance to the match – the populist element may grow and with it internal tensions in the game. I hope referees will play their cards with courage even when it's a matter of star players and important matches, and that clubs use their programmes to welcome their opponents in terms that limit the negative response.

## WOMEN AND TOTAL RUGBY

A group who have attained unexpected importance are women players. Undeterred by the criticism of prejudiced men and women, more and more women are taking up rugby as players. Much of the criticism is unencumbered by fact: those most vocal tend to be those with least direct experience of the phenomenon. Exactly the same kind of criticism greeted the pioneer women players of tennis, track and field athletics, lacrosse, judo, and so on. In due course rugby will become a perfectly acceptable game for women to play.

I've thoroughly enjoyed coaching Loughborough, England, and GB women's teams. A nicer bunch of people and a greater degree of dedication to the game or pleasure in playing, I've never encountered. But as a coach, what stands out is the talent the best women players show for the game. In terms of reading the game, intelligent decision-making, improvising answers to unexpected problems, range of skills, the women give nothing away to the men. They are equally committed to attack and defence, and equally whole-hearted in contact. When you consider that none of the players has any experience pre-dating higher education, their feeling for the game is remarkable.

This registers with spectators. I've seen spectators converted in a matter of minutes: they come to watch a 'women's rugby match', and almost immediately find themselves watching a 'rugby match', indeed a high-quality match. All of my teams have played total rugby, and the women play it technically as well as any male team.

Moreover, the spirit in which they play – very committed and very clean – is wholly refreshing: the men could learn from it how to make a tough game acceptable to parents and people at large. Their love of the game is reflected not merely in their putting up with uninformed criticism but in their paying personally to represent their country: sponsorship is still spasmodic because public approval is still spasmodic.

Little by little, however, they are achieving media respectability. Still, of course, there's a tabloid desire to focus on the fringe that the women's game shares with the men's: those incapable of making a mark as players try to make a mark as clowns. But this is becoming increasingly dated – they are attracting serious official, TV and newspaper interest, and that reflects and will accelerate public acceptance of the game.

The most significant problem that faces women is resentment of their trespassing in a male preserve. It's serious because those who manage that preserve are precisely those most able to offer help to the women. They need club support – a pitch for Sunday matches, coaching assistance, referees, the use of changing facilities. In exchange they create a bigger, financially more secure club, add a social dimension, and attract media attention.

In this respect, women players have come a long way in a short time. There's no reason for them not to consolidate that gain. If you can, give them your help.

# 4 THE COACH'S RESPONSIBILITY TO RUGBY

## THE COACH AND RUGBY

The word 'coach' is imbued with the notion of skill and attention to detail, and the true concern of a coach is the skill and technical flexibility shown by his players and his team. Some coaches have derived a spurious reputation from the sheer physical prowess of the players they have available. The real question is not '*how successful is that team?*' but '*how successful could that team be?*' and the measure of the coach is how closely the whole team approximates to that potential. This view poses a challenge to those coaches whose clubs have the best players, and offers recognition to those coaches who do sterling work in more difficult conditions.

Beyond that is the contribution the coach makes to the development of the game, and to coaching expertise. Coaches now must accept the fact that the technical development of the game is largely in their hands and part of their responsibility is to the game as well as to their club and players. This is true of the tone of the game as well as its technical content, and in both respects short-term gains – achieved e.g. by condoning violence, preaching hatred of the opposition, or encouraging minimum-risk rugby – may well prove long-term losses.

Becoming a technically proficient coach is a process that never ends: there's always more to learn, and more efficient ways of communicating it. You can:

- pick up other people's ideas – and improve them

- examine them more thoroughly and apply them more effectively

- identify what you don't know, and apply 'ceaseless meditation' (see p. 31) to working out answers

- examine the answers more thoroughly, and refine your methods

- tap your own playing experience, and that of your players, and work to establish the principles behind the intuitive action

- never be afraid to try out your ideas, confident that once you get started you'll see ways of improving them

- go to courses and books with specific questions to which you require specific answers – then set about improving the answers

- be concerned about what you don't know, not complacent about what you do

- be at least as demanding of yourself as you are of the players: you need them to be committed self-improvers with a passion for excellence – that goes for you too; you want them to be actively concentrated throughout the practice – that goes for you too.

In short, you should believe in the possibility of constant improvement in all aspects of your work.

If it's any comfort, I took up coaching schoolboys with the unthinking confidence of an international player: it lasted all of five minutes. At that point I'd realised that:

- I knew nothing about coaching
- I knew next to nothing about rugby
- I had everything to learn, and a duty to learn it
- I'd have to work it all out for myself.

Simultaneously, I was facing the same bleak prospect with A-level English, French and History: I was an amateur in an age of amateurism. In my first match for Scotland, I wasn't told what position I was playing till we were actually in the tunnel. The hill of coaching knowledge may be higher now, but at least there are tracks towards the summit, and excellent prospects at the top.

Paradoxically enough, despite the amount of knowledge available, I don't believe that we've really got started on coaching. The next ten or fifteen years may well see radical innovations in the tactics, techniques and coaching methods used in the game. So underdeveloped are coaching techniques that every coach can expect to add something new of his own – you can always develop personal insights and techniques, and take coaching a step further.

My own aims in coaching are, no doubt, much affected by a background in teaching, and the fact that coaching and being coached are educational experiences. I want to help the player become a complete player so far as his physical, mental and emotional limitations allow. My job is to encourage him to enjoy and extend his abilities, and take a proper pride in them. I specifically do not want him to feel that his chief cause for self-esteem is his rugby, or that a bad game diminishes him as a person – sixty-seven (or thereabouts) out of every one hundred human beings know little of rugby, and they still get by. Nevertheless, if he chooses to play, I'd like to see him measure himself against his fellows, and be given the chance to express himself as fully as possible. To that end, the rugby we play must be total rugby.

Rugby is a tough game, but the most important aspect is the ability to be tough with yourself, to demand more of yourself than your opponent does, and that's not inconsistent with a tone in the team that's generous, positive, thoughtful, honourable.

His rugby on the field has got to provide him with something memorable, some spots of time that will live with him. The wider the range of those moments the better. They may be aesthetic or heroic, expressions of speed, power or judgement, fitness or skill, individual or group – but they've got to be memorable expressions of his youth and talent. He's got to feel the elation of winning well, with a touch of style and class, and especially of winning against the odds. He's got to recognise that he can win as an individual against his immediate opponent and against himself, even if the team loses. I'd like him to remember being magnanimous in defeat, generous in victory. I'd like him to enjoy the sense of belonging to a team, and being proud to belong to it in victory or defeat.

Some of these points I've put in the past tense, because they are a recognition of the best of what rugby has offered me, and because, like thousands of others I'm aware that given the right conditions, rugby is more than simply a diversion over a comparatively few playing years. It's up to the coach to ensure that these 'right conditions' are available to as many of his players as possible, in their interest and in that of the game.

The basic condition is the spirit in which the game is played. In the earliest days, when referees were felt unnecessary (he was there to be 'referred' to in cases in which the captains couldn't agree), there was common agreement that there were things in life more important than the result of a match. Without some sense of a greater good – be it sportsmanship, the quality of the experience or the game itself – the importance of winning can grow to destructive proportions. It's up to the coach to keep some such greater good present to his players.

I don't think that such an approach is invalidated by the pressure of leagues or the lure of money. In this country and across the world, 90% of players are unaffected by the commercialisation of the game, except to the extent that they're affected by televised sport. For them and for their coaches, the values sketched out above are the key to a genuinely fulfilling experience. And even for the 10% the benefit is still available if the coach has the strength of character to embody it.

PART 2

# UNDERSTANDING THE GAME – ATTACK AND DEFENCE

## 5 UNDERSTANDING THE GAME

The basic pattern in the game is that of alternate *concentration* and *dispersal*. The laws were so designed that there would be a constant clearing of the field, with a large number of players concentrated in a small area – at scrum, line-out, ruck or maul – so that there was a large amount of open space for the remaining players. The aim of this was to tilt the balance in favour of the attackers – to give them space in which to work. This was complementary to the single most characteristic law of the game – passing back – which was designed to create situations in which the player had a chance to get past his opponent in the most exciting way: by evasive running.

These intentions have been obscured by the adoption of the rugby-league crossfield defence in suitable situations. At static or very slow moving rucks and mauls, and at short line-outs available forwards move out to join the defending three-quarters. This limits the space available for a clean break by the attacking backs, intensifying the problems caused by an attack line which is flat rather than shallow. But problems are the life blood of coaching: they are what justifies having coaches at all. Eight years ago I suggested a solution in *Think Rugby* and it'll be developed further below.

The space available to the attackers allows them to *stretch the opposing defence*: long passing will force each defender to defend a wider zone and give each attacker a better chance of making a break; short passing will create space on the flanks to release a speedy winger or allow a supporting overload. Tactical points – scrums, line-outs, rucks, mauls and penalties – split the field, handicap the defence, and offer alternative channels of attack, one of which will offer superior advantage from introducing the extra man (see p. 264). At each one, you also have alternatives in kicking attack, both laterally and in exploiting the difficulties of the depth defence: the space they've to cover varies directly with their distance from their goal line.

The action sequence in the game is that of *stop-go* corresponding to the basic pattern of concentration-dispersal. This is of the utmost importance to the game for the following reasons.

## It makes the game possible

Figures produced to show the amount of time the ball is actually in play (25–30 minutes) tend to suggest that there's a great waste of time – but the pauses actually make the game practicable: without them, the physical demands would be too great. Inducing fatigue in the opposition by prolonged pressure – e.g. physical contact, sustained ball speed – both in the short term and the long term is an effective basis for attack, and a recognition of the physical limits within which the game is played.

## It restores order

One aspect of the basic pattern can be seen as order-disorder; the longer the fluid phase of play continues the greater is the probability of disorder. This sets up mental and emotional pressures in the players that correspond to (and no doubt affect) physical fatigue. Restoring order – the 'stop' phase – becomes more necessary as players become tired, and the laws recognise this by linking stoppages to mistakes.

Disorder in defence, however, provides the optimum chance for attack to succeed. Defence depends on systems to reduce the weakness of isolated defenders. If the attack can strike whilst the system is disrupted, that weakness returns, and with it a higher probability of scores. Any delay in launching the attack, however, will allow some regrouping of the defence: delay always favours the defenders. So once you've crossed the defence line and been checked, it's urgent to recycle the ball as fast as you can.

## It creates set–pieces favouring the defence

The basic situation at any stoppage in the game approximates to that at a set scrum (see p. 21).

The *defence line* is the line which the offside laws allow the *pressure* element of the defence to take up.

The *gain line* is the point reached by the ball before the stoppage. For either side to go forward they must get the ball across the gain line.

The *tackle line* connects the points at which respective opponents will meet – which, given a similarity of pace and reaction time, will be midway between the defence line and attack line.

The *attack line* is the line along which the back division expecting to gain possession take up position. To allow the ball to be passed without undue pressure they must make space for themselves and tend, therefore, to lie in echelon (see p. 21). If they intend to kick, the echelon must be shallow. If they intend to do a move then individual players will probably have to alter their positions. It's highly unlikely that the most effective positioning will in fact be a straight line even for passing the ball out (see p. 250 ff.), however, the line in the diagram conveys the basic situation adequately.

On pages 250 and 260 there's an explanation of why a wide, shallow line is a better bet than a deep tucked in line. Both 'shallow' and 'wide' are important – many breaks are made wide. With 'shallow' however, there are real difficulties. It's become exaggerated and then raised to the status of dogma. If you're so shallow that the defence is in your face and solar plexus as you get the ball, you've thrown away the advantage of possession completely. If your fly-half lies so flat that he's under constant pressure, his judgement and his skills will be adversely affected – he's liable to do the wrong thing and do it badly. For the sake of the team and the line, he's got to feel comfortable. If he sees the possibility of a personal break, a signal, and he can run onto the ball at the point where he normally stands – at speed and unexpectedly. And outside him every player is entitled to an acceleration zone – enough space to run onto the ball and set up his opponent. But 'shallow' has often been interpreted as 'flat', which tends to mean taking the pass standing still and becoming a candidate for Intensive Care. What's even more remarkable is that teams persevere with it as if there were no alternative. Don't be dogmatic; don't be fashionable: be realistic. The aim is to pass as nearly flat as the situation allows with the receiver accelerating onto the ball – for this and to be able to move the ball wide, you must make space.

In the diagram, the starting point is a scrum but the situation tends to recur at any tactical point where the ball is not made available quickly. The consequences are that at such points –

- if, as expected, team B get the ball and intend to handle they will take the ball back behind the gain line and to reach it again will have to cross the tackle line: they run the risk of losing the ground between the gain line and the tackle line. Possession is only a potential advantage

- if, unexpectedly, team A get the ball quickly and know how they're going to use it, they ought to be able to cross the gain line before coming into contact with their opponents

- whichever team gets the ball across the gain line will have its pack running forward, which generates the most powerful impetus in attack. So far as the pack is concerned, the greatest advantage, in terms of angle of run, accrues when the ball crosses the gain line close to them. The further out the strike is made the less important this advantage becomes for the same yardage of gain. It's important, therefore, that the team should have planned and practised methods of attacking close to the scrum, line-out, maul, or ruck

- the tackling power of each team tends, as a consequence, to be grouped in the back row to limit attacks close in, and in the front three – fh–ic–oc – to pressurise passing movements, with a joint aim to prevent the ball crossing the gain line against them or to minimise such gain. If they can make their tackles on the tackle line, then their team has gained ground, and their pack is moving forward. Tackling power is an important consideration in selection. Indeed, powerful, aggressive, pressurising defence underlies all consistent success. In every team talk emphasise the need to make the first tackle count:

- this concentration of defenders is one of the first elements to be considered in decision-making: the attacking team must have appropriate methods of taking them on, distracting them, or out-flanking them

- any check in the action of the game, such as those provided by the stop-go pattern, will tend to allow the defenders to regroup in the optimum defensive formation. In first-phase situations this regrouping will be complete, and even from mauls and rucks any undue delay will result in a situation approximating to first-phase. Effective second-phase possession – a situation in which the defence has been put under pressure, the tackle ball has been kept available, and the attacking side has regrouped quickly – will lead to a much better attacking situation. Each of these elements, however, is necessary to produce an effective second-phase situation.

## It simplifies decision-making

The constant occurrence of situations in which the defence positioning and tactics are predictable, and where divergences from the expected formation are significant and obvious, makes the spotting of potential weaknesses easier for the tactical decision-makers.

## It provides a simple basis for team tactics

Apart from a team *strategy*, the team's preferred mode of attack, there have to be team *tactics*. These are the team's response to the recurrent set-piece situations in the stop-go pattern. It is moderately certain, for example, that in every match the team will be awarded a scrum about 15m from the opposing line, and 15m from touch. They will know – by thought, experiment and practice – which attacking gambits are effectively open to them and which are ruled out by the limitations of their players. It's then for the tactical decision-makers to select the best option against these particular opponents on this particular day on this particular ground at this particular moment in the match. Incidentally, therefore, it also provides a simple basis for team coaching, unit coaching and coaching of the individual.

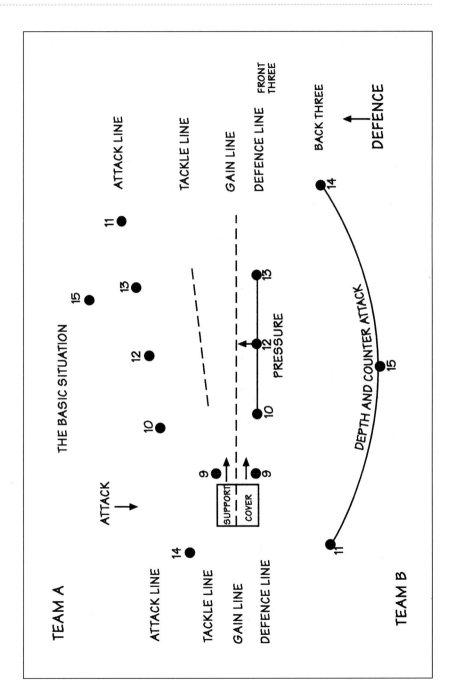

# 6 PRINCIPLES OF ATTACK

What emerge from these considerations are four basic imperatives.

1  Get possession

2  Go forward

3  Support the ball-carrier

4  Maintain the pressure

But these imperatives, narrowly interpreted, can be a recipe for nine- or ten-man rugby. Accordingly, it's useful, while appreciating their truth, to rephrase them as follows.

1  Get the ball

2  Get it into space

3  Be first in support

4  Maintain the pressure

These imperatives recur cyclically in every attack – in first-phase, second-phase, third-phase, and so on. Some teams deliberately seek contact to soften up their opponents, but if they are checked they too have to start looking for space. The most effective form of driving attack in the forwards has each player taking a pass, and driving into space: every check gives time for the defenders to regroup; the quintessential pressure of every attack is speed in going forward into space.

## Get the ball

The minimum realistic possession the team must aim for is all its own ball in the scrum, the line-out, and when your own player takes the ball into the ruck or maul situation. Whatever you get beyond that is a bonus. You must also be prepared to take advantage of any ball gifted to you by way of penalties and misplaced kicks of any kind.

The first priority in any team is to get possession, and the first priority in coaching the units is to ensure that they do. The critical mistake of play-safe coaches, however, is to spend a great deal of time and energy on this at the expense of preparing the team to make a varied and intelligent use of the posession when it wins it.

The use they can make of it is to some extent determined by the quality of ball that's won. Good ball is controlled so that it arrives where it's wanted, when it's wanted, at the speed it's wanted. Ideally, it arrives under those conditions with the opposition going backward so that their defence is off-balance, but that again is a bonus.

It's immensely desirable that the ball reaches the back of the tactical point as quickly as possible. It's equally desirable that there should be variety in its use. If it's always fed to the backs immediately, the opposition needn't commit all their forwards to the ruck or maul or whatever – so that constant quick ball and constant slow ball can lead to the same situation: the backs faced with a strengthened defence. Make no mistake – quick is best – but vary the use you make of it. Keep them guessing so that they become reluctant to commit forwards to crossfield defence.

## Get it into space
The quest for space is the most characteristic expression of total rugby.

It is based on: positioning, passing and pace, all of which are employed to keep the ball alive, constantly moving it away from opponents and forward into space. Of course, even the most skilful of teams will frequently find themselves setting up mauls and rucks, and kicking, and so on, but that's not what they work to achieve. In this they differ markedly from play-safe teams, who customarily use their forwards as bludgeons to crush the opposition by physical impact and serial mauling – they run *at* their opponents, and rarely pass to better positioned team-mates. This is close to the style of weak rugby league sides, hypnotised by the five-tackle rule, and determined not to cede possession by essaying a pass. Teams playing total rugby expect their educated forwards in the loose to move into intelligent *support positions* that will keep the pack running forward into space, with *passing* adequate in quality and variety to that task.

Their coaches are committed to *pace* in the forwards – the great aim, those electrifying bursts that put a player clear and impose impossible stress on the opposing defence. Chapter 24 is dedicated to fitness, and especially to methods of improving the capacity to turn on sprints throughout the match. A pack operating on these principles is one of the great sights of total rugby, and the most powerful form of attack.

The same principles govern back-play. Judgement of position is critical. A slavish commitment to fashionable dogma (especially ill-understood fashionable dogma, e.g. the whole line standing flat off a standing fly-half) is stultifying. The dire efforts of such talented back-lines as Australia in their first '95 Cup match against South Africa, trying the impossible, show the deadening power of conformity, and the absolute need to understand what is and what is not possible from a given formation. The players need education, not indoctrination. So too with handling: no team can tolerate handling mistakes, especially wide, so some coaches decline to play expansive rugby. But the coach committed to total rugby sets out to eliminate handling mistakes by intensive handling practice, and by demanding excellence in all stages of all practice. A coach who allows sloppy handling, or sloppy anything else, is betraying the team.

The third element, pace, is a catalyst: it can transform the situation in attack and defence. Every player should commit himself to a programme of speed work:

- physical – e.g. bounding, hopping, running, ideally up a gradient; work on abrupt change of pace from covering pace; intensive competitive sprint work against players of the same pace

- emotional – the coach can release pace in players by simply telling them that they're running faster, and encouraging them to do so.

Pace will increasingly become a differential in selection in every position. It has always been a selection criterion for the backs. All too often, however, that pace has been underused, with the ball rarely reaching the fastest players. If you have real pace at your disposal you need to work out:

- situations in which the ball can reach the player with least delay – e.g. off one or two passes

- situations in which the player of pace can move safely into strike positions – e.g. the winger appearing on the opposite wing

- how to create the conditions which particularly favour him – some may need to take the ball moving quite slowly to exploit their acceleration; some moving fast to exploit their top speed.

Strikers of quality are strategic figures, with the team pattern of play focused upon them, to bring them frequently into play, and to lull the opposition into complacency about the strike power of other players.

Believe in pace – but, as we'll see later, don't divorce it from all the other aspects of speed in the game.

Both backs and forwards, then, share the core qualities of intelligent positioning, efficient handling, and relative pace. Yes, individual players have specific duties which demand other qualities, but so far as possible these are in addition to these three basic rugby-playing abilities. Don't let stereotypes dominate your thinking, e.g. that forwards shouldn't play touch rugby, that key exercise in applying the three principles, or that props shouldn't be seen in the loose. That kind of dogma (like any other) is simply a way of avoiding genuine thought. The Springboks used touch rugby as their warm-up activity before each match in the '95 World Cup, and the props side-stepped and dummied with the best of them. *Dogma binds; experiment liberates.*

### Get it into space ii

Much of this fluent play originates once a good attacking position has been established. The choice of such positions is the prime function of the TDMs –

they select an axis of attack and a mode of attack appropriate to the established strengths of the team. In varying degrees we can say that the hooker, the no. 8, the halves, the outside-centre and the full-back may be involved in this process – at line-out, scrum, immediately after tactical points, and in initiating counter-attack respectively. In fact, effective control is vested in the halves, at the very centre of the team, handling the ball at the most critical moments, and the full-back, who has the function of choosing the mode and axis of attack thrust upon him by the opportunity to counter-attack.

What these players elect to do determines the nature and effectiveness of your use of the ball and constitutes your tactics, for better or for worse. The questions facing the coach are:

- do I just let them get on with it? They play in those positions so they must have some aptitude for it and experience of it. The team know what they're likely to do, even if it doesn't always work out

- do I impose a pattern on the team, perhaps related to ground positions, and try to groove them into it?

- do I try a programme of education, so that the TDMs (and the team in general) understand better what the team can do, and select appropriate options for a given situation?

These are real questions. The standard answer in the past was the first. If you opt for that, get players to read Part 4 which will help them avoid major problems.

The second answer – strongly encouraging a single pattern of play – can be effective if it simplifies team play as a whole, and produces purpose out of random events. Introduced as an emergency measure, it must start with some limitation, often unfortunately disregarding individual strengths and potential. It works far better if you've time to encourage the pattern of play to develop organically out of existing strengths, and constant reinforcement of its elements in practices.

The third answer – to educate the players, and especially the TDMs – is at once the most radical and the most rewarding. An obvious indicator for trying it is the character of the halves – are they reasonably flexible mentally? Do they pick up ideas quickly? Are they still developing as players? The methods outlined in Mobilising the Team (see p. 85), will allow a virtually painless transition from the present arrangement, and a fair warranty of success.

To have TDMs capable of a flexible, appropriate response to the opportunities and demands of a match has always seemed a matter of luck – of having exceptional individuals with a special gift. But the aim of all coaching is to make the natural gifts of the talented player available to the less talented, and work on decision-making is simply part of that process. Especially, we might say, tactical decision-making, since that's of a scale and kind that make it easier to handle than the micro-decision of when exactly to do your side-step: micro-decisions are virtually unconscious; tactical decisions tend to be rational, and easier to explain. So if you, as coach or player, feel you'd like to undertake some tactical education, you can be moderately sure your work will be fruitful.

Ask yourself how efficient your TDMs are at present. Do they:

- succeed in getting the ball into significantly advantageous space?
- succeed in letting your most talented attackers have adequate opportunities to attack?
- succeed in exploiting weakness in the opposing defence?
- succeed in deploying your tactical repertoire effectively?
- succeed in diverting and inhibiting the opposition defence?
- succeed in determining the proper degree of risk justified by the match situation?
- succeed in maintaining something approaching the optimum tempo for your team vis-à-vis the opposition?
- succeed in maintaining the team initiative by the speed and accuracy of deciding and communicating their decision?

Do they, in short, succeed as leaders? Are they happy, confident, intelligent warriors?

You can see what an enormous bonus it would be to extract a high degree of advantage from each possession of the ball. You have to recognise that *possession of the ball is only a potential advantage*: it's what we achieve with it that counts. It becomes a real advantage only when the team has the *initiative* in using it. Essentially, this means that the team has chosen how to use it, and aren't forced by their own inefficiency or the aggressiveness of their opponents into limited or involuntary actions.

Tactically, having the initiative is the key to total rugby. Any lack of under-standing or uncertainties about the process of decision-making, or its attendant technical requirements will lead to some loss of the initiative, and a failure to exploit fully the abilities of the players. The coach has two equally imperative tasks here.

1  To ensure adequate technical efficiency.

2  To improve and simplify the decision-making process.

Each player in the team must be encouraged to play intelligently – thinking ahead, judging what's going to happen, deciding what he can do about it, and having the confidence to do it. This process goes on throughout the game in an apparently endless set of varying situations, highlighting the need for the coach to simplify the task by providing *principles* of play and *priorities* in applying them – he certainly can't deal with each situation as a discrete event: it would overload the players, confuse them, and embarrass them. Talented players seem to have built in priorities and principles, and one of their tasks as they become coaches is to identify and articulate them.

For the majority of the team, a personal mistake – some infringement of principle or priority – is annoying, but the odds are that a team-mate can cover for them. With key players such mistakes can be critical. Their decision and action directly determine where, how and how appropriately the team is going to use what may be hard-won possession. How you can simplify the task is examined in Mobilising the Team (see p. 85).

## Be first in support and maintain the pressure

The vision that is seminal in total rugby is that of constant support.

Every step we take towards establishing effective support is a step towards maintaining our initiative, the momentum of our attack, and relentless pressure on the defence. We're not talking about magic transformations, therefore, but about steady, often inconspicuous, progress.

Step one is to recognise the factors involved, and to recognise that they apply to everyone in the team.

### Speed of proximity

The nearest player must be capable of acting effectively. Ideally, each specialised forward should be able to operate as a back; each specialised back to operate as a forward, in loose play. Work to expand the range of skills and procedures throughout the team.

### Speed in reading the earliest cues for action

This means constant vigilance – if you have to switch on, you're too late. Everyone should take part in the covering exercises described in Unit v Unit Practices (see p. 290).

### Fast, accurate movement

You cannot afford to wait for precise data: act at once on your general impression. This usually means:

- that your first few steps (especially if you're a forward) will be simply crossfield – but the metres you cover may prove vital

- that this gives way to running responding to feedback.

### Running off your team-mates

- into positions that contribute to moving the ball into space; or
- that reinforce or complement the running line of those ahead of you in defence.

### Speed/accuracy of handling in attack

Sometimes it's vital to be able to move the ball through your hands very quickly; it's always vital that your pass be accurate – don't pass if you can't be sure of accuracy; a mistake might be critical.

In cases like this, intensive handling repays every second spent on it. Don't let the players flop the ball around: put a premium on precision.

You want precise passing, precise positioning and precise timing of the pass, and you get that by demanding precision in all your practices and over the full range of passes. And that implies equal attention to the positioning of the receiver – who must be able to run onto as flat a pass as the situation allows. Keeping the ball alive out of a tackle is a special case, and the key word here is 'control': not passing is often less dangerous than a bad pass. If you're not confident, go with the odds – go to ground and make the ball available. Start every practice handling session with the absolute basics – see 'Intensive Handling' below.

### Length/accuracy of handling in attack

Controlled spin passing can give you the length and accuracy to take out several defenders, and get the receiver into space. This is most devastating when done by forwards – and can be built into tap penalties.

### Urgency in recycling the ball when over the previous defence line

They may tackle you; they should never tackle the ball – make sure as you go to ground that the ball is securely available to the next man. He goes forward if he clearly can – but even slight doubt should see the ball delivered to the line.

### Running speed

The capacity to produce high-speed bursts through the game has to be built up by intensive competitive sprinting in practice for every player. The basic competition is always with yourself: when you hit the line you accelerate abruptly even if you're feeling like death. To produce 110% effort when your body is saying 'no', to run as for your life, demands the best kind of pride and self-discipline.

The conditioning that the coach offers has to change the players' mind-set, their notion of acceptable levels of pain, their sense of acceptable achievement. If, as a player, you don't have such a coach, you must develop it in yourself – which, in the long run, is always the best way. You must become thoroughly acquainted with exhaustion until you come to see it as a friend who lets you drive yourself harder than your opponent can.

# 7 PRINCIPLES OF DEFENCE

For consistent success your defence must be absolutely sound.

If you're trying to reinvent a team you've just taken over, defence is second only to fitness in your priorities. It's a matter of organisation and attitude. An isolated player makes a poor defender: organisation ensures that no defender in your team is isolated. Being defensive-minded is the death-knell of defence – we must always attack. When we have the ball we attack their space; when they have the ball we attack them. We put them under sustained pressure and make every first tackle count. We deny them the initiative: they do what they can, not what they wish. We harry them into mistakes in thought and action. And remember the old adage 'the best form of defence is attack' is eminently true in rugby: keep them anxious about your attacks and their attacks will be less ambitious, less whole-hearted.

There are three elements in defence: pressure, cover and depth. These are necessary whenever the opposition have or are likely to get the ball in set play, loose play, or counter-attack.

**1** **Pressure** is generated by the front three and in specific cases the back row. Its aim is to deny the opposition the initiative, to harry them into mistakes, and if possible to regain possession beyond the gain line. When the opposition are consistently moving the ball wide, the front three and back row may adopt a 'drift defence' to provide cover against overlap attacks (see p. 284).

**2** **Cover** is provided by the pack as a whole with the back row leading. It's concerned with providing safeguards to the pressure groups by creating a wide, deep, defensive pattern of crossfield running (see p. 220). But it isn't restricted to the pack. Intelligent backs are also concerned in supporting players outside them in attack and defence, following exactly the same principles.

**3** **Depth** is provided by the back three – the full-back and wingers. It's concerned with defence against kicks, a third line against running attack, and the generation of counter-attack (see p. 304).

For the pattern to work effectively, you need high morale, a real sense of pride in each of the groups. Each is a mini-team in which the players give each other intelligent, committed support. Other mini-teams may be good, but 'we are the best'. When this is happening throughout the XV you have a great defence: one of my school teams gave away a single try in the course of the season. It's obviously helpful to know your opposing teams before the event. At the top level this has developed into a business – but even at university level, in Japan twenty odd years ago, the week before a championship match, we found ourselves being recorded on half-a-dozen camcorders. Any solid information you can garner is useful. Keep a reasoned log of each match and it may prove useful the following season.

# PART 3

# PRACTICAL COACHING

## 8 COACHING WITH PURPOSE

> 'Great achievers generally work much harder than the rest of us . . . and their achievements come not from effortless inspiration but from ceaseless meditation. If genius really is an infinite capacity for taking pains . . . what makes it possible is the single-minded concentration on the task in hand, carrying it to such a pitch that you bring passion to whatever you do.' (Adapted from a Sunday Times review of Alastair Horne's *How Far From Austerlitz* by Alan Judd – 3.11.96.)

The first thing that the players expect of a coach is that he should know where he's going, and is prepared to find out how to get there.

What convinces them is a continuing sense that every session is planned with purpose, that every activity is meaningful, that they are developing as players, and that their team is heading for a brighter future.

To achieve this the coach needs a substantial constancy of purpose. You need a vision, a glimpse at least, of the rugby you want your team to play. Without that vision, your belief in it, your determination to realise it, you will just be tinkering with the team, plugging a hole here, applying a spot of solder there. There will be no development programme, no sense that there is a more satisfying, more successful, more exciting time ahead. You will lack direction, and it will show.

Whatever your vision, have faith in it. Out of that faith comes energy, determination and enthusiasm. Without it, you'll find it hard to enthuse your players, and you'll find coaching a tough assignment. It's not for the faint-hearted – it demands a commitment of time, energy and emotion to the preparation of the team, week after week. Without faith in what you're doing, it must become a weary grind. But with it, everything is transformed. Every session is an opportunity to take another step forward, every match an educational experience, focusing our minds on the work to be done.

You start with the vision – not a detailed accounting but a clear picture of a moment of play that will characterise the play of your team. Day by day you work to make that vision totally practical, by equipping your players to carry it out and by shifting their mind-set to make it seem natural. You do it by constantly incorporating its elements in individual, unit, and team preparation. There's no need for you to try to articulate it: let it grow organically as the team develops.

Whatever that vision is, no matter how apparently limited, it must be a vision of excellence; it may be kick-and-chase, but it must be the very best kick-and-chase that your players are capable of, and each element in it must go on improving. The greatest compliment to the player is your assumption that he is capable of excellence, in his talent and his character. If you demand only a little of a player, that's what you'll probably get. If you demand a lot, you may finish up with a star. In the same way, you don't plan to give the player what he wants – you plan to give him what he needs. The aim is to convince him of his talent and capacity to the point at which he voluntarily accepts responsibility for making the most of them, where he detests sloppiness with the same passion that you do, where he accepts the need for zero-defect performance as a personal target.

The successful coach, especially one who works with a squad over a number of years, tends to shape a rugby culture. His objectives, his methods, his standards come to seem natural to the team – he has modified their assumptions. As this feeling grows, so too does the confidence and commitment of the team. Their belief in what they're doing lets them play at their calmly efficient best. They train better, practise better, play better. The effectiveness of the team becomes ever greater than the apparent potential of the parts. They don't feel 'this is the way we play rugby', they feel 'this is the way rugby is played'. They have come to share the coach's vision.

This internalising of the coach's values is a critical point in team development. There's no adequate substitute for intelligent, methodical, personal commitment to improvement by the players – that's what maximises the value of club sessions, and fuels voluntary, individual strength/power/speed/skill training.

The coach must aim to conduct himself in a manner consistent with his quest for excellence. Whether he will or not, he leads by example. If you exemplify the slip-shod in your coaching, and in the standards you expect of your players, that's the culture you'll tend to create, until a more dynamic, demanding, focused, and inspirational leader comes along. Your coaching must be as excellent as you can make it: you must expect to work as hard in preparation as your players do in practice, and, like them, keep it up day after day. Do that, and you'll show character traits your players can respect, and seek to emulate.

So too you must be utterly fair-minded in your dealings with the players, encouraging them to be fair-minded with each other. You should show consideration; a player who is doing his best is a man to be respected, and that respect should show, technically, but more importantly, personally. But as a drunken

Hawaiian once said to me, '*I know the kind of man you are, Admiral: you don't take shit from nobody. I like that.*' In general, players not only like it, they expect it. That's not to say that they like the coach. The great thing is that they respect him. If liking develops from that, good, but you never relax your standards to win it.

There's no need to be remote – it's an odd coach who doesn't show his liking for the players, his appreciation of their efforts, his pride in their performance, his concern for their success – but inevitably there's a degree of detachment. You are going to lead, and they, substantially, are going to follow; you are going to pick teams without fear or favour, with contribution to the team as your sole criterion. Neither of these is easy if you're all lads together.

You need to show a balance that they can trust, to be happy without arrogance in victory, positive and forward-looking in defeat. Treat every match as a learning experience rather than an end in itself. Your concern is that the players approach the next game with equal resolve in either case, and with increased insight into how they must and can improve their performance.

Part of that balance is to recognise that, though you work to win every match, winning is not the only criterion of success, no matter how professional the context. Your team can play better than it ever has before and still lose to a team that plays even better. Your players can give all they've got, and it still isn't enough. Acknowledge that, and relieve the pressure on your players. They are *preparing* for victory: they've come closer to their ideal than they've ever done before; some of them will actually have won their personal match with their immediate opponent. Defeat of this kind can be good for the soul: you can emerge bloody but unbowed, and with greater realism and determination in your thinking.

The importance of winning – and no-one should underestimate that – brings us to an ethical question: how much of the tone of the team are you prepared to sacrifice for victory? The successful coach creates a culture, and part of that culture is ethics. Behind every thuggish player is a conniving coach – if he didn't condone dirty play, the player wouldn't hold his place. The coach is as much responsible for that as for the technical skill of the team. If every coach accepted his responsibility, if every referee used his powers, if every union backed up its referees after investigation, rugby could be rid of thuggery. The message is 'don't preach, penalise': take effective action to clean up the game.

You can make a clear distinction to your players between technical offences and thuggery. To be competitive the player must often be on the edge of infringement – a flanker who is never adjudged offside, for example, may not be putting his opponent under adequate pressure. But that is miles away from a physical attack on a frequently defenceless opponent, a typical product of machismo – a mistaken ideal of what it is to be a man. Don't stand for it in your team, even in the form of retaliation. Consider:

- causing you to give away a penalty may be the immediate purpose of the opposition

- giving away penalties is an expensive indulgence – not only does it directly help the opposition, it can disrupt the rhythm of your attack and cancel previous team efforts

- giving away penalties is a sign of incompetence – the best players simply don't do it

- and thuggery is the way to 14-man rugby. One duty of the forward leader is to make sure it doesn't happen.

Whatever else you may say to your players immediately before the match, one point is indispensable: don't give away penalties.

The higher the level at which you're working, the more necessary it becomes to work with the player, discussing the problem with him, and the players around him, but it's desirable at every level. Joint problem-solving is simultaneously a way of creating a positive response to coaching and getting the players thinking about their game. The more positive thought that's going on the better. It isn't, of course, the only way: at different times, with different activities and different people, other approaches will pay off better in speed or energy output. But the truest voice of coaching is quiet and thoughtful. This is most obvious when you are encouraging judgement – getting players to examine the field and the opposition, and picking out the best course of action. In strength and fitness sessions, on the other hand, your voice has got to evoke staggering effort from the players, and it won't do that if you can't be heard.

# How to ease into coaching and build authority

1. As a player, observe your coach, particularly his strengths and weaknesses: you can learn from both.

2. Work to be appointed captain or section leader, so that you become accustomed to thinking and acting like a coach.

3. Start coaching within the area of your own expertise – get accustomed to explaining and commanding on your own turf.

4. Don't necessarily start off with mini-rugby. Coaching kids should be fun for them and for you. If you're on the same wavelength and moderately inventive, by all means start with kids. If not, don't.

5. Offer to help with a junior side.

6. Get yourself onto certificate courses.

7. Start coaching more senior players in the club within your own area of expertise.

8. Prepare beforehand. Really think about what you're doing, and about what you don't yet understand. This will give you the ideal entry into this book: you'll read sections with deep purpose. It'll also give you an ideal attitude for courses – you know what you need, make sure you get it.

9. Keep thinking, keep trying to improve. When the urge to do that wanes, don't be scared to move into some other aspect of club work. If you're not enthusiastic, if you start just turning up, it'll soon begin to harm the team.

10. Ask if you can go along to watch respected coaches at work with their own teams. Provided you don't become intrusive during the session, and hold your questions till he's ready to deal with them, you'll be quite welcome.

# 9 TEAM SELECTION

Without a coherent playing policy you cannot have a coherent selection policy (or for that matter a coherent policy on team development or preparation). To put it at its most obvious: it's difficult to assess a player until you fully appreciate the role he has to play. A player who is admirable in one style of play may be incapable of playing his part in another. You need a moderately detailed *job description* to get the right man. This is not to deny that the player you finally select may be much more talented than the player you looked for, and may expand your whole consciousness of how you can use him – simply that he must have the basic qualifications called for by team tactics.

A second vital principle is that of *complementarity*. In an ideal world we might be able to turn out fifteen omni-competent footballers, each capable of meeting all the varied needs of the game. Part of our coaching programme is aimed at encouraging this all-round competence, providing a sound backing for the specific talent. In practice, however, any player offers a unique set of pluses and minuses and you are seeking in the team and in the mini-teams within the team to create an appropriate blend of these qualities. This entails maximising pluses and counter-balancing the minuses. It's extremely difficult, for example, to play total rugby without an attacking full-back; your wingers, therefore, must be selected in part because they can be depended upon to function well in deep defence. If you intend to attack wide, you need a running outside-centre, and he will function best if the player inside him is a natural timer of the pass, who isn't constantly tempted to have a go himself. If you play a flanker for his attacking flair, you must look to balance him in terms of line-out and maul. The mini-team in which you can least afford to use complementarity as a way of balancing strength and weakness is at half: personal limitation there, in either player, limits the variety of the whole team.

Complementarity recognises that there are many roles to perform within the team. You must make sure that your selection allows adequate flexibility to carry out these roles. There's nothing wrong with selecting eight very large forwards, if between them they can meet all the challenges that the opposition may present. But you cannot select eight large forwards simply because you think they'll win 100% of the ball: they won't, and if they aren't adequately perceptive and mobile they will be run off their feet. Certainly you must select your forwards with an eye to your own strategy – and indeed the forwards available to you will frequently dictate your strategy – but you must have the other eye on your opposition.

A third element is *compatibility* of character traits, personality, and attitude to the game. Team spirit may never develop if personal attitudes are too diverse. You do need a little touch of the heroic, of the player who never knows when he's beaten, and who functions best when things are going badly. It's great to have a joker – but he must take everything up to and including the match seriously.

A fourth element is *leadership*: you need players who have a driving determination to win and are happy representing the coach on the field. You build up the latter quality by giving players responsibility during practice sessions for the work of their particular group, taking care to explain to them exactly what you're after. They have a model for, say, the line-out, expectations of what may go wrong, and a desire to check these expectations out and put right what's wrong. They create a sense of purpose and of pride in their group. You also need tactical leaders – in effect, the halves, who, using the same process, decide the most effective use of the ball at tactical points.

The only foundation for consistent success in selection is *continuity*. At best it is an exercise in continuous forward-planning, looking at least a season ahead. If you are not working ahead like this, you leave no time to prepare against probable contingencies. The short-term application of this is to think always in terms of a squad rather than a team, and to have provisional selections worked out several games ahead. Nothing is so indicative of a lack of policy, incidentally, as radically different squad cover for the same key position – e.g. at half-back or full-back.

Continuity of the team nucleus is a critical example of the general principle. At any level it is a recognition of quality and of the comparative unimportance of temporary variations in form. Lack of this particular continuity probably reveals more about the selectors than about the players. Continuity brings with it the hope of team spirit, of the development of a game plan, and the immediate benefit of shop-floor help in selection. You may not always be able to follow it, but it would be folly to deprive yourself of the advice of your players in completing a team.

The desirability of continuity in the team mustn't blind us to the fact that change is going to occur – very frequently in a university team which loses 30% of its members each year, but steadily in all teams. So far as possible we must prepare for this to happen so that the team continues to evolve without radical breaks. We need continuous forward-planning. The earlier you can spot potential members of the team, the earlier you can:

- make clear to them that you know they're there
- attach them to the squad
- give them a taste of action – to focus their minds on the need to prepare
- identify and set about eliminating their weaknesses
- get senior players/mini-team leaders involved in directing their efforts.

Once you establish such a system, it runs easily. It pays to have periodic meetings with junior team managers, and older players in the junior teams, to make sure that talented juniors aren't being missed. Of course, major new players may join the club – but you can't count on it: it pays to make the most of what you know you'll have.

Selection has now become a technical duty of the person best qualified to carry it out – the coach. Where you have a number of coaches working together, communication between them should be constant and frank. One season I was unhappy about our full-back but it wasn't until well after the start that I discovered an admirable full-back on a rugby course but not in a team. It was partly my own fault: I'd restricted my inquiries to the club instead of taking in the professional courses – but this lad was outstanding and I was sorry he hadn't been referred to me for the team's sake and for his.

# 10 COACHING METHODS

## BASIC COACHING TECHNIQUES

Two questions always face the coach in any activity: *what?* and *how?* I remember very clearly as a schoolboy scurrying down the field pursued by a monstrous opponent who threatened, if he caught me, to bury me, and being exhorted by my Headmaster: '*Run faster, Greenwood*'. This had already occurred to me: it was how to run faster that eluded me. That is precisely the technical role of the coach: *having defined the problem he has got to supply answers, and devise ways of implementing them.*

It's convenient to distinguish two basic situations in defining this technical coaching duty.

**1 The prescriptive case** – for example when introducing a new skill to a group of players. The coach has to:

- *isolate a common problem* – how do we deal with an opponent who has taken the ball and turned to shield it?

- *define a basic form* – we'll pivot him over backward, and put him down on the ground with the ball on our side

- *develop a model* – at contact, we'll throw our right leg across behind him, pull him backward over it, and as he falls pull his left shoulder and push his right to rotate him as we want

- *construct a coaching situation* – once they've mastered it in a l v l static situation, we'll set up a cyclic exercise (see p. 54) in which player A grubber kicks; B falls and gets up with the ball acting as the opponent; C follows up, pivots B and puts him down; D picks up and grubber kicks; A falls . . . and so on. With four players in the group, we'll get quite an intensive dynamic practice of the skill.

The beauty of devising such a coaching situation is that it increases the work-rate: all you need say once it is established is '*OK, three minutes' turn-overs*', and the players will be straight into it. This eliminates those awkward pauses that waste time and check momentum.

The danger of devising such a situation is that we trust in it to produce automatic improvement. It won't. Provided the players have a clear model to follow, and use their intelligence to check what they're doing, they'll probably improve, but you'll certainly find in every group one who's more likely to groove faults than refine strengths.

The phrase 'coaching situation' exactly describes what we've devised: it lets you watch the players perform a skill more frequently in three minutes than they'd do in the next three matches, whilst you are precisely focused on what they're doing. It's a great coaching situation . . . but it isn't coaching. *Coaching is precisely the intervention of the coach to eliminate weaknesses and foster strengths.* The coaching situation gives you every chance to spot which players are making mistakes and what mistakes they're making. At the moment when you intervene to put it right – that's when you start coaching. And you're doing the same thing when you take a player out of the general coaching situation as you do when you sort out the specialist skills of the goal kicker or the hooker – giving him individual attention. It's not teams or units that make mistakes, it's individual players within them – sometimes individual players who lead and make decisions, but still individual players. When you're coaching try to talk to individuals.

**2  The diagnostic case** – the weakest aspect of all games coaching in this country. Pick up the typical coaching manual for any team game and it'll give you dozens of coaching situations, some of them counter-productive, but it won't offer you any help in positive coaching intervention. How can you help people who rely on coaching situations to realise their potential as diagnostic coaches?

- Raise their attention level and direct their attention so that they develop *expectations.*

- Arrange *feedback* devices so that it's easier for them to observe.

- Ask appropriate questions so that they recognise *principles* and how they interact – create a *model* of what they're studying.

- Give them *intensive* practice in diagnosing weaknesses and prescribing remedies in a case with which they're already familiar, and then in cases with a closely-related model so that they build up confidence.

- Show how, with understanding of the *principles* involved, you can build up a *model* of every other aspect of the game, and apply the process effectively.

(In the course of doing this, you are inevitably working with one or more players as a demonstrator. They gain immeasurably from being able to monitor, analyse, and correct their own performance as a step towards the consistent accuracy that is their aim. And for those players who function like coaches whilst leading a team section – the pack leader, for example, proactively marshalling the forwards in the line-out – it's an enabling ability.)

## Get them actively attentive

The first great need is to have the coaches focus their attention much more precisely. So set up an action, and ask them to watch it and describe it after it's been repeated half-a-dozen times. The action I set up is always the same – a moderate scrum-half passing the ball left off the ground – as it can be repeated quickly and without fatigue; it's easy to give the whole course much the same close-up view whilst they sit at ease; it can be done outdoors or inside; it's sufficiently complicated to offer many opportunities for coaching intervention; it furnishes a model that applies to all forms of moving the ball; good scrum-half play is central to total rugby: they need to understand this pass.

We start the session, once the coaches are comfortable, by having the moderate player pass the ball half-a-dozen times. The coaches watch, very seldom intently. They get a rough idea of what's going on, but they don't focus with the precision needed to coach. They watch the passes with their attention decreasing – they've seen it before. Then they're asked to describe the path of the ball. It's amazing how many people don't see that our moderate scrum-half – chosen for his mediocrity – picks the ball up more or less vertically, takes it back, and only then initiates the pass. Once they see it, they never forget it. It becomes one of their *expectations*, and it directs their attention precisely. Suddenly they realise that they've identified a coaching problem, a starting point for coaching. And the aim is to equip them with such expectations for every likely fault. Expectations transform the quality of their observation: they know what they're looking for and they focus intently upon it. It means that they can identify a problem if it appears, and discount it if it doesn't – the basis for all progress.

---

## Two major caveats

Coaching coaches demands the same care and forethought as coaching the best players. You need to make the point to them that the whole set-up, the whole progression, the methods employed, are all part of the coaching. Often you'll find that when they're asked to repeat it with players, they go to what they think is the heart of the solution and ignore the carefully worked out build-up.

Secondly, it pays to emphasise excellence of performance: we don't want players to be a *little* better; we want them to be the best they can be, and we want them to be enthused by excellence, to be passionate about it, to adopt it as their criterion of success. We want them to wince when they see sloppy, slovenly work during practices. We never practise mistakes; we practise eliminating them. And the fundamental way to establish this outlook is to set the clearest example of it. There's only one adequate aim: you want as a coach to be your best. That means a continuing programme of improvement for yourself as well as for the players. What we're looking at now are ways of making your efforts pay off.

---

Philosophically, expectations may be seen as dangerous: they can shape your perception. If I'm looking for red squirrels, I may see a 'squirrel' that turns out to be a broken branch. On the other hand, if I'm looking for squirrels I'll see far more than the casual observer. Broadly speaking, you can say, in coaching as in nature-watching, '*if you don't look for it, you probably won't see it.*'

## Get them looking methodically

As expectations multiply, the coaches recognise that they have to scan methodically. They can't hope initially to check out more than one expectation per performance. But they can get the player to do a series of passes, and check one or two each time. This is always my own first step with a player – put him in a position (a coaching situation) in which he repeats a skill as part of an activity with other players, or ask him to do as a series of e.g. kicks at goal. My attention will almost certainly have been focused on the need for coaching by feedback from match performances. The order in which you scan may be simply chronological or spatial, but very quickly your expectations will create a priority checking system for you – '*it's most likely to be that, and if it's not that, it'll be this*'.

Of course, the solution to particular coaching problems may lie in the conjunction of two or more elements, but that can be treated later. For the moment, the coaches are asked to concentrate on one thing at a time.

## Provide feedback devices

The scrum-half demonstrating is usually set up on a touch line, with the receiver standing astride the line facing him. The aim of this is to make it easy to get accurate *feedback* – precise information on what actually happened. The line gives information about weight and foot movement; the standing target makes it easy to see where the ball actually went – on target, to the left, to the right, at the right height, low or high – and with what power. The coaches are asked to register precisely what happened, and invited to move around to get the best view.

## Get them to account for what happened

They're then asked to account for what they've seen. Why did it go there when the scrum-half intended it to go here? What *cause* accounts for the observed *effect*? The aim now is to get them thinking about the simple mechanics of the pass. It went high, so . . . did he lift his head? That would bring his shoulders, and his arm and hand up. It went left . . . so did his arm rotate with his body? They soon start building a *model* of the forces involved, and for each symptom identify a probable cause – another expectation. When they're at ease and happy with this, it's suggested that there may be several possible causes, but that with this particular scrum-half some are more probable than others. Sometimes the scrum-half will try to put it right but can't – and this points to a more substantial cause, e.g. loss of balance which, once identified, can be dealt with in the same way.

## Demonstrate prescriptive method

Once we've reached this stage, I usually go back to prescriptive coaching, to give the scrum-half a coherent *model*, and feel, for what he's doing. I get him passing one-handed which eliminates the pick up and take back, and ensures a perfect spin as the ball rolls down the fingers. We correct until he's doing this adequately and then bring in the other hand, insisting that as soon as the rear hand touches the ball he initiates the pass. Then we produce a long stick to represent the desired flight path – from the ball at the player's right foot in the precise direction of the receiver's hands. We get the player, without the ball, to go through the passing action, letting the stick control the path of his right hand. This will come as a revelation – it's the line he should be working on, and he's probably never been near it in his life. He needs to stay on that line as long as he can without overbalancing. Take his wrist and take him a few inches further than he's already gone: his shoulders rotate more fully. In due course, when he's passing wholeheartedly, that extra rotation will represent extra power as well as precision.

And all the time we're asking him questions – the same questions we're asking the coaches – posed so that he can answer them, and gain confidence. He ends up with a clear model, able to identify cause from effect, able to answer '*what went wrong?*' as well as any coach, *able to coach himself.* This is the educational element that makes all the difference to his career prospects. I remember in San Diego, a US Army Colonel who said '*That was the most educational experience of my career*'; I remember in Madrid being joined by an All Black scrum-half – he'd travelled a couple of hundred miles to get there – whom I'd worked with as a boy in New Zealand: he still had all the skills, and produced variations of performance to order; I remember in Argentina coaching in the depths of a big soccer stadium, with an audience of ninety players, all of whom, long before the end, were spot on in their analysis of the scrum-half's performance. And most of them couldn't speak English. So what's going to stop you?

## Hands-on experience

What must be made clear right from the start is that in due course all the course members will be expected to apply the system. Without serious personal involvement it's too easy for them to let their concentration wander and for the course to turn into a form of entertainment. They must also realise that what may seem to them decorative preliminaries are in fact part of the learning process: they're there because they're needed.

Get them into threes for maximum participation. In turn, each will act as coach, as apprentice player and as target-man. Remind them of how useful lines are for giving feed-back and allocate a length of touch line or 5m line in which to operate – opposite each other so that you can be closer to every trio as they work.

Start them off on the prescriptive model – it won't matter that they have or haven't played scrum-half before, they're all going to learn. You'll find that they automatically begin to interpret and correct: the diagnostic method is the most natural thing in the world once they've learned to apply it to a technique in rugby. 'They', because though one of them is the coach for this part of the exercise, it may prove difficult to stop the others adding their insights – but as long as they're all learning and listen to each other, no harm is done. Once the first apprentice is passing adequately and the coaching trio are warmed up, switch roles.

You meantime are moving from group to group, helping and advising. Talk about coaching attitude – being positive – encouraging, patient, but deter-mined. Keep asking questions – you're trying to educate these people so that they can apply the method to a range of skills, not merely train them to cope with one. The questions, of course, must be carefully judged, for the course-members must be able to answer them. So don't ask for mental leaps – try to get there step by step. Make the point that the same system of asking their players to answer carefully framed questions gets them thinking about the game active-ly. Try always to establish the principles behind the action, for they are the keys that unlock all the doors on the technical side of coaching. If you read the first part of 'Coaching Sessions', you'll see how easily and effectively what they've learned from the scrum-half pass can be developed into lateral spin passing and spin punting.

Of all the course members it's very likely that the player you chose to work with on the initial pass off the ground – asking him questions all the time – will be the most competent coach in this second phase. This can be turned to advantage: if you've worked on a player's hooking you then have a coach who can work with junior hookers, so that all the hookers in the club – and the hooker turned coach – will benefit. This works a treat in schools where there's little danger of the lads being coached supplanting the 'coach'. (In just the same way, the English scholar-ship group took promising juniors through books they were working on: there's nothing like coaching/teaching to refine your own understanding.)

By the end of this intensive practical work we have some happy, confident coaches, and some fine performers of this particular scrum-half pass. It's an important moment, because diagnostic coaching is at the heart of day-to-day coaching. Its beauty is its speed. You can't afford the time in a normal session to go back to prescriptive basics with a single player while the rest wait, but equal-ly, you can't let a serious fault in a critical player go unaided. If your expectations are honed you can sort the problem out fast. Indeed, you'll find yourself slipping into a habit of coaching at a distance – shouting and gesticulating (in shorthand) to a player on the other side of the field. You work on expectations, on probabilities, on what your analysis of like cases suggests may be wrong.

If it's a difficult case, you have to make time outside the normal session to deal with it. As usual, get the player to run through the action half-a-dozen times so that you get a chance to see what's wrong. To take a simple case: your hooker is quick, and gets to the ball, but it doesn't come back smoothly. You may check the accuracy and consistency of the put-in, go on to examine the depth of strike (your probable expectation – he's not striking deep enough), and end up altering the position of the non-striking foot and the exact line of follow through. Much of this will be experimentation during which you get the various elements clear in your mind and work out how they interact. Provided you don't let worry diminish your concentration – and why should you, we're not talking nuclear physics – you'll get there. If you just alter one thing at a time and really look at the results, you'll get there. And now you have another model, another set of expectations, and the ability to offer fast, effective advice, this time on hooking.

The more detailed your model of the activity, and the clearer your expectations of the cause of the problem, the faster you can work. In practice, you go on refining your model – getting a more comprehensive list of the elements and a clearer idea of their interaction – and your expectations. With expectations, the moment does come when possible causes rank themselves automatically in order of likelihood. Most often you won't get beyond the first couple before you sort it out, but it still pays to concentrate on one thing at a time.

We can now summarise what's been said about diagnostic coaching:

- it's the key to fast, effective coaching intervention

- it's easy to apply

- it's based on four elements:

   **i.** accurately observed *feedback*, on whether a performance was good or bad, and in what respect it was bad

   **ii.** two sets of *expectations* – those that focus our attention on what's likely to go wrong in the team performance of a given activity or in a particular player's performance of a given activity; and carefully honed expectations of what deviations from the model are likely to have caused that particular bad performance

   **iii.** a system of *scanning* that encourages us to look at one thing at a time in the order of probability suggested by our expectations

   **iv.** *models* – the principles involved in the action, and their interaction – to cover as many aspects of the game and coaching as possible.

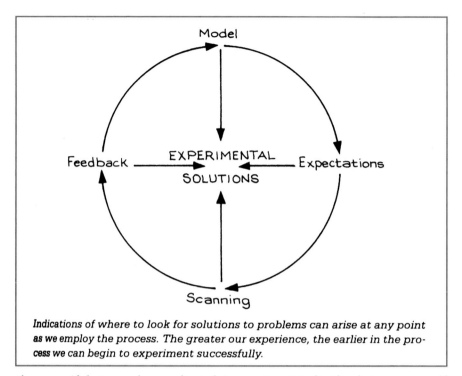

Model

Feedback ——— EXPERIMENTAL ——— Expectations
SOLUTIONS

Scanning

*Indications of where to look for solutions to problems can arise at any point as we employ the process. The greater our experience, the earlier in the process we can begin to experiment successfully.*

I'm sorry if that sounds complicated; in practice, it isn't. It's what you yourself – or your plumber or doctor – apply in tracking the source of a problem, and providing a solution. What I've done is to model diagnostic rugby coaching as simply one more of the problems to be solved in life (see diagram above).

I've used a single example so far because it's clear, and because it's very important: you must have efficient scrum-half passing to play total rugby. But the system applies to every technique in the game (or any other game), and can be applied easily to every other aspect of the game.

The model that lies behind the pass is based on common-sense *mechanics*. You'll find the same model developed in terms of punting and place kicking later in the book, and the same mechanical approach applied to scrummaging and rucking: in each case we're looking at generating and applying bodily force. Look at field athletics and you'll find that that is the central problem – how do you generate power and apply it efficiently in a javelin throw or in the high jump? Javelin throwing and passing the ball, high-jumping and jumping in the line-out are only superficially different athletic activities. Hitting a drive in golf and goal kicking in rugby share the problem of co-ordinating a double pendulum (what we call 'timing'), and ensuring a satisfactory contact with the ball –

any golfer will recognise what causes a rugby ball to swing out to the right instead of going straight to target! There's a lesson here for rugby coaches: your coaching of rugby players in such skills ought to be at least as specific and detailed as the work of good athletics and golf coaches – indeed, our work should be challenging theirs in perceptiveness and precision.

But rugby coaching involves problems more demanding than those in golf and field athletics. It covers a far wider range of activities: it involves interaction within the team, and confrontation, in attack and defence, individually and collectively, with the opposition. And we have to meet all the demands of the game with substantially the same fifteen players. It's a challenge that can last a lifetime – or wear you out in a couple of years.

Yet the consolation is that exactly the same process that you've mastered in terms of the scrum-half pass can be applied just as successfully to every part of the game, from the individual player through the units to the whole team. From mechanical techniques to tactical situations you can design and establish models – prescription – and sort out effectively what's going wrong or is likely to go wrong and put it right – diagnosis and intervention. This book should be a considerable help to you in respect of rugby – but remember: the method has application to all sports. People I worked with on athletics at Loughborough are now coaching Olympic athletes.

You'll find on pp. 76–77 an examination of how you can monitor a complete sequence of programmed unopposed using diagnostic coaching:

- isolate each element in the programme;

- use the model given in this book or clarify the model you normally use;

- get your expectations clear on what mistakes your players may make;

- check the expectations in order of priority, one at a time on each repetition;

- and you'll end up at the end of each run with a set of specific points to improve performance.

As you gain experience you'll be able to test more than one expectation from each element and you'll spot mistakes you hadn't expected. You'll also note what is well done: it's obviously as important to praise as well as criticise. Indeed, even if the performance is 90% bad, it's best to start by praising the 10% that's good. Always be as positive as you can.

Gather the players around and explain when explanations are necessary, reinforce with praise when they've done well. This is altogether more efficient than a general comment. It motivates the players and eliminates particular faults simultaneously. Programmed unopposed – in which you specify what's going to happen – is good as a starting point: you can work on a limited number of models, and get the models, your expectations, and the order in which you'll scan, clear as you prepare the programme. And don't think you need a new programme every session: if your initial programme is well suited to your team, you can use it again and again and see continuing improvements in your players' performance. A further advantage of repeating a programme lies in work-rate – you needn't spend time explaining the programme, you simply get on with it.

## DESIGNING THE COACHING SITUATION

In all aspects of coaching, we're generally moving from *technique* – establishing an effective form of action – towards *skill* – operating the technique effectively in the competitive match situation – by *conditioning* the pressures on the players acquiring the ability. This applies to establishing judgement as well as physical skill. We'll see this process underlying the progression within our structured session – a movement, basically, from easy to difficult (see p. 73). There's nothing particularly demanding about it, but we've got to be aware of it all the time.

There are various elements we can control to alter the pressure on the players: the *numbers* taking part; the kind and degree of *opposition*; the required *speed* of action and repetition; the length of *time* over which we continue the exercise; and the *space* in which we are operating. We must also be very clear about the action we want them to acquire. If it's complex we may have to see whether it can be presented in parts that make sense, and which can be mastered separately without detracting from the final effectiveness of the whole action. And, of course, we can make it easier by explaining as we go, relating the whole to the match situation, and the parts to the whole. The latter requires careful rehearsal: the right words aren't always available when they're wanted, and if they're not right – exact and brief – they simply get in the way.

**1 Numbers:** the greater the numbers, the greater the potential confusion, or the less intensive the exercise for the individual player; start small and work up.

**2 Opposition:** this is a critical factor. Initially we must recognise the need to practise both offensive and defensive techniques – that for each attacking technique there's got to be a defensive technique, and that they're equally important. But in acquiring these techniques we must – until the players reach a very satisfactory skill level – be quite clear which aspect we're working on. We must bias the practice in favour of one or the other, gradually lessening the bias as the competence increases.

At the lowest technical level, we start with *unopposed* practice. The great bulk of the intensive handling, for example, is done unopposed so that the players can concentrate on the ball without worrying about opposition. We can then introduce *passive* opposition – e.g. standing still to provide a focal point for passing, or moving forward for the same purpose but making no attempt to interfere with the operation. You may find difficulty in getting your 'opposition' to observe the conditions. We had a large, craggy and very amiable Portuguese coach on Summer School one year who was nicknamed 'Passive Defence' from his total inability to restrain his competitiveness: his good resolutions lasted till his opponent – working on mauling – made contact, and then it was total war. So when possible, deprive the passive opposition of choice – put them in set positions, e.g. with their arms linked, so that they can't interfere too much. But the basic notion to get across is of a joint learning activity: they'll all get their chance. It's important that they do get to this point for there's got to be a kind of opposition in which they offer more than token resistance but a resistance judged so that the learners go on learning.

**3 Speed of action** is something that comes with practice. At the start it's usually best to slow the whole thing down so that the technique is clearly and effectively carried out. This may involve e.g. carrying it out at walking pace, then trotting. *Speed of repetition* must be controlled in the same way – starting with single attempts and working towards pressure practices once the technique has been mastered. *Speed of progress* is a matter of judgement. Err on the side of thoroughness: you can't build on inadequate foundations. Try to do too much too fast, and you leave the player no more competent, and more confused.

This typical grid pattern will accommodate 32 players, four to a 10m x 10m grid square. Centre square is reserved for the coaches, who need never be further than 10m away from a given player. You also have grid channels, three squares long, which allow continuity exercises, e.g. start outside the bottom of the grid so that you have four lines ahead of you, and you can stage four repetitions of a move. You can have four groups doing this simultaneously, turning through 180° and repeating it, with the coaches still within 10m of a given player.

The grid allows high work-rate, close supervision, much reduced risk of accidental contact, and an interesting format that prompts you to devise fresh practices.

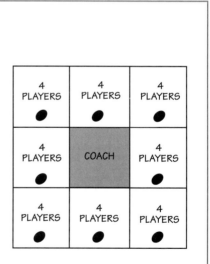

**4** **Time** becomes important with the onset of fatigue. It's certainly true that the skill may well be used in conditions of fatigue during the match, and there's something to be said, therefore, for technical practices to match this as fitness work does. But I've found myself that technical work is best done while the players are fresh and receptive, and that exercises should finish before the interest level drops.

**5** **Space** is important in designing practices, partly from the need to economise in time and energy, and partly from the need for the coach to be near enough to coach. If an exercise involves more movement than is necessary, intensity of repetition is lost; if players are dispersed the coach must be remote from some of them. It's desirable, therefore, to limit movement and it's recommended that this be done physically – e.g. by keeping the work between the 22-metre line and the goal line, or by using grids. Grids – 10–11m square, marked out e.g. behind the dead-ball line – are invaluable for repetition practices. Every coach should use them.

**6** **Feedback** is an important accelerator of learning, and wherever possible we should build it into coaching situations. You can give clearer feedback and make the players more conscious of its importance if you provide the following:

a) *clear guide-lines for action.* Examine the use of a single goal-post, the goal line and the intersection of goal line and 15-metre line in the section on goal kicking. Examine the use of grid lines and partners in the introductory exercise for spin passing, passing off the ground, and punting (on p. 70 ff.)

b) *clear indications of success and failure.* Examine the use of the flat pass and receiving in sequence to provide feedback on successful support positioning and timing in the exercise 1–4 on p. 127. Receiving in sequence means that the designated supporter must be up to receive the pass immediately the previous player gets the ball: the number of paces the ball-carrier has to carry the ball (i.e. be a target) before he can give a flat pass, is a measure of the supporter's inefficiency. Examine the use of a fixed mark for the thrower-in to practise his throwing against (see p. 198)

c) *clear comments from partners and coaches.* Partners may disguise rather than expose shortcomings in performance until they recognise that it's not in their or the other player's interest to do so. The stand-off may give out a soft or backward pass because he reckons the inside-centre will never reach his efficient pass, the inside-centre slows down, as he has to, to take a pass which has been put too close to him. The ball may not go down but there's no crisp acceleration in the exchange. What's needed is a re-evaluation of the moment at which the inside-centre can start his run and how deep he should be to run onto the flat pass at the speed he wants. In the match the compromise is necessary; in practice it has to be avoided. So, too, a jumper may make a thrower's indifferent performance look acceptable by catching a ball in practice that would never reach him in the match.

Encourage your players in all practices and in the game to offer positive comment to immediate partners. It helps clarify their own understanding, and that of their partner.

**7  Attention span:** despite your best efforts to make the session entertaining as well as instructive, they're going to get tired, and their performance will sag. That's a bad way to finish. So as soon as you detect fatigue, prepare to finish strong:

- tell them how well they've done

- set them a challenge that will pull them back into focus. This should be of the type: *'Right, we're going to call it a day. But first, I want you to do it perfectly three times. So remember the main points . . . OK, let's see three perfect performances.'*

In applying conditioning, the coach has got to use his judgement all the time. It's unproductive to start at too low a tempo with the gifted player, or too high a tempo with the less gifted. Nevertheless, the basics are very important: with gifted players the mistake I usually make is to expect too much, and move too fast. The other danger is for the coach to become over-pernickety and dogmatic in the conformity he demands in the form of the exercise. What he needs is to get the principles clear, and effective form established. After all, the game is always developing and the coach's ideas should be developing with it. We should always be learning from our players, and we won't if the players are drilled into a mechanical conformity: we need to get them efficient and get them thinking. In this as in everything else, we need a co-operative venture. A coach should speak with authority based on his experience, his recognition of the essentials, and his willingness to go on learning and experimenting.

## MAINTAINING THE ACTION: THE DRIP-FEED APPROACH

Most players are far better doers than listeners: never strain their attention-span or overload their systems – it'll confuse them, waste time and kill activity. Feed the information to them bit by bit, as it becomes relevant. That way each instruction is crystal clear and easy to follow.

If I see a group inactive, an uncharitable feeling floods my mind towards whoever's in charge. Active sessions – when players are on the move – are happy, productive sessions. Keep them that way by adopting the drip-feed approach.

You want players to grasp a whole process at the start? Don't rely on words; arrange a demonstration. Make sure the preceding activity is familiar and self-regulating and use the time to give a quick learner a crash course in the new skill. When you're ready, call players in, give the demonstration, and in a very few words – referring preferably to incidents in previous matches with which they're familiar – explain the purpose.

From then on it's bit by bit, so that activity is rarely halted for more than a minute. Keep checking individuals and putting things right. If more than a few are having the same problem, call them all together, get a successful pair to demonstrate, and try to pick out the cause and solution of the problem. Let your confidence and pleasure show: jolly them along.

An easy way to move into this method is to start with an established exercise and develop it. Say you've set up a cyclic exercise in which the ball-carrier goes to ground, the next man feeds one of the two other players, who goes forward and then to ground . . . and the cycle continues. You then feed in points as follows.

**1** When you go to ground, get your body at right-angles to touch.

**2** Get the ball at arms' length behind you.

**3** Get onto your feet immediately the ball's gone.

**4** As you feed, take a step to check a defender.

**5** Make space in which to receive the ball.

**6** Don't move till you see the ball in his hands.

**7** Let's get another pass in.

**8** Switch sides at the last moment.

**9** Hit it a lot harder: we need pace.

Imagine telling players that lot (which we can go on developing all session) at one go. But drip-fed it's easy to assimilate.

All set-piece coaching involves a performance by the coach, and before each performance you need to rehearse your part – what you're going to do, what you're going to say (try different versions till you're happy with it), which players you'll address, what bits and pieces of equipment may come in handy. People may worry about your muttering to yourself, making little gestures and grimacing – but it's eminently worthwhile. It exactly corresponds to the mental rehearsal of the player, preparing for the big match, setting himself up mentally and emotionally for a great performance. It pays to prepare.

The same drip-feed principle holds good right through to team practice. At each run through of a programme of unopposed, it's far better to pick out only one or two points to be put right in each element than concentrate tediously on one element whilst those not concerned wonder why they're there and those concerned lose focus. Help everyone keep focus by limiting the amount to be grasped.

# Introducing a new element

'Why,' said the Dodo, 'the best way to explain it is to do it.'
Lewis Carroll: Alice in Wonderland

Most people have a short attention span; if you use too many words, you'll lose them. Activity is the key – if you look around and see players standing about, you're not doing your job.

1. If a skill is at all complicated, don't try it in bad conditions – people who are chilled or soaked have other things on their mind.

2. Don't start the session with it – get them doing something they understand and enjoy, so they're happy to pay attention.

3. While they're doing that, get hold of your brightest players, and get them accustomed to the new skill: they'll be your demonstration group. If you've doubts about their speed of learning, get them out before the session starts, and make sure they can do it.

4. Let the rest see them doing it, and explain the context: 'you use this when . . .' But don't ask them to try the whole action unless you're confident they'll succeed. Break it up into discrete units which guarantee success. You need to think about this, about the content of each unit, what ground situation you're going to use to facilitate the operation (e.g. grid lines, touch/5-metre lines), the words you need to use, and so on. A lot of coaching is showmanship, and you have to consider your lines and movement.

5. If you're coaching coaches, emphasise that the method of introduction is as important as the complete action, and that you expect them to follow it in detail. In due course, they may be able to improve on it but they mustn't do worse.

# 11 EXERCISE FORMS

## CYCLIC EXERCISES

Cyclic exercises provide a high work-rate situation based on looping and hammering home the basic notion – 'do it . . . and run'. They can be applied to many of the basic techniques of the game and offer intensive repetition under easily controlled pressure. They are advantageous in that several techniques can be put into a sequence, and that some degree of opposition can be built in. They are also a good basis for light-hearted relay races. And for the inventive coach they offer an adaptable form that can be developed easily and effectively.

The idea is most easily understood from an example, as follows. Number four players 1—2—3—4. No. 1 has the ball and sets off at a trot from the goal line towards the 22 with the rest following. No. 2 tackles him, and 1 makes the ball available on the ground. No. 3 picks up and passes to 4. 1 tackles 4 . . . and the cycle continues.

The pressure can be increased: a) by cutting out the pass, or b) by decreasing the numbers taking part. You may well find that starting with five players makes for an easier introduction.

It's important that the exercise is seen as a coaching situation, and that accordingly it's introduced at a tempo that encourages learning. You may find a tendency for the ball-carrier to run too fast: he needs to take three or four fast strides to get in front of the other players, but then he must slow down.

Equally, of course, you have to end up in a fully competitive situation, where each player swoops in on the ball, intent on breaking away from the group, and each tackler is determined to catch him in his first stride. Only with this competition will the real value of the exercise come through – only then will the optimum approach be called for. As it gets faster, for example, you'll find the player picking up the ball coming in really low, absolutely intent on the ball. This begins to appear in his approach to any 50/50 situation, and it can transform the loose play of the team.

As in most repetition exercises for the basic skills, you are dealing with antithetic pairs: in broad terms, attack and defence. The players are simultaneously practising carrying on an attack and checking it, being tackled and tackling.

In using such exercises, you need to clarify in your own mind the elements involved so that your coaching is thorough. In all cyclic exercises involving movement down the pitch, the basic elements are as follows.

## Judgement of position and pace
There is no point in a player's rushing blindly in support. He has to arrive in balance. This means judging what's going to happen and running accordingly. Cyclic exercises are an easy introduction to this. The coach has to emphasise this – and initially he'll find ample opportunity.

## Keeping the ball available
Unless the player has quite exceptionally large hands, carrying the ball in one hand is an excellent way of losing possession. As soon as the player comes into contact with an opponent, he will tend to pull the ball into his body, and after that the advantage of being in possession is as good as lost. Keeping the ball available is a matter of control, and the easy way to do it is to keep the ball in two hands.

## High work-rate
To keep the cycle going every player has to 'do it and run': if he doesn't, he won't be in a position to continue the cycle. After the tackle, the coach is shouting '*get up, get up*' to both the players.

Every exercise, however, produces a fresh set of techniques for the coach to comment on and improve. So far as this particular exercise is concerned we can check on these elements as well.

### *The tackle*
When the player is moving away from you, you must aim higher. Check that the tackler is winding his arms round, pulling his opponent's knees together, getting his shoulder in, and keeping his head out of the way.

### *Being tackled*
Stay loose, and concentrate on the ball: that's the important thing. Try to put the ball down on the side away from the tackler – if it goes down near him he'll try to kill it. If you can't judge that, put it down on the side away from the last set-piece – and this can be stipulated by the coach. The ball must not run forward, and must not get covered (unless in the match, you are behind the gain line).

### *Picking up*
To be sure of picking up you must be thinking ahead so that you're in the right place moving at the right speed. If you get right behind the ball, you're in trouble. See p. 159 for a description of the technique. It's a great help if you know where the ball is likely to go down (see above).

## Support position for the pass

Here again, to be fully effective, the player must be thinking ahead. Never run blind: get into a useful, interesting position, and let the ball-carrier know where you are. Call his name – the opposition may be calling as well!

## The pass

The pass has got to be good – see p. 122 ff. Aim to get it away quickly, and give yourself practice in different kinds of pass as the chance arises.

## Work-rate

The coach will start off at a gentle tempo, to establish the form and make his coaching points, but at the back of his mind is the fast tempo that will establish work-rate. He'll move towards that as seems appropriate for these particular players, and he'll cut down the length (in time, or space) of the exercise as the tempo increases. All of these cyclic exercises have the potential to be exhausting.

Once the basic form has been established, it's easy to develop this practice. The obvious development is that the ball-carrier, as he is tackled, tries to get the ball away in a pop-up pass before he hits the ground. The most likely fault here is that they throw the ball back: if it's accurate, fine, but if it goes astray precious yards are lost, and the movement may break down. It's a better bet to pop the ball up in the path of the supporting player.

Each time you alter the practice you will find a need to make conditions. For example, if the ball is being popped up, the whole exercise will go faster, and you may have to add an extra player or limit the running speed still more. Again, if the pop-up is to be successful, the ball-carrier must fight his way round to see his support. The obvious corollary of this is that the tackler must always try to prevent it – but don't point this out till the players have had plenty of experience of rolling and popping.

This first practice is a basic practice for continuity of attack. A similar one which we use a lot deals with the ball on the ground in the open. It's essential that we get possession, and picking the ball up is much slower than diving on it. The attacking dive to gain possession is at least as important but much less practised than the ball in defence. Again in 4s, the players trot down the pitch. No. 1 does a short controlled grubber kick, chases it, in balance, dives onto it, rolls, and either holds it up or pops it for the supporting player, no. 2, who repeats the exercise.

Once again, this is a coaching situation and the coach should get clear the elements involved: the kick, the dive, the support, the feed. This time, though, the ball is less under control – even the best grubber can bounce badly. The coach must, therefore, encourage a wider support pattern, and point out that anyone may be called upon to fall, and that consequently anyone may have to act as supporter.

The techniques involved in cyclic exercises need not be done unopposed. In any of them you can very simply create at least a token opposition. The easiest way of achieving this is for the ball-carrier to drive to the front, put the ball down, carry on for several strides, and turn to act as opponent. You can condition the degree of opposition he offers by controlling the number of strides he takes after putting the ball down, and what he's allowed to do in contact. Once again you balance the need to learn attack and defence in such a way as to encourage the aspect you're immediately concerned with.

A simple mauling practice will illustrate this. Use five players. No. 1 trots ahead, puts the ball on the ground, and turns to act as an opponent. No. 2 picks up and does a power step. No. 3 drives in behind, steps into him and turns to feed. No. 5 goes forward, and the cycle recommences.

The previous forms of the exercise have all started with the whole group trotting in line down the pitch. You can devise useful cycles from other starts.

**a)** Split players into teams of four, about five yards apart. No. 1 stands on the goal line, 2 ten yards infield, 3 ten yards beyond 2, and 4 ten yards beyond 3. This form allows practice of all the scrum-half passes, little cross-kicks, grubber kicks and punts. As soon as 1 has made his pass he dashes ten yards beyond 4, ready to receive 4's pass, and the cycle recommences.

**b)** Shuttle relay allows intense activity without using much space: all the players stay close to the coach. Simple examples will make clear how this form can be used.

*Turning and taking*: No. 1 has caught the ball and turned
No. 2 runs in and turns him
No. 3 takes the ball and runs back ten yards
No. 1 runs after him and turns him . . .

*Picking up the ball*: Nos. 1 and 2 at one end, 3 at the other
No. 1 runs out, picks the ball up, puts it down
No. 3 runs out, picks the ball up, puts it down. No. 2 . . .

*Mauling*: two groups of four players face each other, ten metres apart. Third group with the ball shuttle between them mauling (or rucking) each time they hit.

These forms in particular are useful for work indoors, though even the first form can easily be adapted to it.

The cyclic principle can be applied on a bigger scale just as simply. Take, for example, the forwards working on cover patterns against the back three and behind them, the centres. The forwards follow up the kick from fly-half, catch the fielder and maul the ball back. The fly-half kicks . . . and the cycle continues.

Here is a sample list of cyclic exercises. You will see that the form is easily adaptable to meet the need for intensive repetition. Remember, though, the need to control the tempo, and to use it as a coaching situation.

- 1   pick up    put down    turn
  2   pick up    pass
  3   take pass    put down    turn . . .

- 1   pick up    put down    turn
  2   pick up    drive in and up    offer ball
  3   jack up
  4   complete the wedge
  5   take the ball    put down    turn . . .

- 1   grubber kick    fall    offer
  2   take grubber    fall    offer
  3   take . . .

- 1   trot with ball    get tackled    put ball on ground
  2   tackle
  3   pick up    trot    get tackled . . .

- 1   trot with ball    get tackled    roll ball back
  2   tackle
  3   pick up    trot    get tackled . . .

It's worth pointing out that these cyclic exercises can be adapted to simulate retreating defence as well as attack. If the ball-carrier, instead of putting the ball down and turning, simply stops and puts the ball down in front of him, the next player can be required to get round in front of 'the attack', snap up the ball, and initiate play from there. For example:

- 1   trots with ball    stops    puts ball down
  2   snaps up ball    mauls v 1
  3   completes wedge
  4   trots . . .

And the same effect can be gained, for example, by having 1 do a grubber kick, and defending fall; 2 turning him over as he gets up; 3 passing to 4; 4 doing a grubber kick . . .

## RESISTANCE EXERCISES

A third element in preparation for the bruising contact and muscular effort required in the game – and a longer-term adaptive programme to it – is strength work. The particular variant that works most successfully in the normal session is one that requires no special preparations or apparatus – exercises in which the individual player is pitted against his own body weight or against a player or players of the same build. It has to be interesting, demanding, and carefully monitored; it tends to be very good-humoured and popular. Essentially it involves isolating a strength needed in the game, and devising an exercise that will help develop it. Take an obvious example: building up binding strength in the pack. We want to make the required movement against resistance. One possible solution: two props lie down on their backs, head to head, arms extended sideways. A has his palms up; B has palms down, locked on A's wrists. A tries to clap his hands over his head; B tries to stop him. Work for 30 seconds, then change over.

Or consider the difficulties of getting the tackle ball without landing on the ground yourself. For this exercise, arrange the players in matched pairs, a metre apart, the ball on the ground between them, and their hands on the ball. They lean together in the frog position – legs apart, knees deeply bent, backside sticking out, shoulders crouching forward. They fight to drag back the ball.

You can make such exercises up at the drop of a hat. No area of player preparation offers an easier way of developing confidence in your own inventiveness. All you need do is set up an initial situation, and experiment in developing competition. Here are a sample dozen initial situations. Have the paired players:

- standing facing each other – *position 1*
- kneeling facing each other – *position 2*
- standing back to back – *position 3*
- scrumming position – on the feet – *position 4*
- scrumming position – kneeling – *position 5*
- lying on their backs – head to head – *position 6*
- lying on their backs – feet to feet – *position 7*
- lying on their front – head to head – *position 8*
- lying on their front – feet to feet – *position 9*
- sitting face to face – *position 10*
- one standing; one in any other position – *position 11*
- one kneeling; one in any other position – *position 12*

The other night, for example, in a short session we went through the following programme:

- *position 4*: each player pulling his partner down to the right (*30 sec*); each player pulling his partner down to the left (*30 sec*)

- *position 5*: one player taking his partner up, the other down (*20 sec*); reverse roles (*20 sec*)

- *position 6*: arms sideways, wrists held – one player tries to clap his hands overhead, the other tries to stop him; reverse roles (*30 sec*)

- *position 6*: same position – players move both feet to touch hands on left (5); on right (5); other player's feet overhead (*10 sec*)

- *position 8*: arm wrestling – right hands, left hands (*30 sec each*)

- *position 1*: link fingers of both hands with opponent – push his arms back to his shoulders (*30 sec*)

- *position 8*: press-ups – player A sets the pace and tries to beat his partner (*30 sec*); reverse roles (*30 sec*)

- *position 8*: breast-stroke arm action – (*100 repetitions in time with partner*)

- *position 7*: interlink feet – trunk curls – competition (*30 sec*)

- *position 7*: player A puts feet between player B's feet – A tries to take B's feet out while B tries to push A's feet together (*30 sec*); reverse roles (*30 sec*)

- *position 7*: feet off floor – A writes 'Loughborough Colleges' in the air with his feet; B stays with him.

Some basic principles emerge from the structure of this session – e.g. exercising the different body areas in sequence with concentration on upper body and stomach; moving from exercise to exercise with minimum change of starting position; keeping both players working simultaneously; using set times for each exercise; working with matched pairs of players; getting them to compete with each other. What it doesn't capture is my own performance – in there exhorting maximum effort, and trying to suggest the amusing side of it (after all, I wasn't doing it!). There's no place for an extensive description of possible exercises but a few categories may help you:

- direct muscular confrontation – e.g. wrestling

- strength versus body weight – e.g. lifting a partner; carrying a partner

- using partner's repetition rate to spur the player working against his own weight e.g. star jumps; press-ups.

We finished the short session with a minute's complete relaxation, and a cycle of breathing: breathe out for 15 seconds; hold it for 15 seconds; breathe in for 15 seconds; hold it for 15 seconds, and repeat. The idea is to maximise lung expansion and contraction, and gradually to extend the time unit towards a (for most people) hypothetical minute. I encourage players to empty their lungs whenever they can during the game to increase their oxygen uptake and restore their composure.

You'll find an account at the end of the book of how these exercises can be used in high-intensity fitness work. But one of their principal functions in the structured session is as a familiar morale-booster and invigorator. Once the warm-up and stretching have been done, you need to raise the players' expectations of the hard work and fun to come. A few assorted resistance exercises are excellent for this: it shifts gear from the quiet and the slow to the powerful and explosive, and the players really enjoy it. It's ideal, too, for giving players who may not be running units or sub-units an opportunity to take over some light responsibility for team preparation.

# 12 PRESSURE PRACTICES

These are the natural culmination of work on any aspect of the game, at individual, unit, or team level. Their aim is to drill the players so that they maintain a disciplined, effective performance under stress. The stages of producing such a performance are:

- introduction: prescriptive coaching and diagnostic coaching

- habituation: coaching situation and diagnostic coaching

- tempering: pressurised coaching situation and diagnostic coaching after the event.

The essential element in pressure practices is high work-rate. The action to be established is repeated:

- more rapidly than would be encountered in a match

- more often than would be encountered in a match

- with increased intensification as the players adapt to the pressure.

Pressure practices are a test: they examine how effectively the preceding stages of practice have been assimilated. So preserve confidence by using pressure sensibly: start with a realistic target and alter the pressure in terms of their success. The players want to finish knackered but triumphant. They can be triumphant only if the preceding stages have been thorough, and their focus on what they're doing has been maintained throughout.

The following are examples to show coaching situations being turned into pressure practices.

## Individual players: tackling
*Coaching situation*: three players trot across grid and back. Fourth player puts in ten tackles. Then change over.
*Pressure practice*: same set up. How many tackles can you put in in thirty seconds? forty seconds?

## Unit: forwards – line-out
*Coaching situation*: line-out on goal line – scrum-half calls for each of 12 throws.
*Pressure practice*: line-out on goal line and line-out at deadball line. Players shuttle from one to the other with scrum-half making his call on the way. Perform three sets of three line-outs, each set faster than the one before it ... building to two sets of nine against the clock. Calls varied each time. Line-out ends when ball reaches scrum-half.

## Unit: backs – sequences

*Coaching situation*: ball on right touch. Backs spin ball to outside-centre, who puts ball down to simulate tackle. Scrum-half attacks blind with full-back and wing.
Pressure practice: play the sequence left, then right, then left again, trying to eliminate all pauses whilst players get into position. Time first attempt covertly. They have to beat this on runs two and three.

## Team: programme of unopposed

*Coaching situation*: receive kick-off, attack blind, ruck. Spin to outside centre, ruck. Attack blind with full-back and wing. Wing feeds forwards who interpass and score.
*Pressure practice*: as above but time first run covertly. Trot back to places for runs 2–5. Aim to clip the time taken each run.

You can see how easy it is to devise and complicate such exercises. Stick with playing patterns you use: you want to get them slick.

## Team: opposed

Pressure practice: three-minute match, 1st XV v 2nd XV. Each team takes it in turn to have possession or defend. They have to score in three minutes/keep the opposition out for three minutes. Start from scrum – initially on the midpoint of the 22, later midpoint of half-way.

## Tempo control

Pressure practices are an effective preparation for playing the match faster than the opposition would like. You can apply them to any facet of play. As a result, you can be well into your tap penalty before the opposition have organised their defence; get your back row attack underway whilst they're settling in for their eight-man shove; get your drop-out 22 away while they're still trotting back, and so on. Immediate purposeful action turns a potential advantage into a real one. Dictate to the opposition. They must feel constantly that they're reacting to your initiative. And that's as true when you're 'defending' – i.e. attacking their possession, and depriving them of the initiative in how they use the ball – as when you're attacking.

What we're encouraging is speed based on:

- early decisions – or even established policy

- getting there first – superior fitness and commitment

- role security – knowing exactly what you are expected to do

- controlled action – appropriate to the present skill level after pressure practices

- introduction in a sequence of matches of one element at a time.

## So what must we foster?

**1** A habit of early decision-making and calling wherever co-ordinated play is required. Most of the pauses that relax pressure on the opposition are the result of indecision. Nominate your decision-makers and work with them. For example, intersperse your unopposed with penalty calls, so that you respond fast. Work out where you will do what – perhaps two options at a given point, in case weather interferes with your first choice. Know what your goal kickers can do and don't ask them to do more. Put your scrum-half in charge – he's almost certainly going to be involved in the action.

**2** Very thorough preparation of each element – as a coach, demand excellence; as a player, expect it of yourself. Be prepared to work to get it right. Most coaches I've seen think the job's done after three repetitions of doubtful quality. Get it right.

**3** Intensive drilling of each element and appropriate pressure practices.

**4** Make clear to players that as they approach a point, they should be rehearsing what they're going to do. Be prepared: stay cool.

**5** Pay special attention to critical situations – e.g. within a couple of metres of either goal line, where hope or anxiety can interfere with performance.

Of course, there *are* times when you want everything slowed down. Delay always favours the defenders, allows them to reorganise, make rational decisions and restore their morale – which is why players in defence occasionally collapse with obscure ailments, why the ball goes missing, and why scrums take ages to go down. This may not exactly be time-wasting, but it certainly slows down the proceedings. However, the defence's desire for delay should reinforce your resolve to step up a gear in attack and let them play catch-up.

Playing at this intensity of concentration and effort is tiring: no team can expect to go through an entire match like that. But it's an invaluable resource for the captain to be able to call for just a few minutes of such output, and be certain of getting it. Make sure that he's aware that this possibility exists – with some players unless you actually spell it out it may go unobserved. Focus his attention on – the beginning and end of each half; when you're near their line; immediately after a score for you or against you. But if at any point he suddenly becomes aware that your team is playing at the opposition's pace, he should do something about it at once.

Once you're satisfied with the standard of performance of a particular skill, you should automatically rely on pressure practices in your sessions. The complete session ought to be an exercise in fitness, and pressure practices contribute to that end, by maintaining high work-rate, and getting more done in the time available.

## Saturation Attack

A characteristic expression of total rugby is the saturation attack. This tends to be the culmination of growing momentum, when the team commits itself to an all-out attack, determined to score:

- it's the culmination of an attack rather than its inception
- it tends to be launched down the axis of the previous tactical point, so that forwards can join in quickly on good lines of run
- all available backs should join in – wing, halves, full-back, inside-centre
- the aim is to get more players into the attacking zone than the opposition can muster in defence
- all the players seek effective support positions so that no ball-carrier can be isolated. The forwards think: width, depth, run from deep, run for space, keep the ball alive. To ruck in such an attack is a kind of failure: support is to hand – keep the ball going forward
- the passionate purpose is to convert all the effort into a great score
- it's devastating at any time – but especially at one of the key periods outlined above.

Preparation for this type of attack can be built into unopposed or opposed practice. As soon as the initial break is made in your opponent's half of the field, the call is 'Blitz', and you strike with the power of lightning. You may start 30m out, and gradually extend it, so that the practice gets more and more demanding. Take a spare ball with you to kick back into your half of the field – checking that your remaining players are giving what cover they can. Encourage every player to feel that he can always beat one man if it's necessary.

# 13 COACHING SESSIONS

## PRE-SEASON – THE DEDICATED SESSION

During the season, I'd recommend that you adopt the structured session described on p. 73 as the basic pattern of your practices. It's designed to keep all aspects of play moving forward together, but is flexible enough to let you concentrate on immediate needs. Out of season you can make a major assault on extending the range and quality of your players' individual skills, and the following is a worked example of how you might do this for large numbers, with economy in space and time.

The coach consistently wishes:

- to improve the quality of routine skills

- to introduce skills which he has just identified

- to extend to all, skills usually associated with a few.

He'll find that players – especially the most talented players – welcome the chance to take part. They all want to extend the range of their skills and refine their quality, and the more successful they are, the more enterprising your team's rugby can be – you can extend its range, and you can take what might, for other teams, be unacceptable risks.

It sounds a formidable task to combine the various coaching methods, coaching situations, and coaching exercises described above, but each, in fact, simplifies the real task of educating the players in the form of:

- establishing high standards

- having the players understand the principles behind what they're doing.

Both of these suggest the high regard the coach has for the players – he believes them capable of excellence in performing and in understanding. His final aim is to encourage them to accept responsibility for their own development, to become, as it were, their own coaches.

His first step in this is to ask questions rather than simply give answers. What you're after is a balance between asking and telling. Ask a question at an appropriate level – the whole point is that they should be able to answer it – rephrase it, offer alternative answers, signal the answer through body language, offer a single possibility – '*do you think it might be . . . ?*' It normally takes far less time to reach an answer than to detail the methods, and that time decreases as you get to know the group, and they get to know you.

You help the process by proceeding wherever possible from the known to the unknown – the known is very reassuring, and encourages speculation. This is true even down to the immediate environment: once the players have experienced how you use grids, they feel at ease in them.

The key to gaining the co-operation of players is the way you greet their efforts. If they're only 10% near the answer, praise them for the 10% . . . and go on to elicit more. If you feel an urge to slap them down and show your superiority, you're in the wrong game altogether.

So let's see how the various factors interact to accelerate learning, and leave the players – who may well be coaches – with a comfortable sense of their own abilities. They'll experience:

- prescriptive and diagnostic coaching

- a carefully controlled coaching situation

- high involvement and work-rate

- effective implantation of skills

- understanding of principles

- easy transitions from the known to the unknown

- large numbers accommodated safely in limited space and time.

We'll start with a known, the passes used by the scrum-half, and expand to lateral spin passing and spin punting. This is possible and desirable because they all depend on the same mechanics, and it's a very important model for the players to grasp – it covers every attempt to move the ball by throwing, passing, or kicking. Moreover, most of them will have experienced applications of the model before, in golf, field athletics, table-tennis, or tennis.

## The model

**a)** Determine the required line of flight.

**b)** All of the energy and the direction are transmitted through the hand behind the ball, i.e. the right hand on a pass to the left.

**c)** The longer that hand or foot is in contact with the ball on the desired line of flight, the more accurate the flight will be – rifles are more accurate than hand-guns.

**d)** Other things being equal, a spinning ball will go further, more accurately than a non-spinning ball – rifles are more accurate than muskets.

**e)** Any deviation from the desired line of flight – unless there are external factors involved (such as the wind) – can be traced back to the movement of the hand or foot relative to the ball and the desired line of flight.

**f)** The length of flight is governed by the speed of the hand or foot in contact with the ball, and the quality of that contact.

**g)** The speed of hand or foot is largely a product of bodily forces, notably weight-shift and rotation.

**h)** The quality of contact depends on how nearly the force is applied to a plane through the centre of the ball, and on the ball's being properly inflated.

What you have here is a set of principles that interact to produce consistent effective performance. Let's see now how productive we can make them in a single session.

### Get the coaching situation clear

Work in lined grids.
Work in threes.
Work with one ball to each three.
Work in trainers.
Work on the dominant hand – establish success first.

### Preliminary activity

Get the players warm and happy: play keepball, with one trying to intercept the ball; tag, with the chaser carrying the ball; resistance exercises (see p. 59), starting easy and working up. Get them laughing and active. Any time they look less than happy and active, go back to these activities.

### Scrum-half pass from a maul – i.e. with the ball already in the hands

Take the place of the nearest player, and put his partner on the end of the grid line, facing you, as receiver. Ask them what the advantages of a spin pass are.

Put the long axis of the ball at right angles to the long axis of your hand, and gently spin it off your fingers up into the air, so that they can see where the spin comes from – your hand is right behind the meat of the ball, and all the available energy will go into the ball.

Face your partner, with the whole of your right arm and shoulder vertical above the line. Ask them what the line represents. Step out on your left leg, right shoulder low, and spin the ball to your partner. As you move over your left leg, lift so that the ball is lifted into the pass.

Repeat, correcting and explaining if the ball hasn't gone exactly where you expected. Talk about a long movement, and the need not to block. The players repeat, with the coach commenting, and sometimes bringing them around to explain a point, till they're competent. Whenever you can, ask them about it with a precise, simple question. As they practise, bring their attention to one thing at a time:

- keep your arm vertical

- keep your right shoulder low

- push your right shoulder through the pass

- start low and lift off your left leg

- make sure your left leg isn't blocking

– and keep helping the individual, offering encouragement because you're sure he's trying. Ask about cause and effect for the off-target pass. Get partners commenting on each other's performance. Get a good pair to show what they can do.

Now move one line of players back half a grid, and introduce the idea of using the index finger to push the ball's nose forward and slightly up on release. Let them try it, and then challenge them to put the ball precisely into their partner's hands, three times on the trot.

Explain that when the scrum-half gets the ball, he'll be facing the maul, and will have to pass across his body. Turn both lines of players 90° to the right, on either side of the line, so that they can still use it as a guide. They now have the ball in both hands, but the right hand continues to do all the work. They also have to deal with rotation at hip and shoulder. Keep feeding in material and questions:

- start with your weight on your right foot

- step out on your left foot parallel to the line

- what must you be careful not to do with your left leg?

- what kind of movement are you aiming for?

- push your right shoulder down the line

- if you push your right shoulder through, you'll stay longer with the ball: what will that increase?

- if you push it through, who will you end up facing?

Tell them they're scrum-halves receiving the ball direct from the line-out. Now each player has to flip the ball gently into the air, receive it, and go into the pass.

By this time you'll find that the lads understand what they're doing, and, if encouraged, can comment on each pass they receive, what's right and what might be improved.

## Scrum-half pass off the ground

The coach announces he's going to use the same model for scrum-half pass. He selects a demonstration pair. One faces his partner, feet astride the line at its far end. The other puts the ball on the intersection of the line of pass and the base line. He places himself for a right-handed pass, with his right foot on the base line, in line with the ball and four or five inches behind it. His feet are comfortably together.

He goes down by bending his knees, so that his hand is behind the ball, as it has been in all the sessions so far. One-handed, he spins the ball to his partner, stepping out on his left foot as he does so. If you prefer to have the left leg in position, remember – no blocking and weight on or near the right foot. He pushes his shoulder through the pass down the line. When he's successful, the coach puts the receiver further back. Depending on his sense of the group, he suggests they watch the passer's left leg and foot: is it good? (i.e. is it not block-ing?). He asks them to watch the passer's left arm: is it good? (i.e. is it flinging away from the body to increase shoulder rotation speed?).

The other players copy, with partners commenting and coaching. The coach produces a flag-stick, and uses it with his selected passer to show the line of pass (i.e. its point is at the intersection of the two lines, its length is in the plane of the line of pass, and it's inclined to point at the receiver's waist). The player steps out, running his hand up the stick: it'll come as a revelation to him. The coach can pull his hand further up the stick to suggest the need to stay with the ball as far as possible: it will pull his right shoulder through the pass, and complete the rotation of his upper body.

The other players take a good look, and try to copy. The odds are that by this time you've got some beautiful passes, and your regular scrum-half is looking worried. Two points about this scrum-half pass:

- *scrum-half pass to the right*: most players find it difficult to co-ordinate the shift of weight and the strike of the hand. It's desirable that regular scrum-halves be able to pass off the left hand. They may find it easier to extend the right leg first, limit the weight shift, and whip the ball out with the upper body, arms and wrists. For most players, the answer is a pivot pass – in which you do your right-hand pass with your back to the opposition. I wouldn't bother with it in this session

- *the one-handed pass amply demonstrates the truth of point a) in the model*, and even untalented players will whip the ball off the ground without a pick up or take back, delays which neither the scrum-half nor the stand-off can afford. As soon as you put a second hand on the ball, you'll find that there's a universal ten-dency to pick the ball up. Emphasise the need to have the hand behind the ball moving down the desired line of flight immediately it touches the ball.

## Normal spin pass

The coach asks the two lines of players to turn so that their right hand is on the outside of their grid, and their right foot on the base line. The grid line still marks the direction of pass. Their weight should be on the right leg, which is slightly bent, while the upper body should lean forward to allow the right arm to swing vertically. The left toes should be extended to touch the ground and keep their weight to the right. Now both lines practise swinging their arm across their bodies, and extending the movement down the line of flight by pushing their right shoulder in the same direction. Repeat with the ball, spinning it off the fingers as before.

The coach suggests shifting the left foot slightly back, opening the hips, and so facilitating the movement. He suggests keeping the front shoulder low on all lateral passes. He asks what would happen if the front shoulder were high (model). He asks if there are any particular problems, and invites explanations from the players (expectations), and input on how to put it right (model): he can count on getting some precise answers. He challenges them to repeat with the left hand. Then he turns one line, so that partners are facing in the same direction, and they trot down the lines, giving and taking spin passes: they have to be flat; they have to be accurate. The coach keeps commenting and praising. They turn and come back, still passing. Each pair discusses problems, and refers to the coach those they can't sort out. They repeat the trot, slightly further apart, and with increased emphasis on good positioning by the receiver, so that the ball-carrier's flat pass is always into space.

(Spin lateral passing is currently popular. How would you feel if your scrum-half didn't spin the ball? Why? Does your stand-off complain about the spin pass? All the same advantages apply to spin passing in general play.)

## Spin punting

The coach explains he's going to apply the same model to punting. He rolls the ball down his hand to remind them. He then extends his right foot, so that the toes just touch the ground, and releases the ball over the right ankle, so that it rolls down the middle of the foot. He lets them see what happens when the ball goes down right or left of centre. They repeat.

The coach then faces a partner, 5m away. He steps in on his left foot, his right knee high, toes down and back; the ball is released on the ankle.

As it rolls down his foot, he pushes it to his partner. He repeats, reinforcing the points: 'step in' . . . 'knee high' . . . 'toes down' . . . 'on your sock' . . . 'push it to him'. Some people won't put it down on the middle of their foot: 'watch it onto your foot'. The players have a go. Check that after the kick they remain in balance: they should be able to return their right foot to the ground alongside their left. The coach goes up and down, commenting and eliciting answers from the players. The ball doesn't spin? They've put it too low on their foot, or they've turned their toes up. It goes right or left? They've put it on the outside or the inside of their foot. The coach puts them twice as far apart. He talks about the need to put it into their partners' hands: a kick that goes too far or not far enough is as bad as one that goes in the wrong direction. He tells them to put their left hand slightly forward, with the long axis of the ball still parallel to the ground – the equivalent of pushing the pass with their index finger. This is to reduce air resistance.

Once they're performing adequately, he challenges them to kick left-footed. They go right back to the start, and work through. The critical factor is balance: they must be able to put the left foot back on the ground beside the right when they've finished the kick. Now it's the right hand that's pushing forward . . . but the ball's still got to roll down the extended foot, and if they push their hand too far forward, it can't.

He explains that the ball will tend to move in the air in the direction it's pointing, and that they can compensate by starting with the active hip slightly further back.

He explains that to get more power, they've got to lengthen the levers: hold the ball further out, leaning back slightly, and let it drop further. But he emphasises that successful kicking is accurate kicking: it's got to go to a precise target. He challenges them to put it right into their partners' hands within three kicks. He tells them he expects to see them practising these skills when he next comes out. He praises them . . . and that's the end of the session.

## Reflections on the practice

In this practice, you can see all of the coaching methods in action. The coach adopts a model, designs a coaching situation, clarifies his expectations, and intervenes to correct faults. Well before the end of it, the players will be following the same process: they'll be accepting responsibility for improving their own performance, and understanding how to set about it. They'll be moderately competent in all they've done. They'll think the coach is pretty competent, too. Turn now to Setting up the Structured Session (see p. 75) and you'll see exactly the same kind of process at work, on a much bigger scale, directed at the improvement of individual, unit and team performance, and employing a wide range of models. The method remains the same: the use of models for individual, unit and team performance, the refining of expectations, selective scanning and coaching intervention. And the results are of the same kind: enhanced performance and greater understanding of principles among the players.

To keep the technical progression clear, I've left out the fun activities that spice up the practice – small side games, intra- and inter-grid, resistance exercises, impossible challenges, and so on. Keep it fun. Get as much well done as you can, but tailor it to the people you're working with. And remember, your energy, enthusiasm, enjoyment and good humour condition the response of the players. The first requirement for any teacher is that he be happy.

## IN-SEASON – THE STRUCTURED SESSION

In many ways, the most critical step the coach can make is to adopt a structure for his sessions. Whatever structure he accepts will exactly mirror his aims, and the absence of such a structure can only suggest a lack of definition in his aims.

The structure should aim to give purpose, variety, progression and some degree of inclusiveness to each session. It should limit mistakes and build confidence by moving from easy to difficult, simple to complex, low pressure to high pressure, small units to larger units, more basic to more sophisticated. It should encourage the coach to give a thoughtful coverage to all aspects of the game within his immediate resources of players, time, and facilities. It should give maximum activity in the time available.

Any step towards adopting a structure, even a rudimentary one, is to be welcomed, since it implies an awareness of more elements that require attention. Naturally enough, the structure that seems best adapted to the needs of total rugby has to be fully inclusive. Nevertheless, the structure is simple, strong and easy to use. It satisfies all the criteria of the previous paragraph.

*Discussion of the previous game* (see p. 78)
*Warm-up* – loosening (see p. 121), intensive handling (see p. 122 ff.), strength exercises (see p. 59)
*Individual techniques* (see p. 138 ff.)
*Unit techniques* (see p. 170 ff.)
*Team patterns* (see p. 288)
*Fitness work* (see p. 315)
*Clinic skills* – these are basically individual positional skills that need a lot of the coach's attention. Since you cannot keep numbers of players waiting while you work extensively with one or two, you must make time for this kind of work before or after the session, or while the rest are actively engaged in exercises that demand less of your attention.

The outline of this structured session is also the structure of the whole of Part 5, and details of what can be included under each heading will be found in the relevant chapters.

It's obvious that you cannot do more than a selection of exercises in any one session, and the coach must use judgement in deciding what is to be included on a particular evening. Most clubs at any level have a minimum two sessions a week, and expect their players to work on their own – e.g. weights, physio – outside the sessions. Players giving up this time are entitled to expect that the time will be well spent. Careful preparation is, therefore, absolutely essential.

There are four requirements: *selective planning, intensity, quality* and *coaching*.

## Selective planning

Your *selection* will be guided under each heading by:

- observing what was unsatisfactory in the previous match

- having a clear idea of what will be needed for the weeks ahead, and (for the players and the club) the seasons ahead.

Your *planning* will be guided by:

- the *structure* you've adopted

- a clear, detailed idea of the team practices with which you wish to finish the technical part of the evening: you must build towards them so that their success is assured. You must finish strong.

You may very well find that you have to omit whole elements of the structure – that on a particular evening you cannot find time for a discussion of the previous match or work on individual techniques – and that you can devote only a short time to others. Nevertheless, awareness of the structure will help you over a sequence of sessions to get an appropriate balance. It would be futile to indicate how much time you devote to what – it depends precisely on your judgement of what your particular team needs at that particular time. The only element I cannot imagine leaving out is intensive handling, if only in the form of touch rugby: even if we spent all but the last fifteen minutes on discussing the game and sorting out problems, we'd have a quick handling session.

## Intensity

You demand high *work-rate* from your players in the match – 'pass and run', 'tackle and *run*', 'jump and *run*' – and you must expect the same work-rate of the players and yourself in the practice. Of course there are times when you need a slower tempo – to solve problems, or get players thinking, or simply to give them a rest – but the emphasis in general has to be on cheerful, organised, activity. To achieve this you need:

- to have the programme clear, in your mind and on a piece of paper in your pocket – we don't want awkward pauses

- to have a list of points you must concentrate on – preferably reduced by forethought to work with particular players in particular situations

- to have players in charge of each unit, each with clear (preferably written) instructions on what has to be done – this helps free you for your list of points

- to have in staple activities – e.g. handling, or scrumming – set times, or number of repetitions for each activity

- to have one ball available for every four players

- to have the spaces used clear and limited, and therefore economical and safe – and for this you'd be well advised to have say, nine 10-metre square grids marked out behind the deadball line, and the scrum-machine in position

- to build up a repertoire of coaching situations, so that you can minimise time spent on explanations.

## Quality

There is no point in practising mistakes – a sloppy practice in which players fail to concentrate on improving their performance is worse than no practice at all. If you feel they need a rest, give them a rest; if you feel they need a light-hearted games session, give them one. But don't confuse these needs with a coaching session.

As soon as you sensibly can, set *quality standards* – e.g. if the ball is dropped in a handling exercise, start that exercise again. But remember the need to move from easy to difficult: don't start with the difficult *and* high quality standards. The aim is to tune them up with steady success.

Try to *let no mistake go unchecked or unhelped*. You must be in there, exhorting, cajoling, but above all *explaining*.

Quality is not something that happens overnight. You have to work, perhaps for years, to attain it. And you have to work to maintain it – even to the extent of indoctrinating the coach who will eventually replace you.

## Coaching

Getting quality work from the players and coaching go hand in hand. To a marked extent your enthusiasm, your commitment, your sense of standards and your energy output condition those of the players. If something goes wrong, there's a reason for it, and your job is to point it out and put it right. No exercise does good of itself – it may simply ingrain existing faults: get in there, and coach. If you can, introduce something new every session, even if it's only a variation on an existing practice. But remember that coaching is basically concerned with the hard, unglamorous work of making sure that your players do everything effectively, and that entails repetition and untiring attention to detail.

## SETTING UP THE STRUCTURED SESSION

Nothing gives as much pleasure and satisfaction on our courses as the preparation and implementation of structured sessions. Each syndicate is given a scenario – the past performance of a team, and the opposition it's about to face – and the responsibility for designing an appropriate session.

'Appropriate' is the key word: meeting and putting right actual problems is the true test of a coach, though he's also got a major role to play in expanding the rugby consciousness of his players.

At the end of each session, the player has to feel happy and more confident in himself, his unit, his team, and his coach. He has to feel that problems are being solved and that he and his team are improving. The team element, therefore, at the end of the session should be totally convincing – a demonstration of confidence-building efficiency, especially in areas where there has been weakness.

The simplest way to ensure this strong finish is for the coach to work out what he can reasonably get his team to achieve, and to design his team exercise to show it. Incorporated in this are his concern for what was weak in the last match and what is needed for the next. He then works back through each element of the session, making sure that whatever is needed for that final team exercise is adequately rehearsed in terms of handling, personal skills, and unit skills. If a back row attack to the left is called for, that'll be worked on in unit skills; if the backs have to strike wide to the right, that, too, will have been covered; if a particular form of handling, or a particular form of support is needed, it will be covered in the appropriate slot in the session. So the whole session becomes extremely purposeful, related directly to the team performance.

The exact nature of the team exercise will itself reflect the concerns of the coach. If he's concerned with reinforcing team patterns of attack, he may have the team playing programmed unopposed; if he's concerned with defence, he may have them playing opposed situations. Whichever it is, he's still got to balance these particular needs with the continuing staple practice, e.g. of scrummaging or spinning the ball. He may not, in any one practice, therefore, be able to derive the entire programme from the final sequence, but that shouldn't stop him from deriving as much from it as possible: it's a great source of strength.

Once the coach has completed his plans for the structured session, he has to start thinking how he's going to cover each section. Immediately, he can get help from the basic coaching technique: he knows he has to get his *model* clear – exactly what he wants his players to be doing; check out his *expectations* of what or who will go wrong; and resolve to scan with those particularly in mind. As mentioned above, there will be times when he has to delegate the management of part of the session – e.g. unit skills – to one or other of the players, and he's got to organise that carefully in a form that makes it easy for him. By and large, though, handling, personal skills, and even unit skills have a limited scope; the team exercise seems very complicated . . . but you cope with it in exactly the same way. Say you've decided on programmed unopposed, and that you've six elements:

- receive kick-off right

- attack blind to ruck
- strike wide left with full-back to tackle
- forwards handle to ruck
- attack blind to link with forwards
- forwards handle to score wide on left.

This programme reflects elements you want to strengthen, e.g:

- speed to support the catcher receiving kick-off
- speed to support the ball-carrier in forward attack
- positioning of stand-off in second-phase attack
- positioning of winger in blind-side attack.

You'll already have prepared many of these elements at appropriate slots in the structured session. You'll probably have refined your expectations at the same time – you know what's likely to go wrong, who's likely to make a mistake. Keep thinking of each of these elements as separate; concentrate on one point in each element through the sequence: you end up with six points to make – to put right or to praise – at the end of each run. It's the old story: if you try to see everything, you'll see nothing; if you concentrate on one thing, you can eliminate it. And with practice it gets very easy. But it's extremely important, because after each run you can comment effectively on half-a-dozen points. If you do a dozen runs, and put right even two or three points each time, the overall performance will improve dramatically. You'll finish strong, and everyone will feel good.

With growing experience and confidence, you'll find that you can make these sessions increasingly rich and enjoyable. I think what really impresses the coaches on our courses is how much they can get done in the time available, how purposeful the whole session becomes, and how much the team improves.

Perhaps the best note to end this section on is that of ease and support. In the beginning, you can fit your most effective exercises into the structure, and you'll find that they seem more relevant. As you use the structure, you'll build up a repertoire of staple activities, which your players get to know so that you get a speedy, accurate response. Indeed, you need to avoid putting too much that's new in on any one occasion: it would require too much explanation, interrupting the steady rhythm of action. And once you're accustomed to the structure, it guides your thoughts, supplies ideas and gives you confidence, taking the load off your shoulders, and carrying you happily through the session.

# 14 INFORMATION TECHNOLOGY

## TEAM TALK

The coach's job is to create steady progress for the individual and the team. Provided they're properly prepared and structured, team talks are eminently worthwhile as aids to this.

We tend to talk on a Monday about the previous Saturday's game. This gives us time to assimilate what actually happened. I very rarely talk about the game until I've given myself time to sort things out, to talk to the players individually, and to hear what spectators are saying. Listen to everybody – any little point may come in useful. The other valuable thing about not talking immediately is that it gives you time to get back in balance. It would be a remarkably philosophic coach who didn't get involved emotionally in his team's fortunes – its one source of energy and commitment – but it's not a good basis for decision-making. I restrict myself to the most general of good-natured remarks until I'm ready to talk to the team.

Even then, the first thing I do is to get each member of the team to talk. It's very important that each player should get a chance to express what he feels and what he's noticed. He's got to feel that he's an active part of the team, and that he's got a respectable contribution to make. We start at full-back and work straight through to no. 8, with the captain contributing the last word. We discuss each point as it comes up. As each player finishes, he's asked two questions: what he learned from the game, and what he's got to work on in the coming week.

This works most effectively when the players are accustomed to it. The coach's job in this first phase is to keep the discussion positive and to act as chairman. The positive atmosphere is vital. This is a great way to get petty moans and grievances out in the open and fully aired. The key method in achieving a positive atmosphere is to plug the notion that the people who feel worst about mistakes on the field are the people who make them, and that what they need, on the field and off, is support. One for all, and all for one is every team's motto. I've never understood the point of haranguing a player who already feels bad. What's needed is to build up a proper pride in the individuals, the units, and the team. You can do more by talking as if what you want to be true is true, than by bemoaning its absence. By telling a winger he's very quick, you can, remarkable though it sounds, make him quicker – and so on for every position. If you want a player to think, compliment him on his thinking. It may not work at once; it rarely fails in the long term: a lot of a player's – or a team's – ability is conditioned by his belief in himself. That has got to be built up, and kept in proportion by the quality standards set by the coach.

Much of what you want to discuss will have come up during this first phase. In the second phase, we generally try to clarify the main issues on which decisions have to be made for the units and the team. At this stage, the coach is more evidently in charge, but if he's chaired the first phase intelligently there should be general agreement about what he puts forward. The aim is to reach agreement, but the essential thing is to make sensible decisions, and the coach must take the lead in this: you cannot coach by committee.

The third phase sets out the arrangements for the week so that we all know what we're going to do and any difficulties can be ironed out.

The same principles apply when the talk is focused on the next match rather than that just past. It would be ridiculous not to use any information available, and much of that may come from the players. But in looking forward to the next game we are less concerned with the opposition than with preparing ourselves – getting ourselves into a frame of mind in which we welcome the opportunity to show what we can do. This seems a much more fruitful attitude than encouraging either of the twin dangers – unreal optimism or unreal anxiety. With younger players especially these are real underminers of performance. What we need to ripen in all our players is an honest dignity of endeavour – a willingness to go out and take pride in producing our best as an expression of the self rather than a simple response to external events.

## MATCH ANALYSIS

The coach (or selector) can rarely afford the luxury of being a mere spectator at matches. You give up the simple pleasure of enjoying the game, of being entertained, as soon as you accept responsibility for improving the play of the individuals, units and team. This means that you have to be on your guard against the viewing habits of the average spectator. It's worthwhile examining what these are:

- he *ball-watches* – which immediately focuses his attention on *what* is happening rather than *why*. As a coach you have to view more widely, taking in as many of the elements concerned as possible. You must see what's happening (or what happened) off the ball that affected the immediate situation.
  A further result of this is that the spectator tends to see much more of the *attack* than he does of the *defence*, and this exaggerates his underlying preference for the excitement of attack. The coach, intent on seeing more of the game, must watch the defence just as closely as he does the attack. Secure defence is the only possible basis for a winning team, and it's vital that he monitors the team's defence in every match

- the spectator assesses performance *impressionistically*: he tends to be unduly impressed by single moments of play in which a player does uncharacteristically well or badly. He tends also to be unaware of negative evidence: if a player isn't in view, even though he certainly ought to be, his absence isn't noted. The coach must give the player a clear notion of what he ought to be doing, and judge him in that frame of reference. Equally, if he wishes to assess a particular player he must be prepared to concentrate on him, on and off the ball, for perhaps two or three minutes at a time, at least twice in the match

- the spectator tends to be *blinded by his allegiance* to the team, and his judgement is clouded by his assumptions. The coach has far greater reason to be involved – it would be an altogether exceptionally well-balanced man who could give a great deal of time and energy to the team without being in a high degree affected by its performance. Nevertheless, like a good player his mind must go on working dispassionately throughout the hurly-burly of the game. He may find that *distancing* himself *physically* – putting himself at a remove from the action – may help, but it's more useful to distance himself *mentally*, by some objective process, such as writing notes (which presents information in a much more accessible form than talking into a recorder) or doing some kind of analysis such as is dealt with later in this chapter.

Even when he has overcome these tendencies the coach must face one fact: he can never see more than a limited amount of the game. He may change his position during the match, but he can't be in more than one position at a time – and the action may be 100m away from him. Much of what he's watching involves numbers of players at close quarters, when it's impossible to see what's happening. He can only make educated guesses at the psychological state of his players, and the reasons for it. But the radical problem is the sheer quantity of action, on and off the ball, that may be relevant to his coaching.

In view of these difficulties, the coach has got to accept that he shouldn't attempt to do too much too quickly. He must see analysis as a continuing process, in which he will concentrate on only a very few things in a given match. The key to effective analysis is accurate expectations – prediction of which elements of the team's play are most likely to require improvement. Prediction allows effective concentration so that instead of being distracted by a potential overload of information the coach can look at what counts. This isn't an exclusive concern, for the coach will register a good deal that isn't in predicted focus for him – indeed it's more than likely that the specific concern will be limited to specific phases in the play, and so in other phases he will be free to watch the rest of the team.

In all analysis, as in the whole coaching process, having clearly defined expectations is an enormous help in simplifying the apparent complexities of the action. If, for example, you have a clear model of your defensive shape, it's much easier to see what's going wrong. In this respect, rugby is a much easier game to examine than soccer: rugby can be reduced to a whole series of predictable situations much more easily than the very fluid, very open, 360° game of soccer. This applies to the individual, to the unit, and to team play. As coach you should have clear expectations in respect of each, and so be able to spot discrepancies. The order in which you scan will be dictated by your sense of team priorities.

## BASIC ANALYSIS FORM

| Ball | | Pass | | Run | | Kick | |
|------|------|------|------|------|------|------|------|
| good | bad | good | bad | good | bad | good | bad |

At this stage you may seek to reduce your observation to figures. This forces you to watch consistently, and it crystallises your observation. It's of even more value in focusing the attention of your players: they may have doubts about your subjective assessment of their play, but figures they must take more seriously.

This is already done at a fairly low level – e.g. strikes against the head, or line-out possession. It's very easy to extend it to such aspects as possession from rucks or mauls where we took the ball in, or when they took the ball in; possession of the ball when one of the backs is tackled. These are basically either/or situations, and, therefore, easy to check. Rather more difficult is dealing with a multiple choice – e.g. a scrum-half's use of the ball. But it's still simple enough to produce a basic analysis form.

This is objective insofar as it establishes what proportion of the ball he received, he passed, ran with, or kicked. It's subjective in its estimate of performance quality, though the subjective element could easily be reduced by introducing definitions of 'good' and 'bad' – e.g. 'good ball' allows the player freedom of choice, a 'bad run' leads to possession being lost, and so on.

The use of this kind of form provides basic information for the coach – it helps him identify the area on which he must concentrate. It may, for example, reveal that even with good ball, the scrum-half's passing is bad. The objective figures will help focus the scrum-half's attention on the need to improve his pass. The coach can then take his analysis a stage further, concentrating on the passes and trying to identify a categorical weakness – passing to the right, pivot passing, or whatever. This movement from wide to fine focus is the typical progression in analysis.

For years I made comprehensive notes, in chronological order, of the match. They were all 'subjective' – the notes were my reading of the situation: that a given player was out of position, was off-balance as he place kicked, and so on. It was an excellent discipline, and it meant that the players were given specific advice. Looking back, it seems likely that any ability I now have in analysis, or in

# Post-match think-tank

After each match, you go through a process like this. You probably already do – but it may help to have it articulated:

- what are your quality deficits?
- how do you prioritise them?
- can you identify the critical factors in the most important?
- how will you sort it out?
  - talk it through with the player and those around him
  - clarify your model
  - establish your expectations
  - work out how to test them out
  - who else can help you out: coaches, players, retired players, books, local coaching society?
- if you can't sort it out immediately, can you avoid its recurrence in the short term?
- how will you fit the work into the session without depriving the rest of the squad for too long?
- how will you make sure the player concentrates on the new form in the next match?
  - praise in the practice
  - words immediately before going out to play
  - reminders (and praise) from the section leader
- if he gets it right, how do you use the fact in the next team talk?
- remember, praise the player for his efforts.

ideas of how it should be done, were fostered by this habit, and that perhaps other apprentice coaches could adopt it with benefit.

Increasingly, however, technology is making it easier to study the match behaviour of your own players and opposing teams. My first glimpse of this was in Japan in 1980 when our next opponents sent a team equipped with six camcorders to record us in action. By early 1996, Dave Whitaker, then Olympic hockey coach, was using a full suite of equipment for analysing a match in progress to allow tactical changes to take place immediately. The WRU have now appointed Keith Lyons, the Director of the Centre for Notational Research at Cardiff College of Higher Education, as a consultant in this field.

Recorded material yields results using the same methods of match analysis previously described. You can pinpoint where your own attack or defence broke down, which will focus your attention on what needs to be done with both players and systems. Now, however, you have a fuller opportunity to examine the opposition.

The game-plan of the '95 All Blacks against England is a fine example. The England side relied heavily on Rob Andrew's place kicking. From anywhere in the All Black half he was a threat. England, therefore, were intent on setting up situations where NZ might give away penalties, and NZ were intent on eliminating them. One nice example will make this clear: for several minutes in the second half, Catt, the England full-back, kicked every ball that reached him down over the NZ deadball line – which was then legal – in the hope that the subsequent short drop-out would be controlled by the English pack, the All Blacks being lured off-side to allow a penalty attempt. When Mehrtens took the drop-outs he put in the longest kick he could muster, deep into the England half. Even when NZ had to kick-off to England at the centre they weren't prepared to risk a similar situation: they split their forwards, and kicked 'the wrong way'.

They knew too that England depended greatly on rolling mauls. Much of Andrew's tactical kicking was deep into the corner and aimed at the 'certainty', as it was thought, of a very large England pack dominating the line-out, and setting up a roll close to the line. Such a roll might not get across the line, but had proved a good source of penalty kicks at goal. The All Blacks used short lines, however, that let athleticism flourish, and devoted themselves passionately and intelligently to checking the roll.

One further important recognition was the mismatch between Tony Underwood and Lomu. They then made absolutely sure they could get the ball to Lomu, and he proved unstoppable.

It was sad to see how the prevailing culture in the England camp had stifled the talent of the backs. They turned to the backs when everything else had failed, and they did moderately well against a relaxed defence, in broken play. But the NZ forwards showed real urgency in making the ball available when they were checked. The England forwards, on the other hand, were imbued with a desire to hang on to the ball, and release it only after a struggle – by which time there wasn't a great deal on for the backs, except, of course, kicking.

The analysis of the tapes went something like this . . . 'This is what they do . . . Why do they do it? What advantage are they after? What is the supposed advantage based on? . . . How can we avoid it? Nullify it? Exploit it? . . . What is the downside of their style? How do we exploit it? . . . What is the downside of their selection? How do we exploit it?'

There's a lesson for all here in the total lack of complacency in the NZ camp, and their determination to understand exactly what changes of emphasis they would have to make to maximise their chance of winning.

# 15 COACH RECRUITMENT

I don't believe it's possible to coach more than a single team effectively, and then only by careful organisation and delegation of responsibility. Once the players are accustomed to the way you work, you can handle maybe two teams, but not so well.

If you're going to coach a large group of players you must devote a fair amount of energy to increasing the number of people who can share the load. To have one coach per serious team, and one to jolly along the social players, is what the club must aim for. Fewer than that and the club is failing in its responsibility to the player.

At representative level it's now customary to have a team of specialist coaches and trainers. Money well spent if it means consistent success.

The first essential is to get your decision-makers assuming responsibility for their units, reflecting and confirming their position on the pitch. Briefing them properly for the practice is part of their own preparation for taking charge on the pitch. The more players you can put in charge of sub-units the better.

Finding other coaches is often difficult, and compromises may be necessary. You can start with limited objectives. For example, it doesn't take long to equip an apprentice coach to master a single aspect of rugby, e.g. scrumming, and be able to do good work. From that basis he can broaden out, but almost from the start he's going to lighten your load. Again, it's not unlikely that the local schools have P.E. teachers who, given the chance, would come and help: I was in that position myself for years. Both specialist coaches and people from the school will need support to establish themselves with the players: don't make your invitations half-hearted. Put the players fully in the picture, and give the apprentice coach the support he needs.

Use local coaching resources just as you use the local terrain: make the most of where you live.

In some ways the most important job is to prepare your successor. The minimum assets you're looking for are strength of conviction and the energy of long-term purpose. Without those he's likely to follow rather than lead, and if you don't lead you can't be a coach.

# PART 4

# THE INNER GAME OF RUGBY

## 16 MOBILISING THE TEAM

You've got the players fitter than ever before, you've extended the range of their skills and substantially improved their standard of performance. You've established efficient forms in their unit work. Now you need to mobilise them as a team.

This is more demanding than organising a team – it's aimed at getting a greater contribution from the individual by improving his reading of the game, his judgement, and his decision-making.

Even in seemingly mechanical routines, there's an element of judgement that focuses performance accurately. The flanker applying his power to the scrum should be responding to the needs of the prop, and his reading of what's about to happen: over the game even this adds up to a distinct advantage. But in the loose his judgement is the difference between tries being scored or not scored, between applying energy to maximum effect or wasting it.

If we could get maximum effect from all fifteen players, we'd transform team performance. It's not wholly impossible within a sequence in the game – an attack, for example, to which so many people contribute that it seems magical. You get such moments with the Baa-baas and the Lions, and they're magical for the players too. However, even in teams such as these, they're serendipitous, not to be taken as a realistic specific coaching target.

But if we can establish greater forethought in the players, and apply that forethought to our methods of attack and defence, the basic organisation of our team, so that everything is done a little more appropriately, a little more efficiently, our team play will certainly benefit – and that's a realistic target.

This section deals with developing the ability to look ahead and make better decisions.

### Helping players to read the game
We talk about reading the game. To understand this phrase, you need to distinguish between the two meanings of the verb 'to read'. The first has to do with a

mechanical ability, more or less passively identifying words. The second is when we read with purpose, thinking ahead, extracting the significance of what's being said, seeing the implications, and searching for further clarifying clues. When we talk about 'reading the game', it's this active, interpretive, searching interest that we mean.

We want all our players to read the game actively so that:

- they search for what may be significant

- this triggers a search for further evidence

- they act decisively to exploit what they've seen.

We've all seen a no. 8 keeping his head out of the scrum till the last moment, looking for clues about what the opposing halves intend. He's checking on them at every tactical point. A nod, a wink, a glance, a gesture – any of these can announce that there's something happening. A casual glance towards the wing by the fly-half triggers the following thought process . . . *their winger's drifting wide . . . our winger's not going with him . . . if I go now, I'll catch him a couple of yards out . . .* He commits himself to the appropriate line early, so it may look like magic when he makes the tackle. But it's not magic – it's a function of intelligent interest in the game: you're trying to out-think your opponent, and trust your intuition enough to make a decisive move.

In the same way, a particular situation may focus your attention: you can be under a maul, unable to see, but guess the opposing fly-half's going to strike blind into the corner, because the opening is there, and you've an inexperienced winger. You are shouting '*the blind, the blind*'. The whistle blows, and you emerge to see the fly-half walking back from the corner with the ball in his hands . . . not the outcome you wanted, but a vindication of the process.

The nature of the opposition's mix – the likelihood that they'll kick, or that they'll handle – comes into the reckoning; weather conditions may tilt the balance. You're basically asking '*what would I do if I were you?*', and backing your guess.

You can exercise this function as player, coach, or spectator and it will transform your involvement in the match. Whenever a player shows this ability spontaneously, praise him for it – a sure way to reinforce his use of it. Prompt him to refine it, but do it sensibly. If you make too much of it, you may find the player spends more time watching his mental processes than he does the opposition.

The vast majority of players, once they're relaxed and comfortable in the game, employ the ability at some level – though physical limitations may stop them translating it into effective action. The coach's job is to make them increasingly accurate at it. Look at the various covering exercises in chapter 23: they're specifically aimed at getting players to make more accurate guesses. Look at the exercises in defence for the front three backs. Working on defence is the easy way into getting them focused on probabilities.

However, the process is equally important in attack. Your TDMs need to be looking at how efficient the opposing team is, so that they can focus attacks on the perceived weakness. You'll see how to coach this below. It's best approached in a fairly informal and non-intimidatory way. Your halves already recognise the centrality of their roles; they almost certainly do try to read the game. They may not relish, however, having the title tactical decision-maker hung round their necks. Make it easy for them: let them wake up one morning, and find that that's what they have naturally become.

## Establish the core routine

Words like 'routines' and 'habits' don't please sports psychologists, who see them as indicating reduced attention; yet acquiring good routines is an excellent way of focusing one's attention on what's needed. The whole section on p. 73 ff., for example, is about one large routine that will transform the output of your practices, because it directs your attention to each element in the coaching agenda, and ensures a coherent, purposeful practice. Here, we're concerned with setting up a routine to guide the TDMs through the process of decision-making. It will help all players, but it's of massive importance to the TDMs.

You start in unopposed and call tactical points at appropriate moments, e.g. when you think the ball-carrier would be tackled, call for a ruck. Stay alongside the fly-half, and direct his attention through questions: '*Any moment now there'll be a ruck – where will you attack next?*'.

The aim is to prompt a *provisional decision*, and to move it from late in the sequence – when the ruck's on, and the ball's coming back, and there's no time left – to early on, when there's less pressure, and more time to size up the situation. The extra time also allows communication, a vital part of co-ordinated play, to the other players concerned, so that they can arrange to contribute effectively to the call.

The decision is provisional because things may not work out – there may be a bad ball, an inaccurate pass or a late defensive move by the opposition which would rule out the prime intention. So, as soon as he has called the play, you ask him: '*What'll you do, if you get bad ball?*'. He needs a *provisional alternative*, to make the best of a bad job. This will probably be a kick, but early thought allows a better choice of kick (an undefended area, near enough for the kick to be precise, with the kick high enough to make the team follow-up effective). It takes a second, but it improves the subsequent action significantly.

You needn't use terms like 'provisional decision' with the players, unless you're sure it'll clarify what they're doing. Concentrate on asking the question. You needn't start with a ruck: start with a scrum or line-out, where there's more time available – but still demand that early decision. You begin to slip in advice: '*Look at that blind side*' . . . '*Where will their forwards be?*' . . . '*Let's bring x (our ace striker) into play*' . . . '*Let's see you chip back over the scrum*', and later 'What would chipping back like that do to their back row?'. Then tell him you're tired of asking questions: you'll just listen for the calls he makes. I don't ask him to announce alternative decisions – it may overload the other players,who are busy rehearsing what they're going to do on the main call.

Later he can call his own tactical points – gauging where each will occur, reading the pattern of play, accustoming himself to the continuous process of assessment. To summarise: you've now clarified and are aiming to establish a core routine through:

- constant assessment of the developing situation
- an early provisional decision
- communication
- a provisional alternative, if things go wrong.

If you did no more than this, you'd have made a substantial step forward: you'd have improved the quality of decision-making and the readiness for combined play.

You may find a need to alter the TDM's perception of their most valuable skill. They've got to value their decision-making – their judgement and application of the routine – above any particular personal skill. You obviously need to employ those other personal skills, but they mustn't be allowed to play a disproportionate part in the team mix. So whenever you can, pay tribute to their decision-making.

## Help establish their authority

As with coaches, TDMs cannot do their job if they don't exercise *authority* and work *proactively*. A clear sense of *purpose*, a belief in what you're doing, is the key to both. You build *confidence* through monitored practical experience.

- Demand in every phase of *team* or *unit* practice that at every tactical point the player communicates, and, given good ball, carries out his call. Get him accustomed to the routine.

- Make sure that the TDMs function as *mini-team* leaders. Creating an acute sense of pride in the mini-team is an invaluable aid to quality control, and the effective delegation by the coach of authority. The mini-teams are flexible units:
  −the back three (fb + w + w) + oc
  −the halves + ic + oc

–the back row + sh
–the front five (front row + locks) + sh.
They form natural units throughout intensive handling, individual skills, and unit skills practice (where they begin to coalesce). In the match, each unit is out to demonstrate its superiority. In both there is excellent opportunity for the practice of *leadership*. Say you as coach need to work closely with one unit – the leaders of the other units get a written outline of what you want their unit to do, and they are responsible for keeping players hard at work and focused on quality. In the practice and match situation each is the coach's representative – exercising authority, putting things right, making sure they don't go wrong, building pride.

• Make sure that the mini-team leaders work especially closely with whoever, for example leads in all practices, and are involved in and understand his purpose and method. Whoever leads the pack needs to have:
  –a *model* of the line-out identical to the coach's
  –*expectations* of possible problems and how to avoid them
  –*expectations* of possible problems and how to put them right.

Once again, this is an excellent opportunity to develop leadership and authority based on respect. I've never found difficulty in transferring these coaching attitudes to players. As you'll see, the problem-solving methods of the TDMs are identical to those of the coach.

## Provide a repertoire

If you want the TDM's call to lead to efficient action, it's got to be immediately comprehensible, and trigger a practised reaction by the players involved. It's got to emerge naturally from the work they've done in practice, so that they can operate confidently and easily as an efficient unit. Whatever any part of the team is practising from a tactical point, the TDMs should be making calls. That's the time for the rest of the unit to bring up questions – e.g. of where the call's appropriate, and under what conditions it's appropriate. Once you agree and define the situation, you can apply the call most effectively.

The main thrust of your coaching is to establish the basic objectives and structure of your unit and team play: your *strategy* and *tactics*. Once you have these in place, always being polished in practices, and they become a natural environment for your players, you'll enjoy considerable success by simply concentrating on them, and trusting them to reveal opposition weakness. As the match goes on, the TDMs get feedback on what is more and what is less successful, and emphasise the successful.

Your team *strategy* is your characteristic, preferred mode of attack. This will derive straight from your vision of how you'd like to see your team play. You work hard on the technical requirements, aiming for zero defects; you build it into unit practices; you use it as a staple activity in team practices. You constantly seek to devise new practice situations to eliminate weaknesses from it. As I write, I'm thinking of the development of back play, the growth of confidence in it, the commitment to it, the growth of pride in it, and finally the unquestioned assumption that this is not merely how we play rugby but how rugby is played. But that process will apply to whatever your starting vision entails. I don't think I've ever articulated the basic vision to the players: we've just realised it together through constant practice of its elements. Your belief, your know-how, your enthusiasm make it happen.

The easiest way of defining your strategy is to locate the typical area in which the team strike will be delivered. Once you have that, you have a rationale for team development, and all your coaching becomes purposeful and progressive:

- you have a set of job descriptions for coherent selection

- you have a priority list of skills to be honed

- you have defined the delivery system to get the ball into the strike area, and can focus on ways of disguising the delivery

- you have targeted the need to devise variety in the actual strike

- you have defined probable requirements in support

- you have added purpose in individual, unit, and team practice.

This – your preferred, characteristic mode of attack – requires a secondary area of strike if it is to be successful. It is secondary only in its not being the prime component of your vision. It has to be designed with equal care, cultivated with equal imagination, and practised with the same commitment to excellence as your main strike. It isn't an add-on extra: it's best seen as a furthering of the prime attack by other means. It threatens the opposition's commitment to defence against the prime strike by creating equal danger elsewhere.

If, for example, your vision focuses on the wide strike, just inside or outside your wingers (on the open or the blind), you complement it by creating a strike force to cripple their drift defence – striking at or inside the opposing fly-half. But the most immediate intention of those taking part is the same as in your prime strike: to create a situation where the ball can be taken across the gain line, and possession maintained; ideally, to have a player or players running forward into space. By maximising strike power in a particular area, and mobilising support so that even if checked the attack continues, the coach hopes to create optimal conditions to achieve these aims.

Recognising the importance of both strikes is a way of maintaining team morale. It's easy for a talented, international back-division to be demoralised by team commitment to a single area of strike based on forward power. If that is checked, the backs underperform because their morale is low, and they lack conviction in their role.

Once you've identified your secondary strike, all the points made above can be applied to it, from coherent selection to practice material. The secondary strike described above to complement the wide attack is of great importance as:

- the closer you strike to the tactical point, the quicker you're over the gain line – the basic criterion of going forward

- the closer you strike to the tactical point, the more efficient the running lines of your forwards in support

- the closer you strike to the tactical point, the better your defensive position if things go wrong

- the closer you strike to the tactical point, the more disruption you cause in your opponents' pressure or drift defence – you can't concentrate on either if you are being bypassed on the inside.

You can understand from this the attractions of selecting such an attack as your prime strike: it combines efficient attack and efficient defence, and all at minimum risk. In practice, however, few teams who use this as their basic strategy maintain team morale: coaches are seduced into selecting with a single purpose, and coaching with a single purpose – the team can be conspicuously successful, but if the basic attack is checked, they lack alternatives. Their predictability tells against them. Of course, a team that combines driving forward play with intelligent distribution of the ball and confident backs has the best of all worlds: they're playing total rugby.

The saddest thing about the team centred on multiple rucking – pick up and go is a better alternative – is its inability to develop further, even when the players acknowledge – its limitations: it imprisons them.

Within the decision-making that creates the structure of your rugby, the best strikers are assured of getting a chance to show what they can do. At the same time, the pattern of play creates chances for the other players – the defence develops expectations that they can exploit. If the opposition are galloping across pitch to take the wide men, those in the middle find channels opening up to take them between the posts. Every player is free to take the chance that opens up to him, but if his option doesn't work out fairly regularly he has to take responsibility for it.

Your strategy typifies the use you make of the ball, but the coach must also develop *tactics* for exploiting the opportunities predictable at representative recurrent situations. You know that in any short series of matches you're going to be awarded a scrum in the middle of the opposing 22. Look back on last season: how well were your team prepared to exploit it? Had you worked out the most promising gambits from this predictable situation, not for some ideal team but for your own team, with their particular strengths and weaknesses? Take the scrum 5m forward, or 5 or 10m backward: it's still basically the same opportunity – so it's representative and all the more recurrent. The same if it's a few metres right or left. So if you had prepared for that scrum on the 22, you'd have equipped them for a set of possible tactical points. You almost certainly do this already, e.g. for kick-offs, and receiving kick-offs. Why not extend it, at least to the critical situations where getting 5m forward means a try?

You can examine such situations or tactical points, because the opposing defence is predictable at each, and any deviation from the expected pattern signals a weakness. The way your own backs line up dictates how the defence will assemble. You can use this to create space, or to isolate defenders – and isolated defenders are very vulnerable. Walk across the field, 5m out from the opposition try-line, and examine ways you'd attack from the tactical points – scrum, line-out, penalty, ruck or maul. Such an examination brings desirable results:

- it may throw up ideas you hadn't considered

- it draws your attention to weaknesses in personal skills and in the unit and team repertoire, clarifying your coaching agenda

- it involves the whole team, and as you practise your chosen strikes, they begin to recognise what's likely to be the call in a given situation, so that they can all respond efficiently

- at the very least, it minimises wasting match possession, which tends to happen when we try something that we're not really equipped to do, and none of us has done before.

The ideal way to test your choices is, after practice, to play through them against the 2nd XV. Emphasise the need for match focus: they get one chance, and it's got to work; encourage the defence: they need to hold out for only a couple of minutes. When you get gambits that work, incorporate them in the TDM's repertoire of calls.

You can gradually build up the number of situations that you're well prepared for. You can create a guiding network using the 15-metre lines and an imaginary line down the centre of the pitch; the half-way, the 22s, and an imaginary line 5m from either try-line. At each intersection, you've a focus of thought. There's no question of having a separate repertoire for each point – you'll find that many will respond to the same tactics. You certainly don't want a large number of possibilities at any point: keep life simple but rewarding for the TDMs.

## Make them aware of cues for action

When a prompter in the theatre gives you a cue, he's focusing your attention on what you should be doing next. When one of the opposing front three persists in coming up in defence too fast or too slow, he's doing much the same: 'Look at me,' he's shouting, '*I've just left a gap for you*'. Unfortunately he uses body language which sometimes goes undetected. What can be done to improve reception of such cues?

You can start by having the team read Tactical Guide-lines (see p. 102 ff.), in which cues, both positive and negative, are identified and appropriate actions outlined. This should alert the players to the kinds of cues that are on offer, and bring home to them the need to communicate with the TDMs. Two-way communication is a must for efficient action.

Already, you'll have linked your basic gambits to the conditions which favour or rule out their use:

- some gambits will depend on whether you're stronger or weaker in the pack than the opposition

- some gambits will work only if the weather's kind

- some gambits will be very popular with the team – perhaps because they involve your best strikers – and you know that in a crisis they can be depended on

- some gambits will be new and unexpected.

But you'll find that in certain situations you can apply cues provided by the opposition to focus your attack precisely:

- system weakness: every defensive system –

   **a)** can leave individual players, e.g. full-backs, wingers, centres in a split field, isolated and vulnerable

   **b)** may give players two incompatible jobs – e.g. blind winger covering against run, and covering against kick; open winger the same but under less pressure

   **c)** buys strength in one area at the expense of weakness elsewhere – e.g. tight front three leaving space wide; stretched front three, offering spaces in-between; powerful back row good at close quarters but weak against wide strike; blanket defence leaves a weakened pack.

- individual weaknesses: every team will have players who are the weak link in the chain for various reasons –
   **a)** they may have weak technique, e.g. unreliable at catching, kickers

with a short range, players weak in the tackle . . .

**b)** they may have physical limitations, e.g. lack of size . . . lack of pace . . . lack of stamina . . . suffering from injury . . .

**c)** they may have weaknesses of character, e.g. less than wholehearted in tackling . . . easily intimidated . . . worried about catching . . .

These all provide indications of what should prove effective action. We now need to encourage the TDMs to develop *expectations* of where such cues are likely to exist, in a given situation, so that his *scanning* of the field is as economical as possible. This is reinforcing in tactical terms what he's already applied in coaching his mini-team. We can establish this:

- by offering a very clear, easily grasped example as a starter: when it's our put-in at a scrum with a workable blind-side in opposition territory, we *expect* the opposing winger to have a problem.
  Should he lie up to stop a handling attack?
  Should he lie back to cover a chip into the box?
  Act the situation out, with yourself as the opposing winger, so that all the players, and especially those directly involved, can immediately recognise it. We've now created an *expectation*, especially in our scrum-half, blind-side wing, and back row of what to look for in that situation

- by working our practical methods of exploiting the situation: what must we be able to do if he's lying up?
  –**Front five:** stop an opposition wheel into the blind-side.
  –**Back row:** move to support the wing, and keep the ball in the box.
  –**Scrum-half:** chip very accurately so that the ball rolls on, but not into touch, with a range and height that will put our wing in contention.
  –**Wing:** get his position and timing right, so that he's onside, running, as the kick is made, going down the touch line to give him the maximum chance of keeping the ball in play, and conscious of a need to control the ball rather than hack it on.
  What must we be able to do if he's lying back?
  –**Scrum-half:** take up position on the open side to suggest a back row attack in that direction.
  –**No. 8:** (in normal position) control the ball, and give an accurate pass that lets the wing run onto the ball.
  –**Wing:** get his position and timing right, so that he's onside, on the run, as the ball arrives, balanced to move either way, inside or outside his opponent.
  –**BSF:** understand the need to stay bound till the wing is past him, and then

support on the inside.

Once we've worked out these answers, we must make them effective by intensive practice. 'Intensive' does not mean one or two perfunctory run-throughs. We need to establish the *confidence* that makes them work in the match.

Then we can take in other factors that may affect the situation, and work out the influence they'll have. Get the players to be totally realistic. They have a way of letting you carry on without interrupting to put forward the practical problems they face, which may make them disinclined to use the moves in a match

- by pointing out that we can *model* situations. We've just modelled one situation, and we can do it because defence positioning is either predictable or weak. The orthodox defence has attained that status because it generally works, and teams tend to stick to it. We can usually control the positioning of that defence by the way our backs line up in attack, and by giving false expectations of where we intend to strike. We can shift our wing into midfield and:
  −strike in midfield if their wing stays blind, *or*
  −strike up the blind using e.g. fly-half and full-back.
  A couple of chips into the box will prepare the way for a handling attack, and vice-versa.

Once again, you can see the utility of the diagnostic method, and the variety of uses to which it can be put:

- players place the situation in terms of known representative *models*
- they have *expectations* of weakness from practical study of such situations
- their expectations direct their *scanning*: is there weakness as expected?
- they exploit the weakness using methods established in practice
- they are alert for *feedback* to refine the attack if the situation is repeated.

The great thing is that it's based solidly on practical experience, and that they *know* how to exploit it.

And from that it's an easy step to the generalised form:

- being alert to *feedback* from events
- *expectation* of similar behaviour in similar situations
- expectation-directed *scanning*: is it happening?
- a readiness to exploit a situation by focusing an attack on it using part of the established repertoire.

If these seem difficult, the difficulty lies in the wording rather than the idea and the practice. They are basically a single process applied to varied situations, and the final version is a product of habituation to the process.

We've looked at an example of a *system weakness* caused by a comparatively isolated player being left with two duties. We've examined it in the concrete form of a *situation* – which lets us experiment, e.g. to establish just how wide we need the blind-side to be, and which makes it very easy for the players to recognise it in the match. You may find it worthwhile to look at the situation from the defensive point of view:

- get your players into accepted defensive positioning

- run through the team to establish which players are least happy about their defensive role, and why

- examine how this cause for unhappiness can be intensified and exploited as a further aid to focusing attack

- spend time working out how your players' defensive worries can be reduced – without creating worries for someone else.

This work can be done pre-season, and remain good for seasons to come, or at least until the Laws are changed. As with everything else in this book, treat it in single steps, one situation at a time – but do take that first step, that's the one that counts. You'll find that your worries fade away as you put it into practice, and start looking for the next situation you'd like to tackle.

The key to exploiting *individual* weakness is good two-way communication. Each member of the team should be assessing his own opponent and others in the immediate vicinity, and once he reckons he's got the beating of them, he's got to get that information to the TDMs so that they can create the opportunity to exploit it. It's useless a player coming off the field proclaiming he could have beaten his opponent if he has failed to communicate that fact during the match.

Focusing an attack on a weak defender is comparatively easy. A neat practical way of developing it is to use a couple of reserves, in alternate phases, to place the weak player's position on the field during unopposed, with the TDM employing an interesting way of launching a strike at that point. You can do the same on a skeleton basis (e.g. the halves and back three) to represent weakness in the opposing back three, and give the halves practice in dropping the ball on that point.

Finally, in opposed unit practices, you can nominate weakness in the defence, run the attack once, demand communication, then exploitation. It's worth reminding you that, whatever the call, the individual player always has the right to try to exploit what he sees as a chance. If he does so frequently and successfully, he's a good player; if he does so frequently and gets it wrong, he's not.

The odds are that none of this will be wholly new to your TDMs. What these exercises can do, however, is to clarify their thinking and practice. Once they get into the rhythm, they'll start working things out for themselves, and it will pay the coach to listen to them, and extend his own understanding. You'll find much more about this side of coaching in the companion volume *Think Rugby*.

# 17 EVOLVING A GAME PLAN

Developing a coherent approach for a team or club is largely a matter of continuity. A coherent playing policy leads to coherent selection policy – and coherent selection policies tend to lead to continuity of personnel. Most successful teams show few changes that aren't forced by unavailability, and in the event of changes can draw upon a small number of well-prepared reserves, who know precisely their role and what is expected of them. Building a team, and keeping it in good repair, is a continuous job, that leads on from season to season, and is characterised by forethought and early preparation.

Continuity is the key to team spirit, to a sense of the group and a loyalty to it. It fosters that sense of the other player's likely action that is the subtlest expression of team play. It also allows the conscious development of a detailed game plan. A game plan is a joint production between players and coach that seeks to establish the way that the team will handle all the situations that arise in the match in terms of time in the match, position on the field, and immediate situation. It's based on experience of the possibilities in attack and defence open to the team, and a conscious selection of what seems most effective. A very simple example will make this clear: how do we handle drop-outs at the 22? Provided that everyone knows what we are going to do, we can extract maximum advantage from the situation by acting fast and efficiently. The fuller the game plan, the simpler the process of decision-making, and the more effective the execution. Continuity is the essential element to allow a game plan to go on developing. At representative level, indeed wherever there's a professional squad there's ample opportunity to develop the game plan and bring the whole squad to the point where players coming off the bench are fully in the picture. At that level too, you will have a full knowledge of your opponents and what problems and opportunities their team presents. The last couple of pages of the chapter 'Information Technology' cite an actual case of shaping your game to nullify an opposition strength. It's evident that the more fully you have equipped your players, your units and your team, the easier it becomes to effect necessary changes: the more fully you've prepared your players, the more adaptable they become and the easier it is to nullify opposition strengths and exploit their weaknesses. The supply of substitutes will also help to shape your thinking on these points.

This detailed game plan contains material which is deployed to meet the particular challenge of the next match. If you are working at a serious level, you need to know exactly what the opposition are likely to want, and make sure they don't get it. It may be that in first-phase they rely on a bullocking centre to get the ball in front of the pack: make sure that flankers, fly-half and centres delight in the head-on tackle focused on the opponent's solar-plexus, and aim to put him over backward. You also know what you want, and what you can reasonably expect to get against these particular opponents: get the relevant players constantly meditating on how to get it and how to use it.

It pays, in all matches, to take the field with a simple, strong, initial programme – we want to get points on the board early, and we want to minimise the chance of the opposition doing the same. The sooner you get comfortably ahead, the sooner you can settle into your customary rhythm; get behind and the team's emotional stability is threatened.

So we set out initially to:

- get the ball into the opposing half and keep it there

- keep the ball in front of and close to our forwards

- focus our energy on pressurising the opposition into mistakes

- make every first tackle a final tackle, and every loose ball our loose ball.

This is realistic – given our mastery of the necessary skills, and our total intelligent commitment. If we are masters of the skills, i.e.:

- if, under pressure, we combine to produce good ball

- if our kicking is pre-planned and accurate

- if our following-up is an organised unit activity

- if our contact is focused on knocking the ball loose

– it's much more than expedient play for a limited purpose.

And, if our game plan repertoire is adequately developed, we can add the element of surprise:

- our forwards go forward in mini-groups of two or three so there's always a chance of breaking into space by keeping the ball alive

- inside backs are set up to choose angles of running that can get the ball back in front of the forwards . . . but also to take advantage of opponents' assumptions that that's where they'll go

- our scrum-half, who will substantially mastermind this phase of play, creates variety – passing and chipping, feeding forwards, blind-side wings and full-backs, running himself off switches with first receivers.

In other words, we must look to develop the basic purpose in an intelligent and unexpected way that keeps the opposing defence off-balance – we don't let them get in a series of energy-sapping counter punches. This is important if you have parity up-front; if you haven't, then it's essential.

Similarly, you must try to keep the opposing pack off-balance at set pieces:

- at kick-offs, work hard on variations. For example, split your forwards on either side of the field

- at line-outs, keep varying the length of your line, so their lifting units have to adapt

- at penalties against the wind, make sure you have tap penalties immediately to hand, so that at least you can push them 10m back, and perhaps within range of a kick at goal.

Of course, it all demands preparation, but that's what coaching is about. Identify the big problem, and concentrate, with the players, on getting it right: practise, practise, practise . . . refine, refine, refine.

Throughout the match there are critical moments when increased concentration and effort are called for:

- at the beginning and end of each half – to impose your dominance or deny theirs;

- immediately after a score by either side – to refocus: we don't want happy thoughts or sad thoughts, but positive action to take advantage of happy thoughts or sad thoughts in the opposition;

- when we're close to either line and are determined to score or to stop them scoring;

- when the opposition attack starts threatening to develop momentum.

This fourth point calls for a supreme effort because it may alter the whole course of the match. It's futile simply to try to relieve the pressure; you've got to try to regain the initiative. This is the time to exercise the ability to change gear – to put into effect what you've learned in intensive, opposed team practice. I've written about '3 minute-rugby' in *Think Rugby*, the latest edition. The title is self-explanatory: it's an opposed practice of limited duration, during which the defenders have to hold out and the attackers have to score. This is extremely intensive, forces complete concentration and brings forth efforts far beyond the normal. (The three minute limit is also an effort to prevent war breaking out – you need a strong referee.) You can start from a variety of positions to reflect the attacking power of the team in possession. At the end of each mini-match there's time for each team to decide what went wrong and what went right and they'll have two more chances to repeat their role more convincingly. Then they'll switch possession and seek their revenge. That's eighteen minutes flat-out effort but effort channelled according to team plans and their knowledge of the opposition. It's an ideal preparation for the critical moments listed above. Think especially of the last minutes of the match – the need to score and the need to stop them scoring.

It's important to keep reminding them in the intervals of the need for composure and clarity of thought in the midst of this supreme physical effort. How they apply their effort dictates whether they're gaining from it or simply squandering it – it's got to be precisely targeted. The forwards too, should be conscious of the need to set up dynamic – i.e. fast-moving attacks with several forwards breaking out, determined to use their evasive skills and handling to keep up the speed of attack and to draw in opposing forwards who've been thinking about reinforcing the three-quarter defence. And the backs should accept what may be a higher level of risk to dance through the opposing defence. Always, as with the forwards, we need composure and a calm centre to make the most of our efforts. Breathe easily, relax your arms and hands, visualise what you're going to do and then do it with pride.

Three-minute rugby also affords a unique chance to compare the strengths and weaknesses of squad players. Watch with a positional specification in mind and check each point in the eighteen action-packed minutes. Even if you can't instantly make a selection, it will give you a clear idea of what specific coaching each needs.

Much of this directly involves the forwards, the enforcers of the team. But never lose sight of the need to maintain a balance of morale in the team, or the fact that attacks by your backs can slice quickly into space, and that forward and back attacks benefit each other by denying the opponents the luxury of simple concentration.

# 18 TACTICAL GUIDE-LINES

Apart from the positive side of tactics based on the possibilities open to your particular team at given situations, you have to offer guide-lines to the players – and especially, of course, the tactical decision-makers – for coping with or exploiting the situations outside their direct control, in particular the attacking or defensive power of the opposition, and the weather. This is one of those aspects of coaching rarely examined – it's usually left to the imagination and growing experience of the player – mainly, one suspects, because as coaches we haven't given it adequate thought. It's broadly speaking true that a team's tactics in uncoached rugby are a simple expression of the players' limitations.

## DEALING WITH OPPOSITION PRESSURE

### Pressure from opposing front three

- Fly-half takes ball medium-deep with centres lying up, runs and chips over the opposing centres to the right of the full-back;
- Attack the blind-side – taking the ball shallow and where possible bringing in your full-back;
- Play miss moves – i.e. fly-half to outside-centre, or inside-centre to full-back; or multiple misses if you're confident in your accuracy;
- Use change of pace – fly-half runs onto pass slowly and full-back comes into the line at speed between the centres, with outside-centre moving out;
- Kick into the box;
- Encourage scrum-half and back row to attack close to scrum or maul.

The most obvious answer to overall sustained pressure in your 22 – the fly-half taking the ball deep and kicking – is limited. Unless he has an exceptionally long kick, he will tend simply to relieve pressure but not gain the initiative. Under sustained pressure, especially in your 22, the time comes when a decisive attempt to take the initiative, even at some risk, is a better bet than what increasingly tends to be the vain effort to hang on. The fly-half must keep aware of the morale of his pack, and, when the pressure begins to tell, go into attack rather than simply make it safe.

### Pressure from opposing back row

- Engage them by attacking close to the set-piece – e.g. peeling off mauls, and line-outs, and attacking in the back row from scrums;

- Holding the ball in the tight;
- In line-out, throwing long to keep them engaged, or using a push-down to set up a maul;
- Take ball wide at fly-half or inside-centre, and kick back over their heads;
- Use switches between fly-half and inside- or outside-centre to take the ball back inside them, or dummy switches to check them while the ball is carried into space.

Broadly speaking, effective pressure groups do not expect to be taken on, and may not be well prepared for it – if you show a willingness to run at them in numbers (e.g. back row attacks supported by the whole pack) you can take them out of their stride.

These pressure situations are at their most intense at set scrums. In most respects, the situation at a set scrum is the archetypal situation in rugby – all the elements present in line-out, ruck or maul are present here in a higher degree. Being able to cope with them and if possible turn them to advantage is the best gauge of a team's ability.

In most matches, the set scrum offers the highest probability of a good ball, and so the soundest basis for decision-making. It also offers various split-field situations which provide predictable advantages in introducing an extra man, and the possibility of drawing the defence across and switching play to the far side of the scrum. These are substantial advantages which repay attention in training sessions.

The proximity and organisation of the opposing defence make early decision-making vital: it's not only pointless but dangerous to play off the cuff at scrums. Lack of decision and inefficiency in execution are liable to be punished, and this has led some coaches to take refuge in statements about the need to simplify the play – by which they mean kicking possession away. There is, in fact, virtually nothing that you can do, say from a line-out, that you cannot, with adequate coaching, do from a scrum. Indeed, the extra space available from line-outs is balanced by the depth of the opposing defence, and the extra time that the defence therefore has to cover the field. If the risks at set-scrum are greater, so are the potential gains. A basic rule in coaching is that you prepare for the most difficult situation: if you can cope with that, the rest is easier. The coach must prepare his team to attack from the tight, and the first set of guide-lines offered aims to help them deal with the pressure situation, and if possible turn it to advantage.

## Sustained opposition pressure

In all invasion games – of which rugby is one – there's a phenomenon we may call 'momentum': when the opposition start rolling and imposing sustained pressure on us.

Under that pressure, there's a temptation to seek momentary respite by kicking to touch: we're glad to get the ball off the pitch for a moment. But momentum is usually generated by a powerful opposition pack, which is grinding down our pack. The momentum is the result of their constantly getting possession. In those circumstances, kicking to touch is simply checking them for a moment: they'll get possession again, and continue to grind.

There comes a point where our halves have to recognise that kicking to touch is simply delaying the inevitable, and exhausting our pack in the process. At that point, we have to recognise that we're playing the game they've imposed on us: we've completely lost the initiative. Our only hope then is to act decisively to regain the initiative.

The earlier we recognise this, the better: it allows us to select a better opportunity to raise the siege. We must select an attack wide that we're confident in, tell the line that next time we get the ball, even if we're on our goal line, we're going to launch it, and then have a go. If that opportunity is denied, it may well be better to kick the ball as far as possible into space down the pitch rather than into touch: look at their back three, judge the wind, and have a go.

## Being driven back in the loose

This is a good point at which to reiterate the advice: '*never try to play rugby going backward*'. Under pressure, it's fatal to start throwing the ball about in the hope that the next player can perform a miracle. If, as ball-carrier, you find yourself pressured, the best thing to do is grit your teeth and – even if it's only a pace or two – run at the opposition. The odds are that you'll be able to miss the first one: just try – it's amazing what the average player has never learned about his own abilities. Maybe it's something to do with appearing brave – but let fear lend wings to your feet and you'll be surprised how elusive you can be. When you're running into big battalions, drive in low, get to ground, and put the ball at arms length behind you. You've then done the safest thing for the team – created a little time for support to arrive.

## Opposing line drifting

- Take the ball wide, then chip back (e.g. from outside-centre) to the forwards.

- Adjust the timing of your moves – i.e. delay the strike till you are in a position where they'll find it hard to react fast enough to stop you.

- Switch between stand-off and inside-centre, who will bring the ball back to forwards who have dropped back from the scrum or line-out and switch with them, so that they can launch an attack behind the opposing defence.

- Launch forward attacks at their stand-off, and inside the stand-off: drift defence hinges on the ability of the opposing back row to cover the stand-off area in the absence of the stand-off. This has become more difficult from scrums so launch a forward attack with the scrum-half as striker, and the stand-off sailing up on the outside as immediate support. Do that once or twice, and the opposition will have to revert to a pressure defence, and you can spin the ball wide again against a weakened defence.

If you play running rugby and employ moves, your opponents may decide to hang back with the aim of putting out your timing. If you simply spin the ball, they can then drift out so that there's a majority of defenders out wide. You aim to exploit this by taking the ball as far forward as you can wide, so that their front three and cover are pulled across, and switch the focus of the attack behind them by a chip back to the forwards.

A mechanical use of moves will tend to break down against such a defence – typically the players go into the move too early, and the striker is faced with an undisrupted defence. The key is judgement – taking the ball forward to the right point before actually initiating the move.

## Reinforced crossfield defence

The importation of Rugby League defensive patterns – a line of players, the backs supplemented by spare forwards, spread across the field – is an attempt to deny space for back attacks. When this happens, reflect that the opposition are buying strength crossfield at the expense of weakness elsewhere. The weakness lies in their depleted pack and rests on their belief that your pack lacks the fire-power – skill, determination and pace – to cause serious problems in attack. To demonstrate that you do have the fire-power, albeit against a depleted pack will force a rethink on their part.

Previous editions of this book have emphasised the need to liberate the forwards and prepare them to play a full part in the loose. The structured session sets aside time for preliminary touch rugby, intensive handling, individual skills: all the players take part in all of these and as coaches we're looking to turn out forwards with as nearly as possible the same range of abilities in loose play as our backs. Our whole team should be composed of rugby players happy with the ball in their hands, equipped with excellent ball skills, capable of beating an opponent, eager to get into space, determined wherever possible to keep the ball alive and going forward. I'm happy to say that this is now accepted. A second quote from my headmaster – 'That was a fine try Greenwood, but remember: your job is to give the ball to the backs' – sums up traditional orthodoxy. In fact, there always were forwards exercising a full range of skills – but now they're expected to do so and must be prepared for that role.

All too often however, forward attacks founder for lack of support. Typically, one forward breaks away and keeps going as far as his evasive abilities – heading for any glimmer of space, changing direction, stepping, spinning, rolling, swerving and dancing into it – and determination not to be stopped – accelerating through tackles, handing off, brushing off, running round, over or through the defenders – can take him. To be fully effective he's got to have support. If a back reacts fast enough and runs fast enough he brings an abrupt change of pace which can shatter defensive planning. But if we want forward support we need to identify the situations where 2/3/4 forwards can break together and then practise and practise, and practise until the break-out seems the natural conclusion, so that everyone is rarin' to go. So what are the likely situations?

- rolling mauls, as soon as you've outflanked the opposition. Get a man wide to clear the edge of the maul, give him the ball, he gets the ball back inside to a standing supporter, who feeds the bulk of the break – out on the outside – using a miss pass

- short line-outs with the spare forwards grouped wide and the ball thrown to them. Immediately they're thinking width and depth to create the space to stretch the defence and develop pace

- receiving kick-off, where the opposition can get there but not in numbers. Take the ball down and immediately shift it sideways and once again you're rolling.

- tap penalties – needn't simply mean going forward and rucking. Think in term of a major bluff and a concealed minor strike. Think in terms of what your opponents least expect from the opposing forwards and build it in. See the examples in *Think Rugby*.

- scrums wheeled under control through 45 degrees will outflank the opposing pack and clear the way for an attack on the left.

You need to establish what best suits your pack and what new skills they need to do the improbable, what the opposition won't expect. Practise the bunch-passing exercises detailed later in the book, but also miss moves, dummies and reverse passes. Clear the pack's minds of lingering inhibitions; get them giggling in their bellies; and teach them to dance through the opposition. Do it once and the opposition will have to think; do it twice and they'll have to act – and your whole team will benefit.

## EXPLOITING WEAKNESSES IN THE OPPOSING DEFENCE

### Opposing front three lying tight

- Fly-half runs for opposing inside-centre; inside-centre runs for opposing outside-centre; outside-centre runs into space;

- Use miss moves – fly-half to outside-centre, inside-centre to full-back.

If they lie tight – close together – there's bound to be space outside them, and the aim is to put a player clear in that space. If their open winger is lying close in as well, you look to put your winger clear – and this can be done by diagonal kicks, e.g. from outside-centre, or by moving the ball faster and further than they expect. The long diagonal kick can be very effective if their wing is lying close on their own goal line – but make sure your winger is ready for it, up wide and flat to maximise his advantage.

Of the two basic actions outlined above, it's sensible to use miss moves out to the left.

### Opposing front three lying wide

- Fly-half runs wide and inside-centre runs parallel to him before either straightening for the crash ball (if his own opponent has stayed wide), or coming back inside for the switch (if his opponent is coming in to close the gap).

- Use 'Strawberry' – the open winger slicing back in to take a short ball from inside-centre. If the inside-centre runs across as for a switch, it's easy for the winger to get into position, and he comes into the line with a distinct change of pace.

- Bring in extra man – e.g. full-back or blind-side wing – between the centres.

- Fly-half runs at his opponent, and curves back inside to feed the back row.

Some teams adopt these extreme forms of defensive positioning on principle – e.g. to avoid the chance of a break fairly close to the pack – some because they are aware of weakness – e.g. if they are notably slower than the opposing backs they will tend to lie wide. A consistent pattern of attack will also tend to impose or at least encourage one or the other – if you consistently run the ball wide, they will tend to drift wider; if you consistently bring it back, they'll tend to close up. The good fly-half will seek to exploit the space created by these alignments – but he's got to have his head up and be looking for them, have methods clear in his mind for exploiting them, and have effective communication with all those involved – never forgetting the back row.

## Opposing front three dog-legged

- The player whose opponent is lying back runs for the inside shoulder of the opponent one out from him – e.g. fly-half for the opposing inside-centre. If he comes in, give the pass; if he stays out, get behind him and give the pass as soon as you can.

This is the basic 'gap' that all front three players pray for. A typical case is where the opposing fly-half hangs back, and the opposing inside-centre rushes up. Once the initial break is made, it's always sensible to move the ball on – especially if it's the fly-half who makes the break. Keep your eye on your opponent – if he hangs back, there's always something on. A special case of this is the half-break. In this the player is conscious of his opponent hanging back and creating a slight gap, though not one he can get through. But he runs wide in the half-gap, turning away from his opponent to shield the ball. If the next opponent out is enthusiastic rather than controlled, a slight dog-leg will appear and the ball can be flicked out to the next man coming back on the angle. Against pressurising defences this is becoming increasingly important. To coach it, have the players walk through it and gradually increase the pace. Make sure that the ball-carrier's shoulder is really far forward and that he's tilted forward from the waist: every inch counts. In intensive handling, work on the pass made with arms extended to the front. And, as always, tilt the balances towards the learner: make sure the defender does allow enough space.

These various categories of bad alignment are easy to spot – provided your tactical decision-makers have got their heads up, and know what to look for. The first time they spot it they may not be able to take advantage of it – but it clues them in for the future.

## RELATIVE WEAKNESS OF AN OPPOSING PLAYER

- Get the ball to your player when, where, and at the pace he wants it.

Most teams will possess a player who they feel is likely to be capable of taking his man on; all too often they make no special plans to exploit his skill. You have to establish the three basic needs – when, where, and at what pace does your particular striker want the ball? If he's elusive he may want the ball late to minimise the opponent's reaction time; if he's quick, he may want it early. If he comes inside, he may want the ball set up for him to come inside; if outside, he may want the ball outside his man. If he's capable of abrupt acceleration but limited in top speed, he'll need to be given the ball moving fairly slowly. It's up to the coach and the other players to recognise these needs and be clear how they are going to meet them. Equally, he must be given support – if he can make the initial break, players should be behind him to carry the attack on.

# EXPLOITING WEAKNESS IN THE OPPOSING BACK THREE

### Exploit the winger's placing

Every winger has two jobs in defence – to mark his own man, and to provide depth – and his initial positioning must be a sensible compromise to give him a chance of doing both. This is much more difficult on the blind – where the attack is very quickly mounted – than on the open, though once the ball reaches outside-centre the difficulty is just as great on the open: does the wing come up to guard against the handling attack or stay back to guard against the chip behind him?

If he commits himself to one and neglects the other, then you can exploit his position. Whenever you have a scrum on the left with a fair blind-side, check where the opposing winger is lying – if he's lying back, get the ball to your winger, preferably from scrum-half; if he's up, chip into the box. So too, outside-centre can choose to pass or kick.

What the winger in defence needs, of course, is the assurance of support from his full-back so that as he moves up the full-back moves across behind him.

### Pressurise the full-back

In a badly organised team, the full-back, who should feel that he's a member of a tightly-integrated back three, is often a lonely figure. The fly-half can assume that he's right-footed by preference and when he kicks try to put it on his left, i.e. to his right as you look at him. He can guess at his speed and manoeuvrability and adjust his kicking to exploit suspected weaknesses. Once he's within range he can kick high to assess his reaction to stress.

This is not, by choice, how I like my team to play – it's based more on the other team's weakness than on our strength, and aesthetically it's much less pleasing. But it can be done better or worse, and there's some satisfaction in seeing it done well, by accurate kicking with well-organised support running, as one element in our mix.

### Exploit excessive depth

If there's a strong wind behind you and you've been kicking tactically, the opposing wings and full-back may all lie deep, so:

- chip short behind their centres

- use double miss moves – to the left, if you're not confident – to get your full-back and winger running into space. Encourage your centres to drift out before deciding whether to join that attack – there's space and a limited number of defenders – or to get in position to spin the ball crossfield from a probable tackle and ruck.

## OPPOSITION PRESSURE IN THE TIGHT

### Run with the wheel

The eight-man shove frequently imposes a wheel on the scrum. It will always tend to be clockwise, and will tend to take their left flanker and no. 8 further to their left. This makes any kind of move to our right much more difficult, with the ball-carrier forced to run across and liable to be tackled behind the gain line. But you can turn the situation to your advantage by breaking left. You may find it helpful to shift your no. 8 one space to the left, so that he packs in channel one, and receives the ball there: he can then feed the right flanker, who drops back and left before selecting his line into space on the left. This move can be carried on by the scrum-half, who drops out deep and wide on the left to support him, but if the move is intended, it's best for the no. 8 to start from his normal position, where he gains protection against the opposing scrum-half. This is what you'll have to do if their pack is picking up possession by wheeling you through 90 degrees. So make a virtue of necessity – initiate the move as you start to swing and turn their shove to your advantage. If you get your move really slick and make good ground with the first ball-carrier – your right hand-flanker, for example – and your scrum-half has dropped out open to support him, or to feed your 10 or 14 breaking on his inside, you won't just take immediate advantage, you'll sow a doubt in their minds about wheeling.

If you intend to run a normal attack to the right, arrange for the no. 8 to feed the scrum-half standing back so that there's no chance of the ball being intercepted by the opposing left flanker. It's even possible in this situation for your stand-off to be running against a depleted defence, with the left flanker and no. 8 still in the scrum. Usually, however, if there's space on the left, the stand-off, too, should elect to run with the wheel, away from their back row.

## COUNTER-PUNCHING OPPONENTS

Some teams seek to create havoc by intensive defence. If they can force you into errors on or about the tackle line, they will snap up the ball and launch their own attack into the confusion they've caused in your defensive regrouping. This can be very hard to stop, especially if they are pacy.

You must seek to blunt this by keeping them on the back-foot until they lose focus. You do that by constantly making them turn and go back for the ball, under pressure. It may not be brilliantly exciting, but needs must when the occasion demands it.

Make sure you kick with due respect to their counter-attacking abilities: try to keep the ball in front of your forwards, where it's difficult for the opposition to go forward, or put it high enough for one or two of your players to arrive with the ball.

In handling attack, concentrate on exploiting the blind-side. If they're committing their defence to snuffing out your prime mode of attack, try to take them on elsewhere, where your strike will be surprising. Don't offer them the target for which they're prepared – until you've taken the edge off their concentration.

## CONFUSED SITUATIONS

You don't do the backs any favours by shoving the ball back to them whilst forwards are still milling around. Whenever possible, tidy the situation up by taking the ball forward, and focusing the opposition minds on the need to defend. Once this primary objective is attained, get the ball back fast. You can make ground much faster in the backs, and the ideal time for them to get the ball is when the opposing backs have just been forced to retreat, with perhaps one of their inside backs involved in the ruck or maul. This isn't a contradiction of what I've said about rucks and mauls creating time, even if you win them, for the defence to regroup. That applies once you've crossed the gain line, and they are involved in a stern chase. To get going, you need to open up space, and the best way to do that is to pull sixteen forwards into a tiny area.

## SECOND-PHASE BALL

Good second-phase ball means that you are running against a disorganised defence, and possibly a defence with one of the front three under a maul. To exploit it you need to:

- know where the advantage lies

- react faster than the opposition.

You must get your head up and look at the defensive alignment. Has someone been taken out? If they've lost a player, they'll either all have moved in and the gap is on the wing – spin it for the overlap – or there'll be a gap midfield – set up a break. This isn't the concern simply of the halves – all the backs must be looking for the advantage and moving to exploit it.

The easiest way of losing the advantage in second-phase, other than kicking it away, is to run across. If the ball comes back fast, you may well find that everyone starts running across because they haven't got wide enough or deep enough. This is where fast reaction comes in: it takes discipline to get fast into position, especially late in the game, but it's the only way to be sure of capitalising on possession in the loose. Work to be in position before the opposition are. If you are inside-centre and your fly-half is running across do your best to get much wider and rather deeper initially so that you can straighten the line of attack for him. This applies in any situation, but it's rather more likely in second-phase. But in most second-phase situations every player would usually be better for being a shade deeper and wider!

Good second-phase ball also diminishes the threat of cover defence: it's unlikely that the specialist back row will be in position – they may well be under the maul. Once the initial break is made, you can expect to penetrate deep, which helps sustain the momentum of attack. This second-phase play is at its most devastating in its continuity – it allows no relief from pressure. Every player must be imbued with this notion; he must work to support, to keep the ball alive, to go forward. With this in mind, it's even more important that the nearest player, whoever he is, goes in to get the ball at the tackle. Any check will break down the flowing continuity.

If no immediate advantage has been gained in terms of opposing backs being taken out, the sensible course is to *continue the attack in the same direction*. This avoids running into stray characters who haven't yet reached the maul.

This means that you'll be running into progressively narrower spaces. Any backs on the open side of the maul should, therefore, be preparing for the switch – so that when the *change of direction* occurs, the ball can be moved fast and accurately. This needn't immediately follow a maul: you may attack the blind, see that the odds are against you, check, and get the ball back to the open. Don't jeopardise possession and ball speed. Running across is always dodgy – if you are extremely fast, you may get away with it, but it's not a good bet. What is needed is the line in position ready to move the ball away. Once again, the basic precept – get a shade deeper than you think necessary – allows the acceleration that's needed to maximise the attack.

Attack always gives the player a lift, and makes *high work-rate* easier. High work-rate is the overall key to success in loose running. The game resembles, of course, sevens, and calls for the same qualities of running, support, and getting your head up to look at the opposition. The best preparation for this is small-side touch, which gives every chance to improve judgement of informal situations, and to improvise. Most of the guide-lines suggested there apply to play in the loose.

The more flexible the team is in the loose, the better. Forwards who can see the ball is already under control may do better to get out behind the centres than to go on blindly to the maul. Keep making judgements; never run mechanically.

One clear matter for judgement is the use of space: you can have too many players for a given space as well as too few. If you get into this situation, use miss moves or dummy switches to simplify the situation, or run to take out an opponent and pop up a pass.

## USING THE WIDTH OF THE FIELD

One effect of driving on the attack in the same direction after each maul is that it opens up the width of the field for the subsequent switch. This is most advantageous if the preliminary movement is towards the right touch line so that in the next phase you can really stretch the opposing defence with right-hand dominant passes. As this preliminary drive develops, the backs should be creating more space for themselves to get the maximum effect on the move to the left.

## GETTING THE BALL AGAINST THE HEAD

If we get good ball against the head we can expect to cross the gain line before we reach the tackle line, provided we act fast. Either the scrum-half or the no. 8 ought always to go for the break to the left in this situation. If the opposition are lying deep it's effective to run flat, dummying switches with your backs till you can feed the full-back coming in. The full-back has to judge his approach, so that he can accelerate sharply onto the ball with a significant change of pace.

## GETTING THE BALL IN THEIR 22

Every team works hard to reach the opposing 22; once you get there you must have ways of crossing the line. You can develop these in your work on situations (see pp. 91–2 ff.). Which one you choose, however, is a tactical decision: get your head up and look at the opposition. Have they overcommitted against a particular form of attack? Have they left another area vulnerable? Have they altered the spacing of their front three? Is there a space wide?

This must be done fast and the back row told of the best bet. Otherwise, they may themselves launch an attack without a tactical overview of the whole situation. A dummy attack by them, however, is a useful diversion (see p. 189 ff.). If the scrum is very close to the line, there's always the possibility of a push-over try, best attempted after a half-wheel to distract some of the back row. (In defence on your own line, it's always best to go for an eight-man drive and to try to keep the scrum fairly straight.)

In the backs, remember that the hardest place to defend is the blind-side, and that in the 22 a miss move may make it impossible for the opposing cover defence to get across.

On penalties remember that the opposition will expect you to kick at goal, and if you have your kicker poised he can come up, tap the ball to himself and get across the line while the opposition are still retiring. Some tap penalties, too, are especially well-adapted to making a short gain. You'll find examples in *Think Rugby*.

## USING THE WIND

You must use the following wind intelligently – employing the basic guide-line for tactical kicking (see p. 272), so that you keep returning with minimum energy expenditure to the striking area in the opposition half. Conserving energy in this way is essential since against the wind next half you'll need all the energy you've got.

Naturally, too, a swirling wind increases the chances of mistakes by the opposition and so creates good attacking situations. Once again, the ease of the actual kick (see p. 149 ff.) shouldn't be divorced from the response of the whole team in its pattern of following up – identical on the axis of the kick to the basic elements of all defence: pressure, cover, and depth.

Apart from kicking for position, the following wind can force the opposing back three to lie deep and so open the way for attacks on the flanks – a quick miss move with the full-back in, and the winger running into space. One danger, in fact, is to allow the wind to dominate your thinking, so that you stop examining the precise situation, or in particular what opportunities for handling exist.

In windy conditions, passing demands extra care and common sense – you don't, for example, lie wide apart or try miss moves. Your lying close will tend to bring the opposition defence in tighter, and create more space wide. This can be exploited by diagonal kicks – short, toe-down, low trajectory into the wind, longer and more flighted with the wind behind. These kicks must be in behind the opposing winger, or so placed that your own winger has a good chance of reaching them first.

The prime concern with the wind in your face is to stop the opposition getting the ball – the forwards may need to concentrate a great deal of their energy on first-phase. You may well find that pressurising in the front three becomes a waste of effort, and in positions where they are likely to kick you do better by keeping in line and coming up slowly. The back row may well continue pressurising in the hope of mistakes, and because their fly-half may be a little closer to them and the pass a little less certain. Naturally, though, you adjust to the precise conditions.

Kicking against the wind places a high premium on sheer precision – drilling the ball low across the wind, with the toe down, and going for certainty rather than long-shots.

In defence against the wind, the wingers must support the full-back, and the front three work hard to cover the gaps on the flanks. Basically, this means moving out when your opponent passes the ball, not content simply with supporting the next man, but on getting into the gap. This again is easier if you are not pressurising but hanging back. This is most effective from scrums and mauls when you are already near the gain line: at line-outs, when the opposition are less likely to kick, you need to be moving forward to limit the chance of their running, but with the additional space you will find it easier to cover across as well.

The back three should always be aware of the wind, since it dictates the depth at which you take up initial positions – deep with the wind in your face, more shallow with the wind behind you.

## KICK-OFF AND DROP-OUTS

These are typical recurrent situations in which most teams rely on stereotyped procedures, designed apparently to minimise risk. They can, in fact, offer useful possibilities of attack or at least substantial ground advantage provided that the players are clear about their plans and confident in their execution.

### Drop-out at centre

Kicking the ball in the normal way to the opposition forwards is almost always followed by their gaining possession. Any coach expects his own team receiving the kick in these circumstances to secure possession virtually every time. It pays, therefore, to examine the alternatives, and establish these as your normal tactics.

### *Kick to your backs*

Provided your team is organised for it, kicking open to your backs is far more productive. You need players to go after the ball, and these will normally be your centres and wings. You need cover, in case anything goes wrong, and these will normally be your open flanker, who lines up on the open side, some five metres from the ball, your hooker, who's usually used as back-row in the loose, and your kicker.

Your kicker must practise his kicks to the point where he can stay cool and calm. He inspects the open side of the field at his leisure and, if he decides the kick is on, takes it at his leisure: if he has to hurry, the kick isn't on. He will usually be kicking for your winger, who starts out on the touch to give him the maximum chance of keeping the over-long kick in play, but is basically concerned with getting to the ball. The centres give him immediate cover and support on the inside; the flanker covers him behind.

Your kicker should also consider the possibility of bouncing the ball into touch. You'll often find that your opponents leave only one player to cover 50m of touch. Every season we score tries direct from the kick to the open and very rarely do we find ourselves worse off than from a 'normal' kick. Try to make our opponents play catch-up, setting up problems and forcing them to find solutions. Few teams have more than one player to cover the entire open touch line. The coach must weigh up the advantages of using an unexpected player in the hooker's position against disguising the projected surprise attack. Every season we score tries direct from this kick, and very, very, rarely do we find ourselves worse off than from a 'normal' kick.

## Kick to their posts

A second kick that leads to a better than average situation is the long drive downfield that is touched down for a drop-out, or evokes a touch kick from the midfield area. This again is consistently more successful than the normal kick.

It may, of course, lead to a counter-attack. If you imagine, however, a situation exactly corresponding to the kick-off, but as part of loose-play, you'd have little hesitation in preferring the kick deep into their defensive zone rather than a kick straight to their forwards.

For this kick, once again you need an organised follow-up pattern providing width, depth, and cover. Counter-attack will develop only if you haven't arranged for this. If the catcher looks up to see an organised, balanced pattern covering the field, he'll tend to play safe; if he doesn't, you'll be able to capitalise on it.

## The 'normal' kick

The only time there's a tactical advantage to be gained from the normal kick is when you can guarantee an accurate kick, and have trained forwards to go up for the ball and push it back. Put your jumper wide so that he can run in with his eye on the ball, and arrange – as in following up all normal kicks – for a support pattern that offers width and depth. You don't, in any aspect of loose play, want a thin line of support players. It helps if you aim for a small opponent.

You should also arrange to send a back row player in behind where the ball is dropping to exploit any pat back of the ball by the receivers. If it doesn't come, he back-pedals smartly.

You need to minimise the importance of any mistakes, and in practice this means preventing the ball moving infield. Your open flanker should start off wide (as for the kick to the backs) and come in on the opposing fly-half's blindside, as the latter watches the maul and his scrum-half. The hooker can cover the area between maul and open flanker.

It's sensible, if you expect the opposition to kick, to form your forwards up on the left; if to handle, on the right. If there's a strong sun, use it. If it's in your face, kick, if you can, towards it; if it's behind you make the opposition face it.

## Receiving kick-off

To discourage the kick to the open side, you need at least four players. Your hooker can cover the kicker, and be first in position for a possible scrum. Your open flanker can get some 15m wider, on the 10-metre line, your outside-centre some 15m behind him, and the open-side winger near touch on the 22. If the

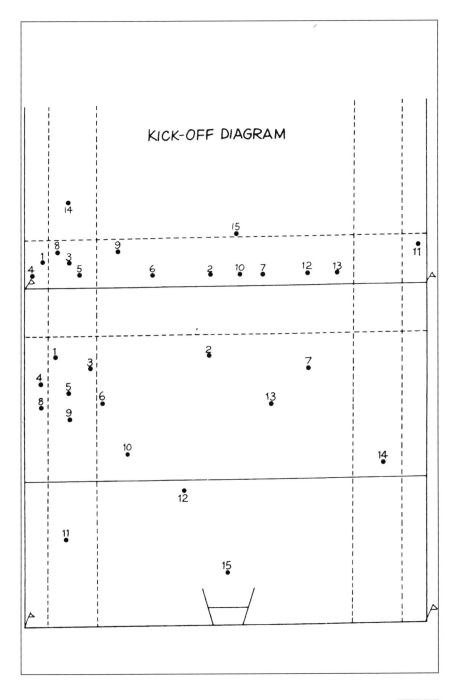

KICK-OFF DIAGRAM

kick is to the forwards, the hooker and flanker go across to the maul only if there's a problem; if not they can drop back behind the centres.

The remaining forwards cover the probable target area – three or four metres behind the 10m line and infield from the 5m line. Position your locks four or five metres behind that so they can move more energetically into their jump. Their attendant lifter works as in the line-out and in aiding the jumper to turn gives him some protection from the immediate opponent. The other forwards should move immediately they see the jumper move, so that he's never without support. We want a close knit maul with the first supporter going in fast behind the jumper to secure the ball and the jumper getting his weight over him, so that he's not easy to pull backwards. As soon as others arrive, you have the choice of feeding the scrum-half or changing the axis of the drive and starting a rolling maul, with the aim of three or four forwards breaking out as an attacking force.

Use receiving kick-off as a starting point in your unopposed: it's an area of the game always worth polishing. Concentrate on:

- an early call – if two players call, the player further back takes it

- immediate movement – as soon as the ball is kicked – to the estimated landing area

- work lock and prop in pairs, to compensate by lifting for static position of lock waiting for the ball, while his opponents are running in to take-off

- wherever possible, avoid patting the ball back: it's rarely accurate, and most opponents will have a player overrunning the landing point to mop up the pat

- the catcher turns as he lands, the first supporter drives in behind: establish the nucleus of the maul at once

- the ball is fed back when, and only when, the scrum-half calls for it

- keep the use of the ball simple, especially at the start of either half, when the opposition defence will be at its most aggressive; go blind only if the maul is on or near the 15-metre line; check depth of the opposing back three before deciding on the nature of the kick

- if the opposition win it, open flanker looks to come in on the opposing stand-off's blind-side.

Whatever course you build into your unopposed, it's got to be sensible, realistic, and reflect genuine match plans.

## Drop-outs

Nothing in rugby shows less tactical intelligence than the standard drop-out from the 22. Looked at objectively, the idea of kicking the ball straight to the opposing pack only a few metres from the 22 is ridiculous: if your fly-half made a habit in loose play of doing so, you'd drop him. And when you consider that the opposing XV have three-quarters of the field to cover, it's even more ridiculous. The basic reason for relying on this kick is lack of preparation for anything different, and lack of confidence in the players.

The plan we follow is very simple and effective: its aim is to get the ball as far away from our 22 as we safely can. Two players are deputed to take the kick. As soon as the touch-down is likely they get into position, one on each side of the field, half-way to touch, far enough back from the 22 to minimise the risk of a charge-down. Immediately the ball is dead, it's thrown to the nearer of the kickers who, with the full backing of the team and the coach, selects his spot, far down the field and away from opposition players, and kicks for it. Every other player works to get back behind him to allow speedy action. Both wings make every effort to chase the ball, and the whole team works to get into the basic follow-up pattern. The best bet, however, is to look for touch near the half-way line.

This is precisely the kind of situation where speed and discipline pay off – in any game the team that moves fastest from attack into defence, or defence into attack, has a substantial advantage. Discipline is the key word, for when both teams are weary, it's the disciplined team that recognises that the little extra effort will reap big dividends.

This is eminently true in receiving the ball from the drop-out. You can inhibit the long drop-out if your players provide immediate depth and width. As always in loose play, it may not be the customary players who provide it – they may be involved in attack. But intelligent players thinking ahead can foresee the need, and provide the cover.

If the opposition delay the drop-out, get back into the normal kick-off reception pattern, with your open flanker out wide, and the hooker at the centre, and apply the same basic rules.

More often now you see attempts in the full-side game to employ the tactics seen in sevens – doing a tiny drop kick to someone close to you, or to yourself. The aim is to retain possession – and often space is available to develop an attack from that possession. Alternatively as I suggested first thirty years ago, you can split your forwards – four on each side of the field – and take advantage of the confusion. But the possibility of accepting a scrum rather than a kick obviously offers a foolproof way of retaining possession, albeit without the element of surprise.

(I'd like to see the laws altered in the half-way drop-out to give the kick to those who have just scored – as happens in American Football and the Grand Prix Sevens.)

## PART 5

# BASIC PREPARATION – TECHNICAL

## The Swansea pack support Marten's break

A major theme of this book is *Space*, and here you see forwards creating it and exploiting it. Note how Marten's immediate supporter has his head up, is looking for space and is moving into a position where he can exploit it; and how the others have created width and depth to give the best hope of keeping the ball alive, and of accelerating onto the flat pass. If the immediate supporter gets the ball, the rest should be moving across to give him the same support, preserving the space until a tackle becomes inevitable and they converge to clear the ball. If they allow themselves unconsciously to converge before that, it makes a check in speed almost inevitable, and every check in speed favours the defenders.

# 19 PERSONAL SKILLS

## LOOSENING

One way to avoid pulling muscles is to do regular stretching exercises, and to repeat them before you do any strenuous activity. And of course if you know that you are liable to have trouble in a particular area this kind of preparation is essential. There's also the possibility of encouraging specific flexibility to meet a particular positional requirement: e.g. the hooker needs great mobility in the hips; the kicker, a long range of leg movement.

The important thing in stretching is to accustom the body to the demands of the game. It does no good to impose sudden strains in your warm-up – that's exactly what you are trying to avoid. So go into each exercise gently, and don't bounce. You aim to stretch to the point where you become conscious of strain. As soon as you feel it, stretch no further. Instead, concentrate your mental attention on that particular part of your body, and hold the position till your muscles adjust to it. Then gently go a little further.

The aim is to try to relax the body even as you stretch it: think loose. You cannot do this quickly, or in time with other people. Get changed early, and spend ten minutes with a minimum of movement – these should be seen as static exercises. Go easy: take a little longer, and your body will work better. It will also last longer.

Which exercises you use is much less important than this leisurely concentration on doing them to best effect. You may find that inhaling and exhaling slowly and deeply helps in this. You may also find that an established routine, in which you move from exercise to exercise up the body lets you slip into the right mood.

Here is a basic sequence of exercises; you can elaborate them to suit yourself:

- *lower leg* – place your hands, hip high, against a wall, and sink your chest below your arms

- *calves* – using your abdominals, pull down slowly to touch your toes

- *hamstrings* – lie on your back, and bring your feet over to touch the ground beyond your head – push your heels further away

- *groin* – sit back against a wall, and bring your feet up, sole to sole, and tucked in. Gently press down on your knees with your hands

- *hips* – link hands overhead, and dip steadily to either side; then describe wide circles with your hips

- *shoulders* – link hands overhead, then reach back to touch either shoulder

- *general* – link your fingers behind your back, and lock your arms. Then gently arch your body backward, dropping your head, and bringing your arms up towards it. Next, bend forward, bringing your arms over and down.

## INTENSIVE HANDLING

Before doing anything strenuous, explosive, or bruising, it's advisable to get the body to its best working temperature. Before working on more advanced techniques in rugby, it's essential to be handling the ball confidently. Put them together and use *intensive handling* as the major part of your warm-up to the structured session.

All of these handling exercises are also *support exercises*. You must hammer home at all times the vital importance of thought in the players off the ball: they must constantly think about their positioning in the movement, and *discipline* themselves to get to and remain in the best position. They must *never* run blind.

The key notion in all passing is that the hand behind the ball provides all the power, all the direction, and part of the control: it must stay in contact with the ball on the line of pass. The key idea in all receiving is to get the far-away hand on the path of the ball – playing down the line, so to speak – and use the other one to trap it.

Every pass must be in front of the receiver – always pass to space – and at about shoulder height. To make this possible, the receiver must be concentrating on his positioning. It should never be a harder pass than is needed on that occasion. Check, too, that the receiver is really trying to watch the ball into his hands. You may find that in trying to run fast he tenses his arms: he's got to relax his arms, and learn to run from the hips down. You may find that as he runs he arches his back: he's got to relax his trunk and run with his head over the ball.

The classic lateral pass, swinging away over the opposite foot, is a unit skill for the backs but even they must have a varied repertoire for getting the ball away. Every player must be able to *keep the ball out of the tackle area*: he may practise passing from *above the head* and below the knee. '*Your opponent may get you – he must never get the ball*'. He must also be able to *pass far* and *give and take* quickly. You must hammer home the paramount need to pass and run. Equally you must hammer home the idea that *you are responsible for the ball until the player you passed to has disposed of it*: if anything goes wrong, you are the nearest player, the one to tidy up – the receiver will certainly have overrun.

In your handling sequence, as with all practices, start easy and build up confidence before you try the difficult: success is a great motivation to keep on going. For example, move the ball left before you move it right, and keep on moving it left till the players are confident.

To get the most out of the time available:

- *use lots of balls* and small groups of players – three in a group will handle twice as often as six

- when you can, *work in natural groups* – those most likely to work together in the match

- *use a small unit of distance* to aid concentration: you get far better results doing four runs of 25 yards rather than one of 100

- *set a definite unit of work*: 'We'll do five twenty-fives of speed passing'

- *set quality standards*: 'If anyone drops the ball, we all start again'.

Once you've said it, do it – so be careful about the standards you set.

In handling practices, the underlying need is to keep the ball spinning around. The player carrying the ball is a target for the opposition. The great aim in practice is to condition the players off the ball to be up in support. If support is always there there need never be a simple target for the opposition. Emphasise, then, speed of passing and quality of support. The simplest criterion of quality support is that the receiver should be immediately available to run onto a flat pass. If you adopt the flat pass rule in your practices, it will transform your support play, because it provides immediate feedback on support performance for players and for coach. If the ball-carrier has to take extra strides, the support is too slow; if he can't pass in front of the supporter, the latter's too flat; if the pass is very short, the supporter's not thinking about space.

The key ideas of total rugby, for every player in the loose, are: positioning; passing; pace.

Intensive handling, focusing on the elimination of handling and positional errors is central to that programme.

## Check list of unopposed handling practices

### *Line passing (3s or 4s)*

- rhythm – move the ball easily at a trot, then faster
- length – spread wide and spin the ball
- speed – give and take as fast as possible
- all passes from above the head
- all passes from below the knee

- alternate high and low
- all passes with arms reaching out (beyond the opponent)
- make up variations: e.g. 1 puts it over 2 to 3 who pushes down to 2 who puts it over 3 to 4 who pushes it down to 3 . . . and so on.

## Switch passing (2s, 3s or 4s)

- switch in pairs
- switch in fours
- switch in threes
- introduce dummy switches

## Looping (4s)

- loop – normal passes, left and right
- loop – passes from above head, left and right
- loop – passes from below knee, left and right
- loop – changing direction
- loop – offer and take at hip level
- loop – offer and take at knee level
- loop – inverted
- pick up and put down

## Bunch passing (5s or 6s)

- 1–4
- 1–5
- over the top

## Combined handling practices

Once your players are handling with pride, put together a string of passes which exercise both their ball exchange skills and their control of positioning, e.g:

**a)** 1 does a miss to 3, 2 loops to outside of 3, 2 switches with 4 . . . who feeds 3 and then 1; or

**b)** 1 does a miss to 3, 2 loops to outside of 3, 2 does a dummy switch to 4 and runs out with 3, 2, and 1 running into support positions.

## Space control practices

A further useful refinement is to call for a change of direction whenever it looks as though the movement may go into touch. If you start the players looping across the field from the corner flag, they'll drift out towards the 22. At the vital moment there must be an instantaneous change of direction while either the looping continues or it is replaced by another form of passing.

## Notes on unopposed handling practices

### Line passing

The basic needs are *rhythm* – so that the next man knows when to expect the pass; *length* – so that you stretch the defence, forcing them to defend more ground and thus creating gaps; and *speed* – so that your players can keep the ball alive under pressure. When I've time I use them separately, one after the other, as a totally familiar introduction. They pass rhythmically, at a jog (but still of course, with maximum attention to positioning), concentrating on establishing an easy rhythm; they spread wide to allow longer passes, all spun, still jogging, still concentrating on position; they come close together, literally moving the ball from outstretched hand to outstretched hand, for speed. Keep reiterating *quality, quality, quality*. Any fool can give a *bad* pass: all our passes must be precise. *Never practise faults.* Our passing must be *perfect*.

Remember that all the power and direction comes from the *hand behind the ball* – the right when passing left, the left when passing right. The longer the pass, the more you must concentrate on *staying in contact with the ball on the line of pass*. And the receiver of the long pass must discipline himself to stay that much further back – the ball will take longer to arrive. *Think, think, think.*

For *passes below knee-level* reach down with the hand behind the ball – try it one-handed. For *passes above the head*, get up in the air and direct the ball down: don't lob it. For both, *concentrate* even harder on placing the ball precisely where the receiver wants it – at hip level, in front – and at an easily-controllable pace.

For *speed passing*, the passer must concentrate on giving the perfect pass, the receiver on reaching for the ball with the opposite hand and swinging it straight across in a single, fast, *controlled*, movement.

## Switches

The easy way to start switches is in *pairs*: get one player on the touch line, one on the 5-metre line, switch in the middle, and go out to the lines before turning for the next switch. Making them go out is the easy way to get them *thinking*. In switches, the player receiving the ball must defer coming in as long as possible to minimise his opponent's reaction time. It's best if the player on the outside of the switch makes the call: he can see what's happening infield, whilst often the ball-carrier can see only him. Remember: the ball-carrier always turns towards the receiver, looks at him, and offers him the ball. *Never practise faults!*

It's very unlikely that you will have a ball for every two players, so once they've got the fundamental form move on to switches in *fours*. Think of each four as two pairs doing switches – as each pair finishes its switch, an ordinary pass gives the ball to the other pair for their turn. Make them *think* about position: the pair waiting for the ball *must* slow down or they'll get in front of the ball. Then go on to switches in threes: centre man starts, runs right and switches with right-hand man, who takes it across and switches with left-hand man, who takes it across and switches with man originally in the centre, and so on. Start your players running downfield between the 5- and 15-metre lines and going out to the line before coming back. Remember, these are basically exercises for grooving a technique of ball-transference. Their weakness, which is all too often to be seen in matches, is that they impose a direction and speed on the receiver. When setting up moves, you should start with the desired end product: putting the receiver away on the line and at the speed that he needs. Look at *Think Rugby* for more on this.

## Looping

This is a great *work-rate* handling practice. It drills home the basic work-rate adage: *pass and run*. Don't loop with single men down the line: the loop used in a back division move has to be precisely set up – it doesn't fit into intensive handling. Instead, *pass and run to the end of the line* so that there is constant support on the end of the line. If they're doing it correctly, the ball-carrier should be able to move the ball at once: if he has to delay (and so become a target) the support is running too slowly. *Don't let it happen.* Get them looping with hip-high, reasonably short, passes to the left. Then do it to the right. Then longer passes – much harder work. Then all passes above the head – still going to the receiver hip-high in front. Then all passes below the knee. Once they're proficient, get them *thinking*. Work across the 22, changing direction of looping each time they come to a line: when a ball-carrier approaches the goal line or the 22, his support players must keep in line to reverse the direction of passing. Then try close-contact looping: in line ahead, taking the ball and offering it, but not passing it – the receiver must take it and in turn offer it. Emphasise the need for the ball-carrier not to turn but to keep driving straight forward. Start with the ball at hip-height, then try it at knee level, then one-handed.

*Inverted looping*
This is a useful variation. Start with the ball-carrier trotting down the 5-metre line, with the rest of his group immediately behind him. Each player stays on that line until he receives the ball. As soon as he receives it, he accelerates sharply out, at an angle of about 40° towards touch. He's creating space for the next receiver by taking an imaginary defender away from the line – get them to imagine they're being pushed out by the defence and must keep the ball in play, or that they're a back row making space by running wide, pulling across a defender, and putting the ball back into the space inside. Experiment with different passes, including one-handed passes, 'out of the tackle', but make sure you're expert on getting up in the air, twisting, and passing to the next receiver trotting down the line. Once you've mastered that, start the players peeling off alternately left and right. Work on that change of pace; suggest the ball-carrier straightens before he passes, build up the pace. (See also Passing over the shoulder on p. 129.)

*Picking up the ball*
Another essential looping practice is picking up the ball. Running in line ahead the ball-carrier takes three or four strides and puts the ball down, the next man drives past, picks up and repeats.

*Make them think*: always put the ball down away from the opposition; always control your distance and pace so that you are in position to pick up – if you are too close or too fast you won't make it.

(See also Cyclic Exercises on p. 54.)

## Bunch passing
The last category of pure passing exercises is bunch passing. They are basically for the forwards, simulating their drive forward up the pitch, but all players should do them. Emphasise the basic support notions of *width and depth* – of getting into useful and interesting support positions. Once again, all *passing* exercises are basically *support* exercises. Work to get into a position where you can really contribute – *never run blind*. Work these bunch practices in 4s, 5s, or 6s. Get the players to number off – having to work in sequence is an excellent inducement to thinking ahead and work-rate. Each player calls for the ball, in sequence with his number, ready to run onto the flat pass.

*1–4*
If the ball-carrier received the ball on his left, he must give it on his left – and the next player in numerical sequence must turn up there, calling out his number; he

will receive it on his right, and must give it on his right. The supporting players are forced to *think* about their position. The effect of this passing is to keep the bunch as a whole driving straight downfield but for the ball to go through what amounts to a series of switches. Hammer home *width*: we must stretch the forward defence, just as our backs stretch the back defence – we must create *space*. Hammer home *depth*: we must have security if the ball goes down, and *time* to select the best direction of attack.

The simplest way of introducing this essential exercise is to start with an even number of players – say four. Number them off. Assemble them on the 22, facing across the pitch, with the odd numbers on one side of the line and the even numbers on the other. Tell them that every pass must cross the line, and that each player in sequence must be shouting his own number and in position as soon as the previous player gets the ball. Once they are doing this, suggest that 3 running into position for 2's pass can run outside 1 as well as inside him, creating, in effect, a miss move; get them all to experiment with this. As soon as they are happy, move on to 1–5.

*1–5*

A more difficult but more rewarding exercise emerges if you add one player to each group. It imposes a further condition on the support running of each player. So far, by insisting that the player turns up in a particular place at a particular point in the sequence, you've made him much more aware of a need to control his support positioning. With the extra man, when 5 passes the ball, 1 has to appear on the 'wrong side of the line' so to speak. He is still up for the flat pass, and he is still a moderate distance away from the ball-carrier. And then, in sequence, each of the other players has to switch sides throughout the exercise.

What you are aiming for, of course, is not a mechanical repetition of the exercise, but a recognition by the player that he must control his support positioning to be effective. When you force him to 'cross the line', it's equivalent to his moving across away from a defender so that he can run into space. You're trying to get him to run with his head up and his eyes open looking for that space. And you encourage him to switch late, to minimise the opponent's reaction time.

*Over the top*

The ball-carrier drives to the front, goes up in the air, and passes to a player at the back of the bunch. He in turn drives to the front, avoiding the players in front of him, and the sequence continues. Emphasise the need for the individual player to think about space, and changing direction: he must make it difficult for the defence. Players off the ball can run with arms high to make the pass harder, or with arms horizontal to encourage a driving position in the runner.

In all of these bunch exercises emphasise the need for *ball speed*: as in looping, the support players must be there immediately the ball-carrier is ready to pass. The number of paces the ball-carrier has to take with the ball in his hands, i.e. as a target, is a measure of the efficiency of the support. The aim is to get all players thinking ahead, confident of running and handling, confident of support. If the ball is dropped, the nearest man drops on it and holds it off the ground. The rest get round behind and set up a maul.

*Passing over the shoulder*

Handling practices are an easy way of extending the players' range of skills – ways of maintaining the continuity of attack. You should be on the lookout for fresh ideas. One came my way in the second round of the Middlesex Sevens. We'd just lost Clive Woodward with a broken leg against London Scottish. The ball was going right across our line, with Alistair McHarg close behind. It reached Roy Black who drew Alistair on and popped the ball back over his left shoulder: we ran straight through and scored – a score made possible by the improvised pass. But why should so potentially valuable a pass be 'improvised?' Why not make it a standard part of every player's repertoire?

You work out the mechanics – easy enough, for like every pass the hand behind the ball provides the power and the direction – and establish match needs – you evidently don't want it lobbed up in the air, so tell them to '*get the hand behind the ball high, and pass in front*'. Then you work on possible exercises till you find one that works. For example, get your players in 4s, trotting down the 5-metre line. Player 1 has the ball. He swerves out to touch, and passes back over his shoulder to 2, who's still on the line. Player 1 has moved out, taken his 'opponent' with him, and popped the ball back into the space he has created. Make sure they practise on both sides: when they've all gone down one side, get them to go back down the 5-metre line to where they started from.

Then get them peeling off alternately to left and right. Then get the player who has just passed the ball to set off immediately after the new ball-carrier as a defender – he'll come from exactly the right direction to be taken out by the pass.

Laurie O'Reilly, that most talented coach from Canterbury in New Zealand, recognised three exercises from this list as the basic support exercises:

- channel support: 1–4, 1–5
- wide support: looping
- line astern support: inverted looping.

They correspond to the forward drive, getting wide as the ball goes across the line, and following up the individual who has made a break. You could certainly concentrate on these as your staple activities, and use others for variety. I ought to emphasise, however, that my primary intention with these exercises is less to increase our group repertoire, than to extend the individual player's capacity to deal with the varied situations he faces – e.g. to encourage him to control his support positioning by having to think ahead, to equip him with a variety of passes he can perform competently, and so on.

## Check list of handling exercises against a conditioned defence

### 2 v 1, 3 v 2, 4 v 3, 3 v 2 switches

The exercises described in the previous section are designed to make the player confident in the basic techniques of handling. The essential move from technique to skill comes with the introduction of some opposition. Again, what every player must aim to develop is *judgement* – his decision-making is what distinguishes the good player from the competent one. Some players, by their position – the best example is fly-half – must be excellent at this, and deal tactically with the whole team situation on the field. All, however, must acquire judgement in the immediate case of when and where to pass, where and how to support.

As in the last section, you start with the easy and seek to build confidence before you go on to the difficult. You may start with a wholly passive defence, standing still, and move through a walking to a trotting defence before exposing the attacking players to a fully active defence.

### 2 v 1

One of the absolutely basic situations towards which any organised team is purposefully working is the simple overlap – the 2 against 1 situation. You'll find, though, that even apparently capable players have some difficulty in dealing with it. Yet the key factors are simple:

- to run slightly out towards the supporting player – this is essential to make the pass easy. (Precisely as in all 'throwing' events, from hitting a golf ball to putting a shot, the hips must be able to pivot: in a pass to the left, the left hip must not block the right.) The most effective – though not philosophically satisfying – advice is to '*run for the defender's outside shoulder*'

- once you have gauged the defender's position, look at your supporting player: '*look early*' is the best advice

- the pass must be made early enough for the ball-carrier to be in no danger of being caught, late enough for the defender to be unable to catch the supporting player. This is the essential nature of *judgement* in passing or in initiating a move, and all players must be given every chance of practising it

- the supporting player must seek:

   **a)** to maintain a position adequately out from the ball-carrier – to 'use his pass', making allowances if it's a left-handed pass

   **b)** to maintain a position adequately behind him, in case of any slowing down as the ball-carrier prepares to pass

   **c)** to look beyond the immediate defender to cover defence

   **d)** to concentrate on taking the ball.

*The coach must emphasise the idea that the immediate 2 v 1 is the only case where a player should draw a man before passing.*

It's easy to devise practices that provide intensive practice of 2 v 1. Here's one I made up for the GB Women's team that seems simple to the point of idiocy but has great results in practice. Midway between the 5-metre line and the 15-metre line plant a row of touch-flags about 15m apart (experiment with this distance). The ball-carrier starts off on the 5m line, and the receiver on the line of touch-flags. The ball-carrier then runs at the next flag and draws this 'defender', before putting in a flat spin pass to the receiver. The receiver meanwhile has to get into space outside the defender – precisely, on the 15-metre line – and be running *straight* down the line as he receives the ball. He immediately swings in to attack the next defender, and his partner works hard to get wide (i.e. on the 5-metre line) and run straight. All the players follow through in pairs, and then turn to repeat the run, with those who passed off the right hand now passing off the left and vice versa. (Yes: it means the ball-carrier is running across, but to run slightly across facilitates the pass, and the rest of the exercise is excellent for making space and running straight.)

### 3 v 2

The coach and a player act as passive opposition to the other players working in groups of three. The aim is to make the players look at the defenders and think. There are three possible configurations of the two defenders as follows.

**1** *The inside man leads* – this is equivalent to a 2 v 1 situation followed by another 2 v 1 situation, and follows on naturally from the previous exercise.

**2** *Both come up flat* – for the ball-carrier to draw the first defender is fatal. He must delay his pass only so long as will prevent the first defender covering the third attacker. He must always allow the second attacker time to set up his 2 v 1 and put the third attacker away.

**3** *The outside man leads* – the ball-carrier must react immediately, checking his own man before swinging hard out behind the outside man and so forcing an immediate break.

These three situations are basic – they cover all the defensive configurations you are likely to meet. Working through them ensures that your players become accustomed to summing up the opposition rather than running blindly at them. All three exercises can be made progressively more difficult by the defenders moving forward – holding position relative to each other – progressively faster on each set. The defenders can go right down the pitch and the exercises then begin to develop the characteristics of a *pressure* practice, with the players having to dash back into position to keep their turn in the attacking sequence.

## 4 v 3

This is a different kind of exercise in which the four are trying to score against the three. Play it between the 10-metre lines. Start beside the half-way line, with the three in behind the four facing the same way. The four trot towards the 10-metre line in front of them, and the three move into whatever formation they wish. As the four turn, they're faced with a new defence and limited time. They must move forward at once and aim to score by intelligent passing and support positioning.

## 3 v 2 switches

This is really a simple development of three man switching previously described, but the addition of even passive opposition allows the coach to refine the running of his players. The diagram shows the basic pattern of the running. The coach can concentrate on monitoring the angles of running and the timing of the pass. I normally stick out my hand as a direction marker to ensure that the ball-receiver is far enough away to be safe from the tackle. You can vary the practice very simply – e.g. by transforming the second switch into a 2 v 1, or by making it into a dummy switch, with the ball-carrier accelerating away on the outside (in the match, the player best placed to decide whether to do switch or dummy-switch is the ball-receiver: he is looking infield and can see much more than the ball-carrier, whose attention should be on the receiver). It's always advisable to insist that, after the switches, the ball is transferred back to the wing where it started – it's good for work-rate and positioning.

## Inventing opposition for particular exercises

For several of the exercises it's difficult to devise appropriate opposition. Here are some examples.

### Looping (see p. 126 ff.)

For some time I'd worried about the effective use made of looping by the French women's team. How could we train our women to defeat it? There are times when the only thing to do is experiment. I got a handling group on the field of

# SWITCH PRACTICES

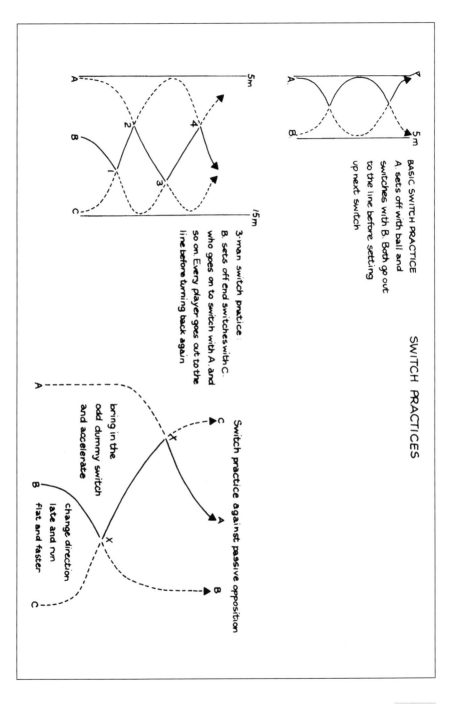

**BASIC SWITCH PRACTICE**
A. sets off with ball and
switches with B. Both go out
to the line before setting
up next switch

**3-man switch pratice :**
B. sets off end switches with C.
who goes on to switch with A. and
so on. Every player goes out to the
line before turning back again

Switch practice against passive opposition

bring in the
odd dummy switch
and accelerate

change direction
late and run
flat and faster

play, the first ball-carrier on the 5-metre line, and the other three infield in a rough echelon ready to start looping. I had the defending quartet off the field a couple of metres ahead of them, in line facing across the pitch. Their aim was to get across and knock down looper after looper, till they gained possession for themselves. Then they became the ball-carriers.

We now had two groups effectively looping, one in attack, one in defence: an excellent high work-rate situation that got the best out of both groups. I was relieved. We started, however, walking through it, then trotting to get the players accustomed to the pattern, and aware of what they'd have to do. In the match, the French started looping again, and I watched our players going after them like tigresses.

*Inverted Looping (see p. 127)*

Devising active opposition to this form of attack was a project I set to course members one summer. The best solution was formulated by a naval syndicate. It works once you've got the players to the point where they're breaking off the 5-metre line alternately left and right. Immediately the ball-carrier passes the ball back inside – to a player who'll be running off to the other side of the line – he becomes a defender, and sets off to tackle the player he has just passed to. The angle he comes from will encourage the new ball-carrier to try passes over the top, over the shoulder and behind the body. And, of course, as soon as the next ball-carrier sets off, the same transformation takes place – the previous attacker becomes a committed defender. It's a typical cyclic exercise.

*1–4, 1–5 (see pp. 127–128)*

The simplest opposition is provided by the line of flag-sticks already suggested for the 2 v 1 exercise (see p. 130). Using them allows you to keep everyone active, warm and cheerful. Start with them 10m apart, and see how much closer you can get them – i.e. how rapidly the players can run through the pattern. Let them have a go themselves – they'll probably find it disconcertingly difficult, till you advise them to treat it as a whole series of 2 v 1s. The ball-carrier runs at the 'defender', and the receiver runs into space outside him. But the structure of the exercise holds good – with support always appearing on the side from which the previous pass was delivered.

You can then go on to live defenders, with limited powers of movement. Stick a couple of posts, one between each 10-metre line and 22 – you now have 'bases' at the 22, the post, the 10-metre, half-way, the 10-metre, the post, and the 22, so each set of attackers will have seven passes each run. The defenders are based on the lines or posts, with authority to run a couple of metres forward or back; they *must* force a pass.

Coaching exercises your ability to face problems as they arise. You are problem solver in chief to your players, and the problems are never ending. But it certainly keeps you interested.

## Handling games

There are many handling games that, in some degree, relate to rugby. But, in fact, I use only three:

**1** keepball (and a variant 'push-down keepball')

**2** benchball (as an indoor lighthearted variation)

**3** touch rugby.

### Keepball

This is played between teams of two. The aim is to make as many passes as possible while you have possession. You gain possession:

- when you intercept the ball
- when you get a two-handed touch on the ball-carrier
- when an opposition pass goes to ground.

It's best played in a grid. The coach emphasises such basics as moving into space in attack, picking up a man in defence, pressurising the ball-carrier, watching the potential receiver rather than the ball.

A more useful variant is what I call 'push-down keepball'. This is exactly the same game except that the defender tries to catch the ball-carrier. The ball-carrier keeps possession if he can fight round and squeeze the ball down to touch the floor – the effective beginning of mauling and rucking. He is then allowed a free pass.

This is an absolutely basic game, and is, therefore, easily conditioned to suit the coach's purpose. Think of the elements you can condition:

- kind of ball – e.g. a medicine ball
- nature of pass – e.g. all above the head
- number of steps by ball-carrier – e.g. none
- method of moving – e.g. walking
- method of losing possession – e.g. two hand touch below the knee
- method of scoring – e.g. scoring tries
- method of dealing with ball on ground – e.g. fall and feed
- number of players – e.g. three a side.

It isn't a bad exercise for coaches to try inventing new games. It's another help in achieving variety.

## Benchball

This is a light-hearted diversion, which we always play indoors, and which offers many of the ingredients of rugby. The ball-carrier can run and pass in any direction. His team lose possession if a player is touched while carrying the ball, or if a mishandling by the team results in the ball touching the floor.

At either end of the gym, parallel to the back wall, and several metres away from it, you place a bench. Each team plays towards one bench, on which some of its members are standing. The aim (the 'goal') of the players on the floor is to get the ball down the gym, behind the bench, and safely passed to a team-member on the bench.

You can condition it easily – e.g. by varying the number on the floor and on the bench: the fewer you have on the floor, the tougher it gets.

It's an excellent game for hammering home another basic in all games: *the need to move fast from attack to defence* and vice-versa when the ball changes hands. It's a critical moment: whoever acts first can gain the advantage or nullify it.

## Touch rugby

Touch rugby is far and away the most important (and most difficult) of these handling games. It's our staple warm-up activity and usually, by the time I arrive, there are one or two games in operation. The beauty of the game is that it offers a variety of handling experience under pressure that is real but not destructive, and it offers the best chance of developing *judgement and foresight*. At intervals there are waves of criticism in rugby circles about its being non-contact – as if all parts of a practice should involve contact! In every practice there must be room for contact elements and non-contact elements. The judicious balancing of these is one function of the coach.

The game is best played between teams of four or five – much larger and the individual player doesn't get an adequate amount of handling. In essence, the aim is to transform the 1 v 1 situation into a 2 v 1. In many ways the game is closest to Sevens once possession has been secured, and it's certainly a key factor in our own success in the short game.

I use two basic conditions which bring out very different qualities in the play – single touch defence, and double touch. In both cases the defenders have to register a two-handed touch on the shorts – any less stringent condition makes it too easy for the defenders. In single touch, the defenders gain possession if they get a two-handed touch on the ball-carrier; in double touch, the attacker can go for the break, forcing it on the first touch and counting on putting a supporting player clear. If the defenders, however, get a two-handed touch on the supporting player, they gain possession. The first form of the game encourages the ball-carrier to hold the ball while support players run off him to create overlap positions; the second encourages quick appreciation by both ball-carrier and support player of a possible advantage and puts a premium on immediate action. Both incorporate basic principles of attack and defence.

These may be summarised as follows:

- the team gaining possession must immediately *stretch* – forcing the defenders to cover more ground and creating bigger gaps for the ball-carriers to attack: the wingers must get outside their opponents

- every attacking player must be *assessing* the opposing team so that the ball-carrier can *feint at strength*, and those running off the ball can then strike at weakness – which tends to encourage using 'the short side'; a moment's reflection will show that the extra man joining a 1 v 1 situation creates a complete overlap, joining a 2 v 2 situation creates a 3 v 2 – which in turn is better than 4 v 3 or any higher figure

- the team formation will always tend (in attack or defence) to have the fastest players out on the wings, where the easiest and most frequent overlaps will occur

- the defending team will adopt a *zone-defence* and it soon becomes apparent to them that all must work together, and preserve a flat-line defence. (This is equivalent to the front-three defence in the backs, and is voluntarily deprived of the essential depth in defence given in the full-size game by the back three and covering forwards, and in Sevens by the sweeper.)

- the defending team will soon realise the need to pressurise the opposition, forcing the ball-carrier to pass, and taking out those he can pass to

- the individual players come to a *proper judgement* of their own attacking ability relative to their immediate opponents

- all the attacking players are made to realise the importance of *ball-speed* and encouraged by the light-hearted atmosphere to improve their own speed of handling

- a vital consideration, that I've left to last – that simply to run at the opposition without a clear idea of how the attack is to develop is to waste the most precious commodity, space. This applies both to the ball-carrier and to the supporting players. Set it up *early*.

It's up to the coach to coach the game – his job is to help make the players aware of these considerations. In fact, beyond a certain level, this must be his *main* preoccupation. Nothing is more important for the potentially very good player than developing the kind of *forethought* and *judgement* I've been describing.

The game itself epitomises loose play in total rugby:

- *position* – the need to run off the ball so that the team can get it into space

- *passing* – the only form of attack allowed – places a high premium on accuracy from every player, no matter what his 15-a-side position, and during four or five-a-side, he'll handle often

- *pace* – the final strike is a test of pace and support.

Don't expect instantaneous success: it's a difficult game – if it weren't, you wouldn't attach so much importance to it. But if you can encourage your players to set it up in the period before the formal session starts, and play it every time they come out, you'll see its effects in the full game: they'll all be much more comfortable with the ball in their hands, and more conscious of the need to help get the ball into space.

The variety of handling exercises and games outlined in this chapter is capable of almost indefinite extension – all the coach need do is watch matches intently and isolate any form of running or handling that seems potentially useful, then devise a form of exercise that allows frequent repetition under varying pressures. We need far more people doing this. We can never have enough different handling exercises to keep our sessions relevant and fresh through the seasons.

I never do a session that doesn't start with handling – concentrating on what seems most needed from the previous game. Sometimes – as at the start of the season or in indoor sessions – handling is the staple of the whole session, punctuated by line-running or strength work. It is a basic requirement for 15-man rugby. Indeed, *passing and positioning* are the most basic skills, and everyone must be proficient.

In designing the handling session, I tend to distinguish between the various groups of exercise – line, loop, switch, bunch, opposed and games – and make sure that as many as I can fit in are represented. If handling is the staple activity in the session, all the players will do all the exercises; if time is limited, the backs may well concentrate in their warm-up on establishing rhythm, length, and speed in lateral passing, and the forwards on the first four points above.

## THE IMPORTANCE OF PERSONAL SKILLS

The wider the range of personal skills available to the player the fuller the part he can play in the team, and the more varied the team's tactics can be. The fundamental skill is handling and support positioning and that is why it's given so prominent a part in the structured session. In every session it's desirable to incorporate intensive handling in one form or another, but it's not possible to do the same for the whole range of personal skills. Nevertheless, over a sequence of sessions, many techniques can be developed to extend the player's range of action.

'Personal skills' covers *the whole range of what the player may find useful* in the match other than those abilities peculiar to specific positions – e.g. propping or line-out jumping. Even then, there's a strong case for every player's being able to perform competently such *apparently specific skills* as, for example, the full range of scrum-half passes. The time needed to make players at least moderately competent in these is not great, and the returns can be high. In the past only a limited number of skills were identified, and those skills were sometimes seen as specific to forwards or to backs. More precise analysis of the game, and a more open approach to the role of the players, should see a very rapid expansion of this area of coaching. The inventive coach has only to isolate an element that recurs in the game, e.g. staying on your feet, or knocking a player down, extract the key factors, and devise a coaching situation. Even more simply, he can take a skill used by a few players, e.g. the cross-kick, and make all his players moderately competent in it.

Broadly speaking, the staple personal skills activity in a structured session tends to be a fairly high pressure exercise designed to give a large number of repetitions in a short time. Although coaching must go on, it tends to be concentrated on a few players with specific weaknesses. A clear, well-thought-out, well-rehearsed explanation – best done, usually, by taking a couple of players through it slowly – and carefully controlled introduction of your basic exercises at the start of the season will do a lot to cut down the need for general coaching in the average session. This is especially true if in each set of four or five players there is one player in charge, keeping an eye on the standard of performance.

The idea behind intensive repetition is to habituate the players to the action, and make them confident of their ability to do it. For some players that will be enough – in the next match, if the chance occurs, they'll use it. For many players, however, another stage has to be gone through, in which the coach encourages them to use it. This takes the form of the coach expressing his own confidence, as subtly as necessary, that the player can do it.

This aspect of coaching needs emphasis. Restrictive coaching – coaching that prescribes a limited role for the player – is bad coaching, and it can seriously impair a player's abilities. If a prop, to take a typical example, accepts that a prop shouldn't change pace, or swerve, he'll lose the ability to do so. But you've only to watch children running in the playground to see that evasive running is virtually a natural gift. It's only in the formal situation, with the bad coach's expectations in his mind, that the player develops inhibitions. The worst aspect of these inhibitions is the mental one – the player can usually be shown his ability in a physical sense, but it's harder to restore the confidence that allows positive judgement of when to use it.

One further technical difficulty ought to be noted. For every attacking skill, e.g. staying on your feet, there's an equally important defensive one: knocking the player down. Sometimes, when there is no direct competition you can coach them simultaneously, as with kicking and catching. Most of the time, however, you must concentrate on one aspect at a time, till you reach the point where skill levels indicate an open competition.

The grouping of skills in the rest of this section is somewhat unconventional but it is designed to make the coach and the player focus on real situations. If the coach wishes to extend the range of skills with which he can deal he's got to work from the situations that arise in the match; if the player is to gain the maximum benefit from an extension of his personal skills, he's got to see them as possible answers to problems that arise in the match. The skills have been grouped accordingly in answer to these basic questions:

- what can I do with the ball in my hands?
- what can I do when the ball is on the ground?
- what can I do when the ball is in the air?
- what can I do when the ball is with an opponent?

## THE BALL IN YOUR HANDS

The earlier the player makes a provisional decision on the best use he can make of the ball the better. This is especially true of tactical decisions where you may need to communicate basic information long before you get the ball. But even with non-tactical decisions, the earlier a provisional decision is made the better – it lets the player set things up a little better. On the other hand, the later he commits himself to decisive action, the more possibilities open to the player, who commits himself last but *keeps the initiative*. Think of the winger who sets himself up to chip ahead, sees the full-back go up to charge down the kick, keeps the ball in his hands instead, and swerves round him. The gifted player is capable in the midst of strenuous action of thinking coolly and clearly, and looking around him.

All of that is easier to write about than to do. So far as coaching is concerned, it's a matter of talking to players, persuading them that they can do it, encouraging them to try, expecting it of them. It's a matter, before matches, of creating a proper positive outlook, in which the players don't freeze up with nerves, but see the match as a great chance to show what they can do; they should be serious but confident. And it's a matter, in the succession of coaching sessions, of providing them with a wider repertoire of skills.

## Passing

Handling has already been covered in some detail. Before the ball reaches him, the player has got to be thinking about the support available to him, both close to and wide. At that moment there's less pressure on him, and thinking is easier. In a well-organised team he'll know what to expect, where his support is likely to be. If he's a good player, he'll be thinking more widely – considering the possibility, for example, of a chip to the winger. Broadly speaking, though, he'll be looking to continue the particular movement by keeping the ball alive and in our possession through handling. Again, in a well-organised team, only those support players who are better positioned will be calling for the ball – shouting the ball-carrier's name.

The wider the range of his handling skills, the more likely it is that the ball-carrier will be able to get the ball away effectively, i.e. in a way that promotes the attack. Attacks sometimes fail not because the pass hasn't reached the support player but simply because it has made him check.

## Evasion

I preach to my players that you can always beat one man. Effective forward handling, for example, often means that you get past a man and give a pass. Neither of these statements is absolutely true, but they are a working basis for attacking play. What's important is not that the players should persistently try to beat a man, but that they should all feel capable of beating a man, and confident of the coach's support when they do so try – if it was really on!

The key idea in evasion is 'run for daylight'. The ability to run into an opponent and keep the ball available is very valuable, but is a second-best: too many things can go wrong at the moment of impact. The aims, therefore, are as follows.

### Run into space

Before the ball reaches you, before the pass has to be made, try, if you can, to get into space. This is a fundamental notion of all team games. Get your head up, look for space. It may be the outside-centre swinging outside his opponent into the gap as the inside-centre prepares to pass, or the winger coming in for the switch as the touch line gets near, or the forward cutting back behind the ball-carrier so that when the ball reaches him he can run forward. Setting it up early so that you can run forward into daylight is the first principle of evasion, but – especially in switches – delay the decisive movement as long as you safely can.

## Change of pace

For the individual, as for the unit or the team, a vital element in deception is changing pace. The three-quarter line that moves comparatively slowly so that the full-back can come in at speed, the team that controls the tempo so that it can briefly work faster than the opposition expects, both are using a change of pace to deceive the opposition. It appears in all the evasive tactics of the individual player – in the swerve, and the side-step, as well as on its own.

In theory change of pace is available to every player. Even if he is not particularly fast, he can run slower than his top speed, and set his opponent up to intercept at that speed, then accelerate past him. In practice, he seldom has a single opponent to beat, and if he slows down he will be caught by the cover defence. The players for whom a simple change of pace works best are those with a high cruising speed, and the ability to accelerate sharply from that.

## Swerving

Swerving is the natural evasive action of the bigger man who lacks the strength-weight ratio that allows the sudden check and acceleration required for the side-step. It conserves the available energy rather than absorbing it and having to create more. Fundamentally, it conserves space on the outside – by checking the opponent – and maintains the direction of run, from inside out. It's much easier as a rule for the average player to beat his man and the cover by swerving than by side-stepping.

It's a mistake to present swerving as a piece of expertise that involves a complicated sequence of foot, leg and body movements. It's far better presented as an intuitive answer to a problem, and then improved by judicious comment.

The thing to do, then, is to set the problem and condition it in such a way that the player can gain in confidence. The simplest way is to split the players into groups of five, four of whom kneel in line about 5m apart, midway between the touch line and the 5-metre line. The fifth player, without the ball, then has to swing alternately outside and inside these players.

Broadly speaking, the further apart the kneeling players are the easier the movement is, but it must be difficult enough to call for genuine changes of direction. The runner must stay between the lines.

With this basic set-up we can provide graded opposition:

- the defenders kneel and try to trip the runner
- the defenders kneel but can fall sideways and try to trip the runner
- the defenders crouch but can fall sideways and try to trip the runner
- the defenders crouch but can dive and try to tackle the runner.

Fundamentally, what the runner is doing is moving round an arc of a circle whose radius is a little wider than the defender's range of action. It is pointed out to him that he needn't worry about his upper body – all he has to do is keep his feet, and later his hips, out of range of the defender. Almost unconsciously he'll change pace, accelerating as he swings round the defender. Sooner or later a defender will get to him and then the coach must drive him on through the tackle – he must keep fighting his way forward, must keep running. By the time he gets past the fourth stage, he can be given the ball. He'll find it easier to swerve if he has it under an arm, and if he finds himself isolated in the game that's where he should put it – wingers may do it, for example, if the ball reaches them cross-field, or if they're quite confident they can beat their man and then the cover, or if they have a very powerful hand-off, or brush-off. Normally, however, putting it under one arm, even if it is the outside one, makes it very difficult to keep the ball available for support. Get them when they can to keep the ball in two hands.

As they become more confident you can suggest that they check the opponent – either by moving the ball to the inside as they begin to swing out, or by turning the shoulders, outside shoulder to the front, so that it looks as if they're going for the inside.

This quantity practice is simply to create in players a confidence that they can make defenders miss them, and for most players, meeting their opponents at close-quarters, that's all that's necessary. For the backs, however, who are likely to get the ball in space and find themselves running against a solitary defender setting them up for a tackle, a little more guidance is helpful.

The first thing that the swerver must do on getting past the first line of defenders is to preserve the space outside him. Unless you have a great deal of space and a lot of speed it's futile simply trying to run away from the full-back. It's good to take him slightly out, making him believe that you intend to out-run him, because it makes your subsequent feint to go inside – the merest check, the outside shoulder thrust forward – that much more credible, but you must preserve space on the outside. You must straighten up.

By going out and taking him with you, you also create a good immediate situation. It's most likely that the full-back will try to force you outside by positioning himself so that you can't come inside. This can be to your advantage as soon as you check him: you want to start your swerve at least on the line of his outside shoulder, so that all the movement is outside him. If you start on his inside shoulder, much of the movement is wasted – you aren't getting much further away from him.

If you are clear of the cover defence, it's useful to slow down slightly so that your change of pace can be decisive. On the other hand, make sure that you still have the energy to accelerate, and that the ground will allow it.

The next stage is for the player to incorporate the swerve in a short sequence that he can practise alone – e.g. pick-up, cruise slightly out, check and swerve, chip the ball ahead . . . and repeat.

The player can then go into a 1 v 1 situation against a defender conditioned to two-handed touch. The defender is given a limited length of the goal line to defend, and the ball-carrier is placed on the 22. The defender must stand on the line of or inside the ball-carrier. The ball-carrier has to start moving out. He gets five points if he can come back inside, and one if he goes outside – so that the defender is very keen not to let him in, and the practice has a greater chance of success.

## Side-step

The difficulty of doing a side-step varies with the speed at which you are moving: the spectacular high-speed side-step demands a very high strength-weight ratio, not unlike that of a good triple jumper; the close-quarters variety, at a much slower speed, is possible for most people.

The most important point to grasp is that it's the movement – and, precisely, the lack of balance – of your opponent that makes it effective. The easiest way to think of it is as a step inside a player committed to taking you on the outside. He is coming across, straining to get there; you check, to let his momentum take him further across; you drive – off your outside foot – in behind him, and try to accelerate clear of the cover. Even if you can't accelerate away, your wrong-footing your opponent may create the time for support to reach you: it doesn't need to be spectacular to make it valuable.

Once the situation is there, you've got to register it: get your head up, and look. Without this your timing may be bad; at close-quarters it will probably be instinctive. You check by letting your outside leg absorb your weight. You step inside by driving off it. It's this combination of absorbing and driving that demands the strength. You can reduce the demands by spreading the check and drive over two outside-leg strides: check, hop, drive. This, however, means you start further away and give him a little longer to react.

Setting up a practice for side-stepping has two phases: unopposed habituation to the movement, and conditioned opposed to help the timing. Get the player trotting down the touch line, and every third or fourth outside foot stride, check and drive across towards the 5-metre line, where he repeats the process off the other foot. Get two players doing this, one a couple of metres behind the other. The player behind can then watch the player in front and use him as a cue, seeking to sidestep as simultaneously with him as possible and in the same direction as he does. You can then go on to a variation of the final swerve practice – but reverse the scoring so that the defender loses five points if the attacker goes outside and one if he comes inside.

This treatment of swerve and side-step is effective, but a little too clinical. One of the problems is precisely to avoid inhibiting the players by suggesting that you are dealing with 'techniques' rather than innate abilities. You can redress this by playing pursuit games in a restricted area: children's games like 'tag' will reveal evasive qualities that your players may have forgotten in the 'serious' world of rugby. This is another indictment of bad coaching.

## Counter-action
'Run for daylight' is the great imperative, but there are times when contact is inevitable, and support isn't at hand. This often happens close to the opposing line, when the ability to break the tackle is of maximum importance. It's then that practice in the hand-off, brush-off, and hip-swing pays off. Get the ball under the outside arm for a start.

### The hand-off
There are basically two forms of this, depending on the size of the ball-carrier. If he is big he can aim to knock his opponent back; if he is light he aims to push himself off the tackler. For both he needs a good target – the base of the neck where it meets the shoulder is much more effective than the head – and he needs to look at it very intently. Don't just see an opponent, see the target area. The critical difference in the action is that the light player seeks to lock his elbow before contact and run round the outside. In both, it's advisable to keep the thumb close to the index finger.

The hand-off is most effective when the tackler has misjudged his tackle, coming in too high or rather too low.

### The brush-off
When the tackler takes off rather too far away, so that his bodyweight is not going to be effective, he finds himself reduced to grasping with outstretched hands. The attempt can then often be brushed aside by a more powerful arm action which knocks his extended arms off course. Look for his hands and drive them aside.

### The hip-swing
The powerful player can sometimes break a tackle by lowering his hips and swinging them into the tackle. This has two effects on the tackler: he finds himself hitting a very much more solid target than he expects, and he hits it before he expected to. Again the key idea is to watch him: the later you lower and swing, the more he will be committed to his false reading of the situation.

At the moment of impact the ball-carrier must be completely committed to continuing his leg action: he must keep running; he cannot trust the hip-swing to be totally effective of itself.

## Contact with opponents

Rugby is a contact sport, and every player must be equipped to deal effectively with the physical challenge of an opponent when he has the ball in his hands. Ideally, in attack, he will have immediate support and need never become a target (see p. 121), but the ideal state cannot always be attained.

### Control on contact

Once we are committed to contact, there is one great imperative: *don't let the opponent get a hand on the ball.* How we set about doing this depends partly on our physical capacity. It's an awe-inspiring sight to see a Lomu-like character ploughing onward: every metre he goes forward makes it easier for his supporters to be sure of getting the ball. When eventually he's approaching a stop, he heaves himself low at the next target, twisting to land on his side, and putting the ball at arms length behind him. His supporters drive over the top, and there's the ball, ready for use against a team still on the back-foot.

At the other extreme is the player conscious of his lack of Lomu-type characteristics, who goes to ground almost without making contact, still trying to get down on his side, with his body as nearly at right-angles to touch as he can manage, and the ball back at arms length. Although the first case creates far greater problems for the opposition, the second is perfectly tenable: he's doing what his judgement and experience tell him are the right things to do.

By going to ground the player makes sure that if the ensuing ruck is inconclusive, his team will retain possession. By putting the ball behind him at arms length, he's making it that little bit more difficult for the first opponent to snap it up, or simply roll him over to leave the ball on the defending side. By getting across at right-angles to touch, he's making it easier for his support to drive over unimpeded by the recumbent body. But if successive players go to ground virtually before contact, the whole attack will lose momentum: each player is surrendering perhaps half a metre. It doesn't sound much, but it makes a great difference to the defence, who aren't forced into retreat, who are balanced to drive forward and snuff out further attacks. If you can, gain those extra centimetres: force them on the back-foot.

We can sum up the advice so far, as follows.

1  If you can, hit the opponent before you hit the ground.

2  Hit the ground with your body at right angles to touch.

3  Get the ball to arms length behind you.

To these we can add a fourth.

4  Tuck your head in against your chest, so that it's not a target.

If you go to ground automatically, it's probably team policy. If it isn't, explain why you're doing it, and be consistent in doing it. Getting the ball back from a contact situation is far more efficient if we know what's going to happen.

So long as the present law continues giving the ball to the team in possession if they've got it on the ground, it's evidently a desirable option, though, of course, it's possible to move smartly from a maul to a ruck.

If you're adequately large, strong, and determined, you can hope to keep possession whilst staying on your feet. Hit the immediate opponent with a hand in the chest or with your shoulder, and roll to present your back to the opposition and the ball to your supporter. It'll help if you can split your feet fore and aft as well as sideways, and if you get your weight (centre of gravity) inside the wheelbase. Reduce the levers: bend your knees, hunch over the ball, keep your elbows into your sides. Be prepared to fight from the hips up. Focus on your first supporter.

Every player, within his own physical capacity, has to become adept at one or both of these methods of keeping the ball available. Once he's done that, the first supporter starts making the decisions.

If he can see space, and the chance of going forward without losing possession, that's what he should do. He can:

- snap the ball up from the ground, *or*

- drive in on the standing player, on the side that promises space, and roll off him into the space.

If he can't see space, his job is to stop an opponent touching the ball:

- if the ball's on the ground, he lowers himself into a driving position, and drives up and forward into any defender trying to get hands on the ball, *or*

- he drives in on the ball-carrier –
  **a)** if the ball-carrier has got round to face him, he drives straight in on him in the classic scrummaging position – shoulder at his waist, hips below shoulders, knees bent to drive forward, feet apart for stability, and to distribute the ball. He becomes the dynamic centre of the ensuing maul. He either gets both hands on the ball, or gets both hands on the ball-carrier's shorts, and drops his elbows to shield the ball. The ball-carrier should drop forward across the supporter's back to minimise the chance of being pulled backward by the defenders. This forms a very powerful unit: the supporter can exert a massive force

  **b)** if the ball-carrier has only got partly round, the first supporter may find it easier to form a wedge. If the ball-carrier's right foot is forward, the supporter gets his left foot in behind it, and gets his back under the ball-carrier's chest, with both hands on the ball. They've now formed a wedge that offers some protection on either side but which is very limited as the nucleus of a dynamic maul. So the supporter, who's facing the back, looks for the next supporter to arrive, comes round to meet him, and between them they set up the situation described immediately above – they've simply moved it one player back.

No matter how efficiently the ball-carrier sets about denying the opposition even a touch on the ball, he's evidently dependent on support arriving to secure possession. To that end it's best if he can occupy the defenders in the Lomu-style, and create time for the support to arrive.

On courses, I've often put players in pairs, and challenged the ball-carrier to find a way of carrying the ball that lets him drive his opponent from touch to 5m without his opponent being able to touch the ball. The only consistently successful way of doing this is as follows:

- drive in with your spine on the line of drive – in the match situation, parallel to touch – and your shoulders parallel to the ground

- carry the ball in two hands back near your thighs – the opponent should never see it: all he should see is the triangle of your back

- drive up into your opponent's belly, hitting him with the top of your shoulder blade, whilst your head is in space to the side of him, chin pushed forward to let you see where you're going. Hitting him in this way keeps your shoulders below your hips and ensures you can always go to ground

- work vigorously to lift him up and back – this helps you stay on your feet

- if there's any danger of his touching the ball, push it behind you

- if you find yourself going down, push the ball back, push your chin forward, and twist to land on the inside shoulder.

I've no doubt that this method is the most efficient way of dealing with a cluttered close-quarters situation. I developed it at Loughborough with a course of second-year soccer-players, making their first contact with rugby. We worked hard on the method described above, which they accepted as the norm. We used the limited resistance, and resisting line exercises described on pp. 224–26 to provide intensive practice. They beat the first-years, internationals and all, and the central feature of their game was their control of the ball on contact.

There's inevitably some measure of danger in driving at close-quarters into opponents. You must get your head into space if you want to keep your spine in line with your drive; if you can't get your head into space, then you must twist sideways, so that there's no risk of putting pressure on your head and neck as you hit the opponent or the ground. You then depend on your supporters being close as you lay the ball back.

What the first supporter does is conditioned by the immediate situation. Please look at the judgement exercise detailed in the section on Cyclic Exercises (see p. 54), and at the description of rucking and mauling in the section on Unit Skills – Forwards (see p. 222).

The coach needs to work intensively on speed into the desired position. Once again, start with the players in pairs, working across the 5-metre area. Have the defender facing touch, half-way across the area, with the ball on the ground between him and the attacker, who's on the touch line. The attacker picks up, drives in – you'll find that the set-up of the practice gets him into a good approximation of the desired position – and tries to drive the defender back to the 5-metre line, where he rolls the ball back. Gradually increase the pressure from the defender. Make absolutely clear to the attacker the need to keep pressure off his head and neck.

When the players are happy with this form of exercise, move on to a variation in which the defender starts with the ball in his hands. He passes to the attacker, who now has to get into the desired position from a standing position. Once again, start easy and gradually increase the pressure.

It would be difficult to exaggerate the importance of the player taking the ball into the tackle/contact area doing the right thing, both in terms of safety and of tactics. If he does keep the ball available, then we'll probably get it back; if he doesn't, we almost certainly won't. We need the same sense of secure possession when we take the ball into contact as we do from the tight scrum.

## Kicking

It's essential both in attack and defence that your key decision-makers be accomplished kickers, and that all your players should attain some competence in kicking as a means of keeping the ball going forward or shifting the axis of attack.

### The punt

The punt in attack is best seen as a set-piece kick. It is a tactical weapon, to be used with judgement and by choice. In the great kickers it's a leisurely activity from good possession and a long pass. I use the following sequence as a basis for long spinning kicks.

**1**   Stand the players in pairs, one on the touch line, one on the 5-metre line. The kicker holds the ball, one hand on each end, at right angles to the long axis of his foot. With his knee high and his toe down, he lets the ball drop high on his ankle and roll down his foot. This roll is the safest way of creating spin. As it rolls down his foot he pushes it, caresses it almost, into his partner's hands. Repeat this till the ball is spinning accurately. Get the players to check their performance – is the ball going down high enough on the foot? Is it going down on top of the foot and not to one side? Is the lower leg swinging straight towards the catcher? Is the knee high and the toe down? Has the kicker got his eye on the ball?

**2** Repeat the exercise over 5m and emphasise the need to judge strength as well as direction. Get them now to start with feet together and take a single step before kicking.

**3** Alter the angle of the ball across the foot. The long axis of the ball stays parallel to the ground but is now at 45° to the long axis of the foot, with the inside point forward. Continue with the exercise.

Once you get to this stage you will find that most of your players are doing fairly adequate punts. They must be in balance, and a check on this – very useful when you come to the non-dominant leg – is that after the kick, the kicking foot comes back alongside the non-kicking foot. You'll find that some players try to make the ball spin by cutting across it – this can work admirably, but it's much less certain than the method outlined.

Gradually encourage your players to open up the angle of the hips to the direction of kick. The ball will always tend to swing left from the right foot, right from the left foot, so get the left hip slightly forward for the right foot kick and vice versa. The distance that the ball is allowed to drop is a matter of compromise. The further it is allowed to drop the greater the length of kick, but the greater the chance that the ball will not land accurately high on the foot. Encourage them to trust in timing rather than kicking at the ball: the knee remains flexed till the ball leaves the foot. Get them to think of the golf club flexing as it swings through and its astonishingly long contact with the ball.

For specialist kickers, e.g. the fly-half, the inside-centre and full-back, it's essential that the ball goes precisely where it's intended. A game that drills this home is played using a goal line as a guide. One player is in the field of play, inside the 5-metre line about 2m from the goal line; the other diagonally opposite him in the in-goal area. Each gets one point for punting across the goal line on the near side of the posts, two for between the posts, and three for punting across the line beyond the posts. He loses five points if he fails to punt across the line. The results will almost always come as a surprise to the kickers. Concentration is essential.

The top-spin on a ball kicked as described ensures that it will tend to roll on rather than bounce up. This is a much better bet for the attacker: if it bounces, it may bounce into an attacker's hands but the odds are long against it; far better to keep it rolling forward to be played with the feet, or seized in an attacking fall.

Once the kicker has attained accuracy in direction and length and the ball is spinning sweetly, you can look to increase his power. How would you do this? Examine each element:

- run in – two or three lively, controlled steps
- non-kicking leg – drive up off the ground
- hips – allowing for a little more rotation
- placing of the ball to allow longer levers – knee less high, foot further forward, ball slightly lower on sock
- upper body – leaning back to accommodate longer contact with ball
- knee and foot – coming through with greater, but controlled power.

What gives length is the flight of the ball: don't sacrifice the spin for power – as in every punt, depress your foot to let the ball roll, push the front of your ankle forward, accelerate the spin, and lift it away.

Where do you practise this? Initially, in a hockey or soccer goal, complete with net, so that you can generate as much power as you like, and get the ball back immediately. But your aim is to burst the net.

Then out on the pitch, preferably with one of the back three who needs catching practice as much as you need punting power. Start within your established range, get the ball dropping on the fielder, and gradually extend the range. Establish the spin, and feed in the power. Get the fielder standing where you'll want the ball to go in the match – deep to the corner, or deep to the posts. Kick from the area where you expect to be operating in the match.

Remember, this is not an attacking kick in the same sense as those we've been looking at. No supporter is going to be able to arrive with this ball. It's a punt to make ground, to set up a good attacking position, to lift morale and put pressure on the opposition. It's got to be good. See p. 272 for the use of such kicks.

The fly-half has got to practise the basic attacking kicks – to the box, high up the middle, and out to the open wing usually from a midfield position. He should also work on the ball that clears the centres and drops short of the full-back: if he can place this accurately on the full-back's weaker side and vary its strength, it's a potent form of attack. For all of these it's best to work in small units first – in this case, fly-half with scrum-half, each time with the code call for a pass standing still, and then as a unit practice with the support players moving up in balance onto the ball. Finally, of course, it will be incorporated in team practices. Punting is far too important a weapon to be left to chance.

## Coaching the goal kicker

Being sure of your place kicking is a fine recipe for competitiveness; no team without consistent place kicking is giving itself a fair chance of winning. And that has evident implications for player, coach and selector.

You may take it that any kicker can be made – or can make himself – more accurate and more consistent. It's a much harder job to take a non-kicker and make him proficient than to turn a reasonable kicker into an excellent one.

It may seem a formidable task if you yourself have never kicked, but, provided you're prepared to set about it intelligently, it's not really that difficult. You already have a model for propelling the ball: now you're going to apply it systematically, with your brain switched on.

The key to improvement is your clear model of the kick, and your willingness to check out one thing at a time. The time to do it is before or after the session proper – you can't devote the requisite amount of time and concentration to one or two players while the rest stand around.

Half the battle is to set up the practice situation carefully so that you get as much feedback as possible. So:

- aim at a single post. This gives very clear indications of height and direction.

- aim at it from the goal line. Lines are a great help in giving very clear targets. If we can get the kicking foot swinging straight along the plane of that line, and through the midpoint of the ball, we're well on our way.

   Lines are also very valuable in giving feedback. If the ball goes on a straight path to the left or to the right, we know we're going straight through the midpoint, but our foot isn't swinging in the plane of the line. If the ball curves to the right, we're coming across the ball from right to left; if it curves to the left, we're coming across it from left to right.

- kick from the intersection of the goal line and the 15-metre line, with your non-kicking foot in the field of play, and your kicking foot swinging down the line. The 15-metre line then provides very accurate indications of the placing of the non-kicking foot, fore and aft, and laterally.

   If you think of extreme positions fore and aft, you'll understand clearly what goes wrong. Too far behind the ball and your kicking foot can't stay long with the ball on the desired line of flight – the tendency is to make contact high, and kick it along the ground; too far forward, and you'll find the kicking foot is coming down through the ball at impact. By far the best bet is to have the toes of the non-kicking foot in line with the ball at first contact.

Laterally, you're involved in a trade-off: further away, and you gain power, but can't stay long with the ball on the desired line of flight; too close, and you can stay with the ball, but you lack power. You're gaining power from increased rotation; accuracy from long contact with the ball down the line. You can't have both, but you can make sensible compromises.

(It's worth noting here that coming in on a curve – the 'soccer kick' – is a natural, comfortable way of increasing rotation: it holds the kicking hip back until just before impact. But from the moment of impact, the line of the foot has to be straight at target, and the rest of the body arranged to facilitate that, if you want a straight line of flight. Avoid coming in at extreme angles: it becomes increasingly difficult to convert the angular energy into a smooth, long, swing down the line.)

You've seen how the 15-metre line helps establish the exact position of the non-kicking foot, but it also helps establish the angle of the non-kicking foot to the desired line of flight. Best results come when the long axis of the foot is at right-angles to the 15-metre line, i.e. parallel to the desired line of flight. To gain accurate information from the 15-metre line, keep smoothing over studmarks between kicks. Do the same with marks that appear along and across the goal line, but not before you and the kicker have had a chance to scrutinise them. The studmarks offer clear evidence of the position and posture of the non-kicking foot, and of the accuracy of swing of the kicking foot. If the kicking foot marks are at all deep, it almost certainly means the player's too close laterally and that he can afford to shift the non-kicking foot a little wider.

The goal line is also an excellent indicator of where the kicker's body weight is going at the moment of impact. Insist that after each kick the kicker stops where he first lands. We know where he should land – down the line of flight. If he lands in the field of play, his non-kicking side has collapsed and he's proba-bly rotating too hard, with too much lateral displacement. He's reaching for the ball, letting the non-kicking knee bend too much to get him there, and leaning infield. We don't want him leaning anywhere: it's an indication of imbalance, and balance is essential for consistency. If he lands in the goal area, a rather more likely fault is that he's coming in too fast or at too extreme an angle. 'Avoid extremes' isn't a bad motto in goal kicking.

Check, too, the angle his feet make at landing with the goal line. If he's at an angle, it's an indication that he's not moving decisively enough from rotation into linear movement.

There's one final piece of information the two lines can give you: how far the kicker moves down the line of kick (where his non-kicking foot comes to ground). This is an indication of how active the non-kicking ankle is. The kick-er's hips should be rising through the kick; if they don't, you'll see a lack of height on the kick. You can initiate this movement, if it isn't already present, by encouraging a heel-toe action on the non-kicking foot. This flexes ankle and knee, and allows the lifting of the hips. I think this active non-kicking ankle is very important and I even encourage kickers, after they've rolled onto the toe, actually to shift, low and fast, down the line. This allows longer contact on the desired line of flight – or at least a far longer follow-through – which in turn guarantees that during the contact phase the foot is exactly on the desired line.

You can see, then, how much you can gain from setting up sessions carefully. I'd never dream of doing a session on scrum-half pass except at an intersection of lines, for exactly the same kind of reasons: you and the player get so much feedback on performance.

This particular set-up also offers twin psychological advantages: it provides an 'impossible' target, so there's far less pressure on the player to succeed, and a correspondingly greater lift when he does it. And if you go intelligently, he probably will. When we were recording for a BBC programme, David Evans, the 13-year-old I was coaching, hit the post four times in six attempts: he had to fake a bad one for the cameras.

We can now turn to the nature of the kick. The word that has occurred most frequently above is 'swing'. It never pays to kick at the ball. Think of your leg and foot as a golf club swinging through the position of the ball and lifting it away. You may well find that if you think of the swinging knee as leading the action, swinging in a long arc up through the ball and along the desired line of flight, it will help. Think of the knee, and let the lower leg and foot, the second pendulum, catch up on it, straightening in its own time.

The contact with the ball has to be precise. Check that the seams on the ball are regular, and then set it up so that the seams point straight along the goal line as a very precise aiming mark. When you're kicking in earnest, and there's no line on the ground to help, that helps you sight on goal. But it's also a precise aiming mark for your foot making contact with the ball: it shows you exactly where your foot has to make contact to get the whole meat of the ball in line with the power. And you need to be making contact on the lower half of that line so that you can lift it as your hips rise.

In this style of kick, we're setting up the ball more or less vertically – a slight inclination back or forward is not important. This allows the extended foot to contact the ball over a substantial area, and gives a wider margin for error.

It is the currently fashionable method of kicking, but that shouldn't, of itself, blind us to other possibilities. In the past, kickers have achieved spectacular success with the ball so teed up that the intersection of the seams at the bottom provided a precise target. The length of the ball was in the plane of the desired line of flight, and it was inclined to coincide with the desired angle of lift. It was kicked with the toe – more precisely with the big toe flexed upward. And it certainly went: the effect of concentrating the impact into so small an area was to create a deeper 'dent' in the ball, and so give greater impulsion to it.

What we have here is a typical case of trade-offs: the current fashion is for a greater margin for error, the earlier went for maximum impact power. Let's proceed on the basis that you've got the ball more or less vertical, teed up to limit the danger of hitting the ground. How about the posture of the kicking foot? You should try to push the toes down and back, to lengthen the lever of the leg, and to allow maximum contact with the ball. How about the contact area? By far the most important advice is that you strike the ball on the bony line of the big toe – the least compressible part of the foot. Most good kickers do this naturally, but if you haven't done it before it won't feel natural. You have to persevere. The aim is to put that bony ridge exactly along the line of the seam, and swing through it in the plane of the goal line.

Even when these directions are understood, it's possible to make contact with the toes before the rest of the bony ridge. They will tend to impact low on the ball, and you'll see the ball revolve quickly, turning over and over. The kick will also look feeble, because the power has gone not through the centre of the ball but along a short secant some distance below the centre.

So far I've said very little about the upper body, though some points are implicit in the foregoing. First it must be comfortable and relaxed: you do nothing positive by screwing yourself up. Check that your shoulders are relaxed. They're going to remain level throughout the kick. If you start dropping one or the other, you'll find yourself off balance and landing off the goal line.

Don't strain to keep your head down: you'll inhibit the arc of your kicking leg. Concentrate on that part of the seam you mean to contact. Aim to be in balance. Use your arms to aid balance – you'll do it automatically – but don't tighten them up.

Concentration is difficult, and concentration on a mass of points is impossible. But most kickers don't need to. With constant practice, they groove their swing. What they're left with is a few expectations of what they're likely to do wrong. Concentration on getting them right is not difficult.

The point at which to have these expectations clear in your mind is the rehearsal point before you start to move in on the ball. I don't say 'run' in, because there's no need to run in for the kicks you should normally agree to take – the kicks within your normal range. Of course, you try to extend that range, and a player with a well-grooved swing can build up to tremendous power, but if you haven't reached that stage, stick with what you know you can do. More people ruin their confidence through trying the extremely unlikely than through any other single reason. Don't do it: it won't help you or the team.

At different stages in your kicking career, the points you concentrate on may change. You begin to build a ritual that will help you relax; you groove a swing that takes care of all the basics. Some things don't change: the need to focus on that seam, and the sense of lifting up and through the ball, in balance.

As a coach, you may now feel burdened by a mass of information. One of the great benefits of working things out for yourself, as I've had to do, is that you develop a working knowledge – but you pay for it in the time it takes to reach understanding! Be assured: assimilating this lot is easier, quicker, and less embarrassing.

Usually, I start by concentrating on the overall purpose – applying force down the desired line of flight. I then set up the ball, and explain the positioning of the non-kicking foot, laterally, fore and aft, and parallel to the line of kick. Lastly, I place the kicking foot against the ball so that the bony ridge is down the seam.

Then the kicker puts in half-a-dozen kicks at the post. During this I'm checking out what he's doing, and making him think about the feedback from what the ball is doing. You can tell fairly quickly if he's got any talent for kicking – rhythm and ease, and the ability to stay in the suggested form. If he hasn't, it's kinder to everyone to say so. I start off checking the feet, and usually intend to check through in the systematic way described on p. 42, but, of course, I've got my own expectations of what accounts for the mistakes he makes, and tend to revert to that method fairly quickly. Once I start to interrupt (and if you don't interrupt, you don't coach), I'm constantly trying to get the kicker to identify what he has done, by referring him to the various kinds of feedback available. I ask questions I'm sure the player can answer; I tell him the answer in body language. The aim is to get him to the point where he can monitor his own performance and become his own coach, in practice and during the match. The first step towards this is to build his confidence, and get him into a frame of mind where he's prepared to cultivate the habit.

Once you're happy with his technique, you must move on to its consistent application in the match. For this, we need to establish *confidence and detachment*. The kicker should feel he can look at the posts, locate his precise target – a dot in that big space – and visualise the path that will take his kick there. He can build this up by regular practice from representative positions within his range. The aim is to accustom him to success, and build up a habit of serious practice. The more confident he becomes of kicking within this range, the more room there is for a gradual extension of the range and variety of kicks. But just as I start our backs – including internationals – with simple handling, designed to reinforce rhythm, length, speed and accuracy in everything, so too you should start each session with kicks at goal that will reinforce players' confidence.

Even when a player is confident, he needs to acquire detachment. It comes from an attitude of mind linked to the insulating routine, the ritual, which we've already looked at. A kick is a kick – divorce it from other technically irrelevant circumstances. Clear your mind of what's going on round you. You're doing what you've practised for, and you're the member of the team best qualified to do it. It's a great chance to show your character. Be calm. Slide quietly into your ritual. Do everything as you've done it so many times before. Settle into it, look for that dot, and do what you know you can do.

Once the kicker's consistent range is established, it can be built into the team's plans for how to exploit penalties. The aim of this is to avoid wasting possession and to avoid wasting time: we want to act decisively and fast. In essence what we need is to treat the basic situa-tional grid in terms of penalties (see p. 91 ff.). We can then incorporate it in unopposed practice – calling for a penalty, e.g. at mauls or rucks, where they're likely to be awarded.

## The drop-kick

Your scrum-half, fly-half, inside-centre, and full-back must all be encouraged to see accurate drop-kicking as a basic requirement. The team must have its drop-out drill at 22m and half-way firmly established, and for this accuracy and length are essential. But inadequate attention is paid to the drop-kick as a simple, effective way of scoring points precisely in that area of the field where defence is at its most committed. From set-pieces and indirect penalties especially, where possession is probable, it can be, with practice, relied on to score points.

The basic conditions are precisely those outlined for goal kicking.

- *Balance* – you must be comfortably in balance to be consistent. Don't try to force it – find your effective range, and wait for the chance. Practise with the player most likely to pass to you: make sure he knows precisely what you want so that you're in balance when the ball reaches you. After each kick check where your kicking foot ends up.

- *Contact* – push your toe down to lengthen the lever and maximise contact. Try meeting the ball along the line of your big toe. Swing through rather than kick at the ball.

- *Follow-through* – to the target, allowing for wind-drift. To allow an easy follow-through you should open your hips, clockwise for a right foot, anti-clockwise for a left foot kick.

- *Placing the ball* – give yourself room. As in place kicking, the last stride is long to let your hips lift into the kick. It also allows a slight backward lean of the upper body, which makes a full follow-through easier. So, a longer left foot stride is needed, with the ball placed near its toe. Make sure it is placed a normal distance to the right: if you put it too far to the right, it will disturb your balance.

- *Control the ball* – so that it bounces slightly back onto your foot. It is vital that you watch the ball onto your foot, that you place it – 'drop' is too vague a word – precisely where it is wanted, tilted slightly backward.

- *The best general concept of what the kicker is trying to do* – he's setting himself up for a place kick, and the only problem is to put the ball down precisely as he'd like it for a place kick.

In your practice, you can follow precisely the same pattern described under place kicking to establish good form. You must then move to the situations where you are going to use the kick to establish your accurate range. Don't play at it: it repays serious application.

## Kicking in loose play

There is a whole category of kicks which are not tactical, but improvised answers to immediate difficulties or opportunities. Typical of these are the chip ahead, the cross-kick, the defensive kick over the shoulder, and the grubber. The kick over the shoulder is essential for scrum-halves, and highly desirable for the back three; the others should be available to the whole team. The kick over the shoulder is also an example of the specific needs of the scrum-half, many of whose kicks must be made in uncomfortable but predictable situations – e.g. from the base of the scrum or from indifferent possession at a line-out. In coaching these kicks, I haven't come across any great difficulties: the important things for the coach are the need to recognise that they can and should be coached, and a reasonably experimental approach to coaching methods.

The chief technical point about all of these kicks other than the grubber is the need to offer the maximum target area on the ball. This is simply done by holding the long axis of the ball at right-angles to the long axis of the foot. These kicks are easier too if the kicker thinks of keeping his knee high, so that he can place the ball fairly accurately. His foot position controls the actual flight of the ball, and he should be encouraged to experiment in keeping his toes down or pulling them up.

The critical point in the grubber is less the technique – toe down, knee forward, pushing the ball forward – than the need to use it only when you are actually in the gap, and the chance of its being intercepted virtually nil.

Most of these kicks can be practised using simple drills – e.g. cyclic exercises (grubber, fall, feed, grubber . . .), grid games (grubber between partners; opponents try to fall), handling exercises (handle the ball to the right in 4s, chip back to the left). What is needed is usually practice rather than coaching – though comment must go on.

Positional kicks may need coaching. For the kick over the shoulder you might, for example, start facing the scrum-half, throw the ball over his head so that he can turn and catch it easily, and get him immediately to kick back into touch over his left shoulder. You can then build up pressure by throwing and following up progressively faster. The next step is to help him kick straight back by rolling backward and kicking as he rolls. Give him support initially by hanging on to his collar and lowering him fairly slowly. Do this in front of the goal posts so that he has a definite target (and, of course, give someone else catching practice at the same time).

In the same way, you can encourage the scrum-half to practise kicking almost as he picks the ball up, getting his knee and toe coming up sharply to get immediate height. Or get the centre to practise bouncing the ball accurately into touch, as he may need to if there's a check in handling. The message for the coach is always the same: look in detail, isolate the element that's likely to recur, make sure the players concerned are given a chance and helped to improve.

## THE BALL ON THE GROUND

As in every other phase of the game, the player faced with the ball on the ground has to exercise judgement and make decisions. If the coach can simplify this by giving some guide-lines it'll speed up the player's actions and effectiveness.

### The player in attack

- If you've got time, and the ball isn't rolling away from you or wet, pick it up.
- If there's only one opponent and the ball's rolling away from you or wet, get your foot to it, then dribble.
- If there are several opponents close, no matter what the ball's doing, make an attacking fall.

### The player in defence

- If you've got time, and the ball isn't rolling away from you or wet, pick it up.
- If you've any doubt whatsoever in a situation, fall on the ball and get up fast.
- If you're isolated from support and near touch, push the ball into touch with your foot.

As with all guide-lines, the moment the player starts making finer, more fruitful, personal judgements, is the moment where coaching justifies itself.

Dealing with the ball on the ground is a critical phase of play – typically it sustains attack after the tackle, and is a corner-stone of defence. Every player must be adept at it.

### Picking the ball up

It's best to suggest that this is what the player does only if conditions are favourable. '*If you've got time . . .*' covers two aspects: the 50/50 situation with an opponent, and the difficulty of controlling personal speed in supporting the ball-carrier.

You must set the mechanics of picking-up in a context. The player tackled puts down the ball on the side away from the tackler – which allows the support player to predict a good line of approach. The support player has to govern distance and speed. It's an absolutely typical support situation, and work on picking-up in the form of a cyclic game is valuable as a basic exercise in support play.

The mechanics of the pick-up are simple. Set it up so that the ball is on your better side – i.e. for most people on their right. Judge your approach so that you put your right foot beside the ball. This gives you greater flexibility in case the ball is bobbing about. Your eyes should be on the ball, your mind thinking ahead. The right hand makes contact first, and scoops the ball a few inches into the left hand. Your hands should be relaxed, your fingers slightly spread.

It's dead simple but needs unceasing practice. Set up cyclic games:

- *pick-up ... put-down*: four players, numbered. 1 trots out, puts ball down, 2 picks up and so on in sequence. Gradually build up speed.

- pick-up/put-down shuttle relay: use four marks a, b, c, d and two balls, one on a, one on c. Each runner picks up the ball and puts it down on the next mark. Start with two players at the a end, one at the d end. Insist on accurate put-down.

- *pick-up ... pass ... put-down ... turn and pressurise*: the exercise goes on but now with a conditioned resistance. After putting the ball down the player turns to offer opposition. The new ball-carrier can drive in as for a screen pass, or get the ball away before contact. The ball can go to either supporter, who in turn puts the ball down and turns.

- *pick-up, tackle*: this is the essential pressure exercise, and one whose usefulness is hard to exaggerate. It's described on p. 54. It brings the pick-up fully into the competitive match situation.

These exercises are, of course, only coaching situations: the coach must monitor the actual performance.

### The attacking fall

At close-quarters, especially if you are outnumbered, or there are opponents ahead of you, the first aim is to secure possession, and the quickest way to do that is by a controlled dive onto the ball. Imagine you're a soccer goalkeeper – dive with both eyes open, and both hands reaching for the ball, pulling it under your shoulder.

Once you've got it you can either roll onto your back and hold it up for a supporting player, or squeeze it back towards your own players, or if you're lucky, get a pass away. If you do pass, pop the ball up gently rather than throw it back.

A cyclic exercise to give intensive repetition of the action is described on p. 56.

## Defensive falls

There are two basic forms of defensive fall. One deals with the situation when the defender is going forward to meet a dribbler; the other, when the ball has been pushed behind him and he has to go back for it. Both call for intelligent anticipation to get into the right position. In the first case, the defender must position himself to force the dribbler to one side, as in tackling; in the second, he's got to judge the path of the ball, and arrive in balance.

**1** You aim to dive on the ball and roll between the ball and the dribbler so that your shoulders and back hit his lower leg. Pull the ball in, and curl round it so that your head is tucked in with your chin on your chest.

**2** You do a soccer sliding tackle onto the ball, and land with the upper body curled round it and the upper hand pulling it into the body. You land on the outside of your lower thigh, with the lower leg flexed out of the way, and the upper leg pushed out in front. The impetus of your slide, and the fulcrum of the upper foot should help you immediately back onto your feet. This is a much more active fall than the attacking fall.

Intensive practices for these falls include the dribble v falling practice on p. 162 and a cyclic exercise – falling and turning him over.

See p. 39 for the way of dealing with a player backing into you. Put your players in threes. No. 1 puts in a short, controlled grubber kick; no. 2 falls, bounces, backs into 3 who is following up; no. 3 turns him over ... and the cycle continues.

## Dribbling

Ideally we want to get the ball in our hands, but dribbling has its place. The key idea in dribbling is to push the ball as far as you need: don't kick it.

Dribbling is a one-footed exercise: two-footed dribbling is far too slow – it allows the cover to get across. You dribble with the outside and inside of your better foot. Treat the ball gently so that it stays close, lean over it, use your arms for balance and not speed. Keep the ball-dribbling ankle relaxed.

I've never improved on the two basic exercises described in *Improve your Rugby* (Penguin):

- mark a spot on the ground, and take the ball round it using the outside of your foot. Curve your toe around the ball, and guide it. Start slowly and gradually find the speed that you can work at. Let your body lean into the centre

- using the inside of your foot and keeping it in contact with the ball as continuously as you can, drag the ball sideways and slightly forward across the pitch.

The player must keep his eye on the ball. The best time to beat opponents is when they are in mid-air for the fall. Practise moving the ball sideways as in the second exercise, and then bringing it sharply back as in the first exercise at the moment you glimpse them falling.

An excellent intensive practice has four players in the grid. One has the ball at his feet and tries to keep possession as long as he can; the other three are all trying to fall on the ball, gain possession and start dribbling.

Dribbling affords another good situation for encouraging intelligent support patterns – giving width and depth to the movement, and immediately responding to changes in the ball's position. Think in terms of a 3–4–1 pack with the ball at the hooker's feet. As soon as the ball player loses control he accelerates ahead and rejoins at no. 8; the remaining players alter position to maintain the 3–4–1 pattern.

There are situations and conditions that dictate kicking the ball on the ground. A full-back near touch, isolated from support, with opponents bearing down on him may have to kick the ball into touch – but 'kick' does not mean a wild 'fly-hack', it requires precisely the same concentration as a place kick. Again, if the pitch is very heavy you may have to kick the ball forward – but again you judge it. Whenever the ball is near touch, for example, you either want it in touch or you don't, and you must concentrate on your objective. When you're following up a kick that takes the ball near touch, you must run to get between touch and the ball, and play the ball back inside.

## Judgement

A highly effective cyclic exercise for refining judgement in handling ball on the ground situations is as follows.

Players 1, 2, 3, 4 and 5 trot in Indian file, 1 with the ball in his hands. He accelerates (the rest do not), places the ball on the ground, goes beyond it, and turns. The critical factor is how far beyond the ball he goes. The spacing he creates should indicate the most appropriate action to take. For simplicity you may categorise these into:

| Defender | First man | Supporters 1 & 2 |
|---|---|---|
| he's right over the ball | ruck him off it | pick up & go forward |
| it's just in front of him | attacking fall | ruck over the top |
| two metres in front | pick up & ruck | join ruck |
| four metres in front | pick up & pass | support positions |

The fifth member of the group is there to start the next cycle. Roles, of course, change automatically every run. Remind them of the need for the rest to pause as the ball is carried out front – the defender must be given time to get into a desired position.

## THE BALL IN THE AIR

The primary concern here is the ball in the air after a kick. Taking a pass is covered under handling, and line-out catching under line-out.

### Defence

Catching practices are basic – being able to defend effectively, and being able to counter-attack, depend upon certainty in catching. Throwing the ball up and watching it into your hands is a simple way of building basic confidence. In pairs it's best to start throwing and as confidence grows, throw higher and higher. Every kicking practice is also a catching practice, but won't be until the kicking is moderately accurate.

The mechanics of catching are simple enough:

- *move to the predicted landing area*

- *if the ball is coming to you, call for it* – if more than one player calls, the player furthest back should take it

- *assess what your opponents are doing early* – do this as you move into position: once you lock onto the ball that will take all your attention. If it's going to be a pressure situation, hang back slightly so that you can accelerate in towards the ball, and get up into the air to take it. If you don't, they will

- *get your lower body set for what you expect to do* – it may be anything from running to taking a tackle – but keep the upper body and arms relaxed: you may find that breathing out helps you relax

- *get your hands out and up to welcome the ball* – this brings your elbows together, so that the ball doesn't slide through

- *keep your head and chest up as long as you can*

- *pull the ball into your chest* – some rotation of the upper body in the direction of your goal line takes the way off the ball, sets you up to take a tackle, and lessens the risk of a knock-on.

In the catching practice it's well worthwhile getting the players to call for a mark: make all your players aware of the possibility, and go through the procedure with them. This will reveal difficulties, such as kicking to touch from midfield.

A player who can catch the ball in his hands, without pulling it into the body, is able to move it much more rapidly, but this is a secondary consideration if the player is in a genuinely defensive position.

Once the catching is efficient, the coach must turn his and the players' attention to the need to support the catcher. He should never have to catch alone – the other players must give him support in defence and for counter-attack (see p. 304). As in all support, width and depth are the key ideas – and here especially depth.

Once these basic abilities are established, the range of catching situations can be extended. In practice it seems adequate if one deals with one further catch – where the ball goes over the catcher's head. This is particularly important for the scrum-half and for the back three – the full-back and wingers. Stand facing the player about 5m apart on the 5-metre line, and lob the ball over his head so that the ensuing catch will be easy. Once he's doing this confidently – observing the rules for an ordinary catch cited above – get him to catch and kick over his shoulder to touch (see p. 158). Once he's doing this confidently, lob further and follow up the lob to try to touch him before he kicks. A natural extension of this is to encourage the player to experiment with beating his opponent by a dummy turn followed by a pivot the other way. Broadly speaking this means a dummy turn towards touch – holding the ball wide on that side – and pivoting infield to give a better angle for the kick or to start counter-attack. It's much safer for the right-footed kicker to try this on the right touch, so that he ends up with a dominant-foot kick.

A sensible general kicking and support exercise puts two pairs of players A and B, C and D in opposition. A kicks to C as accurately as he can; D covers behind C, moves into position for an easy pass, collects the ball, and kicks for B, who feeds A . . . and so on. You can then add a fifth player, E to the A/B group. When A kicks, he can then follow up his kick and pressurise the catcher – and the game goes on. This will allow the catcher to try dummying a single opponent approaching at speed.

## Attack

In a 50/50 catching situation between an attacker on the move and a defender at a halt, it's much easier for the attacker to go up and take the ball early. This can be practised at kick-offs, but is true anywhere on the field. The attacker must always keep the possibility in mind as his first choice of action. More often, however, he will find a situation developing in which the defender will be able to catch the ball. If he's moderately sure of making an effective tackle, that is his second choice of action. If he isn't sure, he should adjust his line of running and his speed, to limit the catcher's range of action. In general he should encourage the kicker to turn towards touch so limiting the possibility of counter-attack, and the range of touch kick.

Many attacking kicks are angled across the pitch, and the supporter's first aim then is to get between the ball and touch. If he cannot be sure of catching the ball, he must make every effort to keep the ball in play with his feet – concentrate on the ball and push it inside. All wingers must practise this.

Just as with the defensive catcher, the attacking catcher following up the kick needs support. Support practices for the forwards are described on p. 290 ff. The team as a whole must follow up kicks maintaining their basic defensive formation – pressure, cover, and depth. The whole team can fit into the forward practice – start in position and follow up as a team.

Kick-off catching and support are dealt with on p. 116.

## THE BALL WITH THE OPPOSITION

The defensive skills are every bit as important to the complete player as the attacking skills, and his attitude in using them must be just as positive. To become 'defensive', for the player as for the team, is to hesitate and lose the initiative. The aim of the coach in dealing with situations when the opponents have the ball is to make the player see them as the basis for another form of attack: *when we've got the ball, we attack their line; when they've got the ball, we attack them.* And this attack needs the same forethought, the same decisiveness, the same skill in execution as attacking the line.

### Tackling

The classic tackles are those that tend to be performed by the back row, the front three backs, and to a lesser extent the back three. They take place in the open, and they tend to form part of a defensive plan – to limit the possibilities open to the attackers so that their attacks become predictable and defensive roles easier to fulfil. See Chapter 22.

Planning can go only so far, and every player in the team may be faced with the need to tackle. Even on the personal level, though, the first aim of the tackler is to set things up so that the ball-carrier's options are limited. What the tackler is always trying to do is to create a situation where the ball-carrier is forced to go in one direction, and preferably forced to run on the outside of the tackler. This allows the tackler's impetus to go into the tackle, and may force the ball-carrier to run further than the tackler. Ideally, too, the ball-carrier is channelled between the tackler and the touch line, or another defender, or a scrum or maul. This imposes a further limitation on his movement.

The other aspect of planning a tackle is timing. Ideally the tackle is made simultaneously with the arrival of the ball: the less time the ball-carrier has to set himself up the better. In loose play, especially, the most effective tackles are made by defenders who have predicted who's getting the ball next, and made sure by intelligent running that he stands no chance of using possession. This is particularly important on the fringes of scrums, line-outs, and mauls or rucks where dangerous situations will develop immediately the ball gets in front of the opposing pack. The easiest time to stop these attacks is before the first ball-carrier gets moving: as soon as he appears he's got to be knocked down. In the backs it's typified by the defender coming in to take the extra man: while he's looking for the ball, you're moving in to take him out – but be absolutely sure you can take man and ball before you commit yourself.

In open play, therefore, it's generally true that intelligent anticipation makes for easy tackles. This is a key idea in all aspects of the game: start fast but arrive in balance. Starting fast means two things: a quicker assessment of the situation than the average player, and quick acceleration. You must get into the tackle area fast, but you must be in balance. A potential tackler running flat out is too easily beaten.

This in turn is linked to personal safety: only a fool tries to damage an opponent at the risk of damaging himself. The easy, effective, tackle is a better bet than the spectacular one. Tackling can be a very effective way of sapping an opponent's morale, and a great way of turning defence into attack. There is certainly a place for the crash tackle – but don't try it unless conditions are absolutely right.

The second factor in safety is that you always aim to hit with the shoulder, and hit something with more give in it than your shoulder – just above the knees, or the solar plexus, are good examples.

The third factor is to keep your eyes open so that you can put your head where it is not going to be hit – generally, behind the ball-carrier's thigh. Create as wide an angle as you can between hitting shoulder and neck. I've seen American players using the head as a battering ram, as if they still had helmets on, but I wouldn't recommend it.

The first aim of every tackle is to put the ball-carrier on the deck and if possible to dislodge the ball. The second is to force him to land with the ball on your team's side of his body: try to revolve him just before you hit the ground. Only in a congested area where he'll want to go to ground should you pick him up – bend your knees and drive them straight – turn him to face your goal line, and hold him up (see p. 168).

The great majority of tackles in the open tend to be from the side and behind; you don't always get the chance to put in the most satisfying of all tackles – the head-on bone-shaker.

### Side and rear tackles

The aim in side and rear tackles is to have the shoulder hit just above the knees and buckle them. This is accompanied by a powerful sweeping action of the hitting shoulder arm operating just below the knees, pulling the knees together and pulling them into the tackler's chest. If the arm is slightly extended before the tackle it brings the hitting shoulder into a more powerful position. The other arm wraps round to bind the tackle. In all such tackles you must allow for the ball-carrier's moving away from you – aim beyond him, and in the rear tackle aim high to come down in the tackle area.

You avoid most difficulties if you accelerate into the tackle, putting the ball-carrier's timing out. The acceleration should give you the initiative.

## Head-on tackle

This is one of the most valuable of all tackles: it's a 'life-saver' close to your own line, when a forward breaks away from scrum, ruck, maul or line-out, or when a centre comes through with the ball. Typically, the opponent hopes to run through you; every centimetre he can gain is a great help to his team. Your job is not merely to stop him but to put him over backward.

To do this, it's a great help if you're meeting him on the reciprocal of his own course. On the fringes of rucks and mauls, for example, it pays, once you are committed to meeting an attack and have broken from the point, to get wide, so that the opponent is running straight at you rather than diagonally across you. If he runs across, he'll force a side tackle on you – easy to do, but allowing him time to get the ball away. Similarly, in the centre: don't let your opponent get wide of you. You want him to go outside, but try to keep him fairly straight.

You go to meet him, lower your centre of gravity, get your head to one side, and focus on driving your tackling shoulder up into his solar plexus. Your arms close round him, but the power of the tackle comes from checking his upper body, and simultaneously, as your legs straighten, lifting his feet off the ground. You then drive through to put him over backward.

This sounds very hairy, but if you practise it – maybe four or five tackles each time – it soon becomes routine. Set it up between touch and 5m and get both players facing each other. Start with A, the tackler, simply waiting as B moves in gently towards him. Leave the ball out of it at the start, and don't let B indulge in evasive manoeuvres. Your aim is to teach confidence in the tackle, and you tilt the balance firmly in favour of the tackler. In due course, B will have his turn.

This is a typical practice in which I'd set up a demonstration. Take two suitable players and while the rest are reinforcing something they know well, take the selected pair through the practice so that they can show the rest what to do.

The basics are easy. Make sure A sinks low enough on the tackling side of his body to be able to drive up into B and lift him off the ground. Get him to wrap his arms around B and break his fall. By the time he's done it a few times he'll find it very easy.

## Knock-down

Very frequently the player is in a close contact position where classic tackling is impossible: he needs practice in knocking a *static* opponent down. This is precisely the kind of practice that is rarely done.

The most effective form approximates to a shoulder charge at the upper body with the leg on that side hooking the back of the knees. It's most effective if the shoulder charge is slightly up to lessen the ball-carrier's contact with the ground.

Start this in pairs and introduce two further competitive players to scoop up the ball as soon as it appears. It's obviously best to work the players in groups of comparable weight. Emphasise the need for the supporter to get down to the ball – don't stand up and grope around, get your shoulder over it, and dig it out.

## Turn over
Quite frequently, the player is faced with an opponent backing into him. The aim then is to put a leg behind him and turn him over so that he lands on the ground between the ball and his own players. Grab the far shoulder and rotate him hard over your leg, and down onto the ground.

*Introduction*
Organise the players into pairs. Player 1 does a short grubber kick. Player 2 executes a sliding fall (see p. 161), rocks onto his feet, and drives back into player 1. Player 1 turns him over. Introduce a third player to snap up or dive onto the loose ball. Build into a cyclic exercise.

## Turning the man
If the ball-carrier is static, turning him over may be difficult. One alternative is to turn him to face your team-mates. The key to this is to lift him off the ground, and swing him round using a wide grip – e.g. one hip and the opposite shoulder – to increase leverage. An effective refinement is to get your arm round his neck to the far shoulder – this gives good leverage and prevents him from tucking down round the ball. The lift comes from your knees, so get them bent, and your back – use it to keep him upright.

*Introduction*
The ball-carrier stands, braced, on the far side of the grid facing out. Turner and supporter trot across. Turner turns him, and supporter takes the ball. At this stage condition the ball-carrier to release the ball easily. The supporter trots back to the far line as the ball-carrier, and the previous ball-carrier becomes the turner.

### Taking the ball
The weakness of turning the man is that it tends to lead to a prolonged wrestle for the ball and a delay that reduces the value of possession. If you're going to use it, you must devise a technique for getting possession quickly, and give your players practice in applying it. If the ball-carrier can wrap himself round the ball, there's no way within the spirit of the game to take it from him quickly. It's essential that the turner should keep him upright. Even then, if he keeps his

elbows in, it's difficult to get enough purchase on his arms to dislodge the ball. The aim is to get a shoulder into his chest above the ball, push down on and behind the ball, and try to pull one of his hands off the ball. A reverse push is quite effective – push the ball up hard so that he is forced to push down, and then quickly push down.

You can develop the previous practice so that an extra support player comes in and two of them with defined roles – e.g. removing a hand, removing an arm, pushing up, preparing to push down – take the ball. But the best solution is to dump him on the ground with the ball where your team want it.

## Isolating the ball

When the tackler is much lighter than the static opponent, he may be able to cap-italise on speed by getting between the ball and the ball-carrier's supporters. This is perfectly legitimate provided he's the first to make contact. This sets up a stale-mate situation which the ball-carrier may well try to resolve by pushing the ball down – and if the tackler is alert he may be able to kick it back on his side.

# 20 UNIT TECHNIQUES – THE FORWARDS

## SCRUMMAGING

The easiest way to play attacking rugby is to dominate the tight scrums. Physically, tactically, and in terms of morale, the opposition are put under heavy pressure and your team are given an equivalent boost. It affects the whole team performance. The opposing halves cannot commit themselves to attack, lose confidence in decision-making, and may find themselves getting a ball of such poor quality that it's an embarrassment. Your own backs have the perfect platform to mount concerted attacks. Moreover, since the team taking the ball into the maul or ruck have the edge in getting it back, you have the promise of effective second-phase play.

Tactically, and this is a point little appreciated, the chance of a break being decisive is greater at a scrum than at a line-out, where the opposing defence has greater depth and longer to cover.

So important is it to be sure of getting one's own ball, that scrummaging power is a coaching article of faith: everyone works to get the most efficient form, and the most appropriate conditioning. The result has been that it's extremely difficult to gain an edge in scrum possession by taking opposition ball. This in turn has made any edge you can get at the line-out that much more important: it really can swing a match. In the '95 World Cup there were more line-outs than scrums. But it would be ridiculous to use these facts as a case for neglecting scrummaging: can you imagine constantly losing your own put-in?

Coaching effective scrummaging is easy: it's a limited, clearly defined, mechanical exercise. With powerful forwards, even a mediocre coach can produce a winning team. Unhappily, all too often that's where the team's aspirations are allowed to stop: a marvellous platform for inventive, exhilarating rugby is used to set up dull play-safe exercises. Time, energy, and thought must be devoted to winning the ball – the pack must work on its scrummaging at virtually every practice session – but equally hard work must be devoted to the way you intend to use it.

The importance of scrummaging is reflected in selection: in all other positions, you can weigh strengths against weaknesses, but a prop who is not first and foremost an effective scrummager is nothing. You hope to get a bonus in terms of loose play – only an idiot would plump on principle for a prop you *don't* see in the loose – but the basic criterion is his performance in the tight. This is a compound of temperament, strength, and shape – controlled competitiveness, natural upper-body strength developed by power lifting, and short levers. All the power generated by your pack is transmitted to the opposition through their spines, and they are in an intensely competitive situation with their opponents. If they are inadequate, it will cripple the efforts of the rest.

Scrummaging is the best defined expression of the pack's solidarity, and for a critical moment of drive every player in your pack must be dedicated to it. Before and after there has to be thought, communication, and prediction, but in the moment of the drive there has to be complete mental and physical commitment. At that moment, you must have four locks, with both flankers committing themselves to that role. A moment's thought will show that the flankers' shove, since it is nearer to the opposition and therefore less absorbed in body structures, is more effective than that of the no. 8. They are also less physically constricted than the locks. They make, in fact, a critical contribution in developing the pack's power. Selection should have an eye to this, and coaches must drum it home.

The emphasis in coaching, once the technicalities have been established must be on concentration. Scrumming is the kind of power event, where, for most people, deep resources are never tapped. If you put an Olympic class athlete in an unaccustomed position – e.g. putting the shot standing with both feet on a line at right angles to the putt – you can improve performance not once but several times simply by calling on the athlete to draw deeper on these resources. The same thing is true of a pack.

Probably once a session and certainly once a week the pack must have a concentrated scrumming session. This must be done, whenever possible, against an opposing pack. A scrum-machine is essential equipment for technical work and for stiff work-outs but it can never supply the confrontational quality of scrumming against opposition.

Such a confrontation must be carefully conditioned. It must be conditioned in terms of numbers of repetitions, defined purposes, and resistance, and it must give the other pack some measure of success.

It must also be conditioned carefully in terms of immediate action after the ball has left the scrummage. It's desirable that each scrummage should lead to a further action by the forwards – drilling home the essential work-rate maxim: *do it and run*. This may be in terms of back row runs and support, scrum-half break and maul, or simply running to specific points as part of a support pattern, each followed by sprinting back to the scrumming point and getting down first. But there's a limit to how many of these a pack can do and retain their composure: you cannot work effectively in terms both of very high work-rate and thoughtful concentration. Mixing the two does not create a good learning situation. Essentially, pressure practices should be kept separate from the coaching of good form. Indeed, I'd prefer always to coach technique using a scrum-machine.

# SCRUMMAGING the basics

## 1 The pushing position – imagine a little man pushing against a wall

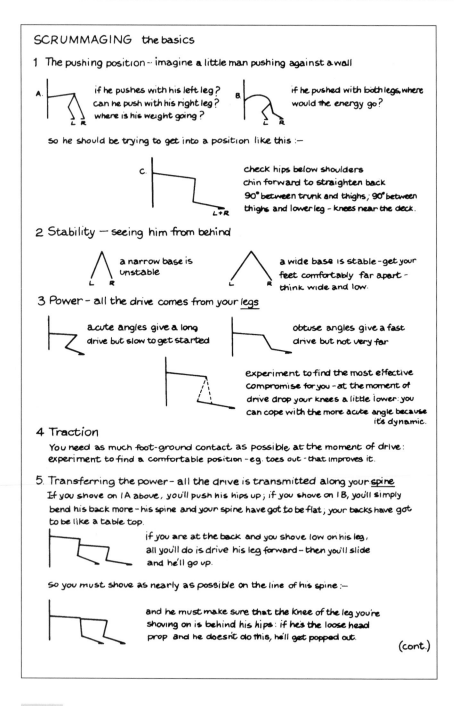

A. if he pushes with his left leg?
can he push with his right leg?
where is his weight going?

B if he pushed with both legs, where
would the energy go?

So he should be trying to get into a position like this :–

c. check hips below shoulders
chin forward to straighten back
90° between trunk and thighs; 90° between
thighs and lower leg – knees near the deck.

## 2 Stability – seeing him from behind

a narrow base is
unstable

a wide base is stable – get your
feet comfortably far apart –
think wide and low.

## 3 Power – all the drive comes from your legs

acute angles give a long
drive but slow to get started

obtuse angles give a fast
drive but not very far

experiment to find the most effective
compromise for you – at the moment of
drive drop your knees a little lower: you
can cope with the more acute angle because
it's dynamic.

## 4 Traction

You need as much foot-ground contact as possible at the moment of drive:
experiment to find a comfortable position – e.g. toes out – that improves it.

## 5. Transferring the power – all the drive is transmitted along your spine

If you shove on 1A above, you'll push his hips up; if you shove on 1B, you'll simply
bend his back more – his spine and your spine have got to be flat; your backs have got
to be like a table top.

if you are at the back and you shove low on his leg,
all you'll do is drive his leg forward – then you'll slide
and he'll go up.

So you must shove as nearly as possible on the line of his spine :–

and he must make sure that the knee of the leg you're
shoving on is behind his hips: if he's the loose head
prop and he doesn't do this, he'll get popped out.

(cont.)

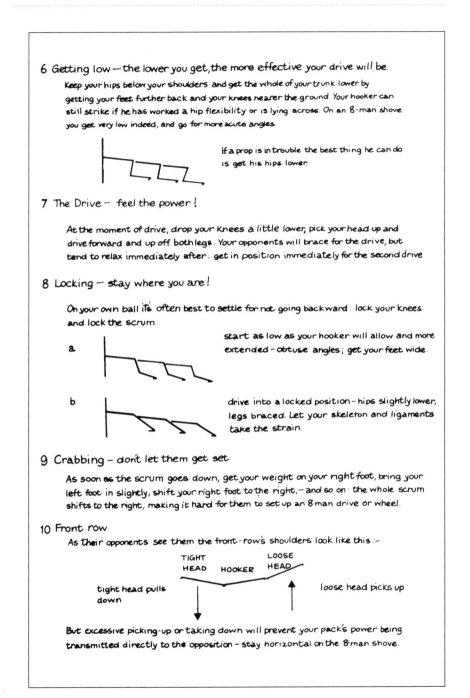

## 6 Getting low — the lower you get, the more effective your drive will be.

Keep your hips below your shoulders and get the whole of your trunk lower by getting your feet further back and your knees nearer the ground. Your hooker can still strike if he has worked a hip flexibility or is lying across. On an 8-man shove you get very low indeed, and go for more acute angles.

If a prop is in trouble the best thing he can do is get his hips lower.

## 7 The Drive — feel the power!

At the moment of drive, drop your knees a little lower, pick your head up and drive forward and up off both legs. Your opponents will brace for the drive, but tend to relax immediately after: get in position immediately for the second drive.

## 8 Locking — stay where you are!

On your own ball its often best to settle for not going backward: lock your knees and lock the scrum.

a     start as low as your hooker will allow and more extended – obtuse angles; get your feet wide.

b     drive into a locked position – hips slightly lower, legs braced. Let your skeleton and ligaments take the strain.

## 9 Crabbing – don't let them get set

As soon as the scrum goes down, get your weight on your right foot, bring your left foot in slightly, shift your right foot to the right, – and so on: the whole scrum shifts to the right, making it hard for them to set up an 8 man drive or wheel.

## 10 Front row

As their opponents see them the front-row's shoulders look like this :-

TIGHT HEAD    HOOKER    LOOSE HEAD

tight head pulls down          loose head picks up

But excessive picking-up or taking down will prevent your pack's power being transmitted directly to the opposition – stay horizontal on the 8-man shove.

## Basic technique

The basic driving position is shown on p. 172:

- *shoulders slightly above the hips* – 'getting down low' means getting the hips down low, and the shoulders come down low as a consequence

- *spine not merely flat, but depressed in the middle*

- *thighs approximately vertical* – it's obvious that the more acute the angle of the knee, the greater the potential range of the drive, but the more strength required to initiate it. Any given player will be strong over a given range of movement – cossack dancers are strong over an extended range, but you have only to go into the full-flexed position to realise that a drive from that position is very much slower and more difficult than a drive from a half-squat. Players tend to assume the position in which they feel most capable of a snap drive. On the other hand, the smaller their degree of flexion, the smaller the range of drive. For a six-foot player, a flexion of 90° at the knee produces a potential forward movement of about one foot, which allows for a snap drive, and the necessary continuation shove. That is more than enough for all practical purposes, and may well be seen as a maximum

- *if points 1 and 3 above are observed, the knee will be quite close to the ground*

- *the feet should be in effective contact with the ground*. It doesn't seem particularly important how this contact is attained. The weakest position is with the feet pointing straight forward with the heels off the ground: the flexion of the ankle is a potential weak point – far weaker than the flexion of knee or hip. This is remedied by shoving more off the sides of the feet, inner or outer. What is essential is that the players feel comfortable and strong

- *in general, every player in the scrum other than the hooker should seek a wide base*. The scrum must be stable, and having the feet close is a source of instability

- *the actual foot placing is most important in the front row, and for the left-hand flanker on his own put-in*. The flanker must have his right foot in position to prevent the ball shooting out of channel one. For the rest of the pack the really important thing is that they should feel comfortable and powerful. If you adopt the 'on your marks' position advocated below, with all four in the second row kneeling on the inside knee, you'll find that they automatically move into satisfactory positions

- *shoulder height in the front row determines how low the pack can get*. From every point of view, the lower the pack gets the better – provided the hooker is capable of striking. It's better to work with your hooker on hip mobility, and on lying 'along the tunnel' (i.e. pushing his head to the right on his own ball so that his body is inclined to the right and his legs are in a flatter striking position) than to settle for a high position. Against the head, it's better to get even lower than usual. What this means is that the props get closer and closer to the basic driving position, with their feet further back and wider, their hips correspondingly lower, and their upper bodies close to horizontal. This has two advantages: it restricts the opposing hooker's strike, and may even prevent it, and it ensures a more powerful and effective drive. It's worth pointing out that most scrum-machines are set too high to allow effective low scrumming practice

- *the only people whose stance need differ in any large degree from the norm are the loose-head prop and the hooker.* The loose-head prop has to counter the downward pressure of the opposing tight-head and allow his hooker a clear view of the ball. To do this he has to keep his feet further forward and his body rather more upright. For effective use of the available strength a stocky figure with comparatively short levers is the best shape for a loose-head prop. For no-one is weight training more important than for the loose-head.
The hooker's main concern, if he is to strike for the ball, is to go down in a position that creates space for himself. In general, this means getting his hips in front of those of the props, staying fairly upright, with knees bent, before he goes down.

## Seven man, eight-man, and locked scrums

There are three distinct organisations of the pack. The seven-man scrum is the normal scrum, with the hooker hooking and the rest driving; in the eight-man, everyone concentrates on the drive (and everyone has to modify from the seven-man position); in the locked position, the side putting the ball in commits itself to not going backward rather than trying to go forward. Each is based on a different appreciation of the situation.

The seven-man shove assumes that a controlled strike by a specialist hooker will minimise the effect of an opposing eight-man shove by limiting the time the ball is in the scrum.

The eight-man shove assumes that the odds are very much in favour of the opposing hooker's getting the strike on his own put-in, that the best bet is to minimise the value of that strike, and that our eight-man can outpush the opposing seven.

The locked scrum assumes that the opponents' eight-man shove will be more powerful than our own seven-man shove, and that the bent knees which are a potential source of power going forward are a source of weakness as soon as the pack moves backward. We, therefore, seek to replace muscle-power by skeletal/ligamental strength, and adopt a position in which so far as possible the body and legs are in a straight line.

### General procedure in scrumming

There are three distinct phases in scrumming – corresponding to 'on your marks' . . . 'set' . . . 'go' in track athletics. The first is concerned with getting the pack into optimum position for engaging with the opposition; the second, with taking the initiative at the moment of engaging; the third, with a co-ordinated snap drive.

### Front row before the put-in: seven-man shove

Before the scrum goes down, it must be organised. The moment of going down, of engaging the opposition, is critical in taking the initiative. It's impossible to do this unless the entire pack can move immediately and as one man into the drive.

It's vital that the props should not move their feet as they go down. They must have their feet in the desired 'set' position before they go down, and must be the right distance away from their opponents: too far away and they will lurch forward and force every other member of the pack to shuffle forward; too near and they will be forced to engage without the desired – or at least permitted – drive. Both have a comfortably wide stance, to give stability and to get their hips adequately low without having the feet uncomfortably far back. Both have their hips, at this stage, behind their feet: they need to counter-balance the pressure from behind.

The hooker's main concern is to keep his hips forward of the props' hips, so that he isn't cramped by their pressure. To do this, he has his feet wide, overlapping the props' inner feet. At the moment of going down, on his strike, he'll shift his right foot alongside his left, and swivel his hips into his desired striking position. In effect, he'll be sitting on his loose-head prop's thigh. The movement of his hips also creates space for the locks' heads.

The binding in the front row must be absolutely solid. Binding over on the left and under on the right gives the advantage of an easier strike – it allows the hooker's right side to sink and right hip to move nearer the ball. However, it is a much more vulnerable binding. The best binding is over on both sides. The hooker's shoulders must completely overlap the shoulders of his props. He binds on their shirts as far round as he can get. The tight-head prop binds on the waist-band of the hooker's shorts: the loose-head on the shirt of the hooker as far round as he can reach at arm-pit level. (If the loose-head binds on the waist-band, he tends to inhibit the hooker's strike with the right leg.) The prop nearer to the ball binds first, and the other binds over his arm: the more important bind is always that nearer to the put-in side.

The hooker is the focal point: he must judge the right distance from the opposing front row. He must also give the word of command for the pack to go down – loud enough for all the pack to hear it and aggressively enough to spark their drive. Before he does do this he must be able to count four heads – a flanker, two locks, and a flanker, all in position, all ready to drive.

To gain the initiative, the pack must meet the opposing pack with as much weight as the referee will allow. From the moment they form up, the front row must be conscious of the weight of the second row behind them. Even if the second row are kneeling, their weight must be threatening to shift the front row forward, so that the front row have to sit back against it. That contact must never lessen: any lessening of it – typically it will happen on the command '*Down!*' – lessens the effectiveness of the scrum.

'Keeping the weight on' becomes a positive, relentless move forward when the hooker calls '*Down!*'. The aim is to meet the opposition as solidly as the referee allows. To use this weight effectively, the props must be ready to transmit it into the opposition through braced spines. As they sit back in the preliminary phase, they also crouch, to get lower than their opponents. They can reinforce this by 'dipping and picking', dropping their shoulders as they begin to move forward, and coming up from below their opponents. In effect, this puts them in a lower and more efficient position than the opposition. A slight movement to the right may also be helpful: this moves the opposition a little further from the ball, lets the hooker lie across a little more, and may disconcert the opposing loose-head who is the key man in their attempt to wheel us.

It's essential that the inside thighs of both props should not be inclined forward once they are engaged with the opposition. If their knees are in front of their hips, the locks will begin to slide down, and the props may be forced into the air – get 'popped out'.

Simultaneously with dipping and picking, the props must bind with their opponents. There are two basic positions for the outside arm of the loose-head prop. He tries either to swing his arms in an upper-cut action up and over the back of his opponent, to bind as far round on his shirt as possible, or he punches straight forward to grasp the waist-band of his opponent's shorts, turning his elbow so that it is on top. Both are aimed at creating a cantilever so that the opponent provides purchase to counter his own effort to keep the loose-head down. In each case, the loose-head's skull is tight in to his opponent's sternum. If he is under heavy pressure he can shift his head to the left, out from under his opponent's chest: this lessens the leverage upon him, but strains the binding of the front row. If his opponent bores in – i.e. tries to drive his head between the loose-head prop and the hooker – the loose-head should make every effort to bind even tighter before going down, should drop his inside shoulder lower than his outer, and (using the second binding position suggested above) try to pull his opponent's hips out, so exaggerating and weakening his opponent's position.

The tight-head prop is in a comparatively strong position and can afford to adopt a mental attitude much more aggressive than that of the loose-head. He has two aims: to bring pressure to bear upon the opposing hooker and his binding with his loose-head prop, and to keep his opponent down. His aim in achieving the first is to get his head close to the opposing hooker's chest as he goes down; in the second, he binds with his opponent's shirt quite close to his shoulders (where the leverage is greatest), pulling down and preventing him from moving his head out. Some tight-head props find they can exert more weight and power on their opponents by moving their outside leg far forward and pulling their opponent down onto the thigh. Whatever he does, however, must conform with the referee's reading of the laws: it does no good giving away penalties or antagonising the official.

Both props will find some advantage in making sure that the outside shoulder is higher than the inside shoulder when they engage with the opposition. This gives them leverage to exert or resist pressure.

The hooker with the put-in is in a favourable position for pressuring his opponent – applying pressure with his head – if his front row have engaged with adequate aggression.

All chins in the front row are customarily thrust forward, to straighten the back and bring head pressure onto the opponents. It's worth pointing out, however, that the hooker striking for the ball may gain an advantage by allowing his head to hang down and so gain a better view of the ball than his opponent. This is less easy than it sounds: we are very unaccustomed to relaxing our neck muscles.

### Front row before the put-in: eight-man shove

The eight-man shove calls for changed tactics by everyone in the pack. The critical changes in the front row concern the position of hooker and the distance from the opposition at which they get set. The hooker is now concerned wholly with binding and driving once the pack is down. His hips are in line – or as close to it as his back-length allows – with those of the props. His feet must be far enough back to let him drive forward, but so placed as not to complicate life for the locks: it's easier if the front row legs don't overlap. All shoulders should be virtually parallel to the ground. Most important, however, is the need to get lower than usual. This is particularly so, of course, for the loose-head, who no longer seeks to pick his opponent up. It means that the hooker must line up a little further away from the opposition so that on engaging all the feet in the front row are further back, and the hips lower. For the eight-man shove to be fully effective, the props must concentrate on transmitting the drive rather than moving opponents up and down. If anything, both props and hooker should be seeking to drive parallel to the ground for the first few inches, and then slightly up to prevent a collapse. The hooker's contribution is to impair his opponent's strike, so that the ball will stay longer in the opposing scrum and the drive have more time to work. He does this by applying downward pressure to the opponent's neck and shoulders by pushing down his own right shoulder.

## *Second row before the put-in: seven-man shove – with the hooker hooking*

The factor conditioning the forces in the second row when the hooker is hooking is the need to allow room for him to strike. Basically, all the force generated by the second row must be channelled away from the hooker and through the props. Accordingly the left lock pushes only with his left shoulder, and the right lock with his right. I've come across the occasional hooker who finds it advantageous to have the right lock push him towards the ball on his own put-in – it's worth experimenting with.

The forces generated by the locks must be counter-balanced by the flankers pushing in – forcing the props inward. The flanker on the left at any given scrum must find a compromise that allows him to be effective in pushing in and gives his scrum-half some protection yet allows him to have his right foot ready to control the channelling of the ball. The flanker on the right has less need to drive in – the tight-head prop needs less support – and more need to drive forward, since the wheeling tendency of the scrum is towards him. In the tight, both flankers must think of themselves primarily as locks on the outside of the scrum.

Binding the second row to the front row is a matter of what works and what the players find comfortable. I don't like any form of binding that encumbers the props since it reduces their efficiency. Binding on the inside leg has the added disadvantage of allowing the lock's shoulders to slide down. Accordingly, I feel that the best forms of binding are either between the legs and up to grasp the waistband, or on the outside of the hips, pulling the prop onto the outside shoulder. Points to look for on the first are that the lock's elbow is thrust far forward – which brings the shoulder into a strong pushing position – and that the grip on the waist-band is more effective if it's across in front of the lock's shoulder.

Whichever binding system is used, the locks must always transmit their power along the line of the prop's spine, and the nearer their shoulder to the prop's spine the better. To push lower down on the thigh is simply to expose the prop to the indignity of being popped out of the scrum.

In the seven-man scrum it is less important that the locks bind tightly with each other at shoulder level than that they should be tight at the hips. Accordingly they should try binding on each other's waist-band. This helps reduce pressure on the hooker.

The flankers should find it fairly easy to push along the line of the prop's spine, especially if the locks are binding under rather than round. There's a theoretical advantage in their binding very tight with the lock, but in practice, to carry out their other job, most flankers find it more convenient to bind fairly loosely with the back of the lock's shirt, and depend on their inward drive to hold the prop in.

Given that the referee is moderately strict in having the scrum take place on the point where he awarded it, and that the opposing scrum isn't hanging back, there's everything to be said for all four players in the second row getting into position with the inside knee on the ground. This automatically gets the hips well below the shoulders and helps all four drive the front row forward without getting high. Practice on the machine will allow you to establish where the feet should be in the set position to get the thighs into an appropriate position for the drive. The vast majority of locks start with the outside foot too far forward for them to move straight into the most effective scrummaging position. They almost always have to shift it back, which is obviously inefficient. They can find the right starting position by reversing the scrumming sequence: get them into a comfortable scrumming position, stop the scrum, and let them kneel on the inside knee. Then check where the outside foot is. Ideally, if the hooker has judged the distance properly before going down, the locks should not have to shift their feet before contact.

The normal placing of the lock's head is against the inside thigh of the prop, and provided the hooker stays fairly upright this is convenient. If he moves over – lying along the tunnel – for the strike, however, it becomes increasingly difficult for the lock to find a place for his head. In the last two seasons we've experimented with the left-hand lock binding on the outside of the prop's hips, with the prop sitting astride his neck. This allows the lock to drive from directly behind the prop, and has proved effective – our present loose-head prefers it. It also allows the hooker to adopt the very desirable 'sitting on the loose-head's thigh' position. The forces operating on the tight-head make this positioning impossible on the other side of the scrum. The standard solution, however, is for the hooker to go down with his hips rotated counter-clockwise through about 30° – a rotation that simultaneously improves his strike and creates space for the lock's head.

### Second row before the put-in: eight-man shove

With the changed role of the hooker, the locks are now free to shove on him as well as on the props: this allows them to direct their drive straight down the pitch. It also enables them to bind tight at shoulder level as opposed to binding on the waist-band. The flankers no longer have to counter-balance an outward drive – they, too, can direct their drive straight down the pitch, and bind more effectively with the locks. In all other respects the second row act as they did for the seven-man shove.

## *At the put-in*

So far we've looked at what happens before and at the moment the packs go down: the 'to your marks', and 'get set' positions. The aim of both is to take the initiative at first engagement, and to get into effective shape for the subsequent drive – the 'go'. This has to be concerted: there has to be concentration in unifying the pack, and then a trigger to fire it. The *concentration* is vital. The coach has got to make the player completely aware of this, driving it home at every practice scrum.

The actual *drive* is initiated by a slight dropping of the hips – this gives a slight increase of angle at the knee, which can be accommodated because the sequence is dynamic, and ensures that hips are below the shoulders. This leads straight into a violent drive forward and upward, by everyone (including, at that moment, the tight-head prop).

The *trigger* has to be either visual or audible. On your own put-in, there's everything to be said for a visual signal. The old '*Coming in now!*' has real difficulties: the scrum-half finds it difficult to co-ordinate the put-in with the words; half the scrum find it difficult to hear; and the rhythm is equally effective for the opposition.

Communication between scrum-half and pack has to be two-way. The first element is that the hooker must tell the scrum-half that he's ready for the ball to be put in. He can signal this by a movement of a finger – and most referees now accept that this is permissible. This signal may also function as a 'put in now' signal, with the scrum-half putting the ball in simultaneously with his perception of the signal. In this case, the scrum-half can deliver the ball down and in in one movement from the knees – giving the opposing hooker a minimum view of the ball. The rest of the pack co-ordinate their drive from the movement of the hooker's foot – everyone must be looking for it, and make sure that they can see it.

For the eight-man shove the time to strike is when the opposition are at their weakest – immediately the hooker has struck. At that moment the hooker is off balance, the props are concerned with sustaining his weight, and with their binding, while others are thinking about channelling the ball. So everybody watches the opposing hooker's feet, and drives as he strikes. It may help if the right flanker talks to his scrum while the opposing scrum-half is preparing to put the ball in.

Any system that delays the put-in will be to the advantage of the stronger pack for the delay allows them to grind away at the lighter opposition. It also allows them to get properly set for the drive. One of the disturbing features of play in the last few seasons has been the effectiveness of the drive in the eight-man shove and the consequent difficulty of setting up enterprising rugby from bad possession. One way of dealing with this is to reduce the delay in getting the ball into the scrum and out again. It can be seen clearly in sevens: we practise by putting the ball in and hooking at the moment of engagement. This minimises the

# THE MECHANICS OF THE SCRUM

## 1. 7-man scrum with hooker hooking

All the power goes through the props, and the basic unit looks like this:—

prop's spine.

prop sits on flanker's right shoulder and lock's left shoulder
lock drives forward and out; flanker forward and in.

flanker's spine    lock's spine

prop's spine is the line of resultant force - so the lock and flanker will probably <u>not</u> push at the same angle.

Put two of these units together, and you get the basic shape

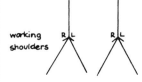

working shoulders    R L    R L

The right unit tends to have the prop angled in slightly, the lock pushing straighter

The hole in the middle is free for the hooker

The left prop drives forward and up; the right prop forward, in, and slightly down

Add the No.8 who shoves rather harder with the right shoulder till the ball comes back, and you get the 7 man scrum. This can be a driving scrum or a locking scrum.

## 2. 8-man scrum – everybody driving

All the power goes through the entire front row, and the basic unit looks like this:—

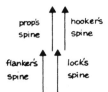

prop's spine    hooker's spine

flanker's spine    lock's spine

Put two of these units together, and you get the basic shape:—

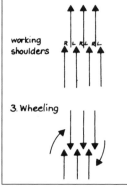

working shoulders    R L  R L  R L

Everyone is driving straight; everyone is lower
The props desist from vertical mayhem.

When you want to wheel, everyone thinks "left shoulder" and channels all his power through it. But make a great effort to go forward on the right before you start.

## 3. Wheeling

The couple on the front row means that there's always a tendency to wheel clockwise in the scrum.

advantages of a side committed to wheeling us. The same thing can be done with a full-scale pack. The pack stays up until the scrum-half is ready to put the ball in, and the hooker strikes immediately the packs have engaged.

Again, the eight-man drive is effective in proportion with the length of time the ball is in the pack: the faster it's out, the less point there is in the big drive. This means more work on the scrum-half/hooker tie-up; more work on the precise line of draw-back by the hooker; and more use of the wide number one channel. Heeling through channel one is the fastest way of clearing the ball from the scrum. But it will cause problems for your scrum-half if you propose to use it often and don't alter your back row positioning to cover it. All you need do is move your no. 8 one space to the left, so that he occupies channel one, pushing (or at least maintaining contact) on the left flanker and lock. You then get a trade-off on back row attack: it becomes simpler to attack left, and harder to attack right.

The third organisational system in the scrum – the locked scrum – is a direct attempt to limit the effectiveness of the eight-man shove. It calls for two basic changes: that the pack and especially its right side should get as low as possible, and that their initial engaging drive takes them into the locked position (see p. 173). The locking on the right provides greater resistance to the wheel, and locking on the left means that we don't actually contribute to it. We've found that adopting the locked position for all our own put-ins is technically effective, and energy-saving, but can lead over a period to too defensive an attitude. It's worth pointing out that locking has to be positive. Imagine a stick propped against the garden wall; now imagine that same stick pushed down in the middle so that its foot comes a little forward, and it's really pressing against the wall – that's what we mean by locking. (And if the opposition wish to destroy your lock, all they need do is shift back a couple of inches: it's their pressure that makes it possible.)

The suggestions above are designed to limit the effects of being wheeled but every team must be equipped with methods of dealing with the situation in which the scrum has been wheeled – e.g. moves that will take the ball to the left, or give it to the scrum-half in space.

### Channelling the ball

There are in practice only two ways by which the ball can emerge from the scrum: between the left-hand flanker and the left-hand lock – channel one, and on the right of the no. 8 – channel two. Channel one, as has been outlined above, has the great asset of speed: it therefore minimises the time for which the pack has to face the opposition. When the pack is under pressure you may have to use it. It has, however, one major flaw: it delivers the ball, under limited control, at a place where the scrum-half may easily be pressured by his opposite number. It's fair to say that even limited control ought to be used – that if the left flanker can check it, take the speed off it, make the opposing scrum-half hesitate, he'll be making life easier for his scrum-half. And if you mean to do this regularly, as has already been pointed out, it's worthwhile shifting your no. 8 into that channel, so that he pushes on left flanker and left lock.

The other channel leaves the ball longer in the scrum, but delivers the ball where both the no. 8 and the scrum-half can use it. To get the ball quickly to the right of the no. 8 is not easy. It demands a carefully angled strike by the hooker, careful attention by the left flanker, a willingness to keep on working by the hooker, and intelligence by the no. 8. The locks don't come into it: if they move their feet, the whole pack will start moving backward. The flanker can correct the angle if the ball is coming back down channel one, and push it over to the right. If the ball gets stuck in the middle of the scrum, however, the person best placed to help is the hooker. All too often, the hooker loses concentration once he's struck for the ball: he ought to be looking for the ball, and be preparing to push it on its way. The no. 8 can sometimes help in this but ideally all he needs to do is move his body over to the left to give the scrum-half maximum protection.

You may sometimes vary the speed of the ball through the pack, unless you're under heavy pressure and want the ball out immediately. Even then, you must concentrate on speed in whatever action you intend to take: there is no point at all in a static hold, unless the scrum-half has called for it to allow some tactical repositioning in the backs. You may hold preparatory to a secondary drive, or when the opposing scrum-half can be trapped offside. You may hold preparatory to a back row move – but once again the aim is to launch it with minimum delay, before the opposition can become fully alerted to what's on.

## Wheeling the scrum

All wheels tend to be clockwise as seen from above. One still hears the odd coach who talks in terms of a wheel to the blind side. So far as I can see this works only when the blind side happens to be on the left of the scrum. It's convenient to distinguish the eight-man wheel to disrupt the other side's possession from the seven-man wheel, in which the side in possession seeks to outflank the opposition by taking the ball out to the left of their back row.

The eight-man wheel must seek to start by moving forward. This calls for a great effort at tight-head to overcome the immediate wheeling tendency against him. However, a wheel without this initial forward movement is never so effective – so it's worth the effort. After the forward drive comes the wheel. The aim is to exaggerate the natural swing in the scrum. The simplest way of doing this is for every forward to think 'left shoulder' and channel all his drive through it. Once the wheel has started it tends to progress fast. If you've got the opposing pack under pressure, you may wish to wheel beyond 90° and enlist the referee's support. But you should note that the wheel opens up a channel on the right of your scrum, with only your scrum-half as defender.

## Hooking

One of the interesting things about the clinic skills – those skills peculiar to certain players at particular moments in the game – is the reluctance of coaches to examine them in detail. They are seen as esoteric almost inscrutable activities. Yet there isn't one, on the technical level, that cannot be reduced to a mechanical solution to a mechanical problem within limits set by the laws and the behaviour of the opponents. In practice, therefore, we can set up an ideal model to which the player approximates within the limits set by the referee and his opponent. Hooking is a precise example of this procedure.

The immediate need is to get to the ball first. This requires speed and reach. The second is to propel it through the scrum at a pace and in a direction required. Speed comes from using short levers – it's evidently quicker to strike with a kicking motion from the knee followed by a draw back than in a sweep from the hip. But this is a short range movement. We can extend it by allowing the support leg to bend, and perhaps by pressing forward off the support foot. We can increase the speed by making sure that the striking foot is not taking any weight, and the range by moving both feet towards the ball. If we can lower his opposite side slightly – i.e. his right side on our ball – that too will facilitate the strike. He will inevitably be striking rather across the line, which increases the difficulty of timing: we can reduce this difficulty by arranging that his whole lower leg comes across more parallel to the ground. To do this he will need to incline his head and shoulders further to the right on his put-in, and his feet to the left – lie more along the tunnel. Correspondingly, against the head he'll need to lean to the left and get his hip and feet further to the right. By applying these ideas we can get speed and reach.

Once we introduce the notion of control and direction we can begin to modify the basic action. All experience shows that a right foot strike on your own put-in gives far more directional control. Accordingly, it's far better to coach a right foot strike provided that, using it, the hooker is getting to the ball first. On the other hand, the left leg is nearer the put-in point and is fractionally longer in reach. It's highly desirable, therefore, that in addition to the right foot strike your hooker should be capable, against good opposition, of striking effectively with the left leg. To be effective, near foot striking has got to incorporate a powerful retracting movement to get the ball back, and the only movement available is that of the heel pulling back towards the thigh. To be able to use this movement, the hooker has to turn his toes and his hips slightly away from the put-in point, and lower his hips. This is the basic position for all strikes against the head as well as for near foot striking on your own put-in.

Once you have organised the basic mechanics of the strike, you can begin to insist on tactics and detail. The most common mistake by hookers is to strike too shallow, and quick improvement can be made by encouraging them to strike deeper than seems necessary. Working with hookers I find it useful to demand an exaggerated action – not just in depth, but in speed and reach. I use a coin (being a Scot, it's usually a penny) and start with a fairly easy challenge: I drop it from a height that makes it comparatively easy to hit before it touches the ground, and at a point that doesn't demand much reach or depth. Gradually, then, we begin to move the dropping point lower, further away, and deeper. All the time, I'm talking about relaxing the striking leg, taking all weight off it, and getting the hooker to imagine the speed of the rattlesnake. As I move further away, the hooker will start to move his feet further over, let his hips sink, and he'll make false starts. This is good: in a very competitive situation, the hooker who doesn't occasionally get his foot up isn't really hooking. It's exactly analogous to the flanker who's never off-side or the sprinter who never beats the gun.

Once the basic action and feelings are established we can begin on the scrum-half/hooker tie up. This is critical and there's never a week that we don't work on it. The first point to be decided is the inclination of the long axis of the ball to the midline of the tunnel. (The long axis must, of course, be parallel to the ground though I've known wily scrum-halves who fed the ball left hand down, bouncing the ball towards their hooker.) Unless the hooker is much more comfortable with a 90° or 180° presentation, there's everything to be said for 45°, with the front point aimed towards the hooker – unless the opposing hooker gets right beyond the ball, any contact he makes with it will be in our favour. The second point is to determine how far into the tunnel the scrum-half should aim to pitch it. This is a matter for the hooker to decide in the light of experience. If it's too far in, the opposing hooker should have less trouble in reaching it; nevertheless most scrum-halves don't put it adequately far in. It's useful to give the scrum-half something to aim at in practice sessions – a mark on the ground under the prop's shoulder line, at the intersection with the right side of his neck, is a good starting point. This is a help to the scrum-half, and it gives the coach an essential check on what is happening: very few scrum-halves can pitch the ball on a given point. It's helpful if he gets into the habit of looking precisely at the point where he wants it to pitch, and he must work on the length till he's accurate.

The flick straight of the lower leg and the draw-back are as continuous as possible. One of the most common faults of hookers is that the draw-back is virtually non-directional. You'll often find that the striking foot comes back against the non-striking foot. This results in shallow strikes with the ball hitting the non-striking foot. The follow-through of the striking foot must be straight to the no. 8. I stand behind the prop – for a practice like this you work only with the front row against a scrum-machine – and show the hooker my hands along an arc from the middle of the tunnel to a line behind his support foot: he has to put

## Breaking from a Wheel

Being wheeled can be to your advantage, provided you break at the right moment: the opposing back-row is wheeled away from its defensive position, and the scrum-half is left to cope with the opposing back-row. But what is admirable about this London Irish break out is the acceleration of Ryan Strudwick. His forward lean allows a full extension of his leg, ankle and foot, which in turn exploits to the full the power available. All pace is valuable, but pace over the first 5–10 metres, in attack or defence, can be critical. Imagine him upright, and you'll see how similar his position is to take-off in the long-jump, which, repeated, is a typical training exercise. Make every training sprint competitive, and announce that it's a selection criterion: hammer the idea of hitting the line and sprinting — look at Ryan's arm drive as well as his leg drive. He had the ball tucked in, but it's justified by the space and the speed. He has support, but I'd prefer to see the player on the right of the photo make more space: there's support behind to drive over the ball if necessary, but he may well be able to break into space.

the ball into my hands.

This is a very concentrated practice, and it's futile to keep players down for long. After two or three strikes we get them up and have a word or two, with the scrum-half, hooker, and props all contributing.

Striking against the head is a matter of depth, length, and strength. I put the ball on the ground rather further away and deeper than is likely in a match, and simulate the put-in by putting my hand on top of it. By keeping my hand on top of it, it's possible to increase the pressure against which the hooker has to draw the ball back. We can then move the ball to encourage greater depth and length of strike. This kind of practice so closely resembles that of the hooker situation in the match that the hooker will tend almost unconsciously to develop modifications that make him resemble a top-class hooker.

The basic reason for the emphasis on depth of strike against the head is that by striking deep, across behind his opponent's leg, the hooker may do enough to let his tight-head prop get a foot to the ball. If the ball can be checked, the tight-head prop has a real advantage over the opposing loose-head: he can set himself up with his left foot wide and his hips dropping in against his hooker so that his right foot is free to strike.

Given a player of adequate strength and reactions, with an aggressive and competitive temperament, you can make highly satisfactory hookers. We frequently have to do this for our team, and very frequently for our seven.

Hooking, in fact, is never simply a matter of form: there's got to be a concentration of will and effort by the entire front row to ensure our getting a little more than our fair share of the ball. They work together: it's a truism that a hooker is no better than his props. If they can put pressure on the opposing hooker, and on the opposing binding, life is that much easier for the hooker. And behind them the four men in the second row must concentrate in just the same way.

Equally, we need to equip our hooker to deal with the case where opposition pressure prevents him from striking from his normal position; in particular, when their front row are so low that they pin him in his starting position. The solution is for him to alter his starting position. He needs to get his left foot far enough back to let him lock his left knee, and approximately parallel to the line of put-in. This lowers his hips, and clears the way for an effective strike. It also allows him to withstand direct pressure from the opposing hooker. He should work on increasing flexibility at the crotch to preserve his depth of strike.

If the opposing hooker is 'lying across', with both feet extended towards the put-in, he should exert downward pressure with his right shoulder: his opponent's position leaves him very vulnerable to that pressure.

## BACK ROW AT THE SCRUMMAGE: ATTACK AND DEFENCE

One fundamental aim of moves in the backs is to set up a handling attack in the forwards. If you can get your pack moving forwards in space with the opposing pack forced to chase them you have created one of the strongest possible attacking situations – the heavy overload. For this you need to involve as many of your pack as possible, to have created in them a keen appreciation of width and depth, and to have brought their handling to a high level. To ensure success they must also be adept at moving from the handling situation to the maul or ruck.

The forwards, however, must be capable of initiating their own attacks. As in defence, you must have encouraged the scrum-half to see himself as being in some phases of the game a member of the back row, and the front five to see themselves as an extension of the back row. The basic reason for the breakdown of back row moves is that they don't get adequate support or adequately quick support. The pack must strike as a pack, just as, in defence, they hunt as a pack. When you practise back row attacks, therefore, you must bring the rest of the pack into them; you must move to the whole pack situation as soon as the back row action has been established.

Unlike attacks by the three-quarters, moves by the forwards must be worked out in principle rather than in detail. It's even more important, therefore, since they are working initially in fairly restrictive situations, to emphasise the need for individual effort, to encourage them to beat or at least wrong-foot an opponent, and to get them supporting intelligently. There's even less hope of their 'going through the motions' of a move and succeeding, than there is with the backs.

### Attack from the scrummage

#### Relieving pressure from the opposing drive and wheel

With the increased use of eight-man drives, getting the ball is sometimes an embarrassment. The scrum is wheeled and the scrum-half finds himself with problems. The back row can relieve the pressure in two ways.

**1** *By the no. 8 feeding the ball back to the scrum-half* who stands a couple of yards behind the scrum. The left flanker and the right flanker give the no. 8 as much protection as they can. The no. 8 gets his feet closer to the scrum and his left foot under his body so that his knees are bent and he's reasonably stable. As his head emerges for the scrum, he picks up the ball, and turns clockwise to feed the scrum-half.

**2** *By developing an attack to the left.* Normally back row moves have gone to the right – away from the opposing scrum-half on your own put-in. The development of the wheel, however, has made it not only necessary but desirable that the back row should be able to break left, able that's to say, not only to relieve pressure from the wheel but to turn it to your advantage. Those with long memories – and especially Scotsmen with long memories – will remember the days when the pack in possession actively tried to create a wheel with the object of outflanking the bulk of the opposing pack, moving them round to a position where they could contribute less effectively to defence, where they were no longer able easily to get between the ball and their line. The theory is identical for any back row break with the wheel; the difference lies in playing the ball on the ground, or in the hands.

*The ball on the ground*
The ball must be checked at the feet of the left lock. The wheeling action of the scrum allows him to get his head up with the ball at his feet. He will immediately be challenged by the opposing scrum-half, and his response is to push the ball left to the no. 8, the scrum-half, and the right flanker going round. The ball goes left into space before going forward. It's vital that each player fights to keep the ball under close control and that as soon as possible the rest of the pack take up a support pattern.

Dribbling is in danger of becoming a lost art. Yet it is one more weapon at the disposal of the complete player, and there are times when it can prove invaluable.

*Handling*
This is essentially a use of the same movement with the ball in his hands. The no. 8 moves to channel one. The ball comes back to the no. 8, who holds it at his feet – better, at his knees. He needs to get his left foot far forward under his centre of gravity to let him pick up the ball in balance. He turns clockwise to feed the scrum-half or right flanker. As soon as the no. 8's head emerges from the scrum, the scrum-half (who has been giving him what protection he can) gets out to the left to support the right flanker's drive. The right flanker has to take the ball at speed. He must wait till he sees the ball in the no. 8's hands. As with all back row breaks he's got to do the running, and the rest of the pack must be in support positions immediately.

## Attack from a heel against the head

Provided the actual heel is fast and accurate, taking the ball against the head is potentially the best possible situation for attacking from the base of the scrum. Given the fast heel, the scrum-half or no. 8 ought always to go for the break.

The initial movement is away from the opposing scrum-half – to the left. Any wheel on the scrum is then to the attackers' advantage, since it will tend to take the opposing back row to the attackers' right, and will make it easier for the no. 8 to get his head up and move forward. The quick heel should also preserve some of the depth in the opposing three-quarters, allowing a freer development of the attack.

The basic forms of the attack will differ according to whether the scrum-half or the no. 8 initiates it. For speed in getting the ball into space the scrum-half has every advantage – he doesn't have to control the ball, get into balance, get his head up, pick up the ball, and disentangle himself from the scrum. His best line of running, provided he's moderately quick, is flat – across the face of the fly-half and inside-centre, to whom he can offer dummy switches – and forward to link with his outside-centre.

The no. 8 cannot hope to move with such pace. His best bet is to go forward, draw any defender near the scrum and feed the scrum-half and right flanker on the outside. The left flanker will probably not be in a position to help directly, but he can cover behind. Once again, the whole pack must try to give width and depth in support. The move is complete only when the entire pack are driving forward.

### Attack when the opposing pack are under pressure

Broadly speaking, the front five make back row attack profitable: if they keep the opposing pack on the back foot, it's much easier for our ball-carrier to get across the gain line. On the other hand, if we are under pressure, it's difficult to launch an attack with enough speed to reach the gain line.

Attack is possible from a stationary scrum, because the attacking side initiate the movement, and that gives them the edge.

The aim remains the same:

- to move the ball forward into space

- to force the opposing defence to commit itself close to the scrum, under conditions in which we ought to be able to retain possession.

It is rarely adequate for the no. 8 to surge to the right intent on keeping the ball to himself. Some of the dullest, least constructive, and least successful rugby I've seen comes from that resolve. The aim must be to set up a player moving into space, who can pose a real threat to the opposition: our minimum requirement is to stretch their defence, and retain possession. Essentially, then, we're looking at trying to overload their immediate defence, on either side of the scrum.

Moving right takes us away from the opposing scrum-half, but into any wheel on the scrum; moving left turns that wheel to our advantage – the wheel opens up ground on our left – but entails facing the opposing scrum-half in the early stages of the move. But we have to develop and establish means of doing both: there's too much to be gained from attack close to the tactical point to let difficulties stand in our way. Successful attack can limit the entire opposition's back division plans for defence; and if we do break through, we've bypassed their forwards, who are effectively taken out of defence.

The team immediately available for the overload consists of the no. 8 and the scrum-half, plus any player coming from deep – e.g. winger, full-back, fly-half. The near flanker is limited in the contribution he can make: he has to wait for the ball to get ahead of him, and he has no acceleration zone to let him add momentum until the break has been made. However, he's well placed to act as a pivot – a player going wide can flick the ball back into him, and he can redistribute it to a runner coming at pace from deep. The scrum-half, too, can act as pivot – going out flat to the right (or slightly back if more time is needed), turning to face the no. 8's pass, and turning a further 90° to watch the striker run for space inside or outside him. The striker might be fly-half, full-back, or right wing, depending on space available, or any combination of that trio, or in midfield, a centre.

But the standard break is into a blind-side, where our right wing has gone wide to encourage their left wing to leave a wide channel inside him, with the scrum-half getting into that channel to take a pass from the no. 8. The no. 8 seeks to draw the first defender before putting the scrum-half away.

The timing for a move like this is as follows:

- scrum-half calls the move, so that no. 8 and winger know what's on

- no. 8 allows minimum time for scrum-half to get comparatively wide and deep

- no. 8 breaks: he runs slightly out, and must pose a threat to the first defender

- scrum-half checks for a moment to let the no. 8 get a little further ahead. This means he can accelerate freely onto the ball – and his speed will be critical to the success of the move.

The background to the move is as follows:

- scrum-half has noted that we're more than holding our own up front, and that we're not being wheeled fast

- scrum-half has noted that there's enough space to make the move feasible.

These arrangements give the scrum-half his choice of a line of attack – he starts running straight – and the advantage of pace. But he needs support, and once the mechanics of the move have been established, the coach should work on getting the whole pack supporting at speed. Drop a marker where the first front five player handles in the action – then challenge them to make you move it closer to the point of origin. We don't want a ruck, we want positioning, passing and pace, but rucks may come, so build preparation for them into your practice.

This move becomes much harder to stop if you can involve a second runner outside the scrum-half. The first defender will be left for dead by a miss move from the no. 8.

A variation on this move depends on your scrum-half having really good acceleration, and going for a wide break – creating space inside him. At this point, your intensive handling practice comes into play – you've practised this situation in 'inverted looping'. But you can increase the scrum-half's pace substantially if:

- he lingers on the left of the scrum till he sees the ball at the no. 8's feet
- he runs back a couple of metres behind the no. 8 to create an acceleration zone
- he takes a pass from the no. 8 as he accelerates away from the scrum.

Moves to the left are made easier if the no. 8 shifts to the left, into space between and behind the left flanker and left lock. This allows the hooker to use the easiest and fastest channel for his strike. As the scrum wheels, and it's an advantage if it does, it rotates the opposing right flanker away, and opens up more space for attack – the no. 8 picks up and turns to prevent the opposing scrum-half getting at the ball. He'll be harder to handle if his knees are flexed, and his feet apart in echelon. He looks for support from the right flanker who will decide whether to set up a maul, or run into space. The scrum-half should have dropped into space on the left to support the right flanker if he chooses to run.

Near the opposing line, especially if the scrum has wheeled, it's possible for the no. 8 to dummy to the right flanker and pivot anti-clockwise inside the opposing scrum-half to drive for the line.

It's a little more difficult to feed the scrum-half, out to the left, direct, and let the right flanker support him on the inside – the equivalent of the variation on the basic right-hand attack described above – but it's a useful variation.

In all back row moves, be alive to the possibility of bringing in a high-speed strike from among the backs. The obvious one is a quick feed direct from no. 8 to the right wing close to the opposing line, with the scrum-half positioned to draw in the opposing winger as the most likely receiver of the pass. And he can feed direct to that winger cutting back behind the scrum on a line attacking the opposing fly-half.

There's a great deal more about back row attack in *Think Rugby*. Such attacks are going to be increasingly important in the foreseeable future: work to exploit the opportunities they offer.

The most economical way of setting up a practice situation is to set up a scrum with both sides locked and feed a ball to both sides – who then both attack to their right or to their left. This creates a virtually unopposed practice. Once the basic form of the attack is established, ask for variety in passing and running lines and gradually get the whole pack to handle, and once they're doing that lead up to a maul or ruck. Then you can go back to using one ball and setting up one team as attackers, one as defenders. You can condition this so that the defenders think first of position – e.g. make it only two-handed touch. If the packs are not evenly matched you can keep both packs in the locked position and get them to wheel as you direct.

The temptation is for the odd player to try too much – emphasise that it's basically a support exercise, and that the usual support priorities apply: speed into position, use of width and depth, variety of passing, variety of running.

Each session should end with at least a few runs in earnest: it's pointless leaving the players with the feeling that if they just go through the moves they'll be successful.

### The secondary drive

An excellent device for getting the pack moving forward is the secondary drive. On your own put-in, there's every advantage in locking against the initial drive – but it precludes the pack's moving forward. Once their initial drive has been absorbed, and the ball is safely at the no. 8's feet, a concerted effort can start the pack moving forward. We use the no. 8 to call 'ready, ready, ready . . . now', and the whole pack puts everything into a drive. Near the opposing line this has led to some beautifully controlled push-over tries.

### Immediate defence at the scrummage

Defence by the pack as a whole is dealt with on p. 291. It's worthwhile, though, emphasising here the need for complete clarity about the immediate actions of the scrum-half and back row when the ball is lost in the tight. It's vital to prevent the opposition getting the ball over the gain line close to the scrum, and highly desirable that the ball never gets in front of the opposing back row close to the scrum. Attacks in that area must be snuffed out at once – and that calls for clear thinking, immediate action, and speed over the first few yards. In this area it's imperative that defence be aggressive – that you go to meet them and knock them down before they get started. You won't go far wrong if you imagine that the off-side line is your goal line: you mustn't get off-side, but you must tackle as far ahead of it as possible.

Your actions, however, must be the result of a decision. Simply to go forward when the ball is already on its way to fly-half is futile – it cuts down your effectiveness in cover. For the same reason, a flanker never goes right round the opposing pack in pursuit of the ball – he comes back behind his own pack and concentrates on getting across between the ball and his line. Try always to avoid being out-flanked, so that you're chasing the ball from behind.

Your tackling has got to be completely reliable, and hard enough to shake up whoever you tackle: imagine he's two men thick, and try to hit the second one. Back row forwards once had access to the head-on tackle – by far the most effective one – at scrums, when they could break when they wished and get out on the reciprocal of the attacking player. That allowed you to drive up at the opponent and put him over backward, effectively checking the momentum of attack. Your side-tackle now has to be equally robust: knock him out of his line of run and hope to dislodge the ball when you do it. You can move wide from a scrum if you're actually behind your own goal line, but that's a choice of evils – drop out and you simplify the push-over try. However, at rucks and mauls you still employ the head-on: read the section on p. 166, and incorporate it in your practices on a regular basis.

The actions of the other two will depend to a great extent on where the scrum is taking place and their estimate of where the attack is likely to take place. Their normal distribution from a midfield scrum is aimed at getting two defenders on each side of the scrum – the near flanker with the scrum-half; the no. 8 with the far-side flanker. If, however, there's a blind-side, these two players may recognise that a single defender can cope with an attack there, and one go across to reinforce the open-side and get into better covering position.

In midfield flankers drive forward if and only if there are signs of an attack aimed at that area; if the ball is going wide, the great aim is to get into the cover pattern.

Two situations create real problems for the back row in defence (and open up excellent possibilities for the back row in attack): the heel against the head, and our pack going backward. The second is too important to be left to chance remedies. If the opposing pack can get the ball and still move forward you have no option but to use an eight-man shove. Losing the ball on your own put-in calls for immediate action by the back row, and more especially the right flanker and no. 8. They must cover the probable attack close to the scrum on their right.

The back row is one of the most important mini-teams within the team. Each member must be capable of sustained concentration and be a habitual reader of the game. Each must be confident of support from the rest. They must talk to each other, off and on the field. The coach can aid this by making the defensive plan clear to them and working through defensive situations. Get two back rows, and two sets of halves, and set them up as for a scrum. The coach stands in the middle of the 'scrum', feeds the ball, and arranges for 'wheels'. The attackers run through attacking possibilities using the back row and halves, and the defenders go through their response – using two-handed touch instead of tackling. The coach ensures that it works realistically, legally, and intelligently. The next stage will derive from full-out scrummaging practice – each scrum that's suitable ending with a back row break and calling for back row defence. It's obviously important that any player likely to come into the team in the back row must

BACK ROW IN DEFENCE

1. Close to the scrum - immediate aims : a pincer, two on each side

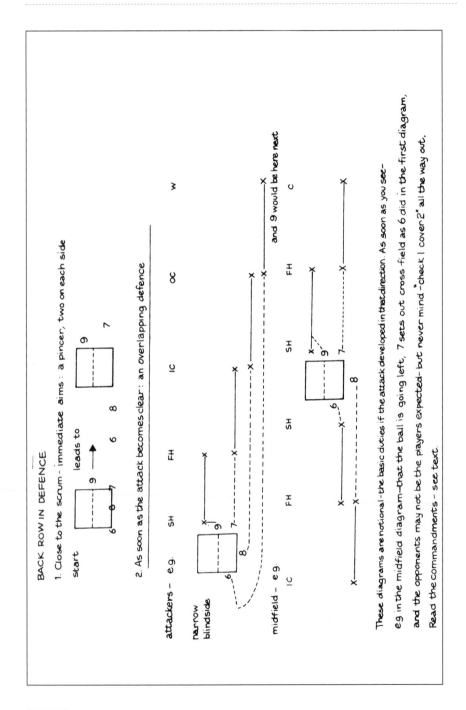

start        leads to

2. As soon as the attack becomes clear : an overlapping defence

attackers - e.g.

narrow
blindside

midfield - e.g.

and 9 would be here next

These diagrams are notional - the basic duties if the attack developed in that direction. As soon as you see -
e.g. in the midfield diagram - that the ball is going left, 7 sets out cross-field as 6 did in the first diagram,
and the opponents may not be the players expected - but never mind - "check I cover, 2" all the way out.
Read the commandments - see text.

know the complete plans in attack and defence and these practices are a step towards ensuring it.

## LINE-OUT

The line-out has long been a problem area for the law-makers, and this is reflected in the difficulties encountered by the players, the referees, and the coaches. The basic objectives of line-out are to bring the ball back into play, to clear the field for subsequent attack, and to involve a different set of skills for the players. The legislators recognise the second objective by limiting the length of the line and the approach of the backs; they would improve it by confining all the forwards, whether or not they are involved in the line-out, to the 15-metre area. Their main difficulty lies in reconciling the third and the first: their efforts to create a straight jumping competition have led to difficulties in obtaining good ball. If they focused simply on the need to get good ball and encouraged all positive attempts to do so – e.g. lifting, double banking, blocking – and penalised all negative, spoiling play, the situation would be easier for all concerned. As a polar alternative, they might simply give the non-offending side a tap penalty on the 15-metre line, with forwards on both sides confined to the 15-metre area – a substantial inducement to keeping the ball in play.

Since that last paragraph was first written, its first suggestion has become legitimised. Supporting and lifting fade into one another, and it's evident that referees have been briefed to concentrate on line-out objectives (see above) rather than the letter of the law.

We have to recognise that getting good ball from the line-out is becoming more and more critical to the winning of matches. As teams become increasingly efficient at getting the ball on their put-in, and getting it back when they take it in to ruck or maul, the ability to get a little more than your fair share of possession at the line-out can alter the whole balance of the match. This means that coaches have to devote more time to improving their jumpers – no matter how big they may be – and more thought to how they can get the ball when the opposition jumpers are dominant. This doesn't, of course, mean that the coach can give less weight to the team's scrummaging. Imagine your scrum being monotonously rolled off your ball, and the havoc that would cause to possession and morale. You need to concentrate on both – which means working smart as well as hard, to do more in the time available.

Getting good ball is the prime concern of the coach. Good ball means:

- giving the ball to the scrum-half when, where, and at the pace he wants it

- being able to catch the ball and bring it down to set up a dynamic maul.

The fact that you can catch the ball with an aided jump shouldn't blind you to the advantages of delivering to the scrum-half from the top of the jump. You need to keep the opposition guessing to slow down their response.

So far as the fly-half is concerned, it's to his advantage, if he wishes to set up a handling movement, to be relieved of pressure from the back of the line-out. For a given length of scrum-half pass, the fly-half and the line outside him will derive more advantage if the ball is thrown long than if it is thrown short (see p. 199). This has to be balanced against the difficulty of throwing accurately over a longer distance when weather conditions are less than ideal, and the need to guarantee protection for the scrum-half.

## The throw

It's impossible to organise an effective line-out if the throw is inaccurate. There's obviously a range of acceptable tolerance, but the coach must be coaching for pin-point accuracy.

Conventional non-thinking prescribes the hooker for this job, possibly on the grounds that it gives him a slightly better chance of avoiding injury, possibly because hookers in the past may have been slightly less large than the rest of the pack. In fact, throwing accurately is in part a talent, and other things being equal the coach should be looking for the most talented thrower.

The only way to give the thrower some feedback on the accuracy of his throws is to give him in practice a fixed mark to throw at. If your jumpers do an assisted sargent jump beside a wall and mark the spot with chalk, the thrower can retreat the requisite distance – 5m plus 1m for every place back in the line – and he can then set about learning to throw accurately. You could, presumably, do this outside but the basic work is best done indoors.

As with place kickers, *concentration* is paramount: both have as much time as they wish beforehand, but only one attempt. The coach may take the thrower through quantity practice initially, but he's got to end up with a limited number of throws that are accurate. And, of course, the practice must end actually throwing to the jumpers – unopposed – and getting feedback from them.

The style of throw is obviously less important than the results obtained. Once he has settled on a style, the thrower will probably stay with it, but it's not a bad thing at first to get him to experiment with the different possibilities. The basic styles are as follows.

*Two-handed throws*
   **a)** Lob from below the waist: this style of throw has a range of disadvantages – e.g. the jumper doesn't see it early; it lacks variety of trajectory – but it is very straight, and is useful for throws over the top of a short line.

   **b)** Soccer throw-in style: this is completely unfashionable but looks as if it could be easily and quickly developed.

*One-handed throws*

**a)** New Zealand bowling action: this allows all the necessary variations, and presents a fairly easy ball to catch.

**b)** Push action: the ball is balanced on the throwing hand, long axis at right angles to the hand, in contact at the base of the fingers, with the middle finger up the seam – a very good, accurate, method of throwing.

**c)** Orthodox spin: the ball is held near the end, with fingertips along a seam to help create the spin – very accurate once it has been mastered but easier if the thrower has large hands and the ball is dry.

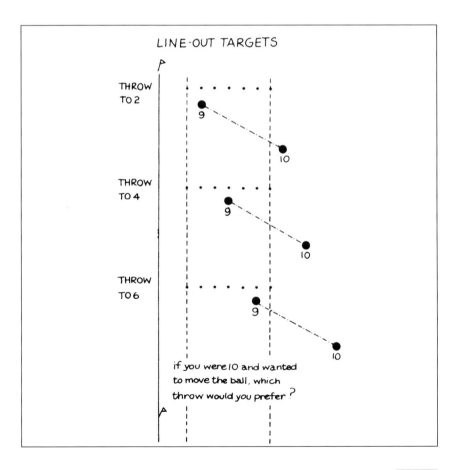

## Coaching the thrower

It is possible to apply the simple mechanical model for passing and kicking that we've already looked at (see p. 67) to throwing-in. Once we've established the point on the basketball backboard at which our jumper wants to receive the ball we go back an appropriate distance (5m + 1m for each position back in the line) and stick a piece of tape on the floor. That's our touch line.

The thrower can now experiment to find the right trajectory. Once that's established, you can begin to advise him on how to be consistent. The key element of the model is to maintain contact with the ball on that line as far as we can. The line will be above the horizontal, so the body has to lift into the throw. Leading this will be the left side which straightens, the left shoulder which mustn't drop (though it may appear lower than the right shoulder), and the hips which keep moving forward as long as possible without the thrower's losing balance. Once the hips stop moving, the chest begins to drop, and it's impossible to stay in contact with the ball on the line of flight. A symptom of this is loss of power, and difficulty in throwing to the back of the line. If the left shoulder drops, it will intensify the inbuilt tendency to swing the ball to the left.

You can give simple advice, starting from the feet. Initially, the weight should be on the back foot. The left foot is out to the front and slightly out to the left to avoid blocking. The whole movement starts with the right knee pushing the hips forward. This starts the weight transfer, and ensures that the chest is up. Keep the head back. As the weight moves forward lift with the left side and rotate the shoulders as the hand goes up the line of flight. Keep the eyes focused on the target.

If there isn't adequate power, suggest the thrower starts with his feet together and steps onto his left foot as he begins the throw (everything else follows as in the sequence above). If the ball moves to the right, the thrower can correct it by applying slight pressure with the little finger on the throwing hand.

There are two basic trajectories: flat, and lobbed. The flat throw is basically for the front of the line. The lobbed throw aids the high jumper – it allows him to go up and meet it. The thrower should be able to adjust between the throw in front of the jumper, and the lob that comes down just behind him – so providing every jumper with alternatives against his opponent.

It's possible for our front jumper to gain an advantage by taking off before his opponent. There are two basic mechanisms for this, both of which the thrower must master. In the first, the thrower takes up position with the ball in front of him, brings it back towards his shoulder and, without any pause, goes into the throw. This allows the jumper to take off while the hand is still moving back, and the ball is immediately whipped, flat, into his spread fingers. In the second, the thrower holds the ball near his shoulder, with his arm ready cocked to throw. The signal for the throw is the first movement of the jumper's feet. Both methods should be used so that the opponent cannot be sure of what to expect. This

## Gloucester make sure of line-out ball

Look at Ian Jones' left hand, and the pressure it has put on Scott Murray. It has stopped him tilting his shoulders, which would give him several inches more reach; it has moved his upper body backwards, destroying the lift from his front supporter, and Scott's face and eyes show that he has things on his mind other than the ball. Jones' lifters are admirably close together — look at their elbows. This means enhanced potential lift. The front lifter could get more lift if his hands — like those of Murray's front lifter — were lower on Jones' thighs, but perhaps the jumper feels better balanced with pressure at about the same level, front and back. His own shoulder-tilt and arm-stretch are admirable. Note how his right hand is behind the ball — playing down the line: he wants to stop it and control it before he delivers it. His rear lifter has moved round naturally, following Jones's right leg — and this offers more protection to the jumper.

kind of throw also has the advantage that any move by our jumper forces the opponent to come forward, so that he's less capable of dealing with the lob (to our jumper going back, *or to the player behind him*).

In throwing to the jumper, the thrower must be absolutely clear about the line-out signals, and concentrate on that point in the air through which he intends to throw the ball.

Once he has thrown he must be immediately ready to take part in the game again – basically, to get into the middle of the 5-metre area and be ready to close it up against attacks around the front. He can be used as an attacking player if from a short throw the ball is pushed back down to him. However, keenness to take up the defensive position mustn't be allowed to interfere with the accuracy of the throw: finish the throw in balance, then nip into position.

On the opposition throw, he should position himself to get a clear run at the opposing scrum-half or the loose ball from a throw to the front. From a long throw he should check that the opposition are not bringing the ball back blind before he sets off on normal covering. This is particularly important near his own try-line.

## Jumping – to facilitate lifting

The key notion for every jumper is *control*. In many ways it's better to have no ball than bad ball. However he deals with the ball – catching, throwing from the top of the jump, deflecting with the inner hand or both hands – his success is to be judged less on the fact that he got to the ball than that he delivered it straight to the scrum-half or to a receiver in the line.

He won't get to the ball unless he watches it. 'Keep your eyes on the ball' is a dead cliché: he's got to see the stitches on it. More than that, he's got to feel 'That's my ball', and that nothing is going to stop him getting to it. Concentration is the name of the game.

He makes contact with his hand. The key idea here is that he plays down the line rather than hooking – that he makes contact with the palm of his hand at right angles to the throw rather than parallel to it. Real control begins when he looks for the ball and stops it, looks for the scrum-half and gives it. The sequence is, of course, continuous and extremely rapid – but it's the consciousness of the scrum-half's waiting hands and the need to pilot the ball there that makes for accuracy. Get the scrum-half to show the jumper his hands.

The hand that makes contact – and even if he *can* catch it, one hand will make contact first – has got to be relaxed, but in a strong position. Strength comes from the ability to keep the arm slightly bent – a straight arm is a weak arm, easily displaced. The aim in jumping, therefore, is not to get the hand high, but to get the *active shoulder* high, so that the hand is high but strong. Concentrate on that shoulder.

*Power* in the jump – the ability to resist body contact or pushing hands – comes from getting the body mass moving in as well as up. This happens either by getting the shoulders in on the line of throw, or by getting the hips in.

*Reach* – how high above his take-off point our jumper can make effective contact with the ball – can be improved if we provide practical answers to two questions:

- how do we increase the height to which he can raise his centre of gravity?

- how do we adjust his upper body position to get his active hand as high as possible above that?

In the first question, the critical factor, long term, is the improvement of strength. It's no coincidence that Javier Sotomayor, the first man to clear 8ft (2.44m) in the high jump, squat-lifts more than three times his bodyweight: he is reputed to lift 660lb (300kg). Virtually every sport has become a power sport, and the ambitious rugby player has to build weight training/power lifting into his training schedules. But it is not a form of training to be undertaken without guidance: it pays to seek qualified assistance.

Other forms of strengthening should appear in every player's preparation – bounding, one-footed and two-footed; hopping down a line of hurdles; two-footed rebound jumps; uphill sprints: all of these will contribute not just to jumping but to running speed.

Repetition jumping at a basketball backboard, employing your full take-off technique, and aiming at maintaining your height over as many jumps as possible up to forty, linked with a diver's belt strapped round your waist and loaded to the point where you can just put your hand flat on the backboard, will certainly improve your whole jumping ability.

But whatever strength you possess must be applied effectively: you must have a clear grasp of the principles behind jumping high. All of the evidence suggests that we should create as much horizontal speed before take-off as our limited space allows. The first suggestion, then, is to maximise that space. Start at the back and move forward with your rear lifter towards your front lifter.

The second suggestion is that you adopt a form of shift that throughout allows a slight upward movement of the centre of gravity. This is intensified sharply, of course, at the moment of take-off. Start with your weight back and low, so that you can move smoothly forward and up into your jump. If you let your centre of gravity drop appreciably, you have to expend energy on checking the drop, and more in compensating for it.

Your aim is to reach your take-off point with your legs still slightly flexed and your centre of gravity moving fast forward and up. As you touch down before take-off, your leg muscles are stretched and – providing that stretch isn't prolonged – produce their maximum energy. Speed is the essence of the take-off: if you linger, your energy is lost. The overall aim is to produce an athletic performance, crisp and controlled, rather than ponderous.

The shape we want to be in the moment after take-off is clear: the trunk upright, the upper arms at shoulder height, and both legs fully extended, as nearly vertically under the body as our tactical purpose allows. This full extension of the legs is important: from hip to toe the muscle groups are propelling us upward. You learn this from bounding. One exercise I found useful some forty years ago was hopping over the high jump crossbar at 5ft 3in, off a three-pace run.

Provided the basic principles are obeyed, the exact nature of the shift is less important. The orthodox method is to have the near foot well forward, and to shift both feet into a two-footed take-off, with the rear foot moving fast to catch up with the front one. This may limit interference by the opposition, and should be effective in conserving upward movement since the near foot shift is short and there is less tendency to sink. We've shown, however (Richard Tong, 1988), what I'd long suspected: there is a gain in lift if we reverse the position of our feet, so that our near foot is back. This allows a single, longer stride that takes the near foot to the take-off point, with the off-side foot shifting to join it in a two-footed take-off. It showed a five per cent improvement in height gained. As you might expect, this style was favoured by those not accustomed to the orthodox take-off. It has tactical advantages that I'll comment on later.

To make the most of our improved jumping – whichever shift we use – we need to lift off from the optimum take-off point. This, ideally, would be directly under the ball – from the midline of the line-out. In practice, it should be as near to that as the referee allows. The referee with qualms about this should consider that it in fact decreases the chance of mid-air collisions – which increases with displacement of the take-off point from the line of throw. One beauty of the reversed feet take-off is that it makes the step into the desired take-off area very easy and very fast. A second advantage is that it allows you to get decisively in front of your opponent. (A third, which I'll deal with here, though it isn't a technical consideration, is that it can be used to disguise the intention to jump. The jumper can stand virtually square on to the line, and move directly into the jump . For the jumper at two in the line, this means that he can fake the start of a peel. Just as important, it allows the prop at one in the line to move directly from his lifting posture into a jump for the ball. The jumper at one has not been adequately utilised in the northern hemisphere, as he is in New Zealand. As an occasional manoeuvre, it's well worth working on.)

So far we've examined how to improve the actual spring of the jumper. Let's now turn to the second point – how to get the maximum reach once we've got the centre of gravity as high as we can. The most obvious advice is to practise the one-handed stop and push. By going up one-handed you can tilt the shoulder to give an extra two to four inches of reach. It's tempting in unopposed practices to let your jumper, especially if he's big, catch two-handed, but it's futile. Always, you should practise the difficult technique against the moment when you'll need it: he'll meet someone just as big as he is, or with a better spring, or superior lifters, and then he's going to need the one-handed, controlled contact. That needs practice.

You will gain another inch automatically, as the lowering of the other arm affects the position of the centre of gravity. You can gain at least another inch by working on your shoulder mobility. You can, in all, possibly gain another six inches on reach simply by working on this method. That six inches gives you an edge on taking your own ball, even if your thrower can't often put it exactly in the area – you will be strong where you might have been overstretching – and it will certainly pay off on your opponent's throw.

Every jumper must have at least two variations to his jump. The basic variations are to get up in front of your opponent to meet the ball earlier than he does, and to vary that with a feint to go forward and an actual jump up behind him to take the ball lobbed over the top. To get the footwork right start with your feet side by side.

A third variation is desirable for the jumper at two in the line. If your opponent at the front of the line has a height advantage you may have to rely on a two-handed drive, forward and up, for the ball thrown hard and flat – a very vigorous action that calls not for wild abandon but extreme concentration, especially on getting your hands across the line of throw. If the front man in the opposing line doesn't get his arms up to prevent this it's probably because he reckons his team get the advantage from your lack of control. A timed jump is a far better bet. Work out with your thrower your strongest position going forward and up for the ball. You then work out with him the timing that allows you to jump – getting up before your opponent who is waiting for the throw – and the thrower to whip the ball into you in that strongest position. Once you've done this, your opponent is forced to react to any forward motion and becomes vulnerable to the lob you take behind your starting point.

At the back of the line even more care is needed in dealing with the ball, since if it isn't controlled your opponents can get to it easily. A further complication is that the ball is a long time in the air and the opponent jumping against you has equal opportunity to react to its flight. The throw, too, will be less accurate than those to the front and middle of the line. As is typical of back row situations, you must rely to a great extent on your own instinct. As deputed jumper you must commit yourself to the ball: all the general principles already stated apply to you. You've got to work on your jumping as carefully as the locks. If you have any problems, push the ball forward towards the middle of the line-out where there's maximum cover for it. For the peel your aim is to get your hand to the ball, stop it, and let it drop on your side of the line – don't pull it down, let it drop. This gives the first ball-carrier the maximum chance of catching it. Try to make sure it drops where your line still offers protection – in front of you – so that the ball-carrier can concentrate on catching it without distraction from the opposition.

It's customary to station your jumpers at two, four, and one from the end of the line. Two offers minimum chance of interference by the opposition – a jumper at one will always be suspected of taking the ball before it reaches the 5-metre line; four gives excellent protection for the scrum-half; one from the end allows your jumper to concentrate on the jump, confident that the man behind him will cover any mistakes. Most jumpers will wish to specialise in a single position. Broadly speaking, the jumper with more spring will do best at four; the jumper with more aggression at two. However, it's desirable that they should be able to switch positions – simply to keep the opposition guessing, or to take one of your jumpers out of a situation where he is being unduly pressured. An effective variation is occasionally to put all three together, all jumping for the ball – this creates a power block when the opposition are making contact a little early, and lessens the need for absolute accuracy when conditions make it difficult to throw with precision. Having a fourth unsuspected jumper makes this even more effective. If, for example, you have one other forward capable of getting up and catching you can use the grouping of the three jumpers at the end of the line to distract attention from the short ball to him at the front of the line. If an opposition jumper stays at the front, then you throw to the back.

It is, of course, highly desirable that at least occasionally you should be able to catch the ball cleanly and hold it. For a long time this was a vain hope for the great majority of jumpers – an opponent going up one-handed had an advantage that made a clean catch unlikely. But now clean catches on your throw, with the help of lifters, are more likely than not.

As I'll show you later, however, the lone unlifted jumper still has an important part to play; indeed, he may now have a better chance of making a clean catch. If that's not on, and he can't be sure of directing the ball to the scrum-half, his best bet is probably to push the ball back towards forwards supporting from the front of the line.

This is useful at all times but especially if the ball is wet. It allows you to use a one-handed jump, but keeps the ball under better control, and closer to your line. The usual target is a designated forward, coming from near the back of the line. You certainly don't want to take a player from the middle of your line – that's an invitation for an opponent to come through, and it leaves a gap which is difficult to fill. Indeed, whenever I've had a really competent scrum-half I've preferred to concentrate on creating a very tight line, and letting him deal with it. If you are going to employ a sweeper, you should consider using the first man in your line. The great advantage he brings is that he's in front of your jumper. The jumper needn't try to gauge where an unseen colleague is and attempt to give him the ball by some form of extra-sensory perception. This is strictly in line with the suggestion I make later about the scrum-half starting on the 5-metre line to offer the same advantage, a suggestion which is now virtually standard practice. And consider the possibility of having your blind-side flanker at one, as sweeper and occasional jumper.

It is occasionally possible for the jumper to give the ball direct to someone not in the line – but he's got to expect it. The jumper at two may well find it possible to push the throw straight back to the thrower, and near the opposing line this is well worth trying. Provided your own thrower expects it, it's much more effective on their throw – push the ball into the 5-metre area, straight towards touch, and let him run onto it while their thrower is still contemplating his throw.

## Coaching the jumper

For all line-out work I prefer to work indoors. This may not be possible for all coaches, but I'd certainly recommend that you try to get the use of a gymnasium. Once inside, what you need is basketball backboards. They provide that invaluable aid: immediate feedback on performance from a fixed target.

To improve the jumper's performance the coach must:

- set quality standards

- encourage him to improve his leg strength

- shape and maintain his technique

- put him in a situation where he gets personal feedback.

The most important criterion of success is the quality of ball he provides for the receiver – usually the scrum-half, but often a sweeper, or a forward setting up a peel. Until he accepts that as the qualifying criterion, with everything else simply a means to it, he isn't going to make real progress. After that, yes: he can take pride in his improvement in strength, in height attained, in power in the air, in speed into the jump, and so on. But all are means to that qualifying purpose.

Building strength is the only way to make a radical difference in jumping capacity. The coach's job is to provide guidance on how to acquire that strength and constant encouragement to work on it. Some of it, especially bounding and hopping, he can build in general conditioning sessions. But he cannot afford to spend much time supervising weight training personally. This has to be part of the player's responsibility to himself.

Establishing an effective form of jump, and monitoring its maintenance, is the coach's prime activity so far as the jumper is concerned. We've looked at the principles behind it, and we can now look at a typical coaching session – incidentally describing the last requirement, the provision of feedback. Wherever possible, we should be aiming for high work-rate from the players present. If we are going to concentrate on the jumper(s), we may aim at treating him/them in isolation while the rest of the forwards or the squad do something more valuable than standing by and listening. This is a prime example of what I've called a 'clinic' skill: it requires an intensive input irrelevant to many of the players. So this may take place while the rest of the players are engaged in a fitness session under the captain or, early in the evening, before the official session starts. You'll probably have all of your jumpers there, though, listening, learning, copying, acting as scrum-half and retrieving the missed ball, and you'll probably (not necessarily) want your thrower-in. Incidentally, who'd throw in if your regular got himself injured? It pays to be prepared.

We have the jumper, then, warmed up and ready to go. We place him in front of the backboard, and mark on the floor his take-off point. We can adjust this so that he has to jump forward as much as we want, say for a jump at two, or as little as we need for a jump at four or six, or one. We explain about getting the inside foot as close to the line of throw as possible, and about keeping the referee happy.

On the first couple of jumps, we ask him to hit the backboard with his open hand, encouraging him to hit it hard. This gets his hand in the right plane, at right angles to the line of throw. Remember: we want him to play a straight bat rather than an attempted hook. From then on, we ask him to go up just the same but to place his hand, fingers spread, as gently as he can against the backboard. As always, we aim to receive the ball firmly but gently. When we start throwing the ball to him we can reinforce this – and prepare the way for attacks close to the opposition goal line – by having him go up, meet the ball, and push it straight back to the thrower.

You can talk to him about the need for a strong, i.e. slightly bent, arm, and ask him to jump raising his inside shoulder as high as possible rather than simply his arm and hand. Once he has that, ask him to push the inside shoulder through towards the ball – which can make a difference of several inches in his reach forward. As I write, I'm thinking of the right arm and shoulder: always start off a learning process with what's easiest for the player – we want him as confident as possible.

There's something to be said for next introducing the alternative foot position – i.e. feet reversed from the orthodox. By doing this, you can make a clear break that renders the player more open to suggestions: he realises he doesn't know much about this! It's extremely simple. Jumping right-handed, he now has his right foot back, rather out of the line, and he is facing slightly into the line. His first step, onto the right foot, will be straight onto the take-off point: it should be flat and fast, and the left foot joins it for an immediate lift-off. Let him experiment with this. Encourage him to start with his weight further back and lower, and to be into the jump before his imaginary opponent can move. Get him to try different lengths of the first stride, and different splits between left foot position and right foot position, still keeping the same basic format. There's a lot that's down to personal preference within the scope of a given format.

You may achieve dramatic results from this phase of learning, but if you do it'll be luck. Whenever you make changes in a habitual skill you'll tend to get a lowering of performance while the player adapts to it and he isn't concentrating wholly on, for example, maximum height. However, introducing the new format gives you a chance to alter old habits without seeming to do so.

As soon as he's got the basic form, remind him about the drive up and forward of the shoulder. Encourage him to drive right off his toes in the search for full extension. If you've doubts, get him to do some bounding – challenge him to head (as in soccer) the basketball net off a three-stride run. Then ask him to do the same thing alongside the net, and place his hand on the board. Then go back into the one-step approach.

Explain that the idea isn't to make a radical change in his jumping style, but to equip him with a further possibility, and suggest how the new format can disguise a jump as a preparation for a peel. Then ask him to try the orthodox style again, but to incorporate what he's learned from the new.

By now your thrower, who's been busy elsewhere, should have arrived. You can immediately offer him an absolutely clear indication of the jumper's mean performance – a point to aim for on the backboard. He can then walk back the requisite distance, e.g. 7m for a throw to two (7 strides will make it just about right), 9m to four, 11m to six. You can then spend a moment or two just polishing his form on the lines, and suggest he can practise throws now any time he's in the gym.

When he starts throwing to the jumper, get the jumper going up, assisted, stopping the ball, pushing it back to the thrower. Talk about the shoulder, up and forward. Then introduce a scrum-half, who starts at the 5-metre line and moves as necessary to receive the ball in front of the jumper. The delivery system has to be directional: we don't want a vague flap, but a guided delivery. So, the jumper concentrates on the ball to the moment of impact, switches to the receiver, and directs the ball firmly (not hard) towards him.

This is difficult: be quick to praise, slow to anger. If it's 90% bad, praise him for the good 10%, and suggest a single amendment to the rest: don't overwhelm him with advice.

Keep at it, keep encouraging the player to improve his strength, to maintain his quality standards – and the best form of feedback is the response of the scrum-half, followed by higher reach on the backboard. If he believes that the ball is his by right, he'll improve.

Now: how would you adapt the backboard learning situation to the variation in which the jumper feints forward and goes back to receive the lob? Incidentally, I rarely have a straight competition between jumpers. I prefer when the lines come together to condition one side to concentrate on getting through, and let the other concentrate on their jumping and blocking.

## Making the most of supporters/lifters

It's eminently worthwhile going through the jumping education described above even if you know you can get your jumper higher with outside assistance. The very fact that lifting has been legitimised creates possibilities for the unexpected solo jumper, and there will certainly be times when a solo jumper has to tidy up when a throw or lift in front of him goes wrong. More radically, however, a good take-off by the intended receiver makes the job of the lifters much easier – it lets them apply force more efficiently, and gets the jumper into the air faster. So get him jumping as described above before introducing the supporters, and then use precisely the same set-up to practise it.

Effective lifting depends on two factors:

- the lifter's getting his knee bent so that he's able to apply lift early in the jump, and so that he can generate lift using larger muscle groups before smaller – lift with the legs, support with the arms

- the effort's being applied to a non-slip surface: non-slip pads on the base of the quads are best.

The closest analogy is probably weight-lifting's clean and jerk. As in all lifting, protect your back: get your hips forward fast, whilst the impulse of the jump is still effective, and drive with the spine vertical.

The application of support has to be timed by the jumper. If he is jumping straight up, this is signalled by a small preliminary bounce; if he is moving forward or back, his first foot movement must signal which so that the lifters can shift into position. In either case you need experiment and practice to work out the best compromise for your particular players.

Rendering aid like this can be applied to any player, anywhere in the line. At the moment, established jumpers continue to act as receivers largely because of their ball-contact skills, but you can see that, for example, a flanker might be an effective substitute: he's unexpected, less heavy, usually no less adept at handling. So, too, a flanker at the front of the line, with a prop lifting, is quite likely to create problems on the opposition throw, and be a useful variation on your own.

At the moment, too, there's a clear advantage to the prepared team. No doubt,

The key to success is organised movement. Decide on a basic unit – a number of steps – and stick to it. In A(1) the lifters can grip in the starting position, take three steps, and lift, in a rhythm established in practice. In A(2), the last man in the line is going to lift, and takes up position three paces behind the jumper. The set rhythm benefits not only the lifting unit but the thrower-in.

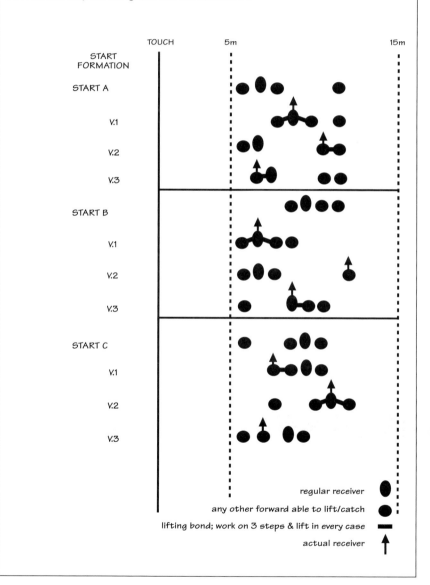

as lifting becomes the norm, that advantage will be eroded. At that point, the short line will come into its own, with movement creating the space needed to get clear possession. See the diagram on p. 211.

Provided your team is adequately rehearsed, the opposition are going to find it extremely difficult to respond in an effective way.

If you find yourself faced with effective lifting, you may not be able to compete in the air. The best bet is to be in first with a drive against the lifting group, and have a couple of forwards ready on the fringe to take out possible runners.

### Protecting the scrum-half

While the immediate lifters are protecting the jumper, the major concern of the rest of those in the line-out is to protect the scrum-half.

Failing a catch or a push-down to a supporting forward, which can lead to a normal maul situation with those on the outside tidying up, and the ball fed back when the scrum-half calls for it, the basic aim is to create a wall. This wall is designed to prevent the opposition following the ball in precisely the same way that a scrum, a maul, or a ruck is a more-or-less organised attempt to stop the opposition following the ball.

The first stage in forming the wall is that everyone stays in the line but moves towards the jumper with the aim of eliminating holes. Once again, this is broadly speaking harder for those behind the jumper than in front. It's got to be done quickly and that calls for concentration. You replace the open-mouthed gazing in the air by an organised movement towards the point to which the ball is thrown. You *compress towards the ball* so that you form a short, tight, line.

If you are using a player to tidy up – because, despite your efforts, the throwing and catching is not efficient, or because bad conditions, or destructive play by the opposition make it necessary – he gets out of the line at once. As I've outlined above, there's much more to be said for having a blind-side at one, and for making sweeping up one of his jobs. He's very well adapted to it, and from that position it's easier for the jumpers to guide the ball to him as he moves down the line exactly as the scrum-half does, but much closer. If you employ someone else, get him from the tail of the line to minimise the need for movement by the rest. He and he alone should go. I believe that the integrity of the line is first priority and that given the wall's protection the scrum-half should deal with the ball. I tend, however, to accept the players' judgement on this.

The players in the wall so far as possible are facing their opponents. Those at the ends have a special responsibility – shared by the thrower-in – to ensure that nobody comes round off-side, and you can't do that facing your scrum-half.

The wall is sealed by binding and the best binding is on the shirts of the players in front of you and behind you: get hold of a shirt.

All the above is simply a codification of practice. Like all the rest of the game, you approach as close to the positive mechanical idea as the referee allows.

## Signals

Signals imply decisions, and decision-making in the line-out is just as much a matter of judgement as in any other aspect of the game. Someone must be thinking ahead, looking for the greatest advantage, weighing the possibilities, and making decisions. Sometimes these are simplified by the quality of your jumpers; too often, however, absence of forethought leads to stereotyped, mechanical calls. The coach must select as decision-maker an intelligent player capable of concentrating and keeping the team's repertoire of throws clear in his mind. In most ways, the ideal position for him is at scrum-half: he, after all, has to deal with the bulk of the ball provided, he can see what's going on more clearly than anyone in the line, and he can communicate easily with the line and the thrower. He's also usually one of the earliest players to approach the position of the line-out, and is well placed, therefore, to call variations in the length of the line before it forms.

Whatever signals you use must be difficult for your opponents to break, and easy for your players to follow. They fall into two categories – visible and audible – and it's customary to provide as much distraction in the shape of irrelevant 'noise' as possible. Visual signals can be given by anyone that the whole line can see – normally the thrower or the scrum-half. Typical examples include:

- skin to skin – he rubs his hands together, or puts them on his knees

- skin to cloth – hands on shirt, shorts

- no contact – both hands on the ball; hands out waiting for the ball

- scrum-half's near foot pointing at thrower – throw to 2

- both feet pointing forward – throw to 4

- far foot pointing back – throw to back.

And, of course, you can alter the meaning to suit yourselves – from match to match, or half to half.

*Audible signals* are effective so long as it is possible to hear them. Once again, they come best from the scrum-half:

- number clusters – 11, 12, 13 – the key digit is, for example, the last in the first number, and you can use 1, 2, 3 for the front, middle, and back, or odd numbers, even numbers and zero in the same way

- letter shapes – curved letters: Orange; straight letters: Tangerine; blended letters: Peach – use them to designate jumpers

- number shapes – you can do the same: 0, 3, 8; 1, 4, 7; 2, 5.

All these signals have a single aim: to identify where the ball is to be thrown. But in a team confident of getting its own ball, there's no reason why other information should not be transmitted, e.g. where it's going and how it's to be used – caught and driven, straight off the top, pushed back to the thrower, setting up a peel, etc. Just don't confuse your own team.

The signals most difficult to crack, however, are those based on arbitrary groupings known to your team but not the opposition. This first occurred to me when coaching a regional team, drawn almost wholly from two clubs, against a touring team. We used the names of players in one club's 1st XV to denote the short throw, in the other's to denote the middle, and anything else for the end. This can easily be applied to the club situation: take any two moderately large, discrete groups known to the players and not known by the opponents and you're away. You use your signals, of course, in every line-out practice.

Your thrower-in is best placed to function as code-cracker on their throw – he can set himself up as an expert on codes, but he'll probably learn more from watching for the unconscious preparation of jumpers about to jump, than watching or listening to the thrower-in.

## Scrum-half positioning

Most scrum-halves stand about 2m back from the line-out. When there's doubt it's probably better to stand a little deeper – it's easier to come forward, than turn and come back.

They usually stand roughly opposite the third man in the line – concealing where the ball is going, but in easy touch with the main jumpers. There's a great deal to be said, however, for their starting on the 5-metre line, and following the ball down the line. This allows them to communicate easily with the thrower and the jumpers, offers a much better target for the jumpers to deliver the ball to, and starts them off facing infield where their partner can signal what he wants. For a two-handed scrum-half, it facilitates passing – they're moving in the direction of the pass; for a one-handed passer, it's fine on one side of the field, but will certainly slow down a preferred pivot pass on the other – he should examine dive-passing. For a pivot pass they're best positioned slightly behind the jumper and turned to face him. For kicking, too, they're better off standing still. But the essential thing is that they must be ready to deal with whatever happens as it happens: in balance, on a narrow base.

This positioning of the scrum-half at the line-out is now orthodox world-wide.

They must be prepared to play an active part in defence. It may be possible to share this, in bad conditions, with designated forwards – e.g. the thrower-in at the front, or one of the back row further back – but scrum-halves who refuse, for example, to go down on the ball are a real weakness in defence.

## Opposition throw-in

Too often line-out practices concentrate on the team's throw, often to the exclusion of practising methods against the opposition throw. Certainly our throw should get greatest emphasis – we must be looking to take our own ball – but the opposition will throw in just about as often as we do, and we need to take some of theirs.

On their throw they will tend to be defensive minded – concerned with protecting their jumper and scrum-half – rather than actively concerned with breaking through our line. We can afford, therefore, to commit ourselves to attack. If we do get the ball, our scrum-half will have a little time to deal with it while the opposition adjust to the situation.

Our jumpers will jump against theirs. You may find that moving one in front of their jumpers is effective, especially if the opponent hasn't worked on the ball dropping just behind him. At the front of the line, our player can stand with his hand up or actually jump for the ball, seeking to push it down to our thrower-in. The jumper at the back of the line should be ready to get up and push the ball back towards the middle of his own line. At the tail of the line-out, at least two of the players should be thinking in terms of cover – one checking that their scrum-half has passed, and going out across the front of fly-half, the other going for fly-half and then inside-centre. The opposition are more likely to pass than kick until the two three-quarter lines are fairly close. If the ball goes loose near the end of the line, however, their job comes back to that of all the forwards not otherwise committed: get to their scrum-half. This player must have his concentration eroded by the pressure of your forwards. If the opposition delay for a moment on compressing their line, our forwards must be half through on him. One player – our thrower-in – has a fairly clear run at him, and should be encouraged to chase him and then run deep. This aggression is possible only through commitment: let the jumpers look after the ball – you look after the scrum-half.

If the opposition move the ball from the line-out, they're likely to strike rather further out than normal, and cover from the line-out should, therefore, start a little deeper than normal, especially for those nearer touch.

There are times when conditions are so bad that the line-out becomes an embarrassment – when the ball is almost impossible to control. At these times, especially, this kind of pressure pays. It's still desirable for your jumper to jump – as an added disincentive to their jumper – but he shouldn't try to get the ball: just make it that much harder for their jumper to deal with it competently. The aim is to get it on the ground, and then to get it with the foot. Keep it going forward, keep it in play. Your thrower-in is the man to keep it in play: try to keep him between the ball and touch.

Once again, the overall aim on their ball is to convert the pack from open-mouthed gazing to simple, committed, action. Simplicity and commitment mean speed.

## The peel

In the line-out, the gain line is only one pace away. It's, therefore, an excellent situation for getting the forwards taking the ball on themselves. One basic way of doing this is the 'peel'.

Teams try this at both ends of the line but the only time a peel to the front is likely to be successful is right on their line. There simply isn't enough space to make attacks there consistently successful. On their line, however, a determined ball-carrier aiming just inside the corner-flag stands a fair chance of success, provided the intention is adequately disguised. The simplest way is to put all your jumpers together further back. If their jumpers move to cover them you may then be able to use a 'non-jumper' – who has practised diligently – to catch the ball and hold it out for one of your big men to take and crash over. If their jumpers don't move, then you throw to your power block.

If you wish to attack the front you're usually well advised to launch a feint attack to the open – by a peel, for example, or getting the ball to the fly-half running slowly – and then switch the ball blind, using the full-back, winger, and thrower-in as strikers.

Far more useful is the peel to the open. For this the ball must be thrown far back in the line, and there's something to be said, therefore, for taking one forward out of the line to keep the throw a little easier. The advantage of throwing to the second-last man is that it allows him to concentrate on the ball, confident that he has support behind him. His aim is to stop the ball and let it drop – not to push it down hard. The ball-collector has a much easier task if the ball is dropping slowly – it allows a greater margin for error in the timing of his run. It's also easier for him if the ball drops to him before he reaches the end of the line: he can concentrate on the ball rather than his opponents.

The ball-collector, however, is virtually certain to be taken out. Even if the end man has managed to make a little room for him stepping across to protect the jumper, the ball-collector is not likely to get far. You must, therefore, discount him as a striker. The really important figure in the peel is the second ball-carrier, and much of the work in preparing the peel is to get him in precisely the right place at the right time. He's got to be right alongside the ball-collector at the moment he passes the end of the line-out. If he's a metre back, the move may well break down.

The second ball-carrier must be picked with great care – speed of reaction, acceleration, and concentration are required. Where he starts from is less important than that he should be in contact and moving fast. However, you'll find that the player standing one behind your prospective ball-carrier offers advantages: he should step back from the line as the ball is thrown, and run alongside the ball-receiver, between him and our line, as a safety factor for the untidy delivery, and as an immediate supporter who expects to get the ball at the end of the line. This has been developed at length in *Think Rugby*. His position, e.g. prop, lock, hooker, is equally unimportant: his qualifications are not positional but personal.

If you find difficulty in getting the right player moving from the front of the line, there's much to be said for having your second ball-carrier stationed at scrum-half. This gives him a clearer view, a shorter distance to run, and a better angle to run at.

The question of angle is important. If your ball-carrier tries to get across the gain line fast he'll be running into their cover, and his change of direction will not improve his speed. He's well advised, therefore, to be moving fast when he takes the ball and get at least a couple of strides in on that line before seeking to go forward. From scrum-half, however, he can go forward without needing to change direction.

You may well find that experimenting with another forward out of the line, stationed near the fly-half, and running straight to straighten the drive and bring more momentum to the strike, adds to the effectiveness of the move.

It's futile, of course, confining a peel practice to those immediately involved: as ever, you should expect the worst, and play through second-phase. Peels tend to be successful in proportion with the number of forwards who get there quickly, in balance, thinking. You seek to develop the attack on the open, supporting as if you were doing a loop practice (see p. 126). Your scrum-half should get right behind the ball so that the ball-carrier if tackled can roll it straight back to him. The rest of the forwards must hope to handle but be prepared to ruck or maul.

Your halves must be summing up continually. The scrum-half may well find that gaps open up round the maul. The fly-half has got to be checking on whether the peel has involved any of their backs, and whether the rest have moved in – if so he'll spin it open, if not he may go himself. He's also got to take a look at the blind-side: it may have been left virtually unattended.

The peel is very much an attacking move, and is often most successful in setting up a scoring situation: use it in their half. There are a number of small advantages in using it on the left. It's also a convenient way of bringing your forwards into the game. You might use it first throw on the left in their half of the field as a declaration of intent.

## *Defence against the peel*

The best moment to counter any close-quarter attack – at line-out as at scrum or maul – is the moment it starts. Your jumper at the back should be committed to getting to the ball and pushing it back towards the middle of his line. If he fails to do that, the end man becomes the key figure. As the jumpers go up he must try to step back behind his immediate opponent, and concentrate on taking the first ball-carrier out of the play. If he can stop him at once, the opposition timing and support may be put out. If he can knock him backward, the initiative is passed from the attackers to the defenders: they are going forward. But every player must be reacting. The thrower-in should stay wide – just in case the attack is switched blind. The rest, while keeping half an eye on their immediate opponents, must get into a cover pattern.

## Variations in the line-out

Any variation you adopt in the line-out capitalises on lack of preparation by the opposition. Some variations have already been described: movement of jumpers; variety of jumps; timed jump; peel.

A most important one has been implied: altering the length of your line. You can gain an irritant advantage by varying the length of your line tactically: if you drop your least effective line-out forward, and the opposition have not thought through the possibilities, their end man may drop out – you have lost an ineffective forward, and they may have lost their open-side flanker, at least for that line-out.

If you drop a couple of forwards, you can leave a gap in your line with a jumper at the end of the first block, and a jumper at the start of the second block. It's likely one of their blockers will cover the gap. If you throw into the gap, your first forward in the second group can move forward into a free jump against him. If they put a jumper in the gap, you can throw to whichever of your jumpers has not been covered by a jumper. Every team should examine this possibility: it is very effective.

For speed to be effective it needs space in which to operate. The optimum number of players for this is the minimum – three. Each player you have above this restricts the movement you can make. Even then you must expect your opponents to have possible ball-winners at the front instead of their regular thrower-in, and in the middle instead of their regular scrum-half. But at least they aren't actually in the line.

Who you play in the line is dictated by the characteristics of your forwards. If your locks are adapted no. 8s, for example, you might be happy to operate with a choice from them and your actual no. 8. If your scrum-half is fast and tough, it might be sensible to play him in his normal position; otherwise, you might replace him with, say, a back row forward.

The more people you drop, however, the more important it becomes to prevent the opposition simply drifting out and making attack impossible. You must, therefore, make sure that the players you drop form a compact, threatening group so placed – e.g. in the 5-metre area or inside the fly-half – that they're available both as a real strike force, and an effective diversion. As a strike force they have one major advantage: timing. They can start to run, and cross the 10-metre line in full stride, because the thrower-in can time his throw from then, and put the ball in their path to coincide with their arrival. Try this from a 2- or 3-man line, say 12m from their line. Equally, the fly-half or inside-centre running against the saturated defence should be aware of the group, e.g. on the left touch, and be ready to chip the ball in front of them.

Dropping players from your line allows you effectively to dispense with line-outs: you can simply throw the ball over the top. In the example above you were throwing it to a group on the move, but you can equally throw to an individual player. This is often the scrum-half, but there may be an advantage in dropping your scrum-half back and throwing to a very aggressive flanker running from scrum-half position. Variations on this kind of move, and the use of a timed jump, are obvious partial answers to the problem of limited size.

Very simple but effective variations on the short line are based on the idea of getting one of your players into space.

- *On every short line, have your end player come into the line from dead astern.* Quite often he isn't picked up and the ball can be thrown straight to him.

- *Throw to the end player running back.* He takes three or four quick steps back with the ball already on its way, and either checks and goes up, or simply lets the ball reach him. He can feed the scrum-half who in turn can either carry on running or pass.

- *Line up with an obvious jumper at the end of your short line, with a flanker immediately in front of him.* If he isn't picked up by one of their jumpers, throw to him. If he is, he sighs, shouts 'Change' and moves on the outside to change places with the flanker. The flanker runs backward and keeps on running with the ball on its way to him in space.

- *Place your two players, 1m apart, 4m back from the 5-metre line.* This allows you to develop such variations as:

  **a)** place your scrum-half between them and the 5-metre line. The aim is to lure their thrower-in to concentrate on covering that gap. Then throw into the gap for your front forward, running forward, to catch and ruck, or to push the ball straight back to the thrower

  **b)** same set-up: both jumpers run into the gap. Throw for the second one to catch and ruck, or feed the thrower

**c)** same set-up: both jumpers run into the gap. Throw over them to the scrum-half, who starts running out as they run in.

In moves like this speed is the essence, and speed means constant practice. Get them refined singly, then do pressure practices, shuttling back and forward between the half-way line and the 10-metre line, with the scrum-half calling on the run, until you can do them fast and efficiently.

It isn't particularly difficult devising such variations. The important thing is not to leave them in a coaching vacuum – what are you going to do with the ball once you've secured possession? Incorporate them in your unopposed and situation practices, talk to the players and work out what are the best bets for your team.

The one place on the field where you do not think of using a short line is within 10m of the opposing goal line – where the bulk of their pack can be closer to the action than the bulk of yours. One place where it is always considered but infrequently used is within 10m of your own line – when, conversely, the bulk of your pack can be nearer than the bulk of theirs. If you are doing well on your own ball you won't need to: a good feed and a good wall give a fine defensive screen, and the more people you have between the ball and the line, the better. The idea of a two-man line, the ball thrown two-handed from under the waist, to a catcher stepping out from the try line 10m out, who feeds the kicker, is very attractive if you can't be sure of coping with the normal line. Most mistakes occur when it's not properly set up – e.g. when the actual kicker is expected to catch – or it's not adequately coached.

## Practising the line-out

What I've said above about practising short lines is equally relevant to practising the full form of line-out. If you can get to the point faster than the opposition; if your call is announced as you arrive; if your players are relaxed, confident and in balance because they've done repeated pressure practices; if your throws are accurate because your thrower's pride in his job has been whetted by good coaching, then you are subsequently more likely to get the ball.

You can use the form of practice outlined above: shuttling from line to line, with the call coming out clear and loud, and everyone knowing his role. Start with six at a moderate pace – efficiency is more important than speed in every aspect of the game. But build towards greater numbers and greater speed.

In unopposed, put balls at each end of every crossfield line. If you haven't got that amount of equipment, make sure you've a player, reserve or injured man to make sure there's a ball ready at the next line. Start on your own line on the left. Play it just as you'd expect – it's a basic situation, part of your tactical game plan – and as soon as that's done, run to the 22-metre line. Play the appropriate line-out sequence there. Then to the 10-metre line . . . and so on right round the field.

As you get into areas where you expect a handling attack, play it through second-phase, and then gallop back to the next line. Once again, start quietly – you must be efficient – but seek to increase the tempo. You can see that this is going to be excellent conditioning of the body and the will to keep going, and it gives very good situation-related practice of this vital area of expertise, the line-out.

## SUPPORTING, MAULING AND RUCKING

The critical question facing every forward in the loose is: where can I most quickly get into the action? This is a matter of judgement – which is, perhaps, why so many coaches avoid coaching it.

The coach can help by giving guide-lines, by setting up practice situations, and by focusing attention on it in all team practices.

The basic guide-lines are simple:

- keep your head up and your mind active: what clues are our backs/their team giving you about what's intended?

- guess what's going to happen, and back your hunch

- make sure you get between the ball and your goal line, as far forward as is safe

- run off the man covering ahead of you: will the attacker come back inside him? You should cover that area. Will he get outflanked? You should run deeper.

The good player is one whose judgement is sound. Some players are overoptimistic – they go too far forward, and find themselves outflanked in defence, or in front of the ball in attack: they fail to get between the ball and their try line. Some players are pessimistic – they go too deep, and rarely get into the action in defence or attack. Mechanical aids to loose play – neat lines in a diagram – are useless. The notion of 'corner-flagging' focuses attention on the ultimate line of defensive running: if you don't catch them on that line, they've scored a try. The idea that a forward would automatically break from a scrum and mechanically set off for the corner flag is ridiculous. He has got to judge his line. The simplest general advice is that most movement in cover is crossfield, with immediate divergence forward or back in view of developments.

Very useful basic exercises are outlined in Varieties of Team Practice (chapter 23), where the pack and backs work against each other, helping the forwards develop skill in following up a kick or covering crossfield. They encourage judgement rather than provide set answers. After each run you check with the pack how effective their running was, and how it could be improved. This allows the coach to drill home the basic guide-lines.

Intelligent use of the group handling exercises described under Intensive

Handling (see p. 122) are another way of encouraging imaginative running. If you keep hammering the basic needs for width and depth in handling attack, with the whole pack creating space to allow the attack to develop, you'll find that it rubs off in support play, both in attack and defence.

All forwards should be encouraged to play small-side touch rugby to help them improve their decision-making, especially in terms of movement off the ball.

A certain amount of help can be given to forwards in attack if, as soon as the tactical decision is made, they are told what it is. This is normally relayed by the scrum-half. They need to know: the direction of attack, the striking point and whether there's to be a switch.

This might come out as 'red–x–cut' – a movement left with attack at inside-centre following a switch. You can make up codes for yourself: keep them simple. This will certainly be a help, but can never replace the judgement from immediate feedback of the individual player.

## Rucking and mauling: developments from support play

So far as attack is concerned, the delay implicit in a ruck or maul, however efficient, is a disadvantage: ideally the momentum of attack should be sustained without check. This implies that a great deal of effort should be devoted to handling and support positioning, so that the ball and the attack can stay alive. The characteristic weakness in forward handling attacks, other than the archaic notion that forwards shouldn't be expected to handle and are, therefore, inadequately prepared, is their failure to create enough space. By remaining tight, they make their assumption – that the pack's role is to maul or ruck – fulfil itself. When they're practising handling, e.g. the basic channel support 1–4 exercise, encourage them to make width and to spin the ball. Talk to them about getting into space – what we're talking about is potentially the most dangerous and effective of all forms of attack in the game.

Once contact is inevitable, however, the forwards need to converge – not after it's happened, but when it's certainly going to happen. They need to be there as soon as possible after contact is made, and for that they must be thinking ahead, guessing what's going to happen, running off the players ahead of them, and rehearsing, however briefly, what they've got to do once they arrive. They have to keep the initiative, and they do that by responding more efficiently and faster. This is true not simply of a running, handling attack, but from potentially confused tight situations, when things are happening very fast and not always as you'd wish. The side that concentrates on what it's going to do, and acts decisively to impose itself, is the side that comes out with the ball. There are no prizes for coming second in rucks and mauls.

A great deal depends on the first moment of contact, and how successful the ball-carrier is in keeping the ball available. This has been dealt with as an individual skill in chapter 19 because every member of the team may find himself in such a role. We also looked at the immediate action of the first supporters, for, once again, the nearest player is responsible for securing the ball. Now we can turn to building up the ruck or maul, and to ways of practising it.

'Ruck' and 'maul' stress differentiation; but in turn conceal the essential sameness of purpose of the players supporting the ball-carrier. Keep it simple: what we're really concerned with is a '*drive*'. Whether we dispose of the ball on the ground or by hand is secondary to our need to construct a drive that is as solid and efficient as a scrum. To get that, we need to emphasise three imperatives, as follows.

**1** '*IN*' . . . Most drives fail because they're wide when they should be narrow; loose when they should be tight. Squeeze IN; drive your weight IN. When you bind, try to get your arm right round the man. If you get up alongside the ball-carrier, you should be as tight to him as any prop to any hooker. If you can get a player either side of the ball-carrier, the ball is safe – provided you're tight. Think first: IN.

**2** '*UP*' . . . People fall down because they get their centre of gravity outside their wheelbase. If you think of driving UP through the players in front of you, team-mates or opponents, you'll automatically get your front foot under your body. If you think of keeping the man you're binding with on his feet – keeping him UP – you'll create the same effect. We don't mean bolt upright: we imitate a loose-head prop.

**3** '*FORWARD*' . . . and this depends on you applying your power efficiently. Never rush in blind; never think that to have arrived is enough: what's important is what you do once you've arrived, and that requires self-control. Take a little longer, and get into a position that lets you apply force as in a scrum. You don't do that by resting your shoulder on top of someone's hips, or your arm on his back. You've got to drive up his spine. Work vigorously as if you were driving yourself up a steep hill. At the right moment, one man's effort can shift the whole mass.

If you're on the outside, remember: your outside arm is to tidy up – don't let opponents creep round.

If you're immediately behind the ball-carrier, remember: your role is that of no. 8 in the scrum. It's you who reaches under to take the ball if we're developing an attack by hand. It's you who controls the release of the ball to the scrum-half in all situations – immediately he asks for it, but not before (which usually means that you keep it moving back without check). It's you who, if we aren't moving forward, can co-ordinate the efforts of the pack with a '*ready, ready, NOW!*', as for a secondary shove in the tight. Listen to the scrum-half: he's the best tactical director the forwards can have. He can see where the opposition defence is weak; the forwards can only guess. If we're going to roll, he'll tell us the best way to go; if you're going to break, he'll tell you the right way to go, and be up for the pass. To break and lose possession is the act of an idiot; draw a man and hand it on.

In rolling the maul, each supporter drives in tight on the previous ball-carrier, his inside arm securing the ball, and his outside arm reaching as far round him as possible, so that as he pivots out there's a solid line of tightly-bound backsides presented to the opposition. Go slow; do it well. Nobody goes alone till the scrum-half – of whom you should have a perfect view – indicates that you've outflanked the opposition. As soon as that happens, you've got to get a player into space and get support to him fast. Outflanking is one justifying purpose; absorbing their back row or opening up a workable blind-side are others. Roll with a purpose, especially if you start in midfield.

Up to now I've been writing about the situation where we take the ball in and our aim is to maintain possession. The other situation is where the opposition have taken it in, or it's in dispute on the ground. If the opposition have the ball under control, we need more than ever to concentrate on driving them back. The key to this is to get lower than they do. It's futile to go on in at a 'comfortable' height: we must get under them, so that we can roll them back.

The simplest way of encouraging this habit is to offer a practice opposition at a variety of heights. I simply get a player to crouch, weight forward, as if he were reaching over a recumbent body to get the ball, at lower and lower levels. The two players practising rucking go in against him together, lifting him up and backward. They concentrate on tightness in the bind at shoulder level: they are squeezing in, and driving up and forward. Shoulders are above hips, and backs are hollowed. When they're really low, they may have a knee on the ground. They need to experience the sheer power available to them if they apply themselves intelligently. Applying themselves intelligently takes a little longer, but it recoups that time in the first moment of the drive.

What follows is a description of various repetition exercises that can be used to habituate players to a team system of retaining/winning possession at rucks and mauls. In these repetitions, keep two purposes clear: establishing the desired form, so that players 'automatically' function effectively, and operating over a severely limited number of repetitions at match intensity. You need to do both, and you need to establish the first purpose before you go on to the second. At all times you should intervene to correct faults and to clarify purposes. At all times you need to judge what your players are capable of, so that you set attainable targets, and leave them successful and confident. Work in a limited area whenever you can.

- *Cyclic exercises*: by this time your players should be at home with the basic cycle, in which the ball-carrier goes out front, puts the ball down, and turns at varying distances to give experience in reading the situation, and, where necessary, setting up the maul or ruck. Now you can develop this. Use your full eight, and depute two players to fall back from each ruck or maul to act as supplementary defenders: this gives greater resistance and teaches another great lesson – that it's what you do when you reach the stoppage that really matters.

- *Resistance with tackle pads*: put your three defenders with backs to a line. It's a great help to have a definite target for the drive. The ball-carrier drives, and the rest play it as the situation demands: if he's half round after the drive, we maul it; if he's facing the way he's come, we ruck it. Get fast into position and drive for the line. Then release the ball, go back and repeat it. The players rotate each time, so that everyone defends and everyone attacks.

- *Limited resistance line*: get seven or eight defenders in a line, with arms linked. This reduces the pressure on attackers learning the techniques. Five attackers are given the task of keeping possession for 3, 4, 5 drives. The ball-carrier drives in, his supporters ruck or maul as called for, they drive, the last player communicates, then sets off on the next drive. The communication includes 'left' or 'right' – the coach, acting as non-playing scrum-half can call it. (In the match, the scrum-half will direct them into space, but the coach directs them into the line: the great thing is that they listen for the call.) Start with a number of retentions that the players can cope with: you need to build up confidence.

- *Resisting line*: once they're coping well, have the defenders free to interfere. Their aim is to get their hands on the ball: the attackers must be determined not to let it happen. Again, start with a limited number of retentions and build up. Things will go wrong: the attackers have got to concentrate on getting it back whatever happens.

- *The cradle*: two rows of players face each other, clasping wrists, and forming a low, tight tunnel. The players working on the ruck or driving maul set up at the entrance to the tunnel, then drive down it. Each time they clear a pair of 'defenders', the 'defenders' join in as attackers.

- *Shuttle*: split your defenders into two groups, facing each other inside any two lines about 10m apart (e.g. half-way and 10-metre, or 5-metre and 15-metre). The defending groups each have a ball. Initially, it's put at varying distances in front of them, so that the attackers can do an attacking fall and ruck over, or pick up and ruck/maul, or even pick up and pass. When they've heeled it, the last man gives a shout and they turn and go for the other end, where the same choice faces them. Limit the repetitions initially. When they're doing this competently, face the defenders out the other way, and put the ball outside them, so that the attackers have to get round and drive back – the start of defensive rucking/mauling. This is an excellent set up where space is limited – if, for example, you're working indoors.

- *Retreating groups*: put one defensive group on the 5-metre line and one on the 15-metre line, both facing down the pitch. Have one non-active player designated as ball-retriever for each group. Start with one group 15m further down the pitch than the other. Each group has a ball at varying distances in front of them. The attackers cope with the first group, just as they've been doing. Once the ball is out, on a call from the last man, set off for the next group. While they're coping there, the first group falls back 30m, so that the same situation faces the attackers. Go right down the pitch like that. On the way back, have them facing away from the attackers, with the ball on the far side of them so that the attackers have to get round behind them, tie the ball up safely, then heel.

- *Immovable opposition*: no matter how efficient you are, you're going to meet many situations where the ruck becomes static, and the ball has to be moved back on the ground. You need players to look for the ball so that it isn't allowed to halt – you must always try to keep it moving relative to the ground, forward or back, and this time you can't take it forward. Be cold-blooded about this: I select volunteers and back them against the wire net round a tennis court, set up a good-looking ruck against them, and start feeding balls in, which must all come out at the back. The attackers must keep the pressure up – listen for the groans – and it's a great opportunity for the coach to check that everyone is actually contributing, pushing up someone else's spine, and not just leaning on the outside. It ought to look like a tight scrum, and those in the middle should feel the pressure *IN*, *UP*, and *FORWARD*.

The majority of these exercises are designed to introduce an element of judgement: it's pointless hoping that things are going to work out just as you'd like them. You must equip your players to deal with a variety of possible starts.

You can see how easily these exercises can be adapted to give practice in rolling or in setting up a loose player to spearhead the next attack. Once it's going well, call in your scrum-halves, and get them to call the next run. Have them practise setting the loose forward away: he's just another stand-off, and must understand the need to get into space and not move till he sees the ball in the scrum-half's hands. Work on the loose forward receiving the ball, cutting back to take out the first defender, and doing a switch to let the scrum-half or another forward run into space.

Make sure all of the forwards understand the basic need to deliver quality ball. The scrum-half should get the ball immediately he calls for it: not before and not after. If he wants it at once, he calls early, and back it should come. This highlights the common-sense need to get the ball into the back of our ruck or maul at once – that's where it's safest, and that's where we can start attacks from. Emphasise the need in the maul to reduce the number of hands the ball passes through. Make sure that the players talk to each other: we don't want them fighting each other for the ball. Make sure they know that if the ball gets pinned by an opponent, the big aim is to get it down to the floor.

No other single factor is as practically useful to the team as being sure that the ball you take in comes back, under control, on our side: it liberates the backs against a retreating or disorganised defence.

## Mauling: defensive tactics

Although the side taking the ball into the maul should always have the advantage in getting it back – they should see losing it as exactly equivalent to losing their own put-in in the scrum – the opposing team must make every effort to deny them an advantage. This has three basic elements, as follows.

### Dealing with the ball-carrier

This must be practised by everyone (see pp. 172–173).

To isolate the ball, or the ball-carrier, calls for a very fast reaction, and clarity of thought. There are three basic methods, each with its own advantages. The first is to *turn the ball-carrier* – i.e. turn him to face his opponents, so that his own body isolates the ball from his supporters. This calls for some superiority in strength and size from his immediate opponent – if it isn't done fast, it isn't likely to succeed. The most efficient way to do it, is to pick him off the ground, swinging him by hip and opposite shoulder to get maximum leverage, and trying to keep his head up so that he can't fold himself round the ball. Once he's round, the ball is isolated and the next aim is to isolate him – to drive between him and his supporters. Once he's isolated, he's got to be attacked. As much downward pressure as possible must be exerted on the ball, and if that isn't sufficient, his hands must be pried off it.

The second way of dealing with him is for the *first opponent to slip in behind him* so that the ball is isolated from his supporters as it is from his opponents. The critical point then is whose supporters can isolate the ball-carrier, driving past so that the ball is in their half of the maul. Single-minded commitment is what's needed. The advantage of this method is that it allows a smaller opponent, who'd have difficulty in turning the ball-carrier, at least to isolate the ball. At worst, it denies the side in possession the chance of a clear feed.

The third and best way of dealing with the ball-carrier is to *knock him down* and put him on the ground. This is easiest if he's backing into you – you can use his energy to put him down. Grab his far shoulder and turn him over your leg so that he falls between the ball and his supporters. As soon as he's on the ground, get your hands on the ball. The big advantage of this method is that it puts the onus on the ball-carrier to release the ball.

## Setting up defence from a maul
The odds are on the side that takes the ball into the maul getting it back. If the opponents have shown that their mauling (or rucking) is of a good standard, it's sensible to back the best bet and make sure that their use of probable possession is limited. The key to this is never to overcommit. You want as many players in the maul as will stop them driving forward, and use the rest to stop attacks close to the maul. It's convenient if your scrum-half always takes the blind-side, but you can't depend on his being available – he may be in the maul – and so you must hammer home the idea of the spare forwards covering both sides and being intent on driving forward as soon as a ball-carrier appears. The best time to stop them is before they get up momentum: hit them before they get started. It's always sensible for the defenders to get a metre or so wide of the maul and drive the ball-carrier into it.

## Making sure that the opposing maul is going backward
Frequently a maul becomes static with the ball effectively locked. A concerted rucking drive can then minimise the advantage of the ball-carrier and deny the opposition good ball. If the ball is on the ground such a drive can often uncover it. The aim is to roll up the maul and deposit it beyond the ball.

The key word is 'concerted'. It is virtually useless to go in singly, though this is the great temptation as players arrive singly. In fact, the most important idea is for the single player to pause and wait for the next player or players to arrive – a matter at the most of a very few moments, but requiring concentration and discipline. Then binding together and driving straight down the pitch they can hit the maul effectively, in the same position and with the same power as in a tight scrum.

As in all contact, there's much to be said for the drive to be *forward and up.* The upward motion is an excellent way of helping the players stay on their feet. As players in front go down, it's highly desirable that those driving do not in turn go down: this means being prepared to keep on driving forward, walking on friend and foe alike. While you're practising, therefore, it's sensible to do this kind of exercise without boots on. Further details appear in the next section.

Whenever possible seek to maintain the momentum of attack. The great aim is for the ball-carrier to be conscious of his support and get the ball away before contact. The next best bet is serial 'pick-up and go' – when the ball goes to ground, the supporter snaps it up and heads for space: he doesn't run at opponents – he runs at a tangent to the mass of the opposing pack, and, if he goes

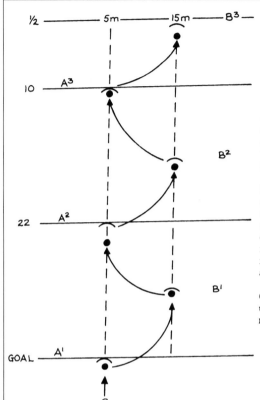

Continuity exercise

Three groups of five players—A, B and C—work in this continuity exercise. In the diagam, A and B are falling back to set positions to provide conditioned resistance for C.

Groups A and B each carry a ball which they place at varying distances in front of them. C deal with $A^1$, $B^1$, $A^2$, $B^2$ and so on, setting up rucks or mauls as they go and leaving the ball behind each time.

When C reach the half-way line, they turn to come back. A and B still face in the same direction as on the first run, and still have the ball at varying distances in front of them. C now set up defensive mauls, moving from $B^3$ to $A^3$ to $B^2$ to $A^2$ and so on.

Vary the exercise by having C carry the ball with them and use support exercises between rucks and mauls.

You can use this anywhere—but it's very effective into a blindside near their line:

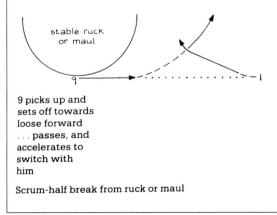

9 picks up and sets off towards loose forward . . . passes, and accelerates to switch with him

last forward to arrive—he faces the scrum-half and, as scrum-half starts his run, he starts his—flat—receives the ball and immediately gives it back to scrum-half

Scrum-half break from ruck or maul

down, puts the ball down on the side that facilitates the next repetition. Convince the players, even a successful ruck or maul is less desirable than keeping the ball going forward fast, and so keeping the opposition defence on the back foot.

## HALF-BACK PLAY

The efficiency of the halves is critical in turning possession into a positive advantage: they must take the initiative by making early choices and having the technical ability to carry them out.

### Their tactical role

The game is so structured that whether they want to or not the halves operate as TDMs. They handle the ball more often and at more critical times (immediately the ball is won from tactical points) than other members of the team, and they operate at the heart of the team. What they initiate is the team's tactics.

Their preparation for this has to be a conscious, continuing element in all practice. They need to be proficient in the skills necessary for implementing the team strategy – its staple, characteristic pattern of play – and temperamentally in tune with it. They must be habituated to thinking in terms of situations so that they respond quickly and accurately. All team practices should be designed to accustom them to the role and to the team response to given situations. Going through this together ensures broad agreement on who has priority of call at any point.

In general, the scrum-half functions as tactical controller of forward play – he's ideally placed to assess what can be done, and where the thrust should be directed – and of blind-side attack. He may also figure as decider of the form of penalties, which should be prepared for as any other situation. The stand-off decides the use of the ball in the backs. Each has to communicate clearly with his section and his partner.

### Their technical role

Any limitation in the personal skills of the halves is a limitation on team tactics. Every extension of their skills extends the tactical possibilities open to the team. All players merit coaching in personal skills, but it's of radical importance in the case of the halves.

### The nature of the link-up

It's easy to accept the existence of two discrete systems of linkage for the halves, based on a running stand-off or a standing one.

**System A** – the standing stand-off.

*Advantages*

It guarantees the depth at which the line will function.

It increases the passing range of the stand-off.
It offers automatic change of pace.
It allows an efficient scrum-half pass, and it simplifies his task.
It simplifies the task of players as scrum half.

*Disadvantages*
It reduces the stand-off's attacking possibilities.
It makes it difficult for both halves to respond flexibly to unexpected problems or opportunities.
Halves trained for it cannot shift suddenly to System B.
You'll find a full examination of the pros and cons in *Think Rugby*, the latest edition.

**System B** – the running or standing stand-off.
*Advantages*
Stand-off remains a potential attacker.
Halves can respond flexibly to problems and opportunities.
It's possible to shift instantly to System A.

*Disadvantages*
It is more complicated and, therefore, more liable to breakdown.
It is marginally more difficult to coach.

The great advantage of System B is that it potentially incorporates the advantages of System A. The critical point is the quality of the coaching and the aptitude of the players. Indeed, System A was largely the result of lack of coaching know-how. If you are prepared to learn how to set up System B, the question becomes not '*Which system?*' but '*How much of each system?*' is appropriate. I'll write as for System B but draw attention to special features of System A.

## Position of the fly-half
The first need is to understand the positioning of the fly-half. It has four components, as follows.

### Depth
The depth behind the gain line at which he takes the ball will depend on his intentions. Broadly speaking, the farther along the line the team intend to strike the deeper he must receive the ball. If he sees the chance to strike himself he'll take the ball flat, to minimise the reaction time of the immediate opponents; but if the strike is to be at outside-centre he must create the space to get the ball out there. Nothing is more revealing of the inadequately prepared team than the fly-half who, after a few tentative steps, is forced into a tentative kick: he needs help with decision-making and positioning.

## Lateral spacing

For the spinning game that's a vital part of total rugby, it's best for the fly-half to lie wide. It allows him to take the ball without the need to run across and it puts him into space outside the immediate pressure of the back row. It needn't deprive the team of the chance to attack the short side: both the centres and the full-back should be able to function capably as fly-halves, and should practise with the scrum-half to that end. For other purposes, however, he may find advantage in positioning himself directly behind the scrum-half – e.g. to counter and take advantage of opponents wheeling the scrum.

## Angle of running

Once he has established the point at which he wishes to receive the ball, the best advice for him is to cross the line of the scrum-half's pass at right angles. If he goes in to meet the ball, he increases the relative speed, makes it harder to take, and makes further difficulty for himself in passing; if he goes out, he makes the ball easier to take, but he makes life harder for his centres – checking them or forcing them to run out – and reduces his own chance of making a break. If he runs out occasionally, it's most likely that the scrum-half is passing the ball too far in front of him.

Crossing the line of pass at right angles has a further advantage: it sets the fly-half up for the action appropriate to the depth at which he takes the ball – running straight upfield off the flat ball, running slightly out for the deeper ball and so setting up an easy pass.

This angle is justified by the ease it brings to stand-off play. But:

- it must be accompanied by the inside-centres lying wider and deeper than usual, so that he and those outside him are not forced to run across

- for particular purposes, e.g. to engage the opposing back row, he'll alter that angle of run.

## Speed of running

The fly-half must be able to choose the speed at which he runs onto the ball. Some passes he will want almost straight to him – if he's going to punt in attack, or drop at goal; some only slightly in front of him – if he's looking for a change of pace as a striker runs onto the ball; and some that he must run onto – so that the whole back line is accelerated sharply. The scrum-half should know precisely what the fly-half needs on each pass: the communication is a necessary concomitant of the early decision, and the early decision is essential for effective action. If the fly-half sees an advantage in kicking then he must *decide* to kick and set himself up to do that as well as he can.

He may choose to commit himself to standing if there are persistent difficulties – if the weather's bad or the ball is difficult to handle, or if the scrum-half is receiving difficult ball from the forwards.

## Combining the halves

It's useful to clarify the respective responsibilities of the fly-half and scrum-half. The fly-half decides his positioning and the speed at which he wishes to move onto the ball; the scrum-half has to provide the ball required immediately it's available, on the appropriate line. If the coach finds that his fly-half isn't moving onto the ball then he checks if the fly-half is calling for the pass to come right to him; if he isn't then the scrum-half is at fault.

The critical factor for combining the halves is the distance in front of the fly-half that the ball must be passed to let the fly-half run confidently onto the ball: any divergences from this are comparatively easy once a code of signals has been established.

It's impossible to establish this distance accurately if the technical level of the two halves is not consistent. The place to start is with the scrum-half: until he can deliver a consistent service, you can't plan further. There's no doubt that the scrum-half is a player who can be helped enormously by intelligent coaching, and it's comparatively easy to do.

### Basic spin pass off the ground

Start with the *dominant hand* – usually the right hand pass to the left – and a *standing target* – the fly-half standing on the line of pass. The scrum-half has to hit him waist-high every pass, and must be encouraged (as soon as he has grasped the basic principles) to account for each inaccuracy: he must be getting feedback from his own performance every time he passes the ball, and like every other player he must in part become his own coach. It's a help if you use a line to pass along – it's not realistic in terms of angle of pass, but it's a great aid to the coach and the player in establishing technical efficiency.

### Moving onto the ball

Start with the ball stationary. Get the player's right foot immediately behind the ball – i.e. directly between the ball and his goal line – with his left foot about six inches away. Encourage him to get low over the ball – knees bent, head low, eyes on the ball. His weight should be on his right foot, and evenly distributed from toe to heel. If his weight goes onto his toes he can find himself out of balance.

Next, get him to move into this position. As in any game, the ball's path can be considered as fixed: the player has to do the moving. Then start rolling the ball so that he has to move to get into position. This he can later do for himself by gently bouncing the ball off the base of a goal-post and getting his feet into position as he takes the ball.

As soon as he's proficient, draw his attention to two further points:

- that if (as he should) he knows in which direction the pass is to go, he should set himself up for it by shifting his start position slightly to the other side

- though it's much easier to learn the basic pass by having his right foot (for a pass to the left) directly between the ball and his goal line, he'll operate better if he has his right toe there, with the rest of his right foot at right angles to the line of pass.

*Weight shift*

The next phase involves getting the body weight moving in the direction of the pass: so far as possible this movement must be parallel with the line of pass. The movement is initiated by the left foot being extended just behind the line of pass – in this case, the line on the ground acts as an invaluable check. It must be just behind the line of pass for three good reasons: so that the arms can throw vertically into the pass; so that the right hip is not blocked as it starts to rotate; and so that there should be adequate resistance to upper body rotation. How far the foot is extended is a matter for compromise: a wide base gives power, a short base speed.

You'll find, incidentally, that even when a scrum-half recognises the need not to block, he may continue to do so. This is because he hasn't diagnosed the basic problem. Essentially, it's a matter of balance: if his centre of gravity is moving forward as he goes for the ball, his lead leg automatically crosses the line of pass to stop him falling. It can usually be traced to one of two causes:

- his back foot is too far from the ball, so that he has to reach forward for it, and begins to topple; *or*

- he's going down for the ball without enough bending of the rear leg, with the same result.

As soon as his weight moves onto his toes, he's in difficulties. So encourage him to get closer to the ball, go down by bending the rear leg, and keep his weight on the rear heel. The problem will disappear.

It's convenient if the left foot is pointing roughly in the direction of the pass rather than across it – it makes it easier to go into a dive pass if that becomes necessary.

To groove this movement of the leg, and the body weight, along the line of pass is very desirable: it establishes the need to move the ball directly away in that direction rather than 'winding up' to the pass. Most players faced with the need to pass 'off the ground' will pick the ball up without positioning their feet, and to get a longer contact – and so greater power – will take the ball back before going into the pass. *Given time, even the best player will do it, and rightly so.* But the good player has to be able to cope with immediate pressure – when there's no time to wind up. So he has to work at moving the ball directly along the line of pass from first contact with the ball.

In System B, the scrum-half is faced with a simpler problem: how to get the ball to a standing target. This allows him to adopt a simpler form of pass. He can extend his lead leg before the ball arrives, which transfers his weight to a static position between rear leg and lead leg. He then takes the ball straight off his rear foot, and sweeps it away with the power of his upper body. It eliminates pick up and take back, so it's quick. Two points arise, however:

- he must delay extending the lead leg till he's sure the ball is available where he wants it – otherwise he finds it hard to adjust quickly: you need to be reasonably sure of a well-controlled ball

- working with an All Black scrum-half (whom I'd worked with when he was still at school), I found he still blocked: he tended to pass round his lead leg, and it wasn't as accurate as I'd expected. In fact, for this pass it pays to be fully in balance, and to have the lead leg a little further back, to give a greater margin for error. He may have blocked because of the sheer power of his arm action.

*Modified scoop action*
As you'll see in The Model (see p. 67), all the power and most of the accuracy of the pass comes from the hand behind the ball. Convincing the player of this is the first step in reducing the tendency to wind up into the pass. Get him into the outlined starting position behind the stationary ball, with his right hand behind the ball. Then get him to spin the ball one-handed, straight off the ground, to his target. The synchronisation of this with the movement of the left foot along the line is automatic in anyone who's going to be even an average scrum-half, and if the player you're coaching finds difficulty in it, find another player. (Passing to the right, however, you may find it useful to suggest that the arm strike starts as the right foot passes the half-way point on the passing base. This co-ordination of weight-movement and arm strike is what causes most weakness in passing 'the wrong way'. Alternatively, have him adopt the System B method: this eliminates the need to co-ordinate weight shift and arm strike. And if that fails, polish up his movement into a pivot pass.) This scooping action effectively prevents any pick up or take back off the ball, and speeds the delivery up greatly. Where there's no very strong tradition of rugby, however, the coach must take care not to be misunderstood: I've met scrum-halves who consistently passed one-handed as a result of this practice. It worked well in the right cir-

cumstances, but the coach has to prepare his player for the time when the circumstances aren't right. The basic need is that as soon as the rear hand makes contact with the ball, it's got to start moving down the track.

*Getting the forces accurate*
Accuracy in propelling anything, from throwing a javelin to hitting a golf ball, is a function of the player's contact time with the implement. It's essential, therefore, that the scrum-half's right hand should stay in contact with the ball as far down the line of pass as possible. A moment's thought will show that this has implications for what the rest of the body is doing. If the left foot – as it frequently does – strays across the line of pass, the right hip is blocked and the rotation is checked. If the head and shoulders come up, the contact time is shortened, and the hand will tend to move upwards rather than along – the usual cause for the ball going high. The head and shoulders must move virtually parallel to the ground so far as they can along the line of pass. For real power, the right shoulder must go right through the pass: towards the conclusion of the delivery the scrum-half's right shoulder blade should be visible from the front. This rotation is helped by the action of the left arm, which tends to swing wide: a follow through on the line of pass with both arms is a phony, and mechanically unacceptable, exercise.

I'd recommend using the flag-stick indicator (see p. 70) as a completely accurate indication of the desired line of flight, both in direction and inclination. Once the scrum-half runs his hand up that line, he'll understand exactly what he hasn't been doing – the more so, if you haul his hand a little further than it wants to go.

What we are doing, precisely, is to delay as long as we can the transfer of rotation from the body to the hand: at the end of the action the rear hand will start to rotate, but by that time the ball's well on its way.

Once the player is at ease with the scooping action and is developing some power, he can go back to a two-handed pass. Immediately he does so, he'll start picking the ball up again. Faced with this, the coach must be realistic: his aim is to encourage the scoop action, and any gain is to be welcomed.

It's desirable for the coach to move around as he coaches: he can see the accuracy of placing the right foot best from the front, but he can see the accuracy or inaccuracy of the right hand best from the target area. He can gain a lot by watching carefully what happens after the pass is complete. Any tendency for the body weight to move off the line of pass is informative. If it tends to fall to the right of the line of pass it generally means that the player has had his weight on his toes; if he tends to topple to the left, it generally means that the left foot isn't adequately far back. Balance is essential for accuracy – and this is what limits the length of contact with the ball: it must stop short of getting the right foot off the ground.

Coach and player must accept completely the notion that for every effect there's a cause, and that each cause of inaccuracy has to be tracked down: until the scrum-half is really consistent it's difficult to go further. However, careful, thoughtful work of the kind we've been examining is usually effective fairly quickly. Once the scrum-half is hitting the target accurately, we can move to the next stage: getting the fly-half running onto the ball. I believe strongly that 'fly-half' should include in each team at least the inside-centre and full-back. It's a great source of flexibility in the team's play that all three should be able to function effectively at fly-half, and should be happy so to do.

*Establishing the lead – System B*
We need now to establish how far ahead of the fly-half the scrum-half must pass to make him run onto the ball without overstretching. This is done by intelligent trial and error.

The coach acts as target for the scrum-half, and the fly-half is set the task of intercepting the ball by running onto it. If the ball reaches the coach accurately and without delay, the scrum-half is doing his job properly and the fly-half must adjust his position.

There are two basic rules for the fly-half to observe: that he must not move till he sees the scrum-half has the ball in his hands, and that he should cross the line of pass at right angles. The first of these is designed to prevent creeping – which reduces the available space, can reduce the choices open to you, and prevents any real acceleration of the line. The fly-half must learn to discipline himself in terms of position and of standing still – both much easier in first-phase than in second. The second point has been discussed.

By trial and error we can establish how far behind the given line of pass the fly-half must start to run onto the ball. Ideally, we want him running on so that the ball comes into his fingers – in front of him but without his overstretching for it. Later, we can begin working on his taking it early and so moving it faster.

This distance has now to be drilled into the scrum-half's head. It's almost always surprisingly large – much more than you'd assume. The scrum-half must see clearly that this is the distance ahead of the fly-half that he must put the ball to make him run, *irrespective of where the fly-half chooses to stand.*

The coach should beware of the kindly scrum-half. He looks at the stand-off, reckons he'll never get to the ball, and puts out a soft pass. The stand-off runs onto it, and it looks fine. But in attack, time is of the essence. The scrum-half must be whipping the ball out. His aim in practices is to reveal the grave lack of pace of the stand-off – to get the ball into the coach's hands before the stand-off can move. That's the only way to establish what the true lead should be. Far better that the stand-off comes up and takes two or three quick paces onto the ball: he needs a shorter lead.

Remember: it's the lead we're trying to establish, not a line of pass.

### Variants on scrum-half pass

The pass we've described is the basic model which we'd ideally like the scrum-half to use. But part of the coach's job is to prepare his players for every likely eventuality.

The most common variant is the *pivot pass*. This is a way of using the strong side when you'd normally have to use the weak one. All it requires is that you do a normal pass, but do it with your back to the opposition. It occurs most frequently at line-outs on the left of the field. To get your fly-half clear of the end of the line, you need a long pass – longer than you can consistently make with your left hand providing the power. You set yourself up a pace or so infield of the catcher and facing the touch line: this will help you minimise the time needed for rotation. Your feet should be comfortably placed; your knees slightly bent to keep the centre of gravity low and provide power. As the ball comes to you, your weight should move onto your right toes to get a longer throwing base, and to allow you to pivot into the pass. As the pass starts you lean slightly forward from the hips so that the arms can swing through vertically. As the weight begins to move, your left foot moves out just as it did for the basic pass, but this time a little upfield of the line of pass. Once again you must get your right hand to stay with the ball – keep your shoulders low.

The tie-up with the fly-half can cause problems. The fly-half often starts to run when he knows the scrum-half must have the ball. But the rotation of the body takes longer to accomplish than the normal sweep pass. The result is that the fly-half receives the ball further forward than he expected. The way to cure this is to rephrase and reinforce the basic dictum – now in the form 'Don't move till you see the ball in the scrum-half's hands!'

Since the scrum-half receives the ball in the air from the line-out we've been describing, having the left foot across the line of pass is rather less important – the right hip will not be so completely blocked. To be consistently effective, however, the left foot should be back, and the right heel on the ground as soon as the pivot is complete. Since there are times – e.g. at mauls and rucks – when the pass will be done off the ground, the scrum-half should aim at getting this right. Some scrum-halves prefer to use it from scrums as well, and the aim then is to get fast into position so that the right foot is to the right of the ball as it emerges, with the body already half rotated as described above.

When the ball is already in the open, or the scrum-half has to move some distance towards it, the *dive-pass* comes into its own. It's true that the dive-pass puts the scrum-half momentarily out of the game, but the importance of this is much exaggerated: if the situation arises he may have to use it, and so he should be helped to do it well.

It's easier to coach the dive-pass using a line – this helps establish that the body weight is moving down the line of pass. Put the ball with its long axis lying along the line. The scrum-half starts a couple of metres behind it, with (for a pass to the left) his right foot on the line. He moves to the ball so that his right foot comes down on the line immediately behind the ball as his hands make contact with it. He cocks his wrists so that his fingers point back towards his right foot. Immediately he has his hands on the ball he's getting his eyes up to look down the line – this simultaneously gets him checking the line, initiates the upward movement that's to follow, and starts the arching of the back that helps power the pass.

He may have to drive off the right foot if he's under pressure but it's mechanically much easier if he can move forward onto his left foot and drive off that. The length of this left foot stride is a compromise between short and faster, long and more powerful. Whichever foot he drives off, the essential message is that he drives forward and up. He must get high enough to give time for accuracy in the pass. If he simply throws himself forward and down, the delivery action will be flurried and inefficient. I tend to stand alongside the line and put my hand out as a target for his head – and gradually take it higher and further away; you can also measure the distance from right foot at take-off to right foot at landing as another measure of the drive he generates.

As the body drives up, the back has to arch to give power. This has the effect of increasing the inclination of the body, which in turn will tend to produce a pass going too high. To compensate for this and get the body into a more horizontal position, encourage the player to get his driving leg high after take-off.

The hands should be kept as far back as possible until the actual moment of delivery – the straighter the arms are before delivery, the greater the potential power.

The pass we've described is the simplest in that all the forces are acting along the same line – there is no vertical rotation of the body to compensate for. You'd therefore expect the scrum-half to land with his body stretched along the line. You're liable to find though, that the dominant arm has a more vigorous swing and affects the landing position. Provided, however, that this doesn't greatly affect the flight of the ball, it's acceptable – it tends to appear only when the scrum-half is trying to exert maximum power. There are cases, however, when the scrum-half may wish to use a dive-pass incorporating rotation – e.g. from a line-out, when he's been facing the line-out as the ball comes to him. For this he needs to practice, as ever, getting his lead leg behind the line of pass and trying to complete his pivot and rotation before he takes off – i.e. for a pass to the left he takes the ball with his weight on the ball of the right foot and as he shifts onto the left foot pivots on the right foot till his shoulders are square to the line of pass. From there on the pass is as already described.

It's worth pointing out that this pass can be spun as easily as any other – a matter of making sure the ball's long axis is lying more or less at right angles to the long axis of the hand, and letting it spin off the fingers.

The last of the passes that the scrum-half needs is the reverse pass. Imagine a scrum, our put-in, from which he wishes to make a quick pass left. He sets himself up as for a pivot pass to the left – weight on the ball of the left foot, left foot to the ball as it emerges, right ready to shift out in front of the line of pass, his back to the scrum. Instead of his left hand going to the far side of the ball, however, it goes to the near side, and his right to the far side, both at the rear end of the ball with the fingers pointing back. He can then fire the ball either with his weight remaining on the left foot, or as it transfers to the right. This pass allows the use of the dominant hand either way, and it is extremely powerful. It's no more difficult to execute or control than other passes, but it's essential that it isn't used blind: the scrum-half really must look for the man running onto the ball.

Although they are identified with a specific position it's desirable that all players should be reasonably competent at least with the spin pass and pivot pass, and that back row players should be a little more than merely competent. There are inevitably times when the scrum-half isn't available and success depends on a decent pass being given. Any moderate games player can learn to do these passes in twenty minutes without the need for individual attention, and the time is certainly well spent. The most important factors are the placing of the feet and distribution of the weight. Stand the players in 3s – one on the 10-metre line, one on the centre line, and one on the other 10-metre line. Start with passes to the left. Put each player's right foot on the line. When his turn comes he puts the ball on the line immediately in front of his right foot. He then scoops the ball one-handed straight to the next player, stepping out onto his left foot as he does so. Explain about the right heel, the left foot, the right hand – one at a time – and very soon you'll have a bunch of players who feel moderately confident. Then you can start a relay to bring some pressure and fun into it. As soon as the first man has passed, he dashes 10m beyond the last man, and so on down the line. You can make up rules as you go.

For the scrum-half proper a little more individual attention is needed as you build up the pressure. For him, too, speed onto the ball is of the first importance: he has to learn to move fast and economically onto the ball. Getting his feet into bad positions and having to shift them is a time-consuming luxury he can't afford. He can do a certain amount by himself – bouncing a ball off the base of a goal post and moving into position – but he doesn't have much feedback on the rightness or wrongness of the lead leg. A useful practice is for the coach to take the scrum-half and another player – not necessarily the fly-half – and half-a-dozen balls. Dump the balls on the ground and start the other player trotting

TIE-UP
SCRUM HALF → FLY HALF → INSIDE CENTRE

1

B width to clear
back row defence

C
this is the
distance that SH
must know-the 'LEAD'

A This will
vary with
intention
of FH

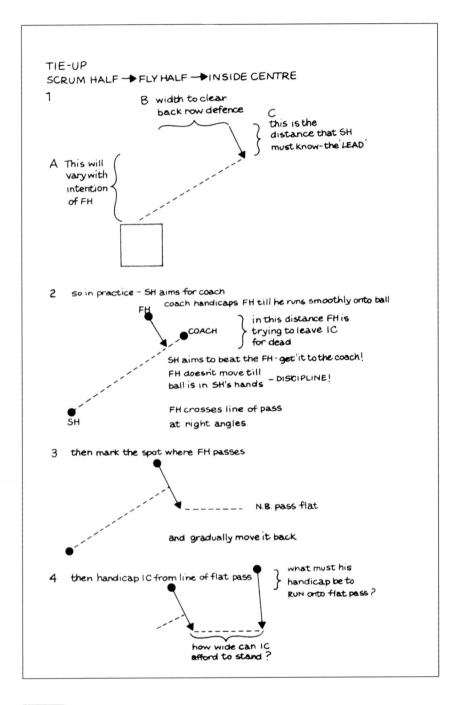

2    So in practice - SH aims for coach
coach handicaps FH till he runs smoothly onto ball

FH

COACH

in this distance FH is
trying to leave IC
for dead

SH aims to beat the FH - get it to the coach!
FH doesn't move till
ball is in SH's hands     - DISCIPLINE!

SH

FH crosses line of pass
at right angles.

3    then mark the spot where FH passes

N.B. pass flat

and gradually move it back

4    then handicap IC from line of flat pass

what must his
handicap be to
RUN onto flat pass?

how wide can IC
afford to stand?

242

in a circle round them. Then walk about and touch ball after ball with your feet – slowly at first, but gradually speeding up. The scrum-half has to get the touched ball to his partner as fast as he can. As with all pressure practices if you don't comment and coach it can do as much harm as good. It is also very hard work for the scrum-half, so have stops for a breather, and don't do too much.

Alternatively, put a line of balls on the ground, and have the stand-off walk along out to the left or right of it, just behind the scrum-half. The scrum-half goes down the line, spinning each ball away to the stand-off as he comes to it – straight to the stand-off, without a lead – and the stand-off puts it down ready for the next run. As a variation, do the same exercise with the scrum-half retreating, so that he has to get round behind the ball before spinning it away. Move from a comfortable to a fast tempo.

Accuracy is equally important. A ball that is even slightly inaccurate deprives the fly-half of a free choice of actions. If he's going to be inaccurate, however, it's better for him to err by putting the ball too far in front than a little behind. At different times, I've hung car tyres from trees and painted numbered squares on walls to give scrum-halves a passing target. I try to fit in a short quality work-out with the halves at least once a week – frequently starting from scratch with the fly-half intercepting a ball aimed at me. Unless the halves are functioning at a high level, there's little hope of the team functioning as a team.

## The stand-off receiving the ball – System B

**a)** He arrives, assessing the situation, and makes his call. He gives a thought to the best alternative if he should get bad ball.

**b)** He works hard to get into position – from rucks and mauls he'll tend always to be too shallow – and checks outside him.

**c)** He checks that the scrum-half knows what pass he wants.

**d)** He doesn't move till he *sees* the ball in the scrum-half's hands.

**e)** He runs to cross the line of pass at right angles.

**f)** He runs at a speed established as effective in practices.

**g)** His great aim is to make life easy for the receiver of his pass: he never tries to buy speed at the cost of accuracy.

## Systems A and B

His actual reception of the ball doesn't differ from reception by any other player.

**a)** He welcomes the ball with his outside hand, fingers relaxed, at right angles to the line of pass: he's playing down the line; his aim is to stop the ball going any further.

**b)** His near hand then retains it. Ideally, as soon as the near hand touched the ball, it would be moving on the next desired line of flight. But he has to be sure of the quality of that pass.

**c)** From a spin pass, the ball should reach him in a position that facilitates his own spin pass.

**d)** He watches the ball into his fingers before turning to look for his target receiver.

**e)** If he finds himself running across, it's because he started late; or the scrum-half has put the ball too far in front of him.

**f)** He works on speed through his hands. Every player who carries the ball for one stride diminishes the space between the lines by two strides; for two strides, by four strides; for three strides, by six strides. If we do that, we must do it by choice, not because we're technically weak. We must use space, not waste it.

*Exercise 1* (in 3s, walking, side by side)
The aim is to habituate the centre player into moving the ball on as soon as his near hand makes contact with the ball. Initially, eliminate passes: as each player reaches to offer the ball, the next reaches to take it and immediately offer it. The ball's motion must be continuously smooth, as if it were on a steady pace conveyor belt. Once it's going smoothly, let them trot, and then do short passes. Don't be fooled by outstretched hands: unless the near hand starts moving the ball on first touch, outstretched hands are no guarantee of speed.

*Exercise 2* (coach as target on line of pass, stand-off running onto ball)
The aim is to set the stand-off increasingly difficult standards in the speed of the pass. Observe the stand-off receiving and passing. Mark the point on the ground at which he passes. Position a helper:
**i)** slightly inside that point, and ask the stand-off to move back inside him – straightening his line of run – as or after he gets the ball away

**ii)** slightly closer to the point at which the stand-off receives the ball, to encourage the stand-off to concentrate on moving the ball faster. As each challenge is met, move the helper a little closer – but keep talking about accuracy and consistency being far more important than speed.

*Exercise 3*: assign helpers to count the strides taken by your front three players each time they move the ball.

*Exercise 4*: use a stop-watch to time the line in repetitions of a given exercise. Don't let them concertina the exercise: put a marker on the ground at the minimum distance to be covered.

**(g)** He works on length of pass. We assume he uses the spin pass habitually (see The Model in Part 3). He operates with scrum-half and a single centre who moves further out after each successful pass to establish effective range.

Points to check:

- that he's starting low, and finishing higher – he's got to spin it up for distance
- that he's getting the nose of the ball raised on each pass
- that as the range increases, he changes his line of run, to let him run slightly across
- that he's conscious of the model of passing outlined in The Model.

You'll see that this section applies to play in general as well as to stand-offs. Your three-quarters especially should be aware of it.

It's essential to read with this the section below, dealing with the positioning of the inside-centre.

## Positioning of first-centre

The angle of run suggested for the fly-half brings howls of scorn from those who haven't adequately thought about it. It's justified by the smoothness and ease it brings to half-back play. Of course, it isn't inflexible: the fly-half will alter his run for particular purposes. For instance, he may run straight at the end of the line-out, forcing the opposing flankers to concentrate on him, and exploiting that by switching with the blind-side wing, or a flanker who's dropped back to meet him. But it's certainly a very useful general rule.

However, it's clear that if we didn't alter the starting position of the first-centre, the whole line would be running across. The vital starting point is that at which the fly-half releases his pass, which, given that it is a flat pass, establishes where the first-centre should receive it. Take the centre to that point, turn him round, and ask him to walk back on the line of attack he'd generally prefer in the match. Get him to select a spot from which he thinks he can run onto the flat pass at the speed he would like, and experiment till it's accurate. Get him to fix that position in his mind relative to the starting point of the fly-half: it'll seem very, very wide, but it works like a dream. I can still remember the excitement of the Canterbury (NZ) back line, as, liberated, they ran onto the ball on whatever line and speed they chose.

## THREE-QUARTERS IN ATTACK – SPINNING THE BALL

The first aim of the three-quarter line is to move the ball into space. As a staple activity for the team, it becomes rather more specific – to move the ball sideways to the point at which a strike has the maximum chance of being successful. Success is primarily scoring a try, and secondarily retaining possession for a subsequent attack.

For total rugby – involving all the players – it's essential that the backs should be capable of getting the ball to the wings. There's no question that the team will always do so – but it must be able to do so when it chooses. And at its most typical, total rugby chooses to do so often – its staple activity is to get the ball to outside-centre, and mount handling attacks from there.

In those distant, bygone days when both back lines took up attacking positions – each set of backs aligned with its own corner flag, so that they attained an optimal defensive positioning only on their own line – it must have been rather easier to move the ball freely than it now is. (No doubt, too, the centres found more gaps with increased space in which to run – at half-way, the gain and tackle lines would coincide, and there would be a premium on attack from your own half of the field. Kicking would be counter-productive. Legislators looking for an elegant and easily administered method of opening the game up might well make this alignment obligatory!) One sign of the increased competitiveness of the modern game is the aggressive pressurising of their opponents by the defending fly-half and centres. This has certainly made it more difficult to move the ball to the wings. It doesn't, however, excuse or even explain the inability of so-called first-class teams to do so. It can be done, for we do it every match.

The legislators have made several attempts to simplify the task – the most notable being their enforcing the 18-metre gap at line-outs – and I've heard reputable coaches declare that only from a line-out should you try to spin the ball wide. Even then, teams at the top level have difficulties, and these difficulties reveal that the problems lie at least as much with the preparation of the attackers as with the pressure of the defenders. The players don't recognise what's needed, and perhaps lack adequate technique to achieve it.

The recognition has two components: an appreciation of the need to create and preserve space, and a commitment by players to the chosen purpose. It's evident that the further out we hope to move the ball, the more space we must create to make it possible. Broadly speaking, the more players who are involved by a decision, the earlier the decision must be made. If the decision is to spin the ball, the decision must be made long before the scrum-half has the ball in his hands. Most failures in attempting to do so arise from a failure to make this early decision. The commitment by scrum-half, fly-half, and inside-centre must be positive – there is no surer way of wasting space than for these players to adopt a 'will I; won't I' attitude: each unnecessary stride with the ball loses some 4m of space. The commitment must be positive, too, in terms of moving the ball faster and further than the opposition expect. It's futile simply to move the ball from one 1 v 1 situation to another: each player must be seeking to provide a slight edge for the player outside him. The basic aim is to stretch the opposing defence, so that each defender has more ground to cover. This is another staple activity – leading to scores, and setting up the opposition for variations. You may not use it every time but you've got to be proficient at it.

You will see back divisions employing a very deep alignment, as in the diagram, tucked in behind the scrum, with the winger a long, long way from the gain line. This is one way of buying space, but it isn't cost-effective. It has a whole list of disadvantages:

- it takes the ball far back behind the forwards – any mistake is going to be difficult to cover, and may be costly

- it takes the tackle line back far behind the gain line

- it gives the cover defence plenty of time to get across

- it's uneconomical in energy – the players further out have a long way to go before they reach the gain line

- it's difficult to maintain satisfactory lines of running – paradoxically, it encourages both running across and, when players are being left behind, running so straight that the opposing defence isn't stretched

- if either of the halves is checked and has to kick, the backs are too far behind them to be able to support the kick.

The alternative method has virtually every advantage, though it calls for a little more technical assurance and coolness. Essentially, this seeks to create all the necessary space at half-back with the fly-half lying deep enough to get the ball wide. The line then lies in a much wider and shallower alignment. The diagram on p. 250 makes clear the difference between the two alignments:

- it relieves the fly-half and inside-centre of immediate pressure

- it keeps the tackle line near the gain line – so minimising the cover defence's chances of getting across

- it's economical in energy

- it makes satisfactory angles of running easy to maintain by the entire line, and facilitates stretching the opposing defence

- it's a much more flexible alignment for coping with late changes of intention, or when the pack unexpectedly lose possession.

It's worth pointing out that the precise alignment of the players is dictated by the varying speed and acceleration of each player – and it's unlikely to be a straight line, even if, as is most effective, there's a *gradation of speed* down the line, with the fastest players at outside-centre and on the wings. How to find this precise alignment is described below.

Although for different purposes, and as a matter of principle, it's essential that the line can function well at a variety of speeds, the one to emphasise in practice is the hardest one – when the line is moving as fast as it can. Here are basic rules for the line to adopt: they've got to be drilled home, by constant repetition, and constant monitoring.

### Rule 1 Get into position immediately, no matter how shattered you feel

The most critical moments in any game are those at which possession is gained or lost: decisive action then is essential, and players must be in position to offer the widest range of choice. The typical mistake is not to get deep enough – with a resultant failure to accelerate, and a corresponding lack of strain on the opposing defence. You must work to preserve your depth and space from the man inside you.

### Rule 2 Run slightly out

Players are frequently told to 'run straight', but nothing (except running across) makes it harder for a line's passing to be fluent. The aim is to run slightly out in the direction of pass. This avoids the inside hip being blocked, and makes passing much easier. The exception to this rule is the intended striker, or any player who fancies his chances: he can run on whatever line will take him into space.

### Rule 3 Nobody moves till the fly-half moves – System B

Just as the fly-half must remain still till the ball's in the scrum-half's hands, so the rest of the line must remain still till the fly-half starts his run. A failure to do this is a certain way of reducing smooth acceleration to the series of halting passes.

### Rule 3 Nobody moves till the ball is in the fly-half's hands – System A

The inside centre's movement triggers the rest.

### Rule 4 Leave the next man behind before you get the ball

To get up real pace, each player must see the man outside him as a rival – the aim is to show how much faster he is than the next man. This has the effect of making both of them run as fast as they can.

## Rule 5 In practices, pass dead flat

This is valuable in two ways. It provides a check on the proper positioning of the players – you adjust each player's positioning so that he runs fast onto the flat pass. If he's running fast and the pass goes in front of him, he's got to move up a little in the preliminary alignment; if he has to check, then he's got to lie back a little. More importantly, the flat pass minimises the covering time for the back row: every pass back gives them that much extra space and time to get across. This applies too, to the defender in a 2 v 1 situation: the flat pass gives him a minimum chance of recovery.

## Rule 6 Flat lines = miss moves

To gain the advantages of the flat alignment, you must expect to use miss moves as a standard item in your repertoire: *miss one* (from stand-off to outside-centre) and *miss two* (from inside-centre to intrusive full-back) are standard moves which invite development – especially with the missed centre moving wide as an extra man. Consider also *miss three* stand-off direct to full-back – and the *double miss* – stand-off to outside-centre, missing the full-back.

## Rule 7 Pass with purpose – to give the next man a little more space

Just as the flat pass allows a precise positioning of the man receiving the pass, so passing with purpose establishes lateral spacing. Broadly speaking, if the ball reaches the next player with energy to spare, he should be lying wider. This is the key to stretching the opposing defence. Naturally, as with the flat pass, judgement of the actual situation comes into it: if the player outside you is slowed by fatigue or injury you keep the ball in front of him, but you keep it where he can reach it; if it's wet or windy you must adjust your pass to suit.

## Rule 8 Unless you or the next player are going for a break, pass at once: never 'draw a man' unless the immediate break is on

This is the least understood of all the basic rules. Every pace the ball is carried towards the opposition surrenders two paces of space – one by you, one by the defender. Against a flat defence, man for man, to run at the first man is to give the second man a great chance to take man and ball: it's the standard recipe for the 'hospital pass'. You draw a man only when the player you're passing to is running into space.

## Rule 9 You are responsible for the ball till the player you passed to has used it effectively: back up – pass and run

The player who passes the ball is the nearest man to the new ball-carrier – the nearest for support in defence or attack. If something goes wrong – if the ball goes down, or the player is tackled – he's got to go in and rescue the ball. The player outside the new ball-carrier will certainly have over-run. If the new ball-carrier is tackled but stays on his feet, support from the inside can lead to great attacking situations; if the pass on the outside is blocked, a pass back on the inside can upset the defensive plan of the opposition by disrupting its timing.

## Rule 10 If tackled, you must fight to keep the ball available

Frequently, it's a back (and very often a centre) who finds himself at the centre of an incipient maul. That's why every back must practise mauling as assidu-ously as any forward. He must fight when tackled to keep the ball available for his own team – ideally the player who gave him the pass, for if he gets the ball it's most likely that the attack won't be checked by a maul. Keep the ball in two

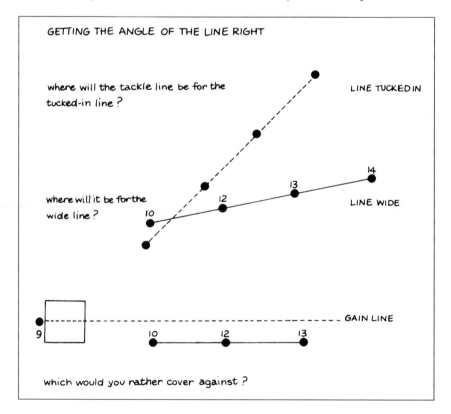

GETTING THE ANGLE OF THE LINE RIGHT

where will the tackle line be for the tucked-in line ?

LINE TUCKED IN

where will it be for the wide line ?

LINE WIDE

GAIN LINE

which would you rather cover against ?

hands, where of course it ought always to be in a passing movement, and fight round to look for a supporter.

## Rule 11 The outside-centre must make a decision

Rule 8 – if there's nothing on, pass at once – applies up to the point at which the next man will be left carrying the ball. When the ball gets to outside-centre that situation is most likely to arise. The wide overlapping attack seeks to move the ball to him, and strike through him, the full-back, and the winger. By the time the ball gets as wide as this, the attackers are liable to be under pressure from the opposition. Indeed, unless they are under pressure they're unlikely to make a decisive break – the whole idea of drawing a man is to get under pressure so that a decisive break can be made. The outside-centre must have a variety of possible activities to choose from. He himself must have a fair amount to offer in terms of individual flair – he's got to be a runner, he ought to have an effective swerve, he ought to be big enough to stay on his feet in the tackle, and he ought to have some facility in decision-making. The possibilities open to him are examined in the next section.

## Building the line

The most economical way of using the time available for coaching the backs during the units practice is to split them into two sub-units. Start with the scrum-half, fly-half, inside-centre tie up. While you are setting up and polishing their performance, the other sub-unit – the outside-centre, full-back, and wings – can run through a separate programme reflecting their needs in attack and defence. These can be summarised as follows.

## Attack – in which they play a major part

- *2 v 1*: outside-centre, full-back, and wing against the remaining wing – outside-centre runs, feeds full-back, who draws the wing and puts his own wing away
  or outside-centre misses full-back and feeds wing, who draws the other wing and puts the full-back clear on the outside
  or outside-centre misses full-back and feeds wing, who takes the other wing out and feeds the full-back on the inside.

- *Switches*: outside-centre swings wide and switches with full-back
  or full-back swings wide and switches with wing
  or wing cuts back and switches with outside-centre
  or any of these switches becomes a dummy switch.

- *Kicks*: outside-centre grubber kicks for wing

or outside-centre chips for wing.

- *Counter-attack*: back three take up defensive positions. Outside-centre kicks to them, and then runs back to join in movement. Back three build up the counter-attack pattern.

## Defence – in which they provide depth

- *Kicking and catching*: our depth defence must be totally secure. That depends not just on being able to catch the high ball, but on support being available for cover and to relieve pressure. Immediate support is also the core of running counter-attack. Play this game: back three (full-back and wings) + outside-centre – split up in pairs, A and B, C and D. A kicks to C – his aim is a dead accurate kick, which in the match he'll put into space or into touch. C calls for the ball and catches. Meanwhile D is running off him to make C's pass easy. Receiving the ball, D kicks to A, the previous kicker, who catches and feeds B . . . and so on. Initially, the supporting player must be deep enough to give cover, and then move to the side the catcher is turning towards.

  For a searching test of accuracy, put A on the 15-metre line in the field of play, and B on an imagined extension of the far 15-metre line beyond the try line into touch in goal. The goal line now becomes touch. They get one point for finding touch on the near side of the goal posts, two for finding touch between the posts, and three for finding it beyond the second post. They lose five if they fail to find touch. (There's a lot to be said, incidentally, for telling your players going for touch to aim for someone in the crowd, rather than just for the line.) You can adapt this for bouncing the ball into touch, and you can play it with two pairs.

All of this needs coaching, and the coach makes time for it over a sequence of sessions. Make sure that they practise close to where you are working; that they have a written list of what to do; that one player is in charge. What they do in a particular session may reflect last week's weaknesses, the probable needs of the next match, or the intentions of the coach.

While they are working on this programme, the coach is laying the foundations for the fundamental ability to spin the ball along an accelerating line. Before they split up, both back sub-units will have worked on basic handling with great stress on quality: putting the ball precisely where it's wanted, and establishing rhythm, length, and speed of passing, at gradually increasing running speed. They will have worked together in the intensive handling warm-up, and this is a final polish.

Even late in the season, it's worth occasionally starting again from scratch with the halves on the basic drill outlined on p. 242. You seek to redefine and sharpen the scrum-half's awareness of how far in front of the fly-half he must pass to get him running fast onto the ball. The inside-centre can function as the fixed mark to which the scrum-half passes while the coach polishes the halves. When he's happy with their performance he adds the inside-centre.

The inside-centre will function in this as himself and as a stand-in for the out-side-centre on miss one – the miss move from stand-off to outside-centre. Choose a point at which you're sure the stand-off will be ready to pass. Get the stand-off to stand there while you ask the inside-centre:

**a)** how far away do you want to receive the ball? Let him choose the point along the flat pass that he wants to receive the ball.

**b)** what line do you want to be running on? Let him choose the line of run – but remind him that if he's going to pass, it'll help if he's running slightly out. You stand at the point chosen in a), and look back down the chosen line of run. The centre retreats down that line. Remind him that he mustn't begin running till the stand-off starts, and ask him to choose the starting point along the line of run that will let him run onto the flat pass at the point where you're standing. Now establish by trial and error where he *should* start from to run onto the ball at the speed he wants.

Once you've done this and got it working, you've liberated the centre: he knows how to work out his starting point to take the ball at any point, running on any line at any speed. Indicate to him how distant his starting point is from the stand-off. The two players will converge because of the stand-off's line of run. Stress how valuable that space is – how, even if the stand-off is driven across by a pass too far in front of him, the centre will be able to run on his chosen line.

At this stage you can ask the centre to act as outside-centre – all he does is move further out, leaving a space for the hypothetical inside-centre. This gives the stand-off a chance to work on his spin pass miss one, and establishes how far out the outside-centre will receive the ball. On this pass, we're moving the ball slightly back rather than flat. When the real outside-centre appears, he can be slotted in to the established pass just as the inside-centre was to the flat pass.

You or a deputy can move out in front of the centres to judge their line of run. If they start running across before the ball reaches them, they've given them-selves too much of a handicap, and should be a little further forward at the start.

You then apply rule 8. If the ball is to go wide, nobody must waste space with unnecessary ball carrying. Check where the fly-half gave the pass, and put a marker on the ground. Encourage the fly-half, taking the ball on the same line, to get his pass away a little earlier – bring the marker back a couple of feet. Skill in this comes with accuracy of pass from scrum-half, and a great deal of prac-tice of the basic speed passing exercise (see p. 244).

How wide the inside-centre stands is established by how hard the ball is going when it reaches him: if it's still got energy, he can move slightly wider, and, of course, a very little back.

Once the inside-centre's position is established, you bring in the outside-centre and repeat the process. Immediately you establish his position, you'll probably see that fly-half, inside-centre, and outside-centre are not in a straight line in their starting positions, even if there is a speed gradient out to the wing, with each player a little faster than the one inside him.

At this point, check on the angles of running of the front three. The fly-half is crossing the line of pass at right angles; the inside-centre is running slightly straighter, but still slightly out; the outside-centre is running parallel to inside-centre. Make the point to the inside-centre that if, in the match, the fly-half starts running across, he must move wider and a little deeper to correct the drift.

Now add your full-back, who must see himself as a third-centre and a key striker. He has a tougher problem than the others in judging his entry, and starts his final move into the line as the scrum-half goes down towards the ball. Ideally, he is running onto the flat pass: if the ball has to be passed back to him, it gives the immediate cover, e.g. the opposing outside-centre, time to get across. He also has problems with the angle of his run: the great majority of full-backs come into the line so straight that they have difficulty in passing. If he intends the break, running straight is fine; if he intends to pass, he must move slightly out. He must get his head up and judge early what's required.

To complete this practice, both wingers join the line together. Their main difficulty is to overcome the fear of being left behind, and their main danger that of getting in front of or too close to the full-back. The easy way to avoid this is to run off the full-back right from the start. As they get into position, they check who'll give them the ball and take their positioning from him. I like the wings to lie wide – though still leaving space outside them – so that if the midfield players have been forced across, the wingers can still run straight. Once they have these basic principles, you run them through, by trial and error, till you find the point they should start from to let them hit the ball at the speed and on the line they wish. Keep making them think about space. As with every other line player, they will tend if they feel they are being left behind to straighten up and arrive closer to the passer than you want.

If you have worked in the right detail you will now have a line moving the ball fast and accurately, and be conscious of their acceleration. This is the basis of everything, the fundamental need for effective back play. Only when this is established can you afford to look at variations and moves. Every session we do, we get the line running sweetly before doing anything else with them.

Once the line's initial positioning is established, the players must discipline themselves to getting back into it. The basic practice is to spin the ball left, check, spin the ball right – and work on getting into position faster each repetition. You then develop this into sequences – which you'll find described in *Think Rugby*. You can then have them run against the pack (see p. 290 ff.), and re-emphasise rules 7, 8, 9 and 10. Specific practice of rule 9 is best provided in Defensive Unopposed (see p. 302).

The toughest situation is in the loose. Here especially, the fly-half's decision-making, and his judgement of the depth at which to take the ball are vital.

You cannot divorce judgement from execution: what is needed is intelligent commitment to the chosen action. A call has to be made, and every player con-tribute wholeheartedly to its execution.

A full account of System A applies in *Think Rugby*, the latest edition. It sug-gests that which system you use depends on the abilities of your centres.

## Wave Attack

I first looked at waves in the mid-seventies, in connection with Sevens. The idea was to split the team in attack into a front three and a back four. The four would accelerate from deep, running for space, creating an abrupt change of pace. (Incidentally, it's running for space that makes the line of run effective, not, as some commentators would have it, the other way round.) You then had a con-tinuation of the attack as the back wave surged forward in support, and the front wave took over the support role.

Substantially, that's how wave theory operates in 15s. You have a standing fly-half, and shallow centres to function as pivots, and both wingers, full-back and a spare forward to function as strikers. Once you get this working, the opposi-tion tend to focus on the strikers, which gives the front three a better chance to strike themselves. They need some such advantage: no-one fancies taking on an able defence from a standing start. If you don't have strikers coming from deep, the front three can be forced into behaving like headless chickens.

The striker's immediate aim is to get into space beyond the gain line – but he must be absolutely determined to go forward as far as he can, intent on giving no-one an easy target. The longer he stays upright, in control of the ball, the greater chance he gives the rest of the wave and the back row to reach him.

The difficulty for the front three is, of course, lack of time. This puts an enor-mous premium on fast, accurate transfer of the ball in a single pass from fly-half to first- or second-centre, or, better, direct to a striker. Don't try anything fanci-er, unless you do have a big advantage in talent. Don't ask the fly-half to do more than he's happy doing – but work on his reception of the ball so he has a few extra micro-seconds to let him concentrate on the pass. There's no reason why, passing to the right, he shouldn't have his back to the opposition, giving him a right-hand pass for the miss or double miss direct to a striker.

You can also create a little more time for the receiver by adjusting his posi-tioning – a little more depth may settle his nerves, and may encourage an uncontrolled rush by his opponent. Practise against a reserve centre, concentrating on trying to get a touch on the receiver before he can distribute the ball, and adjust the positions till it's safe.

There's a curious predilection for the striker to run back inside. Yes, he may get the ball in front of the forwards, he may even be able to do a switch with them so that the ball is taken out into space, but he has to be tough to take on the opposing pack. By all means feint for the inside run, but there's a great deal more space further out.

It's evident that speed off the mark is important for both the front three and the back four. Situations like this are the real test of the quality control that the coach has insisted on in change of pace work in conditioning, and hopefully instilled as a quest for excellence within the players. Training alone, knackered, they must still produce a supreme effort to accelerate at the mark, and hold it to the next mark.

A benefit of wave theory is the creation of a chance for our best runners to get the ball in their hands more often. Of course, it's not the only way: by far the easiest situation to get the ball to the wing is at a moderately wide blind-side, your put-in at the scrum, with your fly-half and centres on the open side, and the opposing winger worried about chips into the box.

Never forget the benefit of being able to launch back row attacks at the opposing fly-half in preparation for an attack in the backs: if you can take him out, and tie in the opposing back row, your back attack is enormously simplified; if he simply expects such attacks, it takes the edge off orthodox defences.

For players liable to come under immediate pressure – e.g. your fly-half and centres in a shallow alignment – it pays to work on shuffling. Watching American footballers, you get the impression that much of their elusiveness comes from their feet staying close to the ground, so that they can change direction quickly rather than having to wait for the completion of a normal running stride. When they want to run, they certainly run, but close to opponents they shuffle, fast.

How would you set up a coaching situation for this? How could you:

- accustom them to quick sideways movement off the opposite foot?

- get them moving quickly with compulsory foot-placings built-in?


## THREE-QUARTERS IN ATTACK – MOVES

There's a rare pleasure for the players and the spectators in a well-executed move. That it is rare is usually the result of coaching that doesn't go into adequate detail in preparing the move, or in creating effective judgement in the players. Even the simplest move has to be thought out and practised in detail, and the players have to execute it with understanding, purpose, and judgement.

It's difficult, for example, to envisage a move much simpler than a loop between fly-half and centre, and yet to be moderately successful the coach has to help the players provide answers to these questions. *Please take a little while and try to answer them yourself.*

1   What indicates the move?

2   When should the decision be made?

3   How far apart should fh/ic initially stand?

4   What should their alignment be?

5   At what point should they initiate the move?

6   What should they do before that?

7   What line should ic move onto?

8   What must the opposing ic be convinced of?

9   How should the ball be transferred?

10   What line should the fly-half turn onto?

11   What's got to happen to his pace?

12   What is his purpose?

13   What will he do if he is checked?

14   Where should oc have started to get into an effective support position?

15   What should he be aiming for in his line of running?

16   Where should the winger be?

17   What cover do you have if the move breaks down?

18   Do you have an alternative form of attack once ic gets the ball?

Once the need to ask these questions is clear, the answers aren't particularly hard to find. The questions fall into eight categories, and several appear in more than one.

## Timing (questions 1, 2 and 5)
You'll find the move works best when the opposing fly-half is up a little faster in defence than his inside-centre, and that's when to use it. It's best called when possession is fairly predictable – e.g. your put-in at a scrum. It's a ball-carrying move so there's a slight advantage in using it moving right to balance the fact

that passing moves – e.g. misses – are best done moving left.

The *decision* has got to be made early for, as you'll see, four players are involved and need to adjust their position, and the scrum-half and back row need to know.

If you start the move too far from your opponents, they'll see what you're doing and snuff it out; if too near, you'll be tackled in possession: you must *judge* the point at which they don't have time to react and yet you have time to do the move.

The last two of these are general principles:

- there are always a fair number of players involved – you must decide early to allow communication and co-operation

- *judging* when you start the move is absolutely vital. If a team start running moves against you *change the pressure of your defence*: if you slow it down, and come up leisurely, you'll see them do their moves in front of you. In attack, therefore, you've got to judge when to start.

It's as well to see the actual decision as provisional, to have a 'cancel' call if anything goes wrong, and to simplify your subsequent action (e.g. kick into the box).

## Purpose (questions 8, 12, 15 and 16)

Everyone involved in the move must act with clear purpose. These questions involve fh, ic, oc and winger – and the scrum-half and back row are involved just as purposefully. It emerges first in their positioning (see below), and goes on to their line of running (see p. 259), but in fact it takes in all that they do.

The basic purpose of the ic is to convince his opposite number that he is the striker – he must look like the striker in his running.

The basic purpose of the fly-half is to get into the space behind the opposing outside-centre.

The basic purpose of the oc is to take his own opponent further out, to open the gap for the fh.

In a wider context, the move sets out to achieve one of the two basic purposes of all moves: to create a 2 v 1 situation in the backs (in this case fh + oc v oc). The other purpose is to get the ball back in front of the forwards.

In the widest context, the move sets out to achieve an overall purpose – to create an advantage for a single player, who must then exploit it by using his flair and judgement. The notion that 'the move gives you a chance and you must make the most of it' has got to be accepted fully by the striker. Moves are no magic formulae for success.

## Positioning (questions 3, 4, 14 and 16)

The strike is being made between the centres so the fly-half should move onto the scrum-half's pass neither very shallow nor particularly deep (see p. 232).

The further apart the fh and ic lie the earlier they must start the move, and the more time the opposition have to react. They must, therefore, be rather *closer* than normal.

Their alignment must be such that as soon as ic has the ball he's in front of fh, so that fh can accelerate smoothly across and forward behind him. The ic, therefore, should initially line up *flat* with fh.

The oc knows that the fh intends to run outside ic – and he must, therefore, lie *wider* to stretch the defence. He knows the fh intends to run across field – and he must, therefore, lie *deeper* so that he can accelerate onto the ball without being forced to check.

The winger knows that oc intends to take his own man wider – so he will lie a little wider and deeper than normal from the oc.

I've expressed these in terms of positioning because that is simpler for the players; it could have been expressed in terms of running speed. The oc, for example, instead of lying deeper – which might alert an opponent – could start very slowly, and then accelerate onto the possible pass. I'd advise starting, though, with positioning.

A recognition of the spatial relationships necessary to the move is basic: it can never work at its optimum without it. If the fh has to check, or the oc has to check, the move will probably not work.

## Line of run (questions 6, 7, 10 and 15)

For simplicity's sake it's advisable to start as predictably as possible – the fh running onto the ball at a normal angle, and the ic running slightly out. They continue to run on those lines till the time is right to start the move.

The ic must then straighten up and pose a threat on the inside of the opposing ic. This also facilitates giving the ball back to fh on the inside.

The fh should run flat behind ic and make no abrupt attempt to turn upfield – which would certainly slow him down: an easy curve behind the opposing oc is what he wants.

The oc starts off parallel with ic's line of run – a little further out and deeper than usual. As fh comes across he must move out so that his opponent is tempted to come with him, and open the gap even further.

## Pace (questions 8, 11 and 14)

If ic is running slowly he poses no threat and isn't a convincing feint.

If fh is going to get clear he must be running fast and must preferably accelerate at the point of decision. He may, therefore, have arranged with the sh for an appropriate pass (see p. 232).

If oc is going to be effective he must reach the possible point of pass running fast – if he has to check he ceases to be an effective threat.

## Cover (question 17)

You must always seek to provide some measure of defensive cover for a move. In this case you have the full-back in position – but he might be employed as a second striker (see below). Your back row will be in position – to cover and as alternative strikers (see below). Otherwise, you'd expect your blind-side winger to move across behind.

## Alternatives (question 18)

You must always have alternatives built into your move, so that if something goes wrong you aren't stuck. The alternatives apply to possible actions by your intended striker, or the provision of other strikers.

- The fh may find that the opposing oc comes in to meet him, or goes out to cover his own man: in the first case he passes to oc; in the second, he runs.

- The ic may drive on as for a crash ball hoping to make a break himself, but most importantly to get in front of the back row and get them handling.

- Most moves work best if they contain two elements, the second being a further surprise to the defenders. The most common of these is to use the move as a distraction to allow the effective entry of the full-back, probably inside but possibly outside the oc. An alternative would be fh going across field to do a switch or dummy switch with oc or fb.

## Techniques (question 9)

It's interesting, on reflection, that the last thing to be discussed here is often the only thing the coach offers in helping the players to do a loop – the mechanics of transferring the ball. This is precisely the same as in any switch – the ball-carrier (ic) offers the ball to the fh, turning towards him, and pushing it out to him. As with any technique, it's got to be grooved so that the players can do it with a minimum of concentration being displaced from the *purpose* of using it.

These eight headings should prove a useful check list for your own analysis of moves, for there obviously isn't space in a book like this for a detailed examination of even a few. A book which shows fine imagination in propounding moves – though not at all in establishing the working detail – is Van Heerden's *Tactical and Attacking Rugby*.

## A MOVE IN THE BACKS

<u>Bone</u> – if you find a good move, try it in a variety of situations
You've got to work and work to establish starting positions and timing

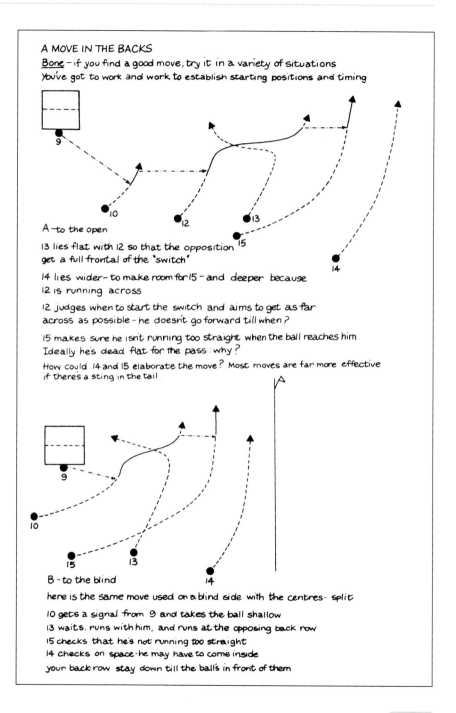

A –to the open

13 lies flat with 12 so that the opposition
get a full frontal of the "switch"

14 lies wider – to make room for 15 – and deeper because
12 is running across

12 judges when to start the switch and aims to get as far
across as possible – he doesn't go forward till when?

15 makes sure he isn't running too straight when the ball reaches him
Ideally he's dead flat for the pass: why?

How could 14 and 15 elaborate the move? Most moves are far more effective
if there's a sting in the tail.

B – to the blind

here is the same move used on a blind side with the centres - split

10 gets a signal from 9 and takes the ball shallow
13 waits, runs with him, and runs at the opposing back row
15 checks that he's not running too straight
14 checks on space – he may have to come inside
your back row stay down till the ball's in front of them

261

## Taking it out and bringing it back

You need two basic kinds of move: one creating overlaps, the other bringing the ball back in front of the forwards. See them both as aimed at scoring tries direct if humanly possible: in both we are fighting to get into space, and beyond that over the opposing line. In each case, every metre we go forward makes it harder for the opposition, but easier for us.

Get the two purposes clear. You'll see from the diagram of the two chopper moves that you get radically different forms of attack from the same move – a switch between stand-off and outside-centre (or winger or full-back) – if you set it up with clear purpose. The two purposes are equally important: prepare for both.

Above all, train your players to recognise that the move is designed to give a single player a better chance to show what he can do: after he gets the ball he has to make the most of it. But he needs immediate committed support to make sure that if he's stopped, the attack will continue. Think of it as a start to our attack, creating a slight advantage that we must work to maximise.

## Moves: general guide-lines

- Use moves with purpose – not just because you happen to have practised them. Relate them to tactical *situations*. Recognise that overlap moves are on when we've the edge against the opposing midfield defence, and that if we haven't they may be futile. You must strike at weakness; you must capitalise on our strength.

- Think in terms of *double moves*: a dummy switch plus intrusive full-back; a switch back to the forwards plus a switch taking the forwards out again.

- Make sure the player you're asking to carry the ball is happy in that situation, and that all the players are happy with the move.

- Play to your capabilities: use miss moves to the left if your players aren't happy with long passes to the right; use running moves, e.g. chopper (2) to the left, to give balance and variety.

- You need a limited range of moves with which you're completely familiar and totally happy. You must work on them intelligently: set them up with regard to space and to time, with a clearly defined end purpose. Then practise them again and again and again.

## Extra man

Quite the simplest way of creating an overload – two of us versus one of them – is to introduce an extra man. You can do this by moves – e.g. the loop, or a missed player looping outside the receiver – but the simplest way is to introduce an extra man – the full-back, the blind-side wing, a flanker who's dropped back, a stand-off crossing behind a scrum or maul.

A very common, very effective, example is the full-back operating as a third-centre in the wide overlapping game. This is a typical feature of fifteen-man rugby, and suggests two basic elements of that game:

- stretching the opposing defence laterally

- striking wide, with oc, fb, and w as potential strikers.

This helps focus the coach's attention on two basic requirements – that his team can get the ball to oc whenever required (see p. 246), and that the outside three should work on methods of striking. They must be conscious of themselves as a small attacking team – a strike force – within the team, and work intensively on the 2 v 1 situations they hope to create. They can also work on switches, dummy switches, and misses (see p. 122 ff.).

In general, however, there are two questions to be answered about the extra man: where and how to introduce him.

## *Where to introduce the extra man*

Look at the figure on p. 276. On introducing the extra man we improve the odds as follows:

4 : 4 becomes 5 : 4 on (open field)
3 : 3    "    4 : 3 on (split centres)
2 : 2    "    3 : 2 on (sh goes blind)
1 : 1    "    2 : 1 on (fb acts as fh)

The improved odds on the short side are one reason for the effectiveness of attack on that side. It's also, by its closeness to the pack, easier to support or cover an attack there.

There are three basic mistakes that account for most failures in attacking the blind-side, as follows.

*Attacking too narrow a blind-side*
Attacks generally need adequate space in which to develop. It's pointless launching a back attack on the blind unless you have at least 15 and probably 20m to play in. You may, on the other hand, launch a very effective diversionary attack on a narrow blind-side provided you've arranged for the ball to come back quickly and then be spun away (preferably to the left) crossfield.

*Attacking the blind-side from too far back*
By definition, the restricted space on the blind-side can be covered quickly by

the defence. Attacks on it must, therefore, seek to minimise the reaction time of the defence. The single most critical factor in this is the depth at which the attack starts – if the fh takes the ball deep, the odds are long against the attack succeeding. This is in line with the basic principles governing the depth at which the fh takes the ball (see p. 233).

*Lack of immediate support by the back row*
Although support should be easy at such close quarters, it isn't always forthcoming. The typical mistake is for the back row to start moving forward in front of the ball. They must stay down till the ball is level with them and then get across behind it. This is simply a specific application of the general principles of support running.

The odds suggest that the team should work on split-field situations – see p. 314 for 'up the sides and down the middle' – as having advantages in attack complementary to the wide strike and the close strike, and that the fb should be trained to operate as a fly-half at least in the blind-side situation.

## How to introduce the extra man
*You can improve the extra man's chances:*

- *by enlarging the gap for him* – make sure that the player on the outside of the gap is moving away, and that the player on the inside runs fairly straight and – if the overlap has been established – draws his man

- *by creating a diversion* – so that the opponents' attention is diverted. Quite our most successful move over the seasons has been 'Bone' – named after John Bone, one of our full-backs – which consists of a dummy switch between ic and oc with the full-back coming on the outside (see diagram on p. 266). Another effective move, of course, is miss one – missing first-centre – which gets the ball to oc faster than expected, and puts out the cover's line of running

- *by creating a change of pace* – if the line is moving fairly slowly the extra man can come in with a substantial injection of pace. This can put him clear of the opposing pressure defence, but he needs support on the outside if the ball is to clear the cover defence. The ability to vary the speed of the line is dealt with under half-back play (see p. 234). It occurs automatically when the ball is carried crossfield before the full-back hits the line – one reason for the success of Bone

- *by varying his point of entry* – so that the opposition cannot settle to a single form of defence. The full-back operates very effectively as third-centre – but he can be equally effective coming in as stand-off on the blind-side, or coming in between the centres. This last entry can be easily combined with entry at third-

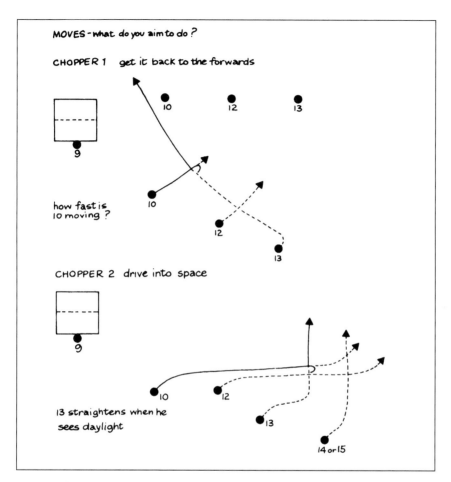

MOVES - what do you aim to do ?

CHOPPER 1    get it back to the forwards

how fast is
10 moving ?

CHOPPER 2    drive into space

13 straightens when he
sees daylight

centre, leaving the full-back to judge which offers the better alternative. Practise with the full-back running directly behind outside-centre, and calling 'in' or 'out'. The outside-centre always sets himself up for the outside pass, but continues his upper body rotation to feed back on the inside, if that's the call

- *by varying the angle of entry* to take advantage of the space available. Cutting back against the grain, provided it's by choice and not an involuntary action, can be very effective

- *by passing straight to him off a miss* – it's marginally harder to stop the extra man when his appearance in the line immediately coincides with the ball, but only if he hits the line at speed. To get the timing right needs a lot of practice and attention by the extra man to the movement of the ball inside

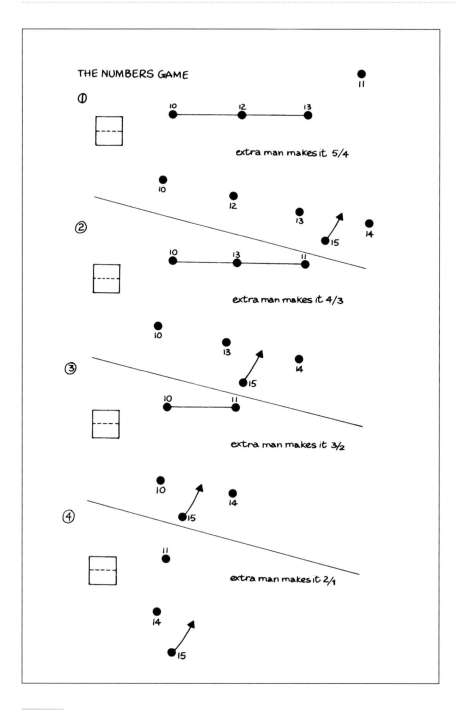

THE NUMBERS GAME

extra man makes it 5/4

extra man makes it 4/3

extra man makes it 3/2

extra man makes it 2/1

him. It's a help to timing if the passer is moving crossfield.

On p. 269 is a move that we've developed and that has proved successful. You'll see that it incorporates several of the points made above.

## Test Piece

Now one for you to figure out – draw it, and have a go at answering the following questions.

In the Oxford v Cambridge match, a scrum-half broke crossfield to feed the fly-half intersecting his course. The scrum-half continued out into the centre. The fly-half turned back slightly to feed the no. 8, who was tracking the scrum-half. No. 8 and scrum-half were now functioning as the first two of four centres.

1 What determines how far the scrum-half can carry the ball?

2 How might he extend that distance?

3 In your diagram, is it possible for the scrum-half to continue his run without obstructing the fly-half?

4 I said no. 8 was tracking the scrum-half; I lied. What line would prove better for the end purpose?

5 What is the most effective pass open to no. 8?

6 Redraw the diagram with a switch between the halves. How would that help the no. 8?

## THREE-QUARTERS IN ATTACK – FLAIR

Flair – that quality of personal performance that goes beyond coaching – is a precious resource, and it's got to be effectively used. All too often the player with flair is not given the help that will maximise its effectiveness: he is allowed to develop an exaggerated reliance on it; he is not given the help that lets him use it with judgement; he is not given the full co-operation he needs in setting up the situation; he is not given adequately organised support.

### Judgement

The player must be helped to recognise the situations that allow his flair to work to best advantage. It's in his own interests, and those of the team, that he doesn't trust blindly, e.g. in his elusiveness: trying when it's not really on alerts the opposition to the danger, frustrates him and takes the edge off his performance, improves his opponent's morale and decreases his. He's got to be taught the virtues of patience – of waiting for the right moment to come, and then delivering a really effective thrust. He needs to recognise the value of establishing a rhythm, a pattern of play, that lulls his opponent and keeps himself fresh, so that when he breaks the pattern it's decisive.

## Co-operation

The team must work together to create this optimum situation for the player of flair. This is basically a matter of giving him the ball when, where, and moving at the pace he wants it and of establishing this as one basic intention with those responsible for his getting the ball. Wingers, for example, are often players of flair who rarely see the ball because of a lack of commitment in getting the ball out, or a lack of expertise in moving the ball, or a failure to recognise that some situations make it easier to give him the ball than others. All three of these points are part of the coach's responsibility. He can establish in the centres' minds, for example, that in given situations they must be prepared to move the ball at once without dilly-dallying over the possibility of a personal break. He can work on establishing the judgement of space in the halves, and the accuracy of passing in all the backs, that will get the ball to the winger in space. He may examine in detail midfield situations in which the number of passes involved is smaller – and the chance of success, therefore, higher. And he can examine miss moves that have the same effect. He's got to make the other players – and the winger himself – aware of the conditions that the winger is most able to exploit. This is usually a matter of angles of running, involving examination of starting positions, and of how far from the opposition he wants the ball. Set even a gifted player up wrong, and he won't do much.

## Support

It's as short-sighted to expect the gifted player to finish off the action, as it is to expect a move to lead straight to a try: it may happen, but it's not a good bet. The gifted player, like the well-executed move, will probably give you an initial advantage – he may well, for example, be able to get past the first line of defence. This is an extremely valuable contribution – it probably means that the entire team can move forward. But it will be of small value if it isn't expected by the rest of the team, and especially the immediate support, or if they aren't equipped to get into effective support positions. The personal gift comes in various forms – to take two polar examples, one player may run like a snipe and be very hard to predict, another may be able to ride tackles, stay on his feet, and keep the ball available. You may, as coach, be able to organise an almost mechanical support play for the second; for the first, you must have got your supporting players thinking ahead. That is always the best bet for the supporters' future.

The important point is to make sure that support is available for the gifted individual, and to make sure that he is aware of the support. He has to recognise

The idea for this move came from a move used by Wales to launch an attack in the 22. They started with the scrum-half running slightly back from a scrum, dummying to the fly-half, missing 12, and moving the ball via 13 to 15. It worked very well. When you see the pattern of such a move, it's always worth trying to apply it with different personnel. Here it has been moved one place out, and launched from the opposition 10-metre line.

- 10 moves onto the ball at normal pace, and goes forward to lure the opposition on. He turns flat when he's just a little further from the opposition than distance A. If we do it early they may be able to recover.
- 12 sets off simultaneously with 10, and parallel to him. He straightens at the moment 10 alters direction. He 'believes' he's going to receive the switch as he did in a previous attack. He reaches for the ball as 10 passes him, running and 'concealing' the ball from the opposing 10 and 13.
- 10, as he crosses 12, takes the ball back to his right hip as if to complete the switch. In fact he's preparing to fire a flat spin pass to 15.
- 15 has worked repeatedly on the timing of the move. He's running slightly out while 13 runs straight or slightly in to keep the gap wide, whilst apparently reaching for the ball. Once he has the ball, 15 swings slightly out.
- 14 is lying wider than usual to increase the gap for 15, and to create a suspicion in the opposing 11 that he's preparing to chase a kick. He runs off 15.

For this to work most effectively, the opposition should be pressurising. So do it from a scrum on the left if your fly-half is right-handed, early in the match after attacking through 12 actually using the switch, and supported by the back row. As with all moves, practice until the players can do it blindfold.

Why did the Welsh scrum-half run slightly back?
Why perform the move to the right?
Why is the pass flat?
Why does 15 move slightly out?
Why is it better that the
opposition are pressurising?
What's the point of running it after
12 has done the switch?

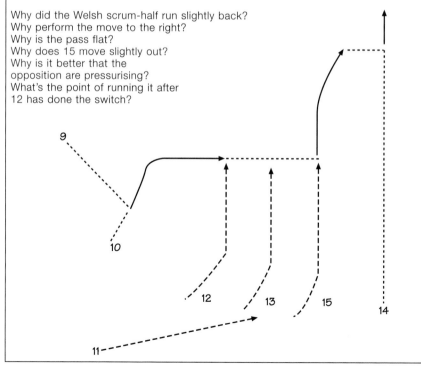

the real criterion of success – that the team secures a real advantage: to beat one man and keep the ball available is success; to beat two men and lose possession is failure. He has to pride himself on being a complete player rather than a great jinker, or swerver or whatever, and the key factor is judgement.

It's fair to say that there are some players very talented in specific directions whom it is difficult to fit into a team. In almost every case, it's because of a failure to convince them of the need to be complete players. The greatest service a coach can do such talented individuals is to convince them that they need to be and that they can be complete players, and to work hard on extending the range of their skills.

Sometimes, of course, it's not possible to convince them. The coach then has to consider his duty to the team as a whole. This is particularly important at half, for a talented kicker at scrum-half, for example, who is reluctant to modify his game, will impose a pattern of play on the whole team: if you play him, you have to build your team and team tactics around him. It may be possible to play him in another position where his particular gifts or attitudes are more effective. Sometimes, however, you have to put the interests of the fourteen other players first.

In the paragraphs above I've concentrated on flair as it is most strikingly displayed and most commonly understood – the flair of the runner. Selectors especially, however, should not be blind to other kinds of flair, less obvious but equally valuable. Your effective runner is often set up by the quality of passing and timing of the player inside him, who does nothing very startling but creates fluency in the line. He and the runner complement and complete each other as has been suggested in Chapter 9. So, too, you may fail to see the player – often a back row – whose talent is turning up in the right place, and moving the ball on, again without pyrotechnics but to great effect.

## DRILLING THE BACKS

'Drilling' is not a good idea, if it's a substitute for understanding. But, in the heat of the action, you need an instant, disciplined, response to the developing situation if you're going to exploit it. You build up such an ability by concentrating preparation on the simple basics of combined play. You must make sure they're totally reliable. Rhythm, length and speed are the three aims I set initially for even the most talented and experienced players. The aim is very high-quality performance of basic passing and positioning.

## Rhythm

Rhythm is important because it prepares the receiver for the pass. We set off at a quiet trot in a single line, running slightly out, giving and taking flat spin passes. Every player knows precisely what to expect, and has to govern his position to let him move easily onto the ball. 'High-quality' means more precise than you'd every predict. I want each pass arriving exactly where it's wanted – not 10cm up, down, forward, or back. The players have done it every session since we've met. They can do it in wind and rain – but they still practise it with great attention to detail.

## Length

In total rugby the ball has to beat the opponent, has to open up large gaps, and has to force the opposition to stretch their defence across the field – at least some of the time. We do this by spinning the ball (see Normal spin pass, p. 71) and getting exactly the advantages that the fly-half gets from the scrum-half. Please read the technical description, Scrum-half pass from a maul on p. 68. It's miles away from the tangential spin that some players try to apply to the ball, both in kicking and handling – it is more effective and more reliable. Of course, positioning is affected: the longer the pass takes to arrive, the deeper you should be to allow you to move easily onto the ball.

## Speed

The promotion of 'fast hands' that operate reliably under pressure. For this we start even more slowly, in a slight echelon, rather less than two arms lengths apart. The aim initially is to eliminate the pass: the ball is moved from extended hands to extended hands in what should appear to be continous movement down the line. (Beware the player who reaches to take the ball, but checks before delivery.) We do this back and forward till it's rippling along. Next we do the same thing with a short pass, and then with a longer pass.

All of this is necessary to get the lads into fine focus. To try to do anything complicated before re-establishing quality handling is a recipe for frustration. I leave them with a short programme to carry out, while I spend five minutes with the halves, working on getting fine focus on the lead. I'll call over the first-centre and check his start positioning before rejoining the others.

**1** We start by *spinning the ball to the wing*. I'll be checking – and injured players will be checking – on things like the running line of the centres, and simultaneous starting down the line. (Where will I be standing for each of these?) Once they're going well we may time ball transfer from scrum-half to wing: do it faster, or move the ball further in the same time.

**2**  We then do *sequences*, to drill players in getting fast into position after a check. Initially, it's spin the ball to one wing, check, spin it back to the other wing. The scrum-half flies across the pitch, and releases the ball when he's happy about positioning. The aim is to get this time lapse down to as near zero as possible. We then introduce a check where we expect tackles to take place – in our case around outside-centre/full-back. The scrum-half arrives, checks the position of the blind-winger – who'll almost certainly have overrun, and not got back deep enough – and carries on into the blind-side. The aim again is to reduce the time lapse. The winger gets the ball back inside, the scrum-half puts it down . . . and the whole sequence reverses direction. If you can do this swiftly twice, you'll find gaps opening up, and back rows dropping like flies.

**3**  We'll then practise *moves* – the various ways we have of getting the ball into the strike area. You can have no idea of how often we go through a single move to make sure it's spot-on for the match. Don't imagine that you've mastered a move when the players can get through it without dropping the ball. That's what some people think, and that's why it fails to work in the match.

It's got to be case hardened and precisely engineered, with everything happening at a higher speed than the opposition can cope with. So you build and build, polish and polish, and when you're ready incorporate it in the sequences. You may choose to use different moves when the ball's going left, and when it's going right. And in the same way, you examine how you can make the blind-side attack harder to stop – a switch between winger and scrum-half, a dummy switch, introducing the full-back, chipping behind their winger. Examine what your team can do, and polish it. Then incorporate it in the sequence, and aim again for reduced time-lapse at each check.

You will see that this is not going to fit into the unit slot in the structured session. It'll be worked on pre-season, and amplified and polished once the season starts. I like, quite often, to spend a whole session with the backs or the forwards, when I think it's needed.

## KICKING

### Tactical kicking

Kicking, especially in its tactical form, is one of the fine arts of the game – at its best, it shows the judgement, precision, ease, and effectiveness that are the hallmarks of the best athletic performances. It's an essential part of the mix even for teams committed to handling rugby.

- It's the simplest way of overcoming the basic difficulty of the game – getting the ball over the gain line and in front of the forwards. It does so with minimum risk of making mistakes behind the gain line, and with a minimum expenditure of energy.

This is particularly important during those phases of the game where any loss of concentration is liable to be punished. Typical moments are at the opening or close of each half, or immediately after you have scored, or when the team, having gone into a lead, are getting slightly complacent. At such times it pays to simplify the game, and concentrate on getting the pack moving forward.

- It's an economical way of moving play into valuable space – the striking zone where the opponents' line is within attacking distance, and the risks involved in handling are much reduced.

The value of distance gained down the pitch can be set out notionally in a diagram (see p. 275). This is based on the notion that a metre at either end may lead to a try, and a metre at half-way is neither here nor there. Economy of effort in getting the ball into an area where the ground is more valuable in front of you than behind you is sensible tactically, is good for your pack's morale and bad for theirs. Playing the game in the opposition half of the field is a sensible guide-line – though, like all guide-lines, it's an aid for the apprentice tactician rather than the craftsman. At the start of the season with tactically inexperienced halves, or an untried back-line, you can suggest the guide-lines on the right of the diagram as a reasonable basis. If you are coaching well, however, your players learn to read the game with greater insight.

- It's an effective way of creating a situation in which handling is easier. Difficulty in handling comes from the attentions of two pressure groups – the front three (fh and centres) and the back row. Both of these groups can be slowed down by intelligent kicking that poses an alternative problem. If the ball is consistently put over the heads of either group – e.g. chips over the front three, preferably to the full-back's weaker side, and back into the box over the back row – it will help create conditions in which neither group can commit itself early to pressurising.

- It's an effective way of probing weaknesses in the opposing back three (fb and wingers), and of imposing pressure upon them. By kicking high you can force the back three into lying deep – opening the way to attacks wide using miss moves, with the opposing wing out of position to counter the handling attack. You can create the conditions where mistakes by the opposition set up excellent attack situations. By kicking centrally you limit the chance of the catcher's making an effective, long, touch kick. By kicking to the weaker side – i.e. usually to the player's left – you can make it difficult for him in the time available to kick at all. If you drop the ball just outside the 22, the return kick becomes much more demanding – it must bounce into touch – and the opponent may be tempted to run. At a scrum or maul with a workable blind-side, the opposing winger is caught in the dilemma of whether to lie up for a handling attack or back for the kick into the box – and the halves can expect this.

- This becomes even easier if there's a strong wind or rain from behind the attackers. In this case it's highly important to play as much of the half as possible in the defenders' territory since in the other half you may well be kept far from their line.

- A final use is as a means of transferring the focus of attack with minimum reaction time for the opposition to cover the new threat. Typical of this is the kick back over the mid-field scrum or maul when the fly-half's initial movement has already forced the opposing pressure groups to commit themselves on one side. This can be even more effective if the kick comes from inside-centre.

The key to all tactical kicking is early decision-making. Failure to make decisions, or to make them early enough, leads to that most depressing of spectacles – the kick that is forced upon you by lack of decisive action, and by your opponents' pressure.

Most tactical kicking is best done when you've set it up. It calls for the same procedure as any other decision. As soon as the scrum or line-out or maul develops, you are examining the possibilities – the point on the pitch, the weather conditions, the line-up for the opposing defence, the morale of both sides – and reaching your provisional decision. Then you communicate to all those immediately involved. The fly-half, for example, on deciding on a tactical kick, must let his scrum-half know so that the ball is passed to him standing – balance is a key factor in consistent kicking, and kicking on the run is an altogether more complicated and difficult exercise. He needs also to alert those immediately concerned with reaching the kick or the catcher – there's no point, for example, in kicking for three-quarters who are lying back as for a handling attack, and are giving the opposing catcher metres more space than they would if they were lying up flat.

The skilled player has a fair tolerance of inaccurate passes, but if his kicking is to be at its best he must get the ball precisely as he wants it. This allows him to set himself up for the kick – to get his hips at the right angle, and to have the leisure to concentrate on his kick.

In most situations, tactical kicking is an exercise in precision – the direction, length, and height of the kick must all be under control, and understood in terms of a defined objective. The direction is implicit in the decision – it's never just 'a kick' – and length and height depend on the purpose. If you want your players to arrive at the same time as the ball, you've got to establish in practices the right mixture of length and height to achieve it. If you want speed and great accuracy – e.g. for a kick to touch when the rhythm of an attack has broken down – you may want a very low kick bouncing in the field of play and rolling into touch. If you're kicking for a player following up, it's best to keep the trajectory low so that the ball rolls forward rather than bouncing up: if the bounce is right, it's marvellous – but if it's wrong the whole momentum of the attack can be lost.

The players following the kick must be just as purposeful as the kicker. If it's a group of players, they must be quite sure of their function and support each other intelligently in width and depth on the line of the landing point. If it's a single player he's got to set off intelligently – e.g. to get between the ball and touch in kicks into the box, and keep the ball in play. The basic rule is to start fast and arrive in balance, to deal with the ball or the catcher. In apparently 50/50 situations, the attacker has the advantage: it's easier for him to go up to meet the ball and if he can't catch it make sure he knocks it back to his supporting players. When the catcher has an advantage, the aim is to limit his choice

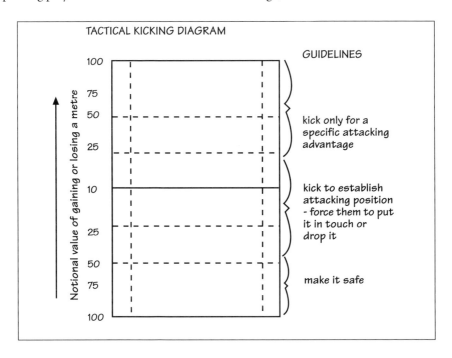

## Dominguez punts upfield

Here is an excellent demonstration of how to punt. Diego has complete calm, complete concentration and beautiful balance. He is under no pressure, though the Wales forwards are close. He has received the ball in space, already knew he was going to kick, and where his target was. As a result, he has – like the best batsmen in cricket – time to exercise his skills fully. Note how high his knee is, how straight his non-kicking leg is as he lifts the ball away. He is leaning slightly back to allow a fuller lift, and better balance. Look at his right ankle and foot, down which the ball has rolled to initiate the spin. He isn't kicking *at* the ball: he is applying controlled power – and controlled technique – to direct it as he wishes.

of actions. If you're sure of the tackle, make it; if you're not, get outside him and push him towards touch, narrowing the angle for his kick.

It's convenient to think in terms of five basic areas for the kick.

**1** *Into the box.* This is overall the most effective kick since it gets the ball in front of the forwards, creates a shift in the direction of attack and limits the possibility of counter-attack. It's most easily done by scrum-halves from the scrum as on either side of the field they can use their right foot for it. The box is also the best place to kick from a heel against the head in a defensive situation – if you kick open you may not force your opponents to turn, and instead present the ball to them with space to move it.

**2** *High up the middle.* This, especially in difficult conditions, imposes maximum strain on the opposing back three, and makes it most difficult for them to make ground on touch kicking. It's also, especially in difficult conditions, a useful alternative to touch kicking in defence. There comes a point where simply getting the ball into touch isn't enough – if the attackers can sustain their attack they will probably, in the long run, score. A player who recognises this should consider the possibility of kicking long down the middle and so moving into attack. The critical question is the depth of the opposing backs: in your own half it's imperative that your kick be long enough to make them all turn and go back. Given that – and the need not merely to relieve but remove the pressure – it's worth trying.

**3** *Behind the opposing centres.* A staple method of creating the space to handle, it's been made easier by the opposing back row being tied down at scrums. It's usually best done moving to the right – partly because it's a marginally easier kick for the right foot dominant fly-half, mainly because it creates difficulties for the right foot dominant opposing full-back. The aim is to put the ball over the centres and to the full-back's weaker side.

There's an advantage in performing this on the run. The very fact of your running gets your centre moving in the right direction and forces your opponents to come forward in case you handle. This opens up the ground behind them. Timing your kick is a matter of judgement: too early and your opponents may be able to turn and kill the ball; too late, and they may be able to charge down the kick. Technically, the kick is more difficult than a kick at the halt. Put the ball at right angles to the long axis of your foot – you need the best possible target. Think of bringing your knee up to get the height. Keep your toe down so that the ball rolls on when it lands. You can practice this running at the posts and chipping just over or under the crossbar. Keep your eye on the ball once you decide to kick.

**4** *Diagonal kick.* Aimed to put pressure on the opposing open-side wing, and bring your own winger quickly into the game. The longer the kick, the less sure you can be of its accuracy, and the more time your opponents have to react. This kind of kick is, therefore, best employed from a midfield scrum when the opposing winger has come up flat with his centres or as a kick from inside-centre.

**5** *Diagonal kick to the corner.* Given that you've at least equality in the line-out, you can always make ground by bouncing the ball into touch. This is a skill to be practised. Get likely kickers in pairs, one on either side of the pitch, and either side of the 10-metre lines. They aim to bounce the ball over the half-way line into the hands of their partner. Once they're doing this easily, tell them they must bounce the ball between the half-way line and their partner's 10-metre line – making it much harder for a defender to deal with.

By far the most valuable of such kicks is the long kick down into the corner. It sets up an excellent attacking position: if you don't actually take the ball at the line-out, you stand a good chance of pressurising your opponents into errors on their line.

It's very much a set-piece – it can come from any tactical point, but you want to maximise your chances, so do it from a scrum, with assured possession, and very limited pressure from flankers. Both fly-half and first-centre should be standing. Moving the ball to first-centre may lure their centres forward and – given that your players' punting ability is equal – add to the range of the kick.

Once more, you want immediate pressure to appear in the shape of your winger, so let him know what's on. You can formalise this by establishing the reliable range of your kicks, with (and without) a wind behind, and have either winger follow up alternately. Then you can agree that the first time you come within range of the corner from a scrum, that's what you'll do – and the winger's got to arrive soon after the ball. If he can't take man and ball, he must shepherd him towards touch – so he must judge the situation as he approaches. It's a great start to either half.

Kicking as described above is an essential element in the team's mix.

On the other hand, nothing is so easily abused as kicking, and nothing is so dull as a team whose sole method of going forward is kicking. It's typical of the play-safe syndrome that kicking is often the only weapon in attack. Typically, the coach concentrates on the pack's getting possession, and leaves the use of it to a fly-half who can kick. Typically, too, such a team lives on the other team's mistakes – they win, as it were, by default, and by good goal kicking.

## Non-tactical kicking

Most incidental kicking in the game is based on the need to keep the ball alive and going forward when the player is under pressure. It's certainly an easier skill than those of swerving and side-stepping, and becomes essential when support running isn't intelligent or intensive, or when the defender's positioning cuts out these possibilities.

The most important case is when some error has checked the momentum of attack. To continue with the move is simply to put the next player in an odds-against situation, and will probably lead to a breakdown behind the gain line. So far as possible, however, the kick has to be purposeful in length and direction – once again, the player who consistently thinks ahead is far better off than one who starts to think only after he's gathered the ball. The neatest solution is often to bounce the ball into touch. This needs practice – two or three minutes of such practice each time you go out is enough. The best bet otherwise is to put the ball in front of your forwards – so limiting the chance of counter-attack. The next – dependent on how much space you've got – is the high kick up the middle.

A second important case is the kick that opens the way for the next man out to run past his opponent onto a rolling ball. This is particularly valuable from outside-centre for the winger, when handling has failed to create an overlap. The opposing winger is faced with the difficulty of marking his man and being uneasily aware of the space behind him: if he's up to take his man, and the full-back is slow in covering him, the grubber in behind him can be devastating. In any kick of this kind, the winger aims to run wide and keep the ball in play – pushing it on for himself, or back behind the full-back for his centres. A place can be made for this kind of kick in normal handling practices – indeed in any handling practice by the backs it's as well to build in variety as the ball reaches the outside-centre, full-back, wing area: if you haven't created an advantage by the time the ball reaches outside-centre, he's got to have some ploys to keep the ball going forward.

The general criteria of success also serve as guide-lines for the kicker:

- wherever possible the defenders creating pressure should be forced to change direction and preferably turn round

- the kick should be judged to create a reasonable chance of regaining pos-session or imposing a weak counter.

In the course of team practices probable kicks should be built in. This is easily done in programmed unopposed: you specify a cross-kick from the right wing, or a grubber from outside-centre, or a chip back from inside-centre, to give practice to both kicker and supporting players, just as you would with tactical kicks.

# 22 TEAM DEFENCE

To the connoisseur, defence is as satisfying as attack. There's a real pleasure for the player and the coach in a team defensive effort in which everyone has a part to play, and which may well lead to a resumption of attack against an over-stretched opposition. Properly, defence always shades into attack and must be regarded as positively as attack is: defence should never be defensive.

There are three basic elements in team defence: pressure, depth, and cover. If you keep them separate in your mind, you'll get a simple, strong, very effective picture of defence.

## THE FRONT THREE

Pressure comes from the front three: the fly-half, and both centres. Their aim is to deny their opponents space, deprive them of the initiative and gain possession beyond the gain line. They also seek to limit the distance the ball moves across the field – to stop it at, and preferably before, outside-centre.

**1** *Get into position immediately, however shattered you feel*

The most critical moments in any game are those at which possession is gained or lost: decisive action in attack or defence at such a moment can turn a match. Discipline – and it's always self-discipline when you get down to it – is at the core of success in defence as in attack. You will need a leader, and the most effective leader in defence for the front three is inside-centre: he's ideally placed to marshal the trio and talk to them. He's got to get that front three into position fast.

**2** *Commit yourself*

Whenever the odds are in favour of the opposition getting the ball, you position yourself to pressurise them. If we do get the ball, then the scrum-half and forwards can launch our attack. What we don't want is our front three in intermediate, uncommitted positions – not in position to defend, not in position to attack. Even if we are on their line, the best thing to do if they are likely to get the ball is to make life as difficult for them as possible: they must all be aware that you are there, and that the slightest hesitation will let you in. You pressure them mentally as well as physically.

**3** *Give them as little space as possible*

The defence line and the off-side line coincide. Leave as little margin for error as your skill and balance allow. Every foot you are behind that line is a foot more space for them.

**4** *Keep inside your opponent*

A key idea in defence is to deprive your opponent of choice. In this case, you must deprive him of choice in direction of running: force him to run outside you. This ensures that he has to run further than you do. Judgement comes in estimating how far inside him you must stand to prevent him coming inside, and how far inside him you can afford to stand to deny him the chance of running outside you. If he's very quick, you'll have to stand wider – and run a greater risk on the inside (see point 8).

Keeping inside your opponent, therefore, doesn't mean being inside him initially at say a static first-phase situation. All the opposing back-division will be running slightly out since it makes effective passing 100% easier. You must be inside him as you approach the tackle area, but you can afford to let him run out towards you, and into that situation. All of you will appear to be outside your immediate opponents before the ball becomes available (see p. 21).

### 5   Go up in line

The front three must move up as one man. The absolute imperative is that you must never go up faster than the man inside you. If he isn't going up as fast as you'd like, you can tell him so afterwards, but at the time you go up with him. If a player goes up faster or slower than the other two then a dog-leg appears in the line, and that dog-leg is the most basic form of gap. As soon as it appears, skilful opponents will take advantage of it.

I believe that the fly-half is always best employed going up on his man. The odds are that his opponent won't be looking for a break himself, but nothing is more likely to prompt the thought than a fly-half who's giving him space. It's possible for the centres to go up, running off a flanker; it's possible for both the centres to come in one, so that inside-centre takes the opposing fly-half – but a miss move by the opponents leaves that for dead. In every way it's healthier that the fly-half should see himself as one of the front three committed to pressure.

### 6   Pressure them by balanced aggression

A key idea in games is 'start fast, arrive in balance'. There's no point in emulating the bull who may once in a lifetime catch the matador, but wastes the rest of the time in futile rushes. Start fast by thinking ahead and being ready to move. Keep glancing at the ball as well as at your opponent. Check that your starting position allows you to get off the mark fast – weight forward, feet comfortably close, nothing in tension. Keep thinking: the man and the ball. Keep checking that you're keeping position relative to the man inside you.

### 7   Take the man who comes to you

It's best to think in terms of a zone defence rather than man-to-man. Switches and dummy switches depend on the defenders being lured out of position by chasing 'their own man'. Think: whoever comes this way is my man.

**8** *Support the man outside you*

The high work-rate maxim 'do it and run' applies here as well: see your man pass . . . and support the player outside you. This supplies a great deal of strength and allows your partner to concentrate on the outside. It's the equivalent of the shuffle of the defence in sevens. It's also the best bet for setting up counter-attack: if your partner makes the tackle, you're the nearest player, and must get your hands on the ball.

**9** *If a break is made inside you, turn with your man*

The only time a player (and this includes the winger) can afford to go in to meet a runner at the expense of leaving his own man is when he's sure of taking man and ball. To go in without that assurance – which is possible only when the player has looked ahead and predicted what's about to happen – is usually a dead loss. At best it may force a pass; at worst, it leaves an opponent running into space. Unless you're so close to your line that allowing the ball-carrier to run on will lead to an immediate try, it's a far better bet to turn inside your opponent and so prevent the ball reaching him. The aim is to funnel the runner onto the deep defence (and specifically the full-back). However, not infrequently, having turned you can simultaneously blank off your opponent, and reach a tackling position on the ball-carrier.

**10** *The tackle is the first stage; the aim is the ball*

Any notion that getting the ball is a concern solely of the forwards is futile: everyone has to see getting the ball as important – more especially since immediate action by the nearest player is the most effective way of getting clear possession. So the tackle isn't simply a matter of stopping your opponent, though that is always the overriding aim. You're trying to stop him in such a way that the ball isn't available for his team.

A centre who can ride your tackle and stay on his feet is an ideal starting point for second-phase play. He must be prevented from keeping the ball available: knock him down if you can, and if you can't, smother him. And remember: if you can get the ball, you must. You should have immediate support from the player inside you – the nearest player on your side.

To be sure of your tackling is essential in the front three. Certainly, it's one of the key qualities I look for, especially at inside-centre. Most difficulties arise not from lack of courage, or lack of desire to make effective contact: they arise from not setting the tackle up correctly – not thinking ahead, not making allowances for your opponent's speed, and coming up out of balance. The only danger comes from loss of concentration. You can hit your opponent low – just above the knees – or high, with your shoulder in his solar plexus: you cannot hit him at his hips. If he sways into you with his hips, he can hurt you. The odd crash tackle can be very effective – but you must make it where he is less powerful and solid than your shoulders are.

## 11 Work-rate

If the pressure is effective, you'll find that your opponents kick a fair amount. If they do, you must get back to offer support to your back three. The outside-centre, especially, ought to be able to get back fast, to offer help in defence or counter-attack. Discipline and work-rate are the bases of good play.

The basic aim of the front three, as defined above, is pressure. There are times, though, when it's most effective not to drive forward on your opponents. If you think of a team that's getting a fair amount of ball against you, and is setting up moves in the backs, you'll see that a constant tempo in your defence may be to their advantage: it allows them to predict, and it simplifies their timing. If you then come up in line at a slower pace you'll find that they start their moves too early. This allows you to see what they're doing before you're committed – you get them to commit themselves first. You don't lose too much if you do this: they will always have more ground to cover before reaching the gain line than you do.

## Defence practices for the front three

The essential things to be drilled home are less concerned with the actual tackle than with organisation – positioning and timing. Tackling practice is better done as outlined in Part 5 (see p. 165), where you can build up a high tackle rate and limit contact power. To build up contact power use a tackle bag and crash-mat indoors. The method is to move the take-off mark further and further from the bag, so that players have to generate more energy and drive to get there. Then I encourage them to get the elbow of the tackling arm well forward, so that the shoulder is in a very strong position. The head should be tilted to the side, and the eyes fixed on the tackle point.

Once this kind of tackling power is established, the aim is to get them thinking very clearly about positioning and timing. The only way to do this is against the 2nd XV backs, and the only contact needed is a two-handed touch on the shorts. I've met mad theorists who claim you ought to have flat-out tackling in practice, but a touch of experience would correct their ideas. It's a joint practice, so there's much to be said for arranging that the pressure on the attackers should increase from a fairly low level to something approaching match pressure. The first thing to look at is lateral spacing – so placing them that at the tackle line they'll be inside their opponents. Initially, the attackers simply spin the ball and continue running. The defender goes up as if his specific opponent were running for a break, staying level with the player inside him. Gradually you can move the defence line forward and encourage the defenders to move up more rapidly but still in balance. As soon as you feel that each is covering his immediate opponent adequately, introduce the idea of supporting the player outside, so that as the attackers move the ball, the defenders go up and then out. You can then ask the attackers to vary their play and test the adequacy of the zoning by the defenders. However, I tend to delay this till the forwards are available to provide cover defence.

## Drift defence

What you've just read is preparation for effective pressure defence. There is an alternative system, however, that can be employed whenever the ball is consistently being moved wide. I christened it a 'drift' defence, and the term is now used everywhere.

A drift defence starts with each player lying wider than normal. The aim is to allow our stand-off to tackle their first-centre, our first-centre to tackle their second-centre, our second-centre and wing to tackle their extra man and wing. This allows our full-back to concentrate on depth defence, and allows our full-back and blind-side winger to continue their cover against a multiple overload.

Many teams employ this method at line-out. The space between the lines often encourages the side in possession to spin the ball wide. For our stand-off and centres to continue trying to pressurise is not merely futile then, it's counter-productive: their going forward prevents them from obeying the first rule of defence – get between the ball and our line. In effect, they contribute to being outflanked.

It isn't, however, of use only at line-outs. Whenever the opposition are consistently moving the ball wide – if they're sensible, employing a miss move – the drift defence comes into its own.

Evidently, drift defence is buying strength wide at the expense of strength in the area of stand-off: who takes the opposing stand-off if he runs? The answer must be one or other of our back row. After their immediate duty (see p. 196), their first priority is to cover inside the stand-off before adopting their normal cover running. From line-outs, rucks and mauls, this is no more difficult than it ever was, but a double problem threatens drift defence from scrums:

- the defending back row are tethered till the ball emerges so they'll be further away from the stand-off than they have been

- it's easier for the attackers to mount back row attacks aimed at the stand-off position, and an absentee stand-off may be sorely missed.

It may be, therefore, that we should think of the scrum as a situation for pressure defence.

Evidently, too, it's more difficult to exert pressure on the opposition. We'll always be forced to run further across than usual, which prevents really hard tackling, and gives an extra advantage to the really swift attacker. I wouldn't recommend the use of drift defence except when the opposition are consistently spinning it.

Setting it up is easy. Get the players to adopt their normal positions against the 2nd XV backs (or the forwards!) and get them moving up together while the ball goes through each pair of hands in the opposing line. Put a spare man wide in the opposition, evidently ready to join the line. Move the stand-off out half the distance to first-centre, and so on down the line. Walk through it, with each defender taking his new opponent. Then trot through it till they're all happy. Don't at this stage encourage the opposition to throw in unexpected attacks: the aim is firstly to get the defence confident in their new roles.

Next bring in the back row explaining that the new system, by providing cover wide, should help cut down on the amount of running the flankers will need to do. Get the opposing first-centre to lie deeper, and their stand-off to carry the ball forward. His aim is to force our stand-off to choose between checking to take their stand-off, or continuing to chase the first-centre and letting the stand-off run. Let the back row see this, and then continue the practice with them providing cover. It's all very simple.

I first saw this applied almost unconsciously by the Fijians in the early '70s. The North were spinning the ball wide to our excellent winger, Keith Fielding, but by the time the ball reached him there were two, three, and on one occasion four Fijians in front of him. They got there without effort, just drifting across to cover. Hence the term.

## THE BACK THREE

The back three have two functions: to provide depth in defence, and to set up counter-attack. The depth they provide is two-fold – against kicks and against running. In both they work together. When the ball is in the air one player must call for it. If two call for it, the player who is deeper should take it: if you call, and you hear a call behind you, it's his ball. But always there must be cover for the player catching the ball – get round him so that you can support him if he makes a mistake, or if the chance to counter-attack is there.

The central defender is the full-back. He must position himself in terms of width and depth. The width – i.e. where he positions himself relative to the ball – depends on his speed. Ideally, he'll be moving across field inside the ball as the opponents pass it. He may find, though, that if he isn't quick he may have to lie outside the ball, so that he can cover kicks to the open side. This leaves him vulnerable to a break on his inside, and to kicks back over his head. Taking into consideration his role in attack, it's obvious that speed is needed in the full-back just as in his two team-mates, the wings. His depth, again, must be a compromise: for tackling he'd like to be close to the point of break, and take his man immediately he comes through; for kicking he'd like depth – it's always easier to run forward onto the ball, and it gives him time to cover effectively. It's best if he allows the cover defence to do the early tackling, and commits himself to covering kicks, and taking the later tackles. He's also got to think of the kind of kicking used by his opponents, and of the conditions on the day. A wind in your face means that you need to get deeper; a wind on your back that – with a careful eye on the way the opponents are using ball – you can move forward.

The open-side wing has two jobs to do – to cover against the long diagonal kick, and to be up to tackle his winger if the ball reaches him. He's best advised to move up steadily as each pass is made – starting when the fly-half passes. As he moves up, the full-back moves across to cover the space he's left. As the full-back moves across, the blind-side wing moves across in turn to cover the space left by the full-back. The three work as a single unit. If the opposing winger beats his man, the full-back should be there to cover him, and if the winger beats the full-back, the blind-side wing must be there to cover the full-back.

All of this demands that the wingers must be able to concentrate throughout the match – the days when they could comfortably rest or look at the crowd have long gone.

The blind-side wing has a great deal of work to do. He is in a difficult position, since a single pass may put his immediate opponent in possession, and a single kick can put the ball into the box behind him. It's a foolish scrum-half who isn't aware of the blind-side wing's dilemma at every scrum, especially near the left-side of the field when his right foot is available for the chip into the box. Broadly speaking, the right wing should be more aware of the kick, the left more aware of the pass. The blind-side flanker must be ever attentive: he is the critical player in supporting his winger against the passing situation. The full-back, directly behind the scrum, provides the support against the chip.

The blind-side winger, immediately the ball goes open must get back to join the rest of the back three – getting his depth first, and then moving across-field. This gives some measure of protection against a delayed kick back across the forwards to the opposing wing.

The back three form one of the most important mini-teams within the team. They have to work hard for each other: as the open winger goes up, the full-back comes across to cover behind him, and the blind-side comes over to take the full-back's central position. When the full-back moves into attack, the blind-side wing gets in behind to guard against any mistakes. When the ball's in the air, each must feel secure that his nearest partner will be behind him providing cover. And when a defensive catch turns into a chance to counter-attack, one element in the equation is the presence of support.

They will frequently practise together while the rest of the back division is streamlining the passage of the ball. On p. 251, you'll find a list of the activities they can work on. A sensible aim is to make them interchangeable.

## COVER

The third element in team defence is cover. This is provided by the whole pack moving crossfield and creating a defensive pattern with width and depth. The basic guide-lines for this are exactly the same in defence as in attack. There are one or two specific points that help:

- the last hope running line against a handling attack is for the corner flag – but if you can't make that, you may be able to force a score far out

- if you are the leading man in the cover, you keep going out – what looks like a switch may be a dummy: if it's a switch, your supporters will take him out; if it's a dummy, you must be there

- any miss move by the opposition means you must run deeper

- if there's a two-man break – e.g. outside-centre and winger – the cover must provide for both: the second man must assume the winger will get the ball, and run deeper

- far and away the most common error is for the back row to go forward and get outflanked: as soon as your immediate job is done, aim where you are sure of getting between the ball and your try-line.

Indications that you should be going forward to pressurise include:

- stand-off getting bad ball from scrum-half – because we're pressurising them up front; because scrum-half's pass is weak

- weather making handling difficult – rain; wind (especially wind in your face)

- stand-off weakness – operating with new partner?; operating at unaccustomed level?; a weak player.

However, there's no substitute for your judgement. Back your hunches – it's the only way you're going to develop that judgement. For the coach, in all unit v unit or team practices, the rule is – teach your principles and talk to individuals: keep them thinking, improving, learning.

Team defence has got to be tight knit, with every player playing for every other. This is especially important for a team that believes in attack, and plays with a sense of adventure. There has to be the same elan, the same sense of constant support, the same willingness to play 15 men in defence as in attack. But remember, *never try to play rugby going backward under pressure – kill the ball, set up a maul, get reorganised, then play rugby.*

# 23 VARIETIES OF TEAM PRACTICE

The culmination of any structured session is work designed for the team as a whole. Indeed, one way of planning a session is to start with what you want the team to be able to do at the end and build the session towards it. Certainly the team practice must run smoothly. It is no place to start on activities that concern only a few, and keep the rest standing about, or to expose weaknesses in the units. What you try on the team level has to have a very high chance of success, likely because it has been prepared for, and necessary because team morale is linked to it.

On the other hand, the team practice is still a coaching situation and it must be used that way. This means that for the most part, and certainly early in the season, you will be working with limited aims and in depth. You will tend to examine a limited number of activities and be prepared to rerun them until the performance has reached a satisfactory level.

When you call the team together you have a whole set of possibilities on which to base the practice.

- *Unit v Unit* – basically the forwards working against the backs to test basic competence, e.g. the backs spinning the ball and introducing moves against the forwards' covering pattern; the back three counter-attacking from a kick against the forwards' covering pattern.

- *Unopposed rugby* – the team working in attack or defence to establish basic forms of both, and especially to establish support patterns. This can be kept realistic because of the constant recurrence of predictable situations.

- *Semi-opposed rugby* – the team working against a limited number of opponents, and so under limited and possibly conditioned pressure.

- *Situations* – since the game consists of predictable situations much of the detail of team tactics can be built up by establishing the team's most effective response, in attack and defence, to representative situations, e.g. a scrum, our put-in, or the middle of the opponent's 22-metre line. These situations can be examined in unopposed or semi-opposed practices, and reach their culmination in inter-team practices.

- *Pressure practices* – once the team can cope adequately with a variety of situations, it's possible in unopposed, semi-opposed, or opposed practices to present them with a series of situations, and to increase the pressure on them by increasing the speed of movement from situation to situation.

## Team tactics

In Part 4 there are some suggestions of the kind of guide-lines that the coach might offer his tactical decision-maker. His grooming and preparation for the

288

job is one of the major concerns of all team practice: he has got to be assimilating not merely the technical requirements for a particular team pattern but the match context that would indicate its use. As well as establishing high technical standards, therefore, the coach must constantly be encouraging the halves – who are by far the players best positioned to assess and control the situation – to develop the habits of mind that will allow them to make effective and early decisions. At every first-phase position they must be able to communicate a provisional decision within moments of the check. This is possible only if their concentration and alertness are continuous throughout the match. The decision-making process has already been outlined in Chapter 16, and is covered in detail in *Think Rugby*. The coach has to make and keep them aware of the three broad categories of information mentioned there. Of these, the third – a knowledge of the team's basic pattern of play and the methods appropriate to particular situations on the field must be embodied directly in the work that the coach sets the team. The other two categories are largely a matter for discussion, and they seem to be best dealt with either in fully-opposed situation practices or in team talks.

It's highly desirable that although the halves are at the centre of this tactical education, every player is involved. The principal reason for this is that the speed with which the team responds to a call is critical to its success. As soon as the call is made, we want the whole team to be rehearsing their own necessary contribution, so that when the movement starts everyone is prepared and committed. It also contributes to team spirit if every member of the team can contribute to a discussion of team performance (as well as unit and personal performance) in team meetings. And it may help players with personal decision-making in less accustomed situations.

The first step – getting the players to recognise and accept their necessary role as decision-makers – is often the crucial one. The abilities required are not uncommon, but are left dormant for lack of encouragement and stimulation. They must see themselves as leaders, and take a proper pride in the quality of their judgement. In all team practices they should be habituating themselves to this role. How the coach fosters their thinking I've tried to suggest by taking particular examples of team practices and working through them in some detail.

In all of this the aim is to encourage a habit of mind, on the field and off – where mental rehearsal is a valuable element of preparation. The moment at which the player produces something of his own better than the coach had imagined is the real moment of success.

It's important, too, to ensure that the rest of the team commit themselves to the decisions made. Nothing is more destructive of coherent rugby – or any team game – than lack of voluntary discipline. There are, of course, moments when an individual player's judgement prompts him to take an immediate and real advantage. What must be avoided is tentative hanging on to the ball in the hope that an advantage will appear. Their chance will come: unless there's something very evidently on for them, they've got to cooperate. This is made easier if all are involved in the tactical discussion in team talks and tactical preparation on the practice field. And every player must be encouraged to take pride in his judgement.

## UNIT V UNIT PRACTICES

When the units first come together, it's useful to test one against the other. It's a comparatively simple situation to deal with, and gives both backs and forwards a chance to start making decisions against a friendly opposition. It's also a useful experimental situation, testing the efficiency of what's been practised, and often suggesting useful improvements.

### The pack advancing behind a high kick

The following three exercises are of value to both units, but they're grouped here in order of introduction to the forwards – it makes no difference to the backs, but it's much easier in this learning sequence for the forwards.

Imagine an up-and-under penalty directed at the posts from centre-field. The kicker is going to kick straight downfield, so his position gives the axis of attack – the axis about which the pack must distribute itself to give *width*, which will prevent the defenders counter-attacking by running outside the forwards. But the counter-attacker may beat the first wave of attack, so we also need *depth*. So we arrange the forwards in order of pace, the fastest at the first to pressurise the catcher, the slower behind to absorb ambitious runners. As soon as it's clear that one forward is going to pressure most successfully, the rest settle into the width and depth pattern, and move forward together. If the kick is off line, the whole block move sideways to straddle the axis of the ball's landing.

This is a very simple exercise but very effective for habituating the forwards to the desired pattern. Once they get the message, the backs give up all hope of counter-attack: the array against them is too intimidating, even without the centres. But they get excellent practice of catching, supporting, and kicking for touch, all under pressure.

### Forwards supporting a diagonal kick

Once again, it's the pack against the back three, this time with the balance tipped in favour of the backs. The pack kneel in scrum formation between touch and the 5-metre line, some 30m out. The kick comes from scrum-half or fly-half, and is aimed to land on the line of the near post, close to the goal line. Experiment to find the point of maximum accuracy, which will be of value to the halves for attack in the match.

To simulate the breaking of the pack, the open side flanker departs as soon as the scrum-half gets the ball, and the rest as the coach counts (fairly quickly) 1 (the rest of the back row), 2, 3 (the locks), 4, 5 (the front row).

The first thing each forward has to do is to gauge where the ball will land. This establishes the necessary first movement of forwards in defence – to make sure of getting between the ball and our line as far forward as is safe on a line through the ball at right angles to our goal line. The movement, initially, for the bulk of the pack, as in most following-up situations, is crossfield rather than diagonally forward. The open-side flanker can afford to run on a diagonal – but not directly at the expected catcher: he'll do better if he too makes sure of getting between the catcher and our line, as far forward as he thinks safe.

The point where the ball looks like landing also defines the axis on either side of which the leading forwards spread to give width – they mustn't be outflanked. Once that width has been established, those breaking more slowly from the scrum fill in behind to give depth – the catcher may beat one man, but he won't beat the rest.

The backs have a real chance now if they can move the ball into space towards the other wing. At first, however, they're concerned with getting in effective defence positions in case the catcher is caught, or pressured into mistakes – the wings must be deeper than the full-back, who is moderately sure to be the catcher given the target of the kick. If all goes well, they can try to mount an attack, or at least move the ball to where they can make a safe and adequate touch. But it's all for real: every player is playing as he would in the match, honing his judgement as he goes.

## Crossfield cover

This is another exercise designed to get the forwards thinking about the general principles of their movement across-field when the opposition have the ball.

The pack kneel down in scrum formation between touch and the 5-metre line. The opposing scrum-half has the ball three or four metres in front of them on the 5-metre line, with his backs in position outside him. Initially, the backs will be using right-hand-dominant passes, and will be told to spin the ball to the wing, and put him clear of the defence.

The coach counts '1–2–3–4–5', starting his count as the scrum-half touches the ball. At '1', the back row can go; at '3' the locks; at '5' the front row.

Each run ends up with a 'score', or the pack setting up a maul. It is immediately followed by discussion of what happened, e.g. are the pack obeying the fundamental rules? i.e:

- get your head up, look at the opposition, back your hunches
- get between the ball and your line

- run off the man ahead of you, giving him the support you think he needs. If you think he'll be outflanked, run deeper; if you think an opponent will cut back inside him, tuck in behind. Think all the time about creating width and depth in the total cover pattern.

  Are the *backs* making the ball do the work? If each player can safely put the ball a metre further, then the winger has four more metres of space in which to get round.

Once this basic form has been used, the coach can start encouraging the backs to try other possibilities. For example:

- *the outside-centre goes as far as he can with the ball before passing* – this creates a second target for the pack, and gives the winger a little more space. The front runner for the pack must go for him: what must the rest do to cover the winger?

- *inside-centre and outside-centre do a dummy switch* – this will probably check the cover, and give slightly better odds on the overlap. What must the covering pack learn from it? That the front-runner mover checks for the switch, but goes on to take the outside runner, that the players behind him must be in balance to take the runner coming in, and that those running deep must run a little deeper in case the overlap comes off. At this point, too, the back row can start scrutinising the opposing backs, and making their predictions of what's likely to happen judging from their positioning

- *the backs can do a switch between inside-centre and outside-centre* – have the forwards' predictions worked? And for the backs, which centre is in the better position to decide on switch or dummy-switch?

- *the backs can do a miss move* – this will probably result in the pack suddenly being forced to run deeper than they had intended, and may well suggest to the backs the desirability of using miss moves in the opposing 22, where the opposing pack cannot run very deep. When the coach is satisfied that the pack are running intelligently – which he may well feel coincides with the time that the pack stop trying to get closer to the scrum-half in the starting position – he can alter the starting point to a midfield scrum. Immediately, the back row defence (with one of the front five subbing for the scrum-half) must start operating their immediate action plans (see p. 194). The practice then goes on in the same way, with the coach commenting and whenever possible complimenting between each run.

It's usually best in the kicking exercises to start without the attacking centres, so that the pack face the worst possible situation, and so that the back three have a reasonable chance of counter-attacking (see p. 304 ff.). But whether the back three can counter-attack or not, they face the situation that will occur match after match – the high ball in the air above them – and get adequate practice in positioning, calling – if two people call, the one further back takes it – and catching. They are also faced with the decision – should they try to counter-attack, or play safe? (See p. 304 ff.)

Once the pack have faced the problem of covering without the centres, the latter can be brought on. Since the decision is to kick they will, of course, lie up flat: their aim, to pressurise the back three. It's useful for the coach to arrange for the receiving catcher to kick the ball back over the heads of the centres occasionally to bring home to them the need to turn and get back fast if it should happen in the match, even though in the match their own back three would be giving depth to the whole move.

Again, once the coach is satisfied that the attackers are moving intelligently, he can change the situation to that of following up a penalty – e.g. an up-and-under. He can then establish in what precise area of the field this is likely to be the most effective way of using the kick. The forwards can begin their run in their follow-up pattern as they will in the match, with the line of the kick as the axis of the pattern. The coach will find, if he hasn't already examined the kick, that most players find great difficulty in kicking the ball high down a given line and he'd do well to have established the best kicker earlier in the practice and given him some coaching (see p. 150).

In both of these follow-up practices, it's best to play to a 'score' by the back three, or possession by the forwards followed by an attack from their backs. Initially, however, the pattern must be established, and the coach will find it more effective to concentrate on that. Later he can introduce the ways in which the forwards can gain possession – how to deal with an opponent who has the ball (see p. 167), how to do an attacking fall (see p. 160), how to set up a maul (see p. 222 ff.). Then he can introduce the backs in the second-phase attack, with the tactical decision being called on each replay according to the positioning of the back three. This helps the fly-half acquire the habit of looking to see precisely where the opposition are positioned. A useful variant on this in all unopposed or lightly opposed practices is for the coach to represent the bulk of the opposing defence – he moves into probable positions, and the team must attack in a more lightly defended area.

It's as well in any opposed practice to remind all the players that they are members of the same team, or at least club, and to moderate the aggression. The practices just described can be substantially carried out using two handed touch as a substitute for actual tackles. When you introduce tackling make it abundantly clear that there will now be tackling.

## UNOPPOSED RUGBY

The various forms of unopposed rugby are a very valuable – I'd say an indispensable – aid to coaching, provided that:

- they are a direct preparation for the pattern of rugby you intend to play in your matches

- they are seen as coaching situations – opportunities to improve individual, unit, and team performances

- they are complemented by a balanced programme of other work.

The aim of unopposed team practices is precisely that of any practice that seeks to reduce the pressure on the players: it allows full concentration on the performance of the techniques. They are practicable since in any of the given recurrent situations in the game the formation and behaviour of the defence is predictable.

It's very important that any team practice should be successful. One of the aims is to encourage confidence in the team, and the growth of mutual respect between the units. What we don't want at this stage is a succession of errors, or more stoppages than those at the end of each exercise. Errors will occur, and a vital part of preparing unopposed work is to drill home the need to deal with them effectively. But the first aim is to create a sense of the team working together. To this end, whatever you incorporate in your unopposed programme should already have been worked on. If you intend to use a back move in the programme, it ought to have been practised during unit skills. At this stage an error by one player affects fourteen others: we want to get rid of errors while as few players as possible are involved.

It's evident then, that unopposed has to be an integrated part of the whole session – one that appears to rise naturally from what has gone before. In practice, this means that the coach has to consider the session as a whole, working in part from the needs of the team backward, and partly from the needs of the individual and units forward. I feel very uneasy when team practices are divorced from the whole session. Indeed, as I've indicated in Chapter 13, I usually plan the whole session as an expansion of what I want the team to be able to do at the end. This means that each of the major requirements will have been practised and polished before it's brought into the team play.

This can be taken further by using the basic technique practices as elements of the unopposed. When the forwards handle, for example, they can be using '1–4' (see p. 127); when the maul is set up, it can be done by a player putting the ball down and turning (as on p. 56 ff.) to offer resistance; when it's to be a ruck, one player puts the ball down and offers resistance, one falls on it, the rest drive over (see p. 222 ff.). This has a further advantage in speed of communication; when I say '1–4', the players know exactly what's wanted.

As with all coaching, it's important to insist on quality standards. Simply to go through the motions does have a place – at a very low introductory level – but by the time we reach team practices we ought to be functioning fairly effectively. What's now needed is precise, crisp work. The team must be absolutely clear on what's wanted, and must expect to work till the pattern is adequately established. This can only happen if there is constant monitoring of what happens, and if the coaching produces an improvement at each scrum. With the players working at a high level of concentration and performance you must limit the number of repetitions and give very specific guidance on how to achieve the improvement.

A number of points call for very careful attention from the coach.

**1**   The single most important point is the positioning of the halves. Without opposition, it's fatally easy for the fly-half to take the ball too shallow – in a position where he'd have in the match to go himself or kick – and then try to spin it wide. His appreciation of depth is the most fundamental thing he has to learn, and the coach must constantly correct him or praise him for the position he adopts relative to what he's got to do.

**2**   Again, a basic aim is to involve the forwards in handling attacks – but it's got to be realistic, with each player contributing to the forward drive and ball speed. This means hammering home the basic support themes of depth and width – of working to get into useful and interesting positions where he can run fast onto the ball and be able to move it fast.

**3**   A third point to check is that everyone – and especially the full-back and the blind-side wing – is fully involved: there's rarely a moment when a player cannot be making a positive contribution, offering support or cover. Keep checking what the players not on the ball are doing.

The whole exercise is conventional and certain specific conventions are very useful.

## The scrum

For this the forwards kneel in scrum formation, and the ball is fed back by the scrum-half. The hooker counts '1–2–3–4–5', starting his count as the scrum-half regains possession at the back of the scrum. At '1' the back row can break, at '3' the locks, and at '5' the front row. This simulates the slow break-up of the real scrum.

## Rucks and mauls

It's best, as suggested above, to adapt a known practice to this. Make sure that it doesn't simply become a rest: the scrum leader has got to be encouraging them – 'squeeze in', 'pick him up'. The critical point – and one highly desirable in the match – is that the ball is not fed back till the scrum-half calls for it, and that he doesn't call for it till the player he's passing to is ready.

## Dropped ball

It must not be dropped, but if it is treat it as a maul situation: fall, offer the ball, set up the maul. It's very important that play doesn't stop because a mistake has been made.

## Ball on the ground after a kick

Treat as for a dropped ball.

# PROGRAMMED UNOPPOSED

This is based on a sequence of events dictated by the coach. Basic principles underlie the preparation of such a programme, as follows.

## Link-up

The forwards feed the backs and the backs feed the forwards. Except for specific purposes – e.g. making sure that the outside-centre must go for the ball if the winger is tackled – the ball shouldn't simply be put on the ground when it reaches the winger, for example. The aim is to get the forwards to see themselves not as drudges moving from set-piece to set-piece but as rugby players able to run and handle. The coach must see to it that the backs are alive to the notion of handling the ball on to the forwards.

For this to happen, the support patterns have got to be established. Emphasise the need for team communication and for observing the basic support laws. Look for individual forwards and check whether they are getting into effective positions. Are they running too shallow? Running too deep? Running with an eye to the man ahead of them?

## Speed into position

The critical moments in attack are the moments of regaining or retaining possession – you must emphasise the need to get into the right position fast. This applies to all the players, but in unopposed keep an eye especially on the fly-half and centres. If they aren't in position they immediately diminish the number of options open to them.

## Decision-making

Even in programmed unopposed, where the sequence is set out, you must expect your tactical decision-makers to be at least announcing decisions. One way of ensuring this is to leave options open – e.g. 'when the ball comes right for the first scrum, I want to see a move in the backs' – so the decision-maker has to decide, and the communications system has to work. And the programme should lead into standard situations which the halves have already considered, e.g. a ruck, our take-in, 5m out from the opposing line and 15m from touch. It's one thing to study this, or to set it up as a single practice, and another to encounter it, under pressure, as part of a sequence.

## Continuity and direction of attack

Continuity – the sustained attack – depends on getting first to the breakdown point and doing the right things (see p. 159). After this has been built up in technique and pressure practices it can be incorporated in your unopposed practices.

So, too, the basic patterns of *extending* your attack, of keeping your attack swinging right or swinging left away from belated defenders until you reach the critical point of attacking the *short side* or switching back open and *stretching* their defence; these have to be built in so that the whole team but especially the decision-makers get a sense of team rhythm.

## Establishing the mix

Your unopposed programme must reflect the mix – that balance of attacking methods appropriate to your team – so that passing, running, kicking, and moves all get an appropriate share. This won't, of course, all happen initially in one session – but all should be represented in a sequence of unopposed sessions.

Moves, for example, are essential to your rugby, not an optional extra, and the whole team must be confident in their use, aware of their weaknesses, clear about support patterns. So you must build in your moves for every unit in the team, and for your penalties. You may leave considerable discretion to the players regarding which move they use at any given moment (and if you have doubts about the decision get them to account for it at the next stoppage) but you can prescribe e.g. 'a back row move', or 'an overlapping move', or 'a get-it-back-in-front-of-the-forwards move'.

## Tempo control

Controlling the tempo of your attack becomes a live issue once the basic patterns have been established, and you've tidied up performance in every phase.

Speed of action – within your players' ability to cope – is one of the most potent weapons against the opposition. Ideally, by the time they arrive at the break-down, the ball's gone, and their weary trek has to continue. But speed can only be based on efficiency: you lose a lot of time if you drop the ball, and it goes forward. Once you've established this, take out your stopwatch, and give it to your wounded player – you yourself mustn't be distracted from actual coaching. His job is to motivate the lads to work faster, more calmly, more efficiently. He can time the whole run, or components of it. Your job is to stop that phase of the practice when you're ahead, before speed becomes corner-cutting.

With these ideas in mind we can now proceed to set up a programme. Initially, it's got to be limited in length – e.g. a single second-phase. If it doesn't involve all the players actively and in an interesting way, you may find it more satisfactory to prescribe a separate exercise for them – e.g. although a winger will certainly benefit from moving across to cover the full-back, it's not adequately rewarding to ask him to repeat it ten times.

Programmed unopposed is wholly concerned with attack, and it's sensible, therefore, to start from an attacking position and end with a score. It's the first stage in situation work, in which you work out with the team its best attacking methods from a given point on the field. Let's say, then, that we start with a scrum, our put-in, on the opposing 22, 18m in from the right touch, with both centres on the open side.

In a situation like this, we might exploit the blind-side, and then switch play across field to stretch their defence. The basic elements are:

1   the backs attack the blind-side

2   the forwards handle and maul

3   the backs spin the ball wide.

**1**   From the various possibilities open to us we select one. We'll have the fly-half take the ball blind, the full-back come in as extra man, and the ball go on to the wing.

The aim is to use the better numbers situation (see p. 263) to punch down the blind-side, and to get the forwards in support either to handle, or, if we're stopped, to keep possession. Either way we should pull their defence across, and open up the field for second-phase.

The points we'll have to emphasise as coach:

**a)** *early decision and communication*

**b)** *positioning: fly-half* stays open till the ball is on its way back; takes the ball *shallow* to attack blind-side; *full-back* stays behind fly-half and starts running (across first and then moderately straight) just before fly-half; *winger* must lie a little deeper so that he won't overrun the ball – the fly-half is coming across

c) *execution: fly-half* runs till challenged then feeds full-back; *full-back* must be up flat with fly-half to deny the opposition further time to cover – we'll have to work on this, varying his starting position and timing. If opposing winger comes in, he'd feed the wing; if opposing winger stays out he'd go himself, and look for support from the forwards; *winger* must run fast onto the pass – we'll have to work on this, varying his starting position and timing; he must keep the ball in two hands, and keep it in play.

**2** The forwards must get across to support the blind-side move. Initially, though, they must make strenuous and intelligent efforts to avoid the wheel: if the wheel takes place, the fly-half should cancel the move. This means locking the scrum, getting as low as possible on the right, and real concentration by the hooker to speed the heel.

The shove must be sustained: it may keep the opposition down a little longer, and should rock them back on their heels. We don't want our back row going into the blind until the ball has passed them: keep pushing.

a) *Positioning*: the key ideas are *width* and *depth*. We want, if possible to have the forwards behind the ball and on either side of the ball-carrier and we want the forwards who break later from the scrum giving depth support, so that if the ball goes down we have cover.

b) *Execution*: as the ball passes them, the back row and scrum-half move wide to get the width and then move forward. If they go forward first they will probably be out of the play.

The players nearest to the ball-carrier shout to let him know they are there: shout *his* name – it avoids confusion.

If space is available we'll go for forward handling – using as much width and depth as possible; if cover is there we'll concentrate on making sure the ball comes back. For the purposes of the exercise, we'll put in four sharp passes 1–4 (see p. 127), the last ball-carrier will put the ball down and turn to act as opposition, and we'll set up a maul.

The coach checks the support pattern, the speed of passing, the fact that they 'walk forward' in the maul. While the maul is on he glances left to check the speed into position and alignment of the backs, and encourages the full-back to get back fast for the second phase.

**3** If the blind-side drive has been successful we've scored – but we practise what happens if we haven't.

The ball comes back from the maul when the scrum-half calls for it, and he calls for it when he's checked that the line is in balance and ready to go. If the ball comes back before the line is ready, he'll have to make an immediate decision – to go himself, or to chip blind, for example. The coach must prepare him for this, and if in the practice the situation arises, then he's got to make his decision and execute it.

*We never want our players to stop judging, deciding, acting: the programme we're working through is a staple for the team, but if it's likely to break down we must have positive alternatives, and people ready to execute them.*

**a)** *Positioning: fly-half* – as ever his judgement of the situation is crucial, and should immediately affect his own positioning. In this situation it's unlikely that his opposite number will have been drawn into the maul. If he has, and the opposing three-quarters have moved in one to cover, there'll be a gap wide, so we'll spin it; if a flanker has gone to fly-half, we'll attack him; if the full-back has moved up, we'd chip over the top. The coach uses the practice to point this out: we've got to coach judgement and decision-making as well as the mechanics of the game.

For this practice, we're going to spin the ball wide, trying to stretch their defence so that a gap appears. This means that the *fly-half* will take the ball fairly deep, and out on the open-side.

*Centres*: at any second-phase situation, the temptation is for the centres to lie too shallow, which effectively retards the acceleration of the line: make sure they're in place both in width and depth to allow stretching and acceleration. Usually I make the inside centre responsible for alignment.

**b)** *Execution*: we're looking for quality in moving the ball (see p. 246 ff.). We want the ball to reach outside-centre with time for him to make good decisions. In this case, though, we'll give the ball straight to the winger and let him score.

Once the players have got the basic pattern, we can begin to develop it, and elaborate it. We *develop* it by creating more opportunities for the forwards to handle and give possession from mauls. A key notion in total rugby is that the forwards should see themselves equally as e.g. props and players in the loose. We need to establish the self-discipline that gets the forwards into effective support positions even when they're weary. We want to build up their work-rate – which means 'scrum – and run; maul and run; pass – and run' – so we don't want them in the unopposed above to give the ball back from the maul, and stand applauding as the winger flashes over the line: they must be there in case he gets stopped. We want especially to create a sense of small team unity in the back row – a real pride in the way they support the ball-carrier and each other. We tend to aim, therefore, for at least two handling movements by the forwards in each programme.

We *elaborate* the programme by examining the different possibilities in each of the basic elements. In the two back movements – 1 and 3 – of the programme we're looking at, we can easily incorporate moves. For example, when the ball goes blind, the fly-half can do a dummy switch with the full-back, with the full-back coming back inside to check the opposing back row; when the ball comes open we can add a dummy switch between the centres and encourage our full-back – weary from his recent exertions – to make the extra man. We try, in fact, to incorporate those elements of our particular mix appropriate to the starting situation.

At all times we must see the programme as a learning/coaching situation. It's useless if we don't go on making individual performances better – calling attention to weaknesses, and suggesting, or working out with the player, ways of improving. To this end, you may run through the programme half-a-dozen times. It's useful to start off on your own goal line and call the 22 the opposing try line; and repeat attacking the 10-metre line, the half-way line, the 10-metre line, the 22, so ending up performing the programme really well in the opposing 22. You should also, where practicable, switch from side to side of the pitch. In this programme it is practicable – though you'd have to check on the scrum-half's pass, and expect the final spinning of the ball to be slightly less effective since it will entail left-hand-dominant passes right down the line. On the other hand, it means that a wheel on the initial scrum will work to your advantage, tending to take the bulk of the opposing pack away from the blind-side drive. When you try it, you can, of course, build the simulated wheel into your unopposed, as you would in setting up back row moves to take the ball left after being wheeled.

What has been outlined here is a fairly typical unopposed programme. It starts from one of the recurrent situations – e.g. scrum, line-out, drop-out, kick-off, tap penalty – at which you can predict possession, and within wider limits, the behaviour of the opposition. You build in the basic patterns suggested by your overall strategy, and use it to explore possible tactics. You monitor very carefully the probabilities, so that players don't try to run through the opposing pack, or ignore the tackle line. You insist on quality, and should have prepared for it in the rest of the session. You keep on coaching and commenting, getting the players to think ahead and make decisions. If you do this, you'll find that the programme does much more than establish a single pattern of play – it helps establish basic principles in the minds of the players.

I've detailed another typical unopposed programme in Chapter 13, trying to give a real feel of how you set out to plan one, and then to monitor it.

## Defensive unopposed

Programmed unopposed is all about methods of attack, and an attitude to attack. We also need a method of encouraging high work-rate and efficiency when we are actually going backward. The situation that fits in most easily is where one of the backs is tackled behind the gain line, so that the pack has to go back to maintain possession or limit our opponents' gain. This is easily simulated, and leads to a very intensive pressure practice I call defensive unopposed.

We start from a simulated scrum facing upfield on the centre of the 22. The ball is played back and spun out left or right. When the coach blows his whistle, the ball-carrier puts the ball down, and the player who gave him the pass nips in and picks up. The first forward takes the ball off him and the rest of the pack maul on him. The two backs concerned get swiftly back into position. When the scrum-half sees that the back division are ready, he calls for the ball, the ball is spun out, the coach whistles and the cycle is under way.

The coach can vary the distance from the pack and the depth at which he elects to whistle and give a great deal of intensive practice in support running in a short time. He must, however, carry on coaching – watching individual players and checking that they are using their heads as well as their legs, watching the build-up of the maul and the continued drive, 'walk forward', as the ball comes back, watching the positioning of the backs so that there's genuine acceleration onto the ball, and so on. Mistakes are never welcome, but at least in this kind of practice they are what the team are working on, and they do ensure that mechanical running is avoided.

This is a very high-pressure practice and the coach should limit its duration – start off with three whistle-stops, and gradually in succeeding sessions extend it.

Defensive unopposed is an excellent situation to drill home two imperatives on how to handle the retreating situation:

- the first aim is to stop the ball going back – don't hand the ball back unless the player behind you actually calls for it

- don't play rugby going backward; set up a static situation that allows time for decision-making and safe execution.

## Conditioned unopposed

Programmed unopposed breeds confidence by laying down in advance what is going to happen. The match situation, however, has a much higher content of the unexpected – basically, the difference between the expected efficiency of the opponents and their actual performance. The whole team, therefore, and especially the tactical decision-makers must be put in situations that call for quick, effective decisions. For this we need a form of the exercise that builds in the unexpected – so conditioned that individual players or units can create the unexpected for the rest of the team to react to. The coach's job is then to monitor the decisions and encourage the whole team to appreciate the reasoning behind them, and, of course, to improve the execution.

He can do this in two ways – by telling one part of the team what is going to happen, but not the rest, or by leaving it entirely to the players working within a few stipulations or completely free.

The first form, by its nature, will tend to be limited – playing it through second-phase will be adequate. Say, for example, that we have a scrum on the centre line with a blind-side of 20m on the right. The tactical decisions have been made and communicated. The scrum-half, however, has been told separately that the scrum are in difficulties and he'll have to attack by kicking. This immediately creates an unexpected situation for the rest of the team. How are they going to react? The way in which they do so is the starting point for coaching. Has the back division moved immediately into its defensive position, giving pressure from the front three, depth from the back three? Has the pack created width and depth on the line of the ball? Has the scrum-half put the rest of the team onside? If he's slow, the job will have to be done by someone else – who? And who will fill the resultant hole?

So far as the execution is concerned, we can start with the kick, its range, height, and direction. The scrum-half can go through this, thinking about the need to get it up quickly so that the opposing back row can't charge it down, about the need to keep it in play, about the need to keep it more or less in front of his forwards, about the need to put it high enough to let the pack get into contention for it. It may well bring home to him the need to get out and work on particular kicks, working in real detail – kicking immediately the ball reaches him, from low down, with the ball across his foot, and his foot going where he wants the ball to go.

The coaching continues with comment on the rest of the performance – e.g. have the front three got into line before applying pressure? If they chase as individuals they're backing outsiders – spectacular if they make the tackle, but unlikely to be successful.

The actual mechanics of the practice will be as in programmed unopposed – the first player onto the ball will secure possession, if in doubt falling on it and looking to feed the mauling pack. The ball comes back when it's asked for, and by that time the decisions about the second-phase play must be made. The forward-leader may well have decided, however, that this particular situation is ideal for the pack to set up a drive from the maul – if the kick has been placed in front of them, there's a good chance that they will outnumber their opponents and be able to attack successfully. If they do, the coach lets them drive and then whistles, the ball is put down and the ex-ball-carrier turns to act as opposition, the maul is set up and the resultant ball can be used by the backs from this new and again unexpected situation. How effectively do they use it? The coach can then talk through the decision with the decision-makers.

The second stage comes with the coach stipulating a starting situation and perhaps a closing situation: whatever shape the attack takes, it must end with a particular form of score – e.g. a score by a forward on the right touch line. This last stipulation postulates an opposition that has left its left flank unguarded. It might equally be weak at midfield – and the score has to be between the posts, and so on.

In the final form of this exercise, the shape of the attack – or the defence, for any mistake, intentional or unintentional, will give practice in defensive play – is left solely to the pack-leader and the back-leader, who shape the events between them. The pack-leader creates the unexpected by calling for mauls or drives, and the back-leader shapes the attack from there. All the basic priorities for programmed unopposed apply, and only when the rhythm of the team is adequately established should this form of unopposed be undertaken. Again, it is only a coaching situation – the coach has to be in there commenting, questioning, suggesting, if it's going to be genuinely useful.

## Counter-attack unopposed

The ball that your opponents give to you by way of badly judged kicks is the starting point for a characteristic feature of total rugby – the handling counter-attack. This counter-attack almost inevitably starts with the back three, the full-back and wings, whose job in defence is precisely that of giving depth against breaks and especially kicks. They must be guided into an appreciation of the factors that govern the profitability of attempted counter-attack, and given practice to build up confidence in their procedures. But the rest of the team are vitally involved, and the final success of counter-attack is often governed by their judgement and work-rate. You need a form of unopposed practice that will give everyone a clear idea of his role in the team effort.

What the coach must first do is establish basic conditions for launching a counter-attack, and a ground plan of how the attack is to proceed. The final aim, as in all help towards decision-making, is the independent judgement of the players, but initially a few key factors can be very helpful.

### Position on the field

The coach may initially suggest that if there's any doubt we should not try to counter-attack from inside our own 22, since a mistake there is hard to retrieve.

Broadly speaking, too, counter-attack is most difficult from a kick into the box when the ball starts off more or less directly in front of the opposing forwards. But the fact that the opposing forwards are close together opens up the way for another form of counter-attack. Once again, it depends on work by supporters – in this case the three-quarters. The aim now is to switch the centre of attack clear across the field, and to do it with one or two very long spin passes to colleagues standing back ready to receive them. You have two practices to do in preparing for this: first the passes (see the section on scrum-half passes, and especially that most powerful of passes, the upright pivot pass) and then practising the whole situation, so that as soon as the ball goes into the box, the players are getting into position, to offer standing targets for the passes.

In either of these situations, safety is initially the sensible priority.

## Indications

There are three helpful indications that counter-attack will work.

**1** *The catcher can go forward himself:* this is the most reliable gauge of pressure. It's possible to counter-attack successfully with the catcher simply giving a pass to a supporting player, but all too often this means that the supporting player cannot accelerate onto the ball, and/or cannot choose his direction of run.

**2** *The catcher has immediate support:* you can expect the catcher to beat one man – especially if his opponent has ignored the basic precept 'start fast, arrive in balance' and arrives out of control – and this may open up fresh possibilities. It's generally best, however, to see immediate support as a requisite.

In terms of the practice, this means concentration on getting the back three to work as a team, on an early call, and on a determined effort to be behind the catcher when the ball arrives. This simultaneously gives cover for the fumble, and allows acceleration onto the pass.

Of the other players, I expect the outside-centre to arrive first, closely followed by the back row. The whole team, but especially these players, must make a real effort to get behind the ball as early as they can. A team that watches the ball go back to the back three and stands waiting for them to bring it forward is never going to be a consistently successful counter-attack force.

**3** *The disposition of the opposition:* counter-attack will always have a better chance when the opponent's kick is a result not of choice but of necessity – when pressure has deprived them of the initiative. If they have prepared for the kick and the front three, the back three and their forwards are all in the picture, then counter-attack has a very limited chance of success.

The back three must keep thinking ahead so that they know the situation that led to the kick, and they must use the time while the ball is in the air to glance at the way the opposition is coming forward.

## Direction of attack

Ideally, we want the counter-attackers to play with the same confidence, judgement, and fluidity as a good sevens team, but once again basic precepts will be an initial help. The most useful precept is that you feint at strength, strike at weakness. What this tends to mean is that the catcher and at least one supporter run at the opposing pack. The aim is to discourage them from spreading crossfield – to keep them narrow when they should be wide. This preserves at least part of the field as a possible attacking area.

When judgement dictates, the supporter switches play towards that area. By the time the switch takes place supporting players – the centres and a wing, at least – should be out there, deep enough to be able to accelerate as a line onto the first supporter's pass.

This can be set up as a unit practice before the team come together. Do it on a small scale, with the coach throwing the ball to the full-back, and at a walking pace, until the basic pattern is established. The front three take four or five paces forward to simulate pressurising their opponents, and then move back into support position. Gradually increase the scale and speed of the operation. This small practice will simplify the introduction with the team.

## Disposal of the ball

Setting up this basic form for counter-attack is equivalent to establishing an efficient form of a move – it is designed to give your striker an increased chance to use his abilities. As with moves, it offers no automatic key to unlock their defence – simply improved odds for your raider.

It's yet another case where judgement is called for. Before the switch is made, the players running into support positions, and especially the first of these to receive the ball, have got to be engaged on the assessment of the situation.

- *Look* – he must have his head up and be looking at the opposition defence, getting facts about them.

- *Judge* – he must be sorting these facts out into what is significant – evaluating the possibilities they offer.

- *Decide* – he must by the time the ball reaches him have made his choice so that he can set up the attack properly.

- *Communicate* – his decision must preferably be early enough to allow communication with those immediately involved (though in a fluid situation he may well find he must depend on their reading the situation in the same way that he does) so that all can . . .

- *Co-operate* – effectively.

This kind of thoughtfulness has to be built up in the players by constant encouragement. The decision is on which of the four possibilities to employ – to pass, to kick, to run, to use a move – and by running through these possibilities in the unopposed situation the coach can help them choose with confidence.

If the counter-attacking player has become isolated – by any of the chances that arise in a match – his choice is restricted to kicking or running. Once again his decision can only be effective if it's based on thinking ahead, and the scope of his choice is limited by his personal abilities – can he chip accurately ahead to find touch or keep the ball in play? Can he kick, perhaps left-footed, back to his forwards? Can he kick high and perhaps deep to expose the opposition's lack of depth? By bringing these possibilities to the player's attention the coach can perhaps motivate him to improve his kicking skill and, mutatis mutandis, his running and evading skills.

## Counter-attack practices

Setting up an unopposed practice to exercise counter-attack is moderately easy. It can be done either as a practice on its own or as an addition to programmed unopposed.

For the first of these, start off with a simulated scrum just inside the 10-metre line with the front three up in defensive positions along the 10-metre line. The coach tosses the ball in the air to simulate the opposing scrum-half's pass. As soon as he tosses it, the front three go forward to touch the half-way line and then immediately get into support positions for the counter-attack. Immediately the coach catches the ball he puts in a deep kick to the back three – and the whole team goes into counter-attack.

Once again, this is a coaching situation: it's the quality of comment from the coach and from the players that makes it of value.

The second form of the practice simulates the situation where your team is attacking, the ball is put down, and an opponent kicks it through. The coach sets up a programme, warns the team what's going to happen, takes a spare ball onto the pitch with him, and at an appropriate moment kicks it through at the full-back. The full-back should have immediate support from the blind-side wing, and together they drive forward acquiring further support as they go. This also allows the full-back practice in the situation where the ball reaches him without support and he has to take the ball forward before kicking it in front of his forwards – again something that requires practice to be consistently successful.

## Semi-opposed rugby

Although the name suggests a form of practice in which the team is opposed by half a team – e.g. a team working against a pack – it tends to be used to cover all varieties of limited opposition.

Limiting the opposition is a basic form of conditioning a practice, a further confidence-building step before the full pressure of the match. Besides limiting them in numbers the coach can limit what they are allowed to do. At its simplest he might station four of them, arms linked, at the point where this programme calls for a maul – to give some contact, and to sharpen the supporting players' awareness of the need to get to the mauling point fast. This can be made more realistic by having only one opponent at the mauling point, and the rest at an appropriate distance away, so that they provide opposition of the standard needed. Put them further away and the team's job is easier; closer and it becomes harder.

The coach can also give a free roving commission to this limited opposition – always ensuring that they play within the laws. In a programme beginning with a simulated kick-off, for example, they can pressurise the initial maul and then work as a back row trying, within the laws, to disrupt play. It's as well to emphasise they're acting legally, for they're obviously tempted to make up for lack of numbers by low cunning and mayhem.

Much more interesting forms of semi-opposed, however, are possible, and in my experience the best of them pits the team against a pack and half-backs. This can be conveniently done with the 1st team against the 2nd, with the spare back division working elsewhere on the field. Each team in turn plays against the opposing pack and halves.

The practice starts with a scrum on the 22, with the pack and halves attacking the near goal line.

When they get possession, either at the initial scrum or at a maul, or at the coach's direction, they are forced to attack in the forwards. The scrum-half and fly-half must do their best to get the ball in front of their pack by running or very accurate kicking, and the forwards have to set up handling movements from back row moves, or rolling off mauls. They win if they cross the line.

The full team score by putting two men clear before they reach the 22. Their aim is to get the ball efficiently and quickly into space, and to make sure that ball speed exceeds the running speed of their opponents.

This gives very intensive practice to the two packs in attack and defence in all normal aspects of the game other than line-out. The coach may have to impose conditions if one pack is markedly stronger than the opposition, but there's no reason why he shouldn't even it out e.g. by switching front rows. The backs have room in which to gain confidence, and the pack's halves have to concentrate on attack close to the forwards.

The intensity of the effort required from the packs imposes a time limit on the exercise – I use it to the point where fatigue or frustration becomes evident, and then switch. And again, this is a coaching situation: you need breaks within the exercise to do some actual coaching and commenting.

If you intend to devote part of the team element of a structured session to this kind of work it obviously pays to incorporate within the skill and unit elements an adequately conditioned preparation, so that the semi-opposed practice goes well. It wouldn't pay to go into such intensive work until the skill level, especially of the packs, was reasonably high.

So, too, must be the coach's control of the players. He is, in fact, creating that kind of confrontation which in play-safe rugby can lead to violence. It's best, therefore, to use a certain amount of conditioning, so that the sharp edge of confrontation is blunted.

## Situations

The final stage before playing a match is usually seen as a practice match. For those coaching or playing at a fairly high level, however, practice matches are of limited value: there's no guarantee that they are going to improve technically the play of the teams. They may benefit the stronger team in terms of confidence, but at the expense of the weaker. Besides which, the time can be better employed working in detail on what is most often, remarkably, left to chance – the establishment of team tactics.

It was suggested earlier that the basic strategy of the team, the notion of the kind of rugby they are hoping to play, starts with a vision in the coach's imagination. The vision in the imagination of the coach committed to total rugby, for example, is that of a team playing flexibly to meet the problems posed by particular opponents and conditions but always aspiring to fifteen-man handling rugby. But within this basic sense of how they intend to play, there's a need for a realistic appraisal of how the team is going to react tactically to particular situations.

By the nature of the game, basic situations are bound to recur in the match and throughout the season. Team tactics are largely based on a clear understanding of how the particular players in the team are best equipped to deal with these recurrent situations.

The tactics must cover both attack and defence. Much of the attacking tactics can be worked on in unopposed and semi-opposed practices, and particular facets of defence and counter-attack can be dealt with as outlined above. The real test of their efficiency, however, comes with their exposure to a full-scale opposition.

Rather than play a practice match it's therefore in the team's interest to work, if possible, with a full opposition on the chief recurrent situations, repeated several times and treated both in attack and in defence.

The aim is to establish what, in a particular situation, the teams are best equipped to do, and to work to make it as effective as possible. As part of the general development programme for the team, the coach is always trying to extend these possibilities, and offer greater variety of attacking and defending measures, but establishing what *at this moment* it can do is an indispensable aid to decision-making on the field.

Decision-making is most effective when it concerns a limited number of possibilities – enough to give variety and keep the opposition guessing, enough to provide alternatives when the opposition can cope adequately with a particular one, but so limited as to allow quick, easy choices. Establishing the right number of possibilities, and developing them to the point where each can be undertaken confidently is part of the coach's job. He can err in providing too few choices – as happens in play-safe rugby – or in offering too many, inadequately developed.

Apart from the right number and adequate preparation of methods, he must also help his team to appreciate the factors that indicate one choice rather than another at a particular moment. These factors are basically the strength or positioning of the opposition, but will also include the actual state, physical and emotional, of team players actively concerned.

At this point in Summer School courses, it's interesting to survey the course members and say: '*Right, think back to last season. Your team's been given a scrum fifteen metres from the opposing goal line, and fifteen metres in from the right touch. What scoring possibilities were open to them, that they'd worked on and trusted and were actively conscious of?*' When the thinking has gone on for thirty seconds, it's too late: the ball is in the fly-half's hands, and the time for decision-making on the tactical level is past. In that time the whole process – looking, judging, deciding, communicating, co-operating – must be complete. What situation practices do is to simplify the task, and to create a habit of mind that's sorting things out even before the referee's whistle goes.

Some time later at Summer School, usually in the bar over a quiet drink, the follow-up question is raised, of the coach's controlling the team, and the game, and converting it into a kind of chess. Some very proper fears are expressed of an American Football situation of the looking being done by trained observers posted on top of the stand and in radio contact with the dug-out, of the coach judging and deciding, of communication taking the form of a substitute sent on with orders, and the cooperation being that of a set of zombies going through pre-ordained movements. I do remember an occasion, sitting in the West Stand at Twickenham for a U.A.U. Final, when at a particular moment Mike Titcombe asked '*What'll they do now?*' and I explained what we'd probably do, and it actually happened. He turned and said '*My God, it's like chess*'. It was, but only in the sense that people who've thought about a subject – e.g. a move in chess, or a tactical decision in rugby – will often come to the same conclusion: it was the sensible thing to do. So far as the mental side of the game goes, coaching sets out to encourage the habits of mind which the gifted player use almost unconsciously, and to bring them within the range of a greater number of players. A problem faced by talented players who turn coach is, in fact, that what seems sensible and obvious to them is by no means obvious to the people they're coaching. What complicates the problem is that to a great extent the process in the talented player is intuitive and he almost certainly will find it difficult to explain what prompts him to his actions. Before he can coach he has to make the process conscious and articulate it.

Considering set situations is a concrete way of solving this problem and of encouraging a like habit of mind in the players. Indeed, it allows the players to make a real contribution. You put them in the kind of situation outlined above and you say – 'Well, what can we do here?' so far as attack is concerned, or 'Well, what are they likely to do here?' so far as defence is concerned. Out of this comes an appreciation of what is needed to make an action work, and what circumstances will make it a poor bet. The great thing is that by recognising such facts in the calm of the practice, the players are less likely to waste possession in the match.

It's a great help to the tactical decision-makers if we – the coach and the players – can establish our most effective gambits at critical tactical points. For each they need two or three live possibilities, and an understanding of the cues that indicate the best choice. There's no question, so far as I'm concerned, of prescribing what should be done in the given situation. It's simply a way of getting all the players to be aware of the possibilities which are likely to be effective. In this, as in everything else, the coach is trying to reach the point where he becomes superfluous, where he can safely leave it to the players, and examining situations is simply an easy path to that point. Initially, the players may depend on it but the great aim is to get them thinking more intelligently and imaginatively than the coach ever did.

The situations you deal with in unopposed, semi-opposed, or opposed practices must justify themselves – i.e. they are certain or very likely to occur, or they are particularly crucial, or they are representative.

They must deal with all the major restarts in the game – kick-offs and dropouts, scrums, line-out, penalties. To be realistic they've got to be continued through second-phase, and this in turn covers the maul or ruck.

The coach cannot treat this full-scale situation, except in a few cases (e.g. short penalties involving the whole team), as an initial learning situation. Whatever can be done in smaller units – e.g. the fly-half kicking into the box, a back row move to the left, the full-back coming in on the blind-side – should be covered before you reach this stage: you don't want half the team standing about.

Although you are dealing with specific points on the ground, and looking at specific possible actions, many of the situations may already be covered by broad principles set down by the coach. For example, the fly-half may have been given basic guidance about kicking, so that he will tend to kick for touch in his 22, kick for position from ball obtained behind his 10-metre line, and open it up beyond that. The coach may have pointed out that you tend to continue attacks checked at mauls and rucks in the direction you were going; that if you continue the direction of attack towards the right touch, you are opening the whole field up on the left to stretch the opposing defence with right-handed passes on the next phase; that you tend to feint at strength, strike at weakness; that broadly speaking it's sensible to pass to the left, and use moves carrying the ball to the right; that it's not a good bet doing miss moves to the right; that some moves can be set up initially more easily from line-outs than from scrums.

And, of course, you will begin to formulate general guidance for your actual team as you examine the specific situations. For penalties, for example, you can establish the profitable kicking range of your kicks, the optimum up-and-under area, the place where particular short penalties can best be used, the places where you'll kick to touch, who is best used for kicks to the left touch and who to the right, whether a pass should be employed to give a better angle, and so on. This leads to a general appreciation and so to better decisions. And, of course, for maximum effectiveness each of these has to be worked on with the whole team to establish the best follow-up patterns, the requisite support, pressure, depth, and width. In general, once these guide-lines are established less time

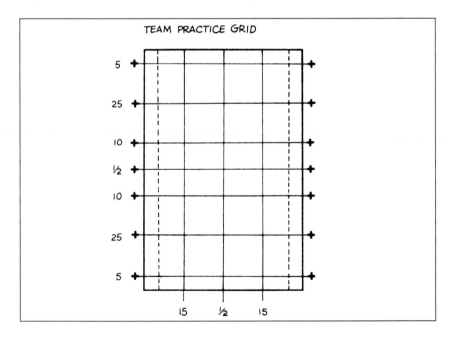

need be spent thinking what the team is going to do and more on the actual per-formance. It allows quicker action in the match – and delay is always an advan-tage to the defenders – and it allows full concentration on the execution.

All the examples used so far have been of attacking play, or at least of using possession we expect to get. Defensive play is equally important but tends to be more general in character – i.e. it isn't greatly altered by position on the field. Much of it can be dealt with in small units – e.g. the pack running crossfield against the backs, or the back row and halves working on immediate defence at a simulated scrum against the opposing back row and halves. Some of it can be simulated in unopposed – e.g. when the coach at a simulated scrum shouts 'ball lost' and the team has to get into defensive formation and prepare for a count-er-attack, or at a kick-off, when the coach puts the ball where it's not expected.

Defence, like attack, however will benefit from being faced with situation practice. It's just as important that the players can deal with the opposing drop out, or short penalty, or kick into the box, or move, as they should be capable of using the attacking possibilities that they present. Situations played against an opposing team afford the best possible test for defensive arrangement, expose weaknesses, and give a real opportunity for improvement.

To cover all the basic situations in at least a representative form, it's conven-ient to think of a line running parallel to touch down the centre of the field. This, with the two 15-metre lines, divides the field into four. This covers a blind-side on the left, a blind-side on the right, and both split-field situations. In prac-tice, these are approximate positions, and for specific purposes – e.g. a right-footed drop at goal, or an attack on the blind that needs a little more space – we'll make necessary adjustments.

For convenience, we can use the 22s, 10-metre lines, and half-way line to com-plete a grid, and use the intersections to establish our representative positions. To cover the most critical situations, however, we have to add two more imagi-nary lines about 5m out, parallel to the goal lines.

We now have a complete grid whose intersections give a good coverage of all the likely points for a set-piece – i.e. any set-piece position will approximate to one of them. The grid has various functions – as an aide-memoire to the coach, as a starting-point and prompter to experiment and devise new ways of attack-ing and defending, and as a fine basis for revision and pressure practices. To go round the circuit, up the sides and down the middle, affords an excellent range of starting points, each calling for decisions. In unopposed, semi-opposed, or opposed it gives the chance to play a whole variety of situations. Pressure can be built up by imposing time limits – how far can we get in four minutes? Can we beat our record for going down the middle? But as with all pressure exercises this can be done effectively only when very sound basic forms of the activity have been established.

313

As a starting point for the use of this grid it would be a useful exercise for the coach to go through it in terms of penalty kicks, planning precisely what his particular team should do at each point. The whole team is, of course, involved in terms of support and defence. Immediately the kicker is faced with the precise problem there is motivation for him to practise and the coach to coach. You can establish the accurate range of your place-kickers – which is in the kickers' interest and the team's – and work out from there the points at which different tap penalties, and up-and-unders, and kicks to touch, can be used. You will find that the grid helps you be thorough in covering the possibilities.

# PART 6

# BASIC PREPARATION – PHYSICAL

## 24 FITNESS FOR RUGBY

The amount of time to be devoted to the physical preparation of players for rugby is inevitably a matter of compromise. The rugby coach needs a keen appreciation of the various requirements of his players in terms of basic conditioning, immediate pre-season testing, in-season sharpening, and specific and general strength work. On the other hand, he cannot afford to devote more than a little of his own time to supervision of such activities. The team's efficiency is the product of its effective work-rate, governed by this physical preparation but conditioned by its freshness and attitude, and its technical and tactical expertise. The coach's specific function is the last element. He must, therefore, set quality standards in physical preparation, devise effective methods of attaining them, encourage personal and group commitment to specific strength work, and where possible delegate much of the actual supervision to particular players or helpers.

### High work-rate
High work-rate in rugby corresponds to the basic pattern in the game – a capacity to produce a sequence of high-energy bursts punctuated by moments of rest. It corresponds to a sequence of sprints rather than to a steady state middle-distance run.

It differs most markedly from track preparation, however, in its context of frequent, demanding fixtures, in which players are constantly receiving minor injuries. Efforts to generate extra income are reflected in additional fixtures which increase the load on the players. To avoid persistent fatigue and staleness, it pays to make intelligent use of the squad, and to keep fitness sessions focused on competitive intensity. The least tractable problem is that of top players with multiple demands upon them.

The team as a whole can impose a pattern on this by a conscious effort in the match to concentrate on high-energy output for say three minutes at a time followed by a conscious effort to diminish energy expenditure and consolidate the gain of the previous peak. This is one function of the leaders on the field – the captain, pack-leader, tactical decision-maker. To be able to produce this sustained, high-pressure effort at the beginning and end of each half, or to reply to a score, or to consolidate a lead – and these are the critical moments – makes a team much more effective in energy use.

For the individual team member, provided he's adequately prepared, the same kind of concentration on the next five minutes rather than the game as a whole is useful in getting a higher work-rate. '*Burn it up in the first five . . . and the next . . . and the next*' is what he must aim for, confident that at the end of each five he can produce the same kind of effort for the next five.

In essence, high work-rate consists of '*do it . . . and run*' – and the 'do it' refers to every aspect of the game. The player who tackles, and lies there for a moment congratulating himself, or misses a tackle, and lies there cursing is a sure case of low work-rate. A fly-half who watches his opponent pass, lets his concentration slip, and fails to support the man outside him, is a case of low work-rate – and so on throughout the team and the game. The coach must convince the team that there's never a moment when you can stop thinking, and – except when the ball's dead – never a moment when there isn't something you can contribute to team play.

The physical preparation of the team through fitness and strength work is one element in high work-rate. The other is the attitude of the team to the match: if they aren't raring to go, it's of little consequence how fit they are. A large factor of this is freshness. The coach can help by judging the mental and emotional needs of his players and providing a flexible, varied, interesting, and if possible entertaining programme of work. He can, if the fixture list is taxing, make sure that his whole squad is involved and that players have a certain amount of time off. He should note that some players not technically first-class can bring a great deal of commitment to the team, and spark it to greater efforts. He can encourage commitment in his players by getting them to see each match as a chance to show what they can do, and by making them focus on the challenge ahead: a psychological charging of the batteries. Commitment to the team is, in fact, the second major factor. The coach has to create a sense of each player's importance in and to the team, and build up pride in the player and in the team. At a high level in any sport there's got to be an element of dedication – willingness to give a major part of your leisure time to a concentrated physical, mental, and emotional preparation for the big match – and the coach must foster this as a long-term investment. If some degree of this commitment is not present long before the match, no team talk in whatever style is going to be effective.

The nature of team talks has already been discussed. If the coach has got the right captain, the right pack-leader, the right tactician, he should leave immediate pre-match comment to them.

## FITNESS AND FLAIR

It isn't simply high work-rate that is affected by your state of fatigue: your whole capacity to play the game to your potential is linked to it.

Consider these aspects of play:

- *judgement* – the most important talent in any game, the ability to read the game, think ahead, select a course of action – calls for unforced sustained concentration. That's possible only when your body is conditioned to withstand all of the demands made on it by the speed, length and vigour of the game

- *skills*, too, call for momentary concentration, and deteriorate as fatigue increases. This is most evident in the critical closing stages of the match

- *morale* is immensely important. One base for complete confidence is the knowledge that the longer the match goes on, the greater your fitness advantage will be. The best expression of this is the player who never knows when he's beaten – who never acknowledges the possibility of personal or team defeat, no matter what the score, because he never acknowledges his own fatigue. Until the final whistle goes, he has no idea how weary he is. The spectator who runs up, pats him on the back, and admiringly says, '*Don't you ever get tired?*' has no idea how close to collapse he is. This capacity to extract the last dregs of energy is a function of that attitude that sets out to make every moment in training as hard as possible, that aims for exhaustion. When you train, you're training not just your body but yourself

- *competitiveness* – your fitness advantage is a set of weapons to be deployed against your personal opponent, who will vary throughout the match. You seek to pressure him where you have an advantage – at a cost to you, but at a greater cost to him – all the way through. Ideally, you overmatch him in every aspect of fitness.

When you look at all of these points, you can see that fitness is a necessity for allowing you to express your potential. If it isn't harnessed to good judgement, of course, or to adequate skills, then it can be squandered: you don't win points for reckless expenditure of energy. Once you've got it, it simply allows you to exercise your judgement and skills to maximum effect; without it, your judgement and skills may be irrelevant. So, aim to get fit and skilful, and make the most of yourself as a player.

### Setting personal targets

What getting fit entails varies dramatically at different levels in the game. At the highest level, you know you must give yourself every physical advantage you can. Your dedication will be reflected in your lifestyle throughout the year – your exercise, your rest periods, your sleep, your diet, your holidays and even your work will be adjusted more or less consciously to prepare yourself for the matches to come. Performing well becomes to your life what the vanishing point is to a painting – it puts everything in perspective. You have a talent, and a limited time in which to enjoy it, and you determine to make the most of that opportunity. And the odds are that the regime is itself enjoyable: it seems fairly natural. It may be enormously demanding physically, but it's mentally and emotionally acceptable.

This degree of dedication may not be for you. It's a talent in itself, just as playing ability is. You can certainly have a go at it, and you may discover that you do have the talent. But if it all seems too much of a strain, accept who – in respect of fitness – you are, and be you as fully as you can: that's what the top players are doing, and it's a target that's attainable and something you can take pride in.

## How to get fit

Whatever your degree of dedication, you'll be getting fit in much the same way, using methods which have always been used. The great change now is that players who are good enough, or who are prepared to spend a pound or two, can expect to get their state of fitness monitored and fine-tuned. Governing bodies or health clubs possess (or should possess) the required facilities and knowledge to give individual players an objective assessment of their fitness – not to compare with the fitness of other players, but to chart their improvement.

It's significant that the expertise required for getting rugby players fit is not directly linked to experience of rugby – rather to an analysis of the demands made upon players, a measurement of actual practice. There's an inherent danger in this – that we prepare players for what has happened rather than for what's going to happen, or what should happen. Props in general don't move fast, but if we accept this, props in the future won't move fast either, because we'll condition them to move slowly. If you're a prop, aim to be one of the next generation of props, not the last one. So, too, with your skills: be the best you can as well as the fastest you can. You want to maximise your potential rather than be imprisoned in a stereotype.

It's obviously true that rugby offers a range of roles to its players, and thereby caters to a range of physiques and physical capacities. These abilities steer apprentice players into given positions, where they tend to compete with players similar to themselves: their qualities fit them for similar functions. Groupings based on these differences have long been the basis of skills training and competitive fitness training: the props and locks work together, as do the hooker and the back row, the halves and centres, the back three. There's nothing fixed about such groupings – you take account of individual abilities. The broad aim is that like competes with like, motivated by that fact (and a suspicion that it may affect selection) to excel. But all can take part in the same core fitness programme during the season, for all aspire to the same abilities. The prop would like to cover ground like the back row forward, because he'd be a better prop if he could; the back row forward would like to have the winger's speed off the mark; the winger would like to have the centre's power of tackle; the centre would like to have the prop's power to rip the ball: all would like to share the best characteristics of the others, because all take part in the great bulk of the game and play in the open. Each, of course, has to supplement the core programme with what he knows he particularly needs, which may well come back to his position.

This core in-season club session is a great morale builder as all work and suffer together: it's an expression of club solidarity. For the good, committed player it's to be seen as a maintenance measure, a way of maintaining and testing the fitness he has built up on his own throughout the year. For the less committed, it may be seen as a more significant move towards match fitness. The difference will tend to lie in the approach of the player – one trying to exhaust himself in each exercise as it comes, the other pacing his effort to ensure survival. But for all, the session must be marked by intensity of effort: it must demand a continuity of effort beyond that demanded in the game, and a competitiveness that may be evaded in the game. The form of the session will be discussed later.

In-season training may be seen as phase three of the quest for fitness. Phases one and two – out-of-season, and pre-season – are where the real differentiation between committed and less committed, and between the various positions, can most clearly be seen. All will be concerned with the same four aspects of fitness, but the quantity and quality of work undertaken out of season will be strikingly different in terms of commitment and position.

The four aspects of fitness are clear enough:

**a)** the ability to keep going, based on your ability to take in and use oxygen, and to reduce body fat – aerobic fitness

**b)** the ability to produce near maximum effort repeatedly with minimum rest – anaerobic fitness

**c)** the ability to produce explosive effort – power

**d)** the ability to overcome resistance – strength.

Every player needs to establish a fitness advantage in a) and b); all will benefit from working on c); some need to devote time to aspects of d). You should be seeking, alone or in company, to establish a fitness advantage in all of them *before the season starts*. What's needed in the first club get-togethers is not fitness training but a series of fitness tests. After that, though playing experience will indicate special needs and big matches will call for an adjustment of overall preparation, you should seek to maintain your level. This reflects the extended nature of the rugby season – too demanding, in fact, to allow top players to function consistently at their best.

The aim at every stage is to get the maximum pay-off in terms of fitness/freshness/enthusiasm. If you lose your freshness or enthusiasm, you've overloaded on the work, and you'll pay for it later. Don't let a fitness trough develop at any time, and seek to build steadily towards match fitness. You should enjoy every session – soon afterwards. The great side-effect is enhanced enjoyment of being alive.

*Aerobic fitness* is the basis of everything. You build it up by running at approximately 80% of your current maximum for about 45 minutes. Former All Black centre Mark Taylor reportedly ran 60 miles a week – e.g. 10 miles every day but Sunday – in the first phase of his training; in the All Black squad, 40 miles is common. These figures are quoted less to suggest norms than to indicate what excellence entails. Keep in mind that these weren't prescribed distances, and that they weren't a chore: they're the expression of an enthusiasm for fitness and for rugby, and a determination to succeed. Find modes of exercise that you can undertake with a measure of enthusiasm, and gradually extend them in frequency, distance, and intensity. Try fartlek, running on varied terrain, at varied speeds, responding to what the terrain and your imagination suggest to maintain variety. Sign up with Outward Bound for a month in the summer as an athletics/expedition officer, and take successive groups of students twice a day for extended runs through the wood and along the beaches of Moray, drifting to the back and then surging through as they, too, accelerate to ensure adequate work. When they run 1500m, you run 1500s; when they run 800m, you run 800s; when they run 400m, you run 400s . . . and so on, with each group during the day. It pays to be a student or a schoolmaster during your playing career. You needn't exclusively run: walk 30 miles in a day, taking in the four top peaks of the Cairngorms as you go and do it every weekend. Find activities that suit you and that are genuinely demanding. Above all, find activities that you enjoy in their own right.

Aerobic fitness is the starting point, but as soon as an acceptable level is reached, you need to be thinking about building up the other qualities. In the course of your aerobic running, you start working on anaerobic fitness, fitting in more and more repetitive speed work. Take that indispensable aid, a dog, along, and put in sprints in which you accelerate away from a slow pace, and try to keep ahead of him as long as you can. Work alongside someone on a bike, and do the same thing: every time you come to a hill, you must beat him to the top; on the flat, you move slowly and then put a sprint in and try to stay ahead of him for every pace you can manage. You can actually reach a point where the dog, sensible animal, will have had enough. Once again, you're doing lots of hard work in an enjoyable setting. For most people, this is more acceptable than following a prescribed routine.

During your aerobic work experiment with breath control. If you impose a pattern of breathing – e.g. breathe out for two strides, in for two strides – on your stride pattern, you'll soon find yourself thinking of the breathing pattern rather than bodily discomfort. This has general application: you can use it profitably whenever you're exerting yourself, e.g. walking up a steep hill, as well as in moments of calm during the match.

The time comes when you need to formalise your *anaerobic fitness* sessions. This measures your adaptation to the basic pattern of the game – frequent short pauses followed by very vigorous action. Your capacity to do this is based on the success of your aerobic work, reinforced by what in essence is change of pace.

You can incorporate this rhythm, and accustom your body to it, in your warm-up: trot ten paces, stride ten, alternately for a mile and a half. Each time you shift to stride, increase your stride length and the power of your arm action. Even at this speed look for a distinct but unstrained change of pace.

But in the serious work you're aiming for an explosive change of pace as you hit the line. No matter how weary you are, you drive over the first few strides: imagine as you hit the line that you're going for a score in the last seconds of the match; run for the next line as if defenders are closing in on you. Keep going as you get tired: give all you've got each time, knowing you'll have more available for the next one. Intensity of effort is the great criterion.

It pays to use a fairly big unit – it's more demanding, and your mind adjusts to it as simply a unit. Try trot-*sprint*-trot-*sprint*-trot-*sprint*-trot-*sprint* as your unit, followed by as short a rest as you can manage. Always start with a trot – you can always trot, and once you're trotting the sprinting is easier. Don't think about the whole session: concentrate on the next sprint. Each sprint should be about 40 yards. You can slow right down on the trot – not for a rest, but to force yourself into a sharp acceleration. Quite apart from fitness, the ability to accelerate sharply is invaluable in the game, in both defence and attack.

You aim to build up repetitions and diminish rests whilst maintaining the quality of your speed work: it's easy to fool yourself with non-explosive changes of pace. After your trot-stride warm-up, try six units. Stay with that till you're moderately proud of your performance. Go on to eight, and then to ten. The USRFU coaching manual cites four plateaux of performance, ending with 45 repetitions of two 40-yard sprints ('jingle-jangles') – equivalent to about 20 of our basic units: 2.25 miles in under 23 minutes. Somewhere between six and twenty you'll find the kind of session that gives you (a unique individual) the maximum pay-off in terms of fitness/freshness/enthusiasm. Then trot-stride for a mile and a half for your warm-down.

By the time the season comes, you should know what you need to maintain peak anaerobic ability. Graham Mourie, the All Black flanker and captain during the '79 tour, would run fifty 50-yard sprints on match days when he wasn't playing. Again, this is an indication of excellence rather than the statement of a norm. For many, a sprint pyramid (4 x 25; 3 x 50; 2 x 75; 2 x 100; 2 x 75; 3 x 50; 4 x 25) ideally done competitively up a slight hill with a trot back down to the start point, is enough. Quality is all once you've established your appropriate session. Each time you give less than 100% you undermine your match resolve. Each time the coach accepts what's offered as the best a player can do, he undermines the player's resolve. By 'intensity' I mean 'blow your mind intensity': anything less is futile.

*Power* is important for all players, because it enhances the quality of your acceleration. For most players this means speed off the mark; for the line-out jumper, it means greater height. The typical form of exercise is bounding, hopping, driving – accustoming your legs to powerful efforts over the full range of their movement. Running up hill fast, or up steps; hopping for distance or height over a short distance; bounding with an exaggerated knee lift; depth jumping off a box – these are typical exercises. But go with care: start easy and build up. Listen to your body. I used to work on hopping over a high jump lath at 5ft 4in (1.63m) off a three-step run. It was good for my power, but not – as I now know – for my knees. With both power and strength exercises, it's best to work with expert help, and expert help is increasingly available. During the season, you're probably best to rely on your anaerobic work – the explosive start to each sprint, for example – to maintain your power rather than on specific power exercises.

*Strength* is becoming increasingly important for all players at top level. Know-how is important – e.g. for the winger keeping the ball available when trapped in a maul – but strength is a great help when you haven't used your know-how fast enough. Paradoxically enough, the players least likely to commit themselves to strength training are those who are weak, and don't care to have their weakness exposed. But the sooner you get started, the sooner that weakness will go.

Once strength has been built up, you can maintain it with exercises using your own or another player's body weight, or in competitive strength exercises (see p. 58 ff). To build it up, however, there's no real alternative to weight training done with expert guidance during the three to four months prior to the season. Once your instructor knows the situations with which you have to cope, he'll be able to prescribe work for you far more accurately than any book.

As a starter, though, I quote the general weights circuit suggested by Jim Blair, advisor to the NZRFU on conditioning, on his tour to Britain. Compared with some schedules it seems very simple, and that's why I quote it. The exercises are in order: 1. leg press; 2. leg extension; 3 leg curls; 4. leg adduction/abduction; 5. calf raises;  6. pectorals; 7. lateral pull-downs; 8. long cable pulls; 9. bent arm pull-over; 10. arm curls; 11. sit-ups.

You aim to work on these (and position-specific exercises prescribed by your weights advisor) with the same commitment you give to your anaerobic work. Your advisor will advise you on form and poundages: listen to him carefully, and work steadily and safely.

The great change in conditioning is implicit in what we've said about weight training: its objectivity allows you and your advisor to measure your progress exactly, and so to provide well-based advice on what to do next. The same principle is obviously applicable to the measurement of running fitness, aerobic or anaerobic. National bodies are already applying such testing to their top players, and can call upon trained personnel to administer the tests and advise on changes to be made in schedules. In due course, such testing may take place at club level. But if you as a player want to apply the principle to yourself, all you need is a repeatable test, a stopwatch, and honesty.

## Club fitness sessions

What we've looked at so far are the out-of-season preparations of the committed player, leaving him substantially match fit as pre-season approaches. I've concentrated on the free individual approach rather than on setting out what's to be done on which day, just as I've chosen to write for rugby players rather than for groups of players in a specific position. The fact that different expert fitness coaches will prescribe different regimes, and all will work, suggests that there's no single magic key beyond the commitment of the dedicated player. He will certainly cultivate the qualities which make him suitable for his position: I'm suggesting standards and the need to acquire the most desirable characteristics of players in other positions. This helps secure the autonomy of the individual, whilst still pointing a way ahead.

It's already been suggested that the club fitness session fulfils several functions as a bonding agent, a builder of morale, a creator of fitness for the less committed, and a fitness test for the more committed. Every club session of whatever kind should be demanding physically, with the players constantly active, and constantly moving towards match performance intensity. The specific fitness session, however, ought to be pushing the players beyond the demands of the match in terms of intensity, continuity, and competitiveness. It ought to offer each of the four fitness components – aerobic, anaerobic, power, and strength – and be filled with challenge, spiced with fun, and aimed at the great product of fitness, freshness and enthusiasm.

## Club sweat session

Just as with the normal session, a structure makes a fitness session easy to design and administer. A very effective structure uses a pyramid of sprints, with each block of sprints followed by a group of power/strength exercises:

| A | B | C | D | E | F |
|---|---|---|---|---|---|
| 8 x 22m | blocked exercises | 10 x 22m | blocked exercises | 12 x 22m | blocked exercises |

and then down again through 10 x 22m and 8 x 22m.

Each block of sprints should be run competitively. All the players work together, but each has a rival to beat on each sprint. Normally this means winger v winger, and so on through the team.

Each sprint starts with the players lying on their back, with their head to the line (22-metre line and goal line alternately). The coach signals and it's a flat-out sprint to the other line . . . and the same starting position. I'd be unhappy if they weren't trying to beat the gun. Make sure they all roll onto their right side as they get up to sprint. This prevents collisions.

This form of anaerobic work is much more effective for most players than simply trotting and sprinting, which too often becomes trotting and trotting faster.

How many sprints you do in each block depends on the assessment you make of the team's needs, but don't sacrifice quality for quantity.

After each block of sprints you have a block of exercises in a sequence. The sequence shifts the effort from muscle group to muscle group, as in circuit training, so that you needn't halt for rests because of muscle group fatigue. You run through the sequence three times, the first time doing 12 repetitions of each exercise, the second doing 10, the third 8, so that at the end of the block they'll have done each exercise 30 times. With really committed players you can change to a time base – 20 seconds, 15 seconds, 10 seconds – and challenge their workrate. As with the numbers, you can alter the times to suit your needs.

The sequence of exercises in each set goes from legs to abdominals to upper body to general. For example, from star jumps, to bent-leg sit-ups, to wide press-ups, to burpees. Competing in peer pairs, you might move from half-squats, with a partner on your back, to sit-ups while your partner pushes you back, to prop wrestling (in scrummaging position) down to left or right, to trying to get up while your partner holds you flat on the ground. You'll find examples in Chapter 11 of the kind of exercises you can include, but you may well find your players can suggest what to do!

Once you've got satisfactory sequences, stick with them till the players move down the sequence automatically. You want to eliminate unnecessary pauses. Working in pairs, each player can monitor his partner's performance.

You'll see from this how easy it is to build in intensive power work (jumping, bounding, hopping), and strength work (lifting, wrestling). And competing in matched pairs ensures a maximum output of effort.

The whole pattern falls into what is now termed Peripheral Heart-rate Training, and thereby gains a certain respectability. In fact, it is a system that generates a great deal of effort and enthusiasm. It also has the advantage of allowing a steady build-up of training effort as the coach increases the number of repetitions or the number of blocks or the distance run.

## Sprint pyramids

A coach who remains conscious of the fitness/freshness/enthusiasm product will recognise that the kind of session just described will not always meet the requirements of heavily engaged players. A short session based on quality sprints to keep the players sharp is one alternative. Once again, competition is the great motivation. Pair players – a prop with a prop, and so on. As each pair trots in to the start, one of them has the right to break first, and tries to maintain his advantage all the way. On the next run, his partner leads, unless it's evident that one needs a handicap. Run through the finishing line.

Ideally, I'd like these done up a slight hill, and on a hard surface, in trainers. I say 25, 50, 75 and 100 yards, but you may substitute 22m, half-way, the far 22m, and the far goal line. But be clear what you're looking for: acceleration as explosive as conditions allow, sustained running speed, courage to continue. Encourage them to trot back after each sprint – '*You can always trot*'.

Prescribe with your mind on quality rather than on quantity: 3 x 25 – 2 x 50 – 1 x 75 – 1 x 100 – 1 x 75 – 2 x 50 – 3 x 25 gives you only 600 yards sprinting, but if it's flat out sprinting, it may be enough; 4 x 25 – 3 x 50 – 2 x 75 – 1 x 100 – 1 x 100 – 2 x 75 – 3 x 50 – 4 x 25 gives you 1,000 yards and, done competitively with a trot back, that's quite hard work. Provided the emphasis from the coach and the players is on intensity of effort, giving all they've got each time, you can afford to limit the quantity.

## Alternatives

There's a lot to be said for diversity of training, even if it can't be easily fitted into an academic schedule. I remember getting teams to run up steep dirt hills carrying boulders, and although they groaned they gloried in it; or allowing a team a night off because they weren't fresh enough; or playing a variety of basketball for fun and enthusiasm. Look around, and ask yourself what the local countryside or town offers. We've done intensive circuits in the gym to pop music; sung our way through ski exercises; chanted 'Loughborough' as we did 200 breast-stroke arm movements whilst lying on our stomachs. Use competition, with other teams, or soccer clubs, or whatever. Respond to the players, and get the players to contribute.

## The committed player in-season

You should use a club session as a good chance to exhaust yourself. Don't measure your efforts against those who aren't committed – you'll just get swollen-headed; measure them against a hypothetical ideal in which you never get out of breath – and work towards it. Set up a routine that you know will get you there for every important game. Remember to keep the balance between fitness, freshness, and enthusiasm.

## Speed training

Speed to a given point, e.g. a breakdown, is a product of playing ability and running speed: the gifted player who starts earlier can compensate for a lack of sheer pace. Nevertheless, it pays every player to be able to run faster. The anaerobic sprint work won't of itself make you run faster; it will simply allow you to maintain your pace till later in the match. However, the emphasis on swift acceleration into every sprint will.

But you can genuinely increase your running speed. Basically, you can develop a longer stride whilst maintaining your leg strike rate; or you can maintain your present stride, but increase your strike rate.

Now, the search for improved speed has developed considerably. A book I wish I'd had available is *How to Run Faster* by George B. Dintiman (Leisure Press, PO Box 3, West Point, NY 10996, USA).

## Technical sessions

Every practice session should be so filled with activity – quite independent of a specific fitness element – that the players finish up happy, satisfied, and very weary. If it isn't phsyically demanding, it isn't a good session: they haven't been worked hard enough. Quiet fresh learning elements must be balanced by intense activity – pressure practices. This is especially relevant early in the season – as the season goes on, you need to balance the demands of fitness and freshness.

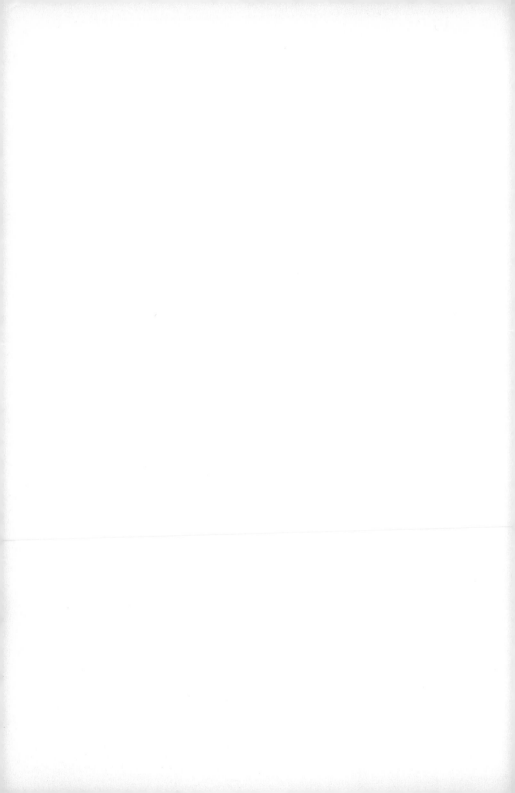